THE EVOLVING CORPORATION

A Humanist Interpretation

William J. Cook, Jr.

QUORUM BOOKS
Westport, Connecticut • London

Library of Congress Cataloging-in-Publication Data

Cook, William J., 1938–
   The evolving corporation : a humanist interpretation / William J. Cook, Jr.
      p.   cm.
   Includes bibliographical references and index.
   ISBN 1–56720–279–9 (alk. paper)
   1. Corporations.   I. Title.
   HD2731.C623   2000
   338.7—dc21   99–462242

British Library Cataloguing in Publication Data is available.

Library of Congress Catalog Card Number: 99–462242
ISBN: 1–56720–279–9

First published in 2000

Quorum Books, 88 Post Road West, Westport, CT 06881
An imprint of Greenwood Publishing Group, Inc.
www.quorumbooks.com

Printed in the United States of America

The paper used in this book complies with the
Permanent Paper Standard issued by the National
Information Standards Organization (Z39.48–1984).

10   9   8   7   6   5   4   3   2   1

Syntagma (2. Antiq) a. A body of persons forming a division of the population of a country.

—*The Oxford English Dictionary*, 1971.

For
William, Samuel, Ashley, and Wallace.

Contents

Preface

Carl Benson, my major professor and good friend, used to remark sardonically that books like this could (and should) be reduced to one really substantial journal article. I can only hope that he would have the same high opinion of this work. Actually, it did begin as a short monograph which I intended to use in my own practice of strategic planning and organization development. During the past twenty-five years, I had come to realize that something was terribly wrong with the corporation-model organization, and that none of the prevalent management and leadership theories even dealt with the issues, much less provided any answers. My experience had been in corporate, government, and professional organizations around the world; and in directing more than four-hundred projects designed to bring about systemic transformation, I was drawn inexorably to the same conclusion. So I intended to write the critical questions.

Then, the subject took over. I discovered early four things that, if the corporation were to be treated fairly, had to be examined at length and together. First, I came to realize just how thoroughly the corporation, both as a specific entity and as a generic organizational structure, had come to dominate the lives of everyone in Western civilization, especially the United States. There was, it seemed to me, nothing I could find that was not either controlled by or patterned after the corporation-model organization — even religious and civic clubs. Second, I came to believe that the aspects of the corporation were the epitome of societal values, particularly in the definition and distribution of wealth. Third, I had known for a long time how debilitating that structure and its culture were. In fact, after years of experience, I could not recall even

one instance in which I thought any person developed his or her full potential in such an organization. The converse was true.

Fourth, I finally decided that there were three reasons why none of the
myriad analyses of the serious dilemmas facing the corporation-model organization could have any effect whatsoever in overcoming the situation. First,
all the books that ostensibly address the problems are written not about but
for the corporation by professional captives of the system. So the commentary and advice become more or less a swelling paean to "improving" the
system — certainly, none dare suggest that it be dismantled; none even dare to
insinuate that it might be anything other than an eternal construct. Second,
those who attack from the outside, as it were, are immediately discredited. It
is a very old tactic. A prophet is without honor anywhere. Monolithic systems
have an overbearing way of developing an intense righteous indignation. All
reformers suffer ignominy and scorn. Third, the only solution to any problem lies within the problem itself. Of all the things I discovered on this venture, I think that this was the most important. It is for this reason that a detailed
historical analysis of the corporation-model organization became necessary.
The emerging system of human affiliation cannot be made apparent except
by a penetrating examination of the existing system.

Having decided to commit myself to the larger task, I was faced with the
cardinal sins of this genre. Most provide exhaustive analyses but no recom-
mendations or even conclusions. So they frustrate rather than clarify. I was
determined to find a better way and to articulate it—if not comprehensively,
then clearly and conclusively. Also, most of these books intellectualize the
trivial. I will admit that much of my own argument is intellectual, perhaps
academic; but I am convinced that no superficial treatment of the matters
involved here would be either fair or revealing. Furthermore, most books of
this kind offer little hope. I suppose that is the most damning characteristic of
all, and the most irresponsible. In my opinion, one ought not put forth observations that go nowhere or questions to which one is not willing to offer some
answer. Finally, most books of the stripe are humorless. The rage for objectivity completely suffocates any personality. So I promised myself that this work
might tease a smile now and then from a real, live person—not a statistic or
stuffed shirt.

To say that writing this essay was an odyssey, ironically, would be true on
two levels. Certainly it was an odyssey of the mind; I traveled great distances,
always trying to make sense of what I thought I was learning and attempting
ultimately to arrive home. But there was a curious parallel in my own actual
travels during this time. In retrospect, I can read specific sections, paragraphs,
and sentences and recall where they were written—Anchorage, Cairo, Vail,
Istanbul, Hilton Head, Buenos Aires, Phoenix, Beijing, San Francisco, Rome,
Chicago, Athens, Victoria, Innsbruck, New York, Venice, Orlando, Paris, New
Orleans, St. Louis, Santorini, and The Hague. In all these places and others,
I was always trying to test the reality of what I was writing against what I was

seeing around me. I really think that without this panoramic perspective I would not have had the insights that inform this study. And, most certainly, I would not have had the courage to tell the truth.

Carl Benson had another saying; his absolute highest compliment for any book was that there was a thesis on every page. I would never suggest that this work has that kind of substance. But would it be immodest to raise the possibility that there might be at least one provocative idea here and there?

PART I

AT LAST REPORT

CHAPTER 1

Introduction

The dawning of the day presented a most melancholy scene. Seven Ships and two Brigs on the same reef with the Convert, a heavy sea running and the wind blowing directly on shore.

Capt. John Lawford, Letter to the Secretary of the Admiralty,
George Town, Grand Caymans, 15 February 1794
Wreck of the Ten Sails[1]

Once upon a time, when the world was supposed to be proper and all things were supposed to be in their rightful place, Samuel Johnson wryly observed: "A woman preaching is like a dog walking on his hind legs. It is not done well, but you are surprised to find it done at all."[2]

If Dr. Johnson were still around, still delighting himself in such waggish terrorism against the perceived vices and follies of the age, there is a good chance that he might recast his famous simile at the organizations the present generation has come to know, love, and abhor. Modern organizations, indeed, are like dogs walking on their hind legs. They do not work well, but one is surprised that they exist at all. A sorry spectacle, indeed. They are unnatural and inhumane, arrogant and predatory—humanity's latest attempt at getting its act together. But, the attempt does not seem to be succeeding.

By now, the universal and irredeemable dysfunctionality of contemporary Western organizations has been generally admitted, if not accepted. It has been lamented by voices as diverse as those of new-age philosophers and ultraconservative Catholic theologians. It has even been reluctantly suggested, at least as a possibility, by corporate turnaround masters faced with the daunting task of salvaging whatever they can from the ruins of once proud mono-liths of the corporate world. It has been proved by the sudden disastrous obso-lescence of thousands of mid-size companies. It has been demonstrated in resurgent labor hostility and societal fractures in the face of downsizing, outsourcing, and globalization. It has been dramatically manifested in the frenetic rush of mergers, acquisitions, takeovers, and serial buyouts—all of which only postpone the inevitable. It has been reflected in the volatility of foreign stock markets, especially those of Asia, particularly the *keiretsus* of Japan. A runaway Dow Jones merely masks the fundamental troubles inher-ent within corporate organizations. On a larger scale, the dysfunctionality of contemporary Western organization has been demonstrated many times over by gridlock and fiasco in the governments and political systems of North America and Europe, utter chaos in Mexico, and confusion and instability in Russia and Central and South America. In fact, it can be argued that never before in the history of the United States has every aspect of its government been so totally out of control. In fact, it can hardly be termed a system.

These conditions of deterioration are at once both the legacy and the end of the organizations that, over a period of three centuries, came to dominate the Western world; in fact, they came to epitomize that civilization, at times even shaping its character, at times being one and the same with it. What was intended to be an adjunct to life became the whole of life. Actually, all orga-nizations of Western civilization (including those of present-day Japan and other Westernized nations) are essentially of a single type—the corporation. I do not mean the corporation in a strict legal sense but as the one basic con-cept and design of organization assumed by groups of people dedicated to any enterprise.

In recent years, many experts of various stripes have dealt with the insistent problems of the corporation-model organization in truly novel ways. The so-called new-age scientists assume a rather dismissive attitude about the entire affair and spin visions out of thin air. Old-line management gurus turned buf-foons pretend to restructure the corporation organization by picking up the pieces during the perennial deterioration of these constructs and cobbling them to-gether in ways even more unnatural than the ones they started with. Tech-nology scions bark out prophecies about the effect of virtuality and velocity on business, all the while retrofitting technology to organizational relics. And political malversers waste billions of dollars in "reinventing" government.

Of course, the corporation no longer appears, if indeed it ever did, in the philosophical purity of the original political metaphor—literally a *corpus*, a single body with its various parts operating as one. Rather, what exists now is that which is left of the original after centuries of imputing various interpre-tations to a splendid metaphor, an interpretation incredibly substantiated by both religion and science. Today there are any number of permutations of the type, and distinct nuances even within each of them. But the fact remains that the structure and character of Western civilization are the structure and character of the corporation. To understand one is to understand the other. More than a half-century ago, Peter Drucker described General Motors, and hence the corporation, as "the representative social institution."[3] As it often happens with prophets, the significance of his words proved far greater than the original intent. It is amazing, indeed, that this type of organization has come to so thoroughly represent Western civilization that there is not a single organization of any kind anywhere within contemporary society that is not formed in this fashion—each a replication of all other corporations—and, consequently, there is not an enterprise of any kind, public or private, that is not at serious risk of imminent demise—for the better, of course. When a catchy advertisement declares "The Corporation is Dead,"[4] there are, perhaps unintended, implications beyond business as unusual.

The passing away of the modern corporation-model organization is as inevitable as its successor is irresistible. Strangely, that is true not just because of the basic flaw in the corporation stereotype or the inherent superiority of the organization to follow but because the societal forces that combine to form the dominant organization of any society have lately converged to prove the corporation obsolete as a way of advancing human enterprise. These forces have also established the conditions, perhaps even the cause, for a wholly new kind of organization to emerge. This is the first of many postulates in this essay: The nature of human organization is determined by the aspects of society.

For example, it is generally held, by those who have thought seriously about the subject, that a society's dominant type of organization coincides exactly with its dominant wealth-producing activity. It logically follows that both proceed from the society's definition of wealth. Some economists cast the relationship in even broader terms, suggesting that the entire structure of a society depends upon its economic system. However, it is specifically the production of wealth, by any definition, that determines organization. Some have even dared to suggest a coincidence between wealth production and value systems. If that be true, then one would expect, following Adam Smith's definitions for the moment, that agrarian, industrial, and information societies would each result in a different type of organization and that is, in fact, correct. Wealth, in all its implications, is always the single greatest influence on the form of human organization.

However, the matter is not that simple. Several other aspects of any society together give the dominant type of organization its full expression. That is not to say that any one of these aspects is in itself a cause; but, taken together, the features become the actual critical attributes of the society's dominant organization. The aspects of society are perceptions of reality, faith, relationships, knowledge, order, system, control, governance, economy, and wealth.

Perhaps the quickest and most direct way to get at this idea is a table (see Table 1.1)—in this case, an admittedly imperfect attempt to graphically present the aspects of Western society and the corresponding organization for the past 2,500 years or so as a prelude to the nature of the system that will domi-

Table 1.1
The Organization of Western Civilization

	Historical Characteristics of Western Society		
Aspects of Society	Phase I	Phase II	Phase III
Reality	Supernatural	Natural	Hypothetical, Mythical
Faith	Theistic	Deistic	Atheistic
Relationship	Spiritual	Empirical, Rationalistic	Humanistic
Knowledge	Revealed	Discovered	Invented
Order	Fixed and Linear	Dialectic and Cyclical	Random, Chaotic
System	Dictated	Fabricated	Symbolic
Control	Personal	Artificial	Superficial
Governance	Authoritative	Democratic	Anarchistic
Economy	Collective	Laissez-faire (Free)	Distributive
Wealth	Agriculture, Mining	Manufacturing	Time
Organization	Family	Corporation	Collective

nate the third millennium. In some respects, this table could be considered the thesis of this study, but it is offered merely as an espalier for the ensuing larger discussion and prophecy which, by the way, are themselves intended to clarify and explain, rather than to defend or propose.

One proviso must be kept in mind throughout the discussion. While the aspects of society and its organization are considered in a roughly historical format, the emphasis has always been on the intrinsic relationships between and among the aspects. For example, it is not merely a matter of historical coincidence that a theistic faith is accompanied by authoritative governance. In each of the phases of organization development, the various expressions of the aspects of society are individually necessary and inextricably connected. It must also be remembered that these features exist as separate factors within the society. Only when they are combined in human affiliation is their inter-relationship fully manifested. So the purpose here is not to offer a detailed historical analyses of these aspects, separate or together, but merely to provide a background against which to discuss the characteristics of the corporation-model organization and its society.

The variations in the manner in which these aspects interrelate, the differences among the corresponding organizations, were all precipitated by a grand-scale contradiction that came to characterize Western civilization, beginning with the first millennium. The modern corporation, by accident or design, is the ultimate accumulation of centuries of dramatic interplay between and among the facets of the society. So it is impossible to understand either the complexities of the modern corporation-model organization or the deleterious implications of its structure and operation on human beings without an appreciation of its irreconcilably contradictory philosophical underpinnings. For most of its long evolution—unlike contemporary sentiment which is intensely practical and pragmatic—its philosophy was taken seriously and was, in fact, the driving force of society. Ideas were once actually in vogue. And, for the longest while, they were the chief motivating force in human life on the planet.

Any critique of the corporation-model organization is, in fact, a critique of the society itself. So it is impossible to draw conclusions or to make pronouncements about the current status of the corporation without at the same time delving into the corresponding issues as they reflect the entire society. That seems particularly true of capitalism and democracy, the pillars of contemporary Western civilization, and of behaviorism and humanism, the foundations of its philosophy. If this discussion, therefore, seems at times to stray from the trajectory of thought directly related to the corporation per se, it is because that kind of organization has come to so thoroughly dominate the entire social order. An analysis of its societal implications serves only to amplify the adverse effects it has wrought in the lives of all individuals in every aspect of their lives.

The corporation is actually built on a faultline, a great divide that runs through all the rational constructs of Western civilization; that is, the inherent schism between Western religion and Western science. In this case, the external conflict manifested itself in the struggle between Christianity and rationalistic science. No other society could have produced the corporation, not only because both the religion and the science were of Western origin but also because no other society would have attempted to reconcile the unreconcilable. At least, no other society yet has even contemplated such a futile effort.

Ironically, the conflict originated in a common dualistic world view; however, any commonality was immediately dashed because that view was seen from two radically different, diametrically opposed, perspectives. So it is necessary from the outset and throughout this study to examine at some depth the fundamental dichotomy of the corporation model both as the coincidental philosophies of the society and the reflections of those ideas evidence the specific characteristics of the corporation.

This study not only traces the philosophical development of the modern corporation but also explores the ramifications of the residual conflicts between religious and scientific assumptions still implicit within its modern constructions and dynamics. Special attention is given to the explicit traits of the corporation-model organization and its world. It is only in this ultimate version of the corporation that the way to future organization becomes evident. As a practical matter, it seems far more important to argue the case for the willing abandonment of the corporation-model organization, the corporation's world, than to attempt an accurate description of whatever is emerging to take its place. Specifically, this study proceeds first by examining the fundamental contradictions within the corporation-model organization—with emphasis on the effect each has had on individuals, on any specific enterprise, and, in a reflexive manner, on society itself.

Next, the very fundamental tenets of the religion that has served, generally unacknowledged, as the foundation of the corporation for 2000 years is examined. Then, this discussion carefully illuminates the major strands of rationalistic science that transformed both that religion and classical science—ideas and forces that were directly reflected in the conflicts within the corporation.

Following that, the discussion turns to the emerging organization. The argument proceeds first by presenting a critical assessment of the current status of the underlying philosophies of both science and religion and then by demonstrating that their present loss of any real credibility has seriously eroded the practical and philosophical bases of the corporation and augers against its continued existence as a viable form of human organization. Finally, it is demonstrated that all aspects of Western society, for the first time in history, have surpassed its dominant yet atavistic organization and have, therefore, created a dramatic epochal cusp between societal orders past and future. During this period of heightened disequillibrium, the emerging forms of human organization, as a practical consequence, ultimately will be brought into congruence with the advancing aspects of society.

Throughout the entire discussion, the overriding question is nothing less than this: Is it possible to create a system of organization that inclusively and completely and continuously serves the universal good of human beings?

NOTES

1. John Lawford, *Our Island's Past II: Wreck of the Ten Sails*, ed. Philip Pedley and Peggy Denton (George Town: The Cayman Islands National Archive and Cayman Free Press, 1994), 2: 19.

2. James Boswell, *Life of Johnson* (London: Oxford University Press, 1904), 309.

3. Peter Drucker, *Concept of the Corporation* (New York: John Day Company, 1946), 5.

4. *Wall Street Journal*, advertisement, February 6, 1995, p. A7.

CHAPTER 2

The Dualing Philosophies

All Gaul is quartered into three halves.[1]

People of Western civilization ought to take great comfort in the knowledge that there is at least one thing on which their religion and their science agree. Well, actually, there are three things, and the third one ends in contradiction if not outright conflict. Both the Hebraic–Christian religion and science, in all phases of their development, have forever either accepted as a matter of fact or hotly pursued as logical argument that the universe and all in it are characterized by four dimensions, three parts, and two sides. Any numbers of examples could be summoned here to illustrate the historically unsung harmony in most answers pertaining to the questions of dimensions and parts. For example, regarding dimensions, Western religion proclaims that both heaven and earth are foursquare, the one having four gates the other four corners. In science, we have moved from the four humors to the four dimensions of relativity, the four quantum numbers of the electron, and the four asymmetrics in the world of atoms. As a matter of speculation, I think it extremely likely that science soon will declare that each of the constituents of the universe (time, energy, action, space, and matter) is the composite of the other four. As for the universality of three parts, there is virtually no end to the accounting. Religion holds to the tripartite division of the universe—heaven, middle-earth, and hell—and to the three components of the person—body, soul, and spirit. The scientific world abounds with triads from novae to atoms. In fact, the four dimensions and three parts are so ordinary, so much the

objects of casual observation, that they need no special context for affirmation. Especially pertinent to the study of society and its organization is the
suggestion by the prodigious historian Will Durant that civilization itself has
four "elements." "Civilization is a social order promoting cultural creation.
Four elements constitute it: economic provision, political organization, moral
traditions, and the pursuit of knowledge and the arts."[2]

So, also, is the universality of the two sides, only here there is implicit
disagreement, division, opposition. The definition of sides is always a matter
of perspective, establishing the human context. For example, the Christian
religion sees the sides of good and evil and attempts to stamp out the evil;
rationalistic science sees the sides as this and the other and attempts to explain and defend the this, while always warily contemplating, or otherwise
accusing, the other. The issue of right and wrong, it seems, also has four
dimensions.

For Christianity, the sides were and are of cosmological proportions—the
eternal war between good and evil, God and Satan, heaven and hell. Christianity assumes a base of good. Orthodoxy holds that God, who is good, created a
universe, which is good, for human beings, who are also good, since they are
made in his likeness. These three assumptions are uncompromising. As to the
first, because good has a single source, it, like the source, is absolute. Good
thus became the only thing in the universe that is not defined by its opposite.
Therefore, it is both the necessary antecedent and consequence of truth.

As for the second, ironically enough, it was by discovering the good implicit within the universe that Newton hoped to prove the existence of God—
that good manifests itself not only in physical terms of order and force but
also as universal moral imperatives, all-sufficient to nurture and guide human beings. The ten commandments delivered to Moses were not impromptu
measures to control rebellion in the wilderness—they were reminders of what
had been central to the original design of the heavens and the earth and
were, according to theology, the issues involved in the Edenic revolt.

As for the third assumption, despite the intense factionalization within
Christianity over the innate nature of human beings after the fall of Adam
and Eve, all sects acknowledge the inherent capacity for goodness within
human beings. Whether and how that goodness is lost and/or (re)gained, or
whether it is simply inviolate, is all a seething font of continuing debate.
Nevertheless, the assumption is that humans desire to be and are, or can be,
good. Not only can they recognize good, but their conscience compels them
to it. Taken to its conclusion, the assumption of absolute good demands the
recognition of absolute right.

Christianity's other side is evil. It must be so: Evil is both the condition and
risk of free will. Free will means nothing unless evil exists as a choice; morality becomes impossible. So does righteousness. Whether by grace or works,
righteousness represents the triumph of the individual's will over evil. But
beyond the choice itself, or more precisely underlying it, is the power of the

individual to choose. This power is the control of his or her own destiny. According to the Hebraic–Christian tradition, the personification of evil is its inventor, variously dubbed Satan, Lucifer, or the Devil. As darkness is the absence of light, so is evil the absence of good; it is defined by what it is not. Evil is not opposite good, nor is it equal.

There are three assumptions in all this that have current implications. First, that evil, like its creator, is absolute; evil means wrong. It abides neither compromise nor accommodation. Second, that the planet earth is being held in a tortuous bondage and is subject to a relentless barrage of terrifying catastrophes and dire visitations that, quite mistakenly, are alleged by lawyers and insurance underwriters to be "acts of God." Third, that since Satan's driving ambition is the destruction of humanity, individually and collectively, evil is an inescapable force in the lives of all people.

For all the petrifying fears that this scenario evokes, it actually simplifies life by crimping a single, stark faultline through the universe. Everything and everybody, everywhere and everytime, falls on one side or the other. But with the advent of science, the world became a seriously complicated place, containing an endless number of two-sided postulates, both sides always relative, floating. Christianity had preached that there is no place to run; science would prove that there is no place to hide. Life would be most intense in that narrow channel between possibility and probability.

The dichotomy of the universe was expanded ad infinitum by the new science, à la rationalism. Whereas religion had simply divided everything into good and evil, modern science, devoid of that moral absolute, proposed to explain all things as the results of equal and opposing natural forces—a dialectic—and to arrange the world accordingly. Order, or disorder, no longer depended on the tension of the person torn between good and evil but on the tensions, from either apposition or opposition, between natural forces—with the person inescapably caught in the middle. The effect on the individual was less than encouraging. Since these forces operated strictly by their own laws and at their own time, the person was rendered more or less ineffectual, having little or no choice in a world at best neutral.

> The man said to the universe:
> "Sir, I exist!"
> "However," replied the universe,
> "the fact has not created in me
> a sense of obligation."[3]

The most a person could do was to try to understand and make allies, albeit dispassionate, of the natural forces and learn to benefit, through submissive adaptation, from the predetermined ends thereof.

It is remarkably ironic that the origin of the fatalistic philosophy referred to generally as "determinism" was Isaac Newton himself. As a matter of fact, by the definition of metaphysics, Newton's laws reflect monism in substance (all things from God), dualism in kind (opposites). Each of his first two famous laws is essentially dualistic in kind: the law of friction and the law of force. The third established the absolute of irresistible interaction that would become the premise of the dialectical concept of the universe and inform the various manifestations of Darwinism in the nineteenth and twentieth centuries. That law is, "For every action there is an equal and opposing reaction."

This law is the basis of predictability. But some explanation is needed. What it argued, ultimately, is that it if were possible to ascertain the position and velocity of every particle in the universe, then the future of the whole universe could be predicted and its entire past reconstructed in exact detail. Accordingly, there is neither chance nor choice. The universe thus becomes a machine; and when the fourth law, gravity, is factored in, admitting the component of time, the universe becomes one gigantic clock.

This metaphor ruled Western thinking for almost four hundred years. Albert Einstein believed it, developed his theory of relativity on it, and defended it stubbornly against all upstart contradictory theories. In fact, the concept was ostensibly validated very late in the twentieth century (1994) when the Hubble telescope discovered an actual black hole. What had once been only a necessary inference, and the hope of scientists who had staked their reputation on classical physics, suddenly became celebrated scientific fact. But simplification has never been the aim of rationalism. The very idea is mind-boggling until one realizes that, if the clock analogy is indeed accurate, all particles of the universe are inextricably interconnected, and their movement is always uniform, consistent, and precise. To know the position and velocity of one particle, therefore, is to know the position and velocity of all particles. Present destiny thus becomes a matter of fact.

Descartes had made the matter of dualism simple indeed. Harking back to the mystery religions, he simply declared that the universe is made up of mind (God) and matter (universe as mechanism).[4] But that was much too simple for the zealots of rationalism. To them, that was about the same as declaring the universe aspirin and nonaspirin. Oh, no. The idea of universal dichotomy presented an endless array of dual forces, and so it became, by the end of the nineteenth century, either more or less than its metaphysical definition. Dualism emerged as a driving dichotomy providing the basis not just of science but also of the sciences. What had once been knowledge became propositions—disconnected propositions.

As human experience and curiosity clustered into ever-smaller logical formations, and as rationalism worked its reductionary magic, a veritable starburst occurred, spraying remnants all over the intellectual galaxy. Whole-system disciplines were spun out, separate, severable, independently seeking their own orbits, all having only one connection, that is, the only remaining indicator of a common source—the motif of dualism—equal and opposite. The age of specialization had arrived, and with it a new phenomenon—fragmentation. For the first time in human history, the universe contracted. Religion had split the universe in two; science shattered it.

It is remarkable that the endless divisibility of the natural universe was heralded at least a hundred years before *Philosophiae Naturalis Principia Mathematica* (1687) by a priest who had the gall to interject human reason into the spiritual universe. Whereas Newton advocated human reason as the means of understanding and applying natural law, Martin Luther, even though he condemned reason as the greatest enemy of faith, urged the same reason as the only means of receiving, interpreting, and practicing the divine will. While it is difficult to tell exactly what influence he had on Newton's own conviction or philosophy, to say nothing of his courage, this kind of thinking in religion eventually forced the Reformation—a great equal and opposite force through which Christianity was forever cast into a schismatic mentality. When Luther nailed his ninety-five theses to the church door in Wittenberg, he established point–counterpoint as the modus that would characterize all Christian theology from that moment onward. And it was not the cosmic battle of good against evil, but the continuous bathetic give-and-take skirmishes over the finer points of doctrine. All the conflicts of all the centuries since were precipitated by one fundamental dialectic—that is, the argument over intent versus interpretation of scripture. Heresy and orthodoxy swapped places. Actually, it would have been more accurate if Luther had instigated his protest with the ninety-five antitheses. Reformation, it seems, has no end.[5]

But it was Newton's grand scheme of mechanistic determination in a universe of equal and opposite action that became the pentimento behind an endless array of designs on the universe. His one-man exhibition quickly turned into a style, then a school, then a movement powerful enough to color every expression of both nature and humanity. And, ironically, it was in precisely these two categories that the sciences developed. For example, in subjects which became known as the physical sciences, it was as if humans had suddenly been given the prerogative of making up their own world.

The idea was simple: Take all the raw material of the universe, lay it out in neat, measurable rows, and develop for each category a self-defining discipline suitable for learning, research, and the decreeing of stately pleasure domes. Just as an aside, some people find it surprising that the academic disciplines of North America were not on the flip side of the tables of stone delivered on Sinai, or, at the very least, part of the *Textus Receptus*. They were, in fact, concocted by university registrars in 1908. What is clear testimony to the inanity of the whole system is that in schools even today biology, chemistry, and physics are always taught in that order—not because of prerequisite progression or any other substantial reason but because of alphabetical arrangement.

To return to the concept of universal duality, this is, after all, the philosopher's stone that turns speculation into science and science into assurance. Newton's third law did more than describe a dualistic universe; it

was itself dichotomous, implicitly establishing two tendencies, if not two categories, of equal and opposite actions: there are those that have a tendency to
equate, and there are those that have a tendency to oppose.

The first category generally is now referred to as the physical and natural
sciences—all based on mathematics and all given to equation. For example,
biology is the study and pursuit of homeostasis; chemistry, equilibrium; physics, balance; astronomy, harmony. From the theoretical to the practical, quan-
tifiable balance in actions, energies, and forces is the essence of Newton's
orderly universe. Any inquiry or pronouncement predicated on that balance
became part and parcel of a great reality usually referred to as "classical"
science. That objective reality is apprehended by the senses and is observable, demonstrable, measurable. That was and is Newton's world.

As one might have predicted, equation proved to be only one side of universal dualism. The other side was constituted by those pairs of actions or
forces that have a tendency to oppose, but with resolution—rather than equation—being ultimately the logical expectation. Georg W. F. Hegel was more
interested in resolution than in conflict, although to hear him tell it, they
were one and the same. There is no question that, in the development of
Western civilization, Hegel was the most influential, albeit most misinter-
preted, philosopher since Aristotle. That is so because of both the universal
scope of his theories and their immediate applicability to human experience.
His intent was to develop an all-encompassing world view, to create a universal context that would provide meaning, for everything and anything.

Oversimplified, which must always be the case in any summary of his work,
his philosophy held that reality is a constant interaction of opposites—equal
probably, but more important, opposite. Working strictly in this realm of ideas
and always seeking to discover truth in the habit of a trained theologian, he
created a kind of syllogism that, in technique at least, reflects his fascination
with Socratic–Aristotlian logic. But there is a fundamental difference between
Hegel's approach and Artistotle's. The difference is in that which is reasoned
as well as the reasoning. Classical logic, filtered through Newton, had established, in its effort to create definitions, the law of contradiction: That is, X is
not Y. That law had ruled Western civilization for centuries.

But Hegel insisted vigorously, even adamantly, that there is no contradiction between X and Y; in fact, there is no between. They are essentially bound
together, they are defined by each other; and neither can exist without the
other. (It is interesting here to recall Hippocrates's observation that opposites
are cures for opposites.) The power of negation sustains the affirmative, creating in the dynamic a third entity as close to "truth" as we can ever come.
This triad he described as "being" and "non-being" and "becoming." The
dialectic thus is an eternal process of fusion, with each successive "becoming" becoming "being" establishing the premise for a new "non-being," et
cetera ad infinitum.

Hegel brought at least two things to rationalism that Newton had never considered. Nor had anyone else. First, there was the postulation that order was more than a matter of set equal actions or forces. In Hegel's world, order was never fixed; rather, order was the dynamic, progressive reality created by the constant tension within a compound force. In Hegel's thinking, this phenomenon transcended natural law—it was a spiritual state. Second, Hegel redefined empiricism. He believed that the human constitution partakes of many experiences that are not apprehended strictly by the five senses. He came to this conclusion very early in the development of his system of thought. The subtitle of his first major work, *The Phenomenology of the Spirit*, is *Science of the Experience of the Conscience*. Hegel used the word *Wissenschaft* (science) to suggest that these nonsensory experiences could be objectified and observed just as surely as the physical attributes of the natural world. This was the *pièce de résistance* of modern philosophy. This concept—called, appropriately enough, "absolute idealism"—became the animus of the human sciences, including history, anthropology, political science, sociology, psychology, and even theology.

All these subjects of inquiry had existed in prescientific forms for a long time, but it was not until Hegel provided the rationale, however misunderstood, that their total-system formation, their disciplining, could take place. It was such a fascinating idea that Lester Ward, a prodigious writer given to uncontrolled fits of Latinate pedanticism, actually devised a hierarchy of natural and social sciences from astronomy to sociology. Lewis Carroll had already listed the different branches of arithmetic as "ambition, distraction, uglification, and derision." It should not be surprising, however, that the human sciences continued the pattern of bifurcation by naturally separating into two logical divisions—one generally called social sciences, the other variously termed but probably best described as "behavioral" sciences.

"Sciences" meant more "knowledge" than ever before. Through the overwhelming influence of those perceived or postulated theories of reality the modern corporation, including government, was brought to its ultimate development. It is poetic justice that the thing that raised up the corporation would bring it down; these two categories of science would deliver a one–two punch in more ways than one. As these twin sciences captivated Western thinking and were transformed from speculation to practice in every aspect of life, they each inevitably created irreconcilable conflict. Whereas the natural sciences had pitted the individual against the universe, human sciences deployed the universe against the individual. I do not believe that either Newton or Hegel had that in mind.

NOTES

1. Old parody of Caesar's *Gallic Wars*.

2. Will Durant, "Our Oriental Heritage," *The History of Civilization*, vol. 1 (Norwalk, Conn.: The Easton Press, 1992), 1.

3. Stephen Crane, "A Man Said to the Universe," *The American Tradition in Literature*, ed. Sculley Bradley et al. (New York: W. W. Norton & Company, 1967), 2: 946.

4. It is very likely that Descartes and other "enlightenment" philosophers were more immediately influenced by Manichaeism via Ming-Chiao. This Chinese religion was most certainly the source of the Western concept of "enlightenment." Interestingly, St. Augustine was a Manichaean before his conversion to Orthodox Christianity.

5. Luther's influence extended far beyond the Church and far beyond his own time. In fact, it can be said that the whole idea of reform — the driving force of nineteenth and twentieth century progressivism in all social, political, and economic arenas — can be traced to him. The irony is that the Church and the established order found in reform their own perpetuating salvation, quite in contrast to the outright rejection and destruction advocated earlier by John Wycliffe.

CHAPTER 3

The Dual Ancestry

And on the pedestal these words appear,
"My name is Ozymandias, king of kings;
Look on my works, ye Mighty, and despair!"
Nothing beside remains. Round the decay
of that colossal wreck, boundless and bare
The lone and level sands stretch far away.
                              Percy Bysshe Shelley[1]

The corporation-model organization, like the society it epitomized, was not
built for survival. Although usually granted eternal life by government in
specific instance, the corporation generically was a coincidental construct
intended strictly as an expedient for the production of wealth as defined at
the time and place, and subject to the conditions and world view of that time
and place. As such, it was obviously supposed to be a means, subservient to
the end. What was not so obvious, however, was its inherent temporariness,
an attribute arising from the simple imperative of continuing, even increasing, effectiveness and efficiency in achieving the declared intent. Any contrary expectation or practice or manipulation has always led to trouble and
disappointment. That is to say, any application of the corporation model to
wealth-consuming enterprises, or any assumption of permanence with regard to either actual corporations or the basic concept, was doomed from the
start. Why anyone would do so remains a mystery. There is a fine line between hypothesis and illusion, and there is perhaps an even finer line between illusion and delusion.

Quite actually, the corporation was a *deus ex machina*. But in this case, the hoary dramatic device suffered from severely limited capability: It could advance the plot, all right, even to climax; but it could not bring about denouement. The problem was not with the engineering of the artifice, so the solution was not "reengineering" or "reinventing" as supposed by most *fin de siècle* reformers—those who, true to form, believed the fix is always to be found in complication. The problem was fundamental. No remedy, however sophisticated or popular, could overcome the corporation's essential dichotomies and, hence, its unlikely design, or its unnatural amalgamation of intellectual and nonintellectual materials, or its jury-rigged arcane construction. Moreover, the corporation had to exist not only within the world that had created it but also in the world of its own creation. All things considered, the corporation, like the civilization it represented, was a system hopelessly at odds with itself, desperately struggling to hold itself together with little more than its own spit.

Conventional wisdom assumes that the juncture of science and religion was the collision of unequal and opposite forces. But that is only partially correct. Actually, there was no collision. It was more of a convergence, increasingly so. Paradoxically, modern science was born in the attempt of religion, or at least devoutly religious men, to "enter the kingdom of God." Any subsequent conflict arose as much from the inquiry as from the answers. However, it is true that to what degree the answers lay in the questions is itself an unanswered question. As for the matter of inequality, there was simply no contest. Command always serves control. Rationalistic science was destined to dominate religion from the beginning, eventually expunging all symbols of its religious heritage, denying any connection with anything sacred, never acknowledging that escape from that heritage would mean self-annihilation.

The worse part of this life-and-death struggle was borne by religion. Actually, religion lost the argument simply by agreeing to the terms of the disputation (faith can never prevail in a rationalistic debate). Consider the implications of Cardinal John Henry Newman's reply to Sir Robert Peel, who had argued vociferously that the study of science "will make men not merely believe in the cold doctrines of Natural Religion, but . . . it will so prepare and temper the spirit and understanding, that they will be better qualified to comprehend the great scheme of human redemption." Newman's reply makes it difficult to determine who is the stronger defender of science.

Science gives us the grounds or premises from which religious truths are to be inferred; but it does not set about inferring them, much less does it reach the inference;—that is not its province. It brings before us phenomena, and it leaves us, if we will, to call them works of design, wisdom, or benevolence; and further still, if we will, to proceed to confess an Intelligent Creator. We have to take its facts, and to give them a meaning, and to draw our own conclusions from them. First comes Knowledge, then a view, then reasoning, and then belief.[2]

The ultimate outcome of this kind of inverted reasoning was the Church's gradual and fitful disappearance. At its moment of greatest challenge, Christianity—especially in North America—was in no position to resist either assault or its own erosion. By the beginning of the twentieth century, Christianity had so fragmented itself—factions from Lollards to Latitudinarians—that it could no longer muster any concentrated effort. Even if it could have achieved some semblance of unity, its real energy had either been spent in the emotional frenzy of frontier bush-arbors or stifled in the rigid hauteur of musty citadels of academe. In fact, it was in these two ways that organized religion would seek to perpetuate itself—both, ironically, results of the insistent overlay and intrusion of science.

The bush-arbors transformed themselves into variously presented traveling salvation shows, ranging from Elmer Gantry to the Christian Broadcasting Network (Enterprises)—complete with glossolalia, music, dancing, magic tricks and souvenirs, and books of warmed-over pop-psych pablum miraculously transubstantiated into healing religious nostrums, to say nothing of profit-making gimmicks from theme parks to memorial bricks and unrestrained capitalistic ventures ranging from communication empires to land grabs in Third World countries. And while a rational, pseudosophisticated world looked upon these shameless shenanigans with pitiful contempt, most religious enterprises outcapitalized capitalism. Jesus saves. He also produces serious tax-free revenue. The other form of religion, intellectual Christianity, "rationalized" itself in position papers and edicts on a variety of irrelevant social issues, in effete, politically correct translations of the Bible and preposterous revisions of liturgy, in chilling debate over textual sources and alphabet authors, in justifying sin rather than sinners—all the while currying academic respectability, social acceptance, and economic advantage. It is a remarkably significant commentary on the lifelessness of rationalized religion that Christianity during the twentieth century produced neither art nor poetry (by 1990, no religious journal even accepted poetry for consideration); and its music was either commercial or political. So much for the human spirit. Probably the watershed event for this kind of intellectualized religion was the ill-fated ecumenical movement of the 1960s. After that embarrassing debacle, the Church spent the remainder of the century trying to redeem itself, or at least justify its existence. Sinners were left pretty much on their own. Back alleys became main street. The moral basis of any social contract disappeared. In 1996, when a psychopath brutally gunned down sixteen elementary school children and their teacher in Scotland, a priest could only complain, "We don't know why this happened." Similar tragedies, with similar pathetic responses, occurred in Kentucky, Arkansas, and Colorado. Surely, ignorance is the greatest sin; irrelevance, the greatest punishment.

With individual or collective salvation passé, religion's last desperate attempt at relevance was its frantic issues-based push into political arenas beginning the 1980s. The Moral Majority, the Christian Coalition, the fabled

"right-wing conspiracy," and other such enterprises represented cynical perversions of the gospel, as well as deceitful manipulations of the fundamental
privileges of democracy. By the end of the century, mainstream Christianity,
for all practical purposes, had become nothing more than a fragmented political party, rendering unto Caesar, advocating special interest agendas, fight-
ing off scandal, and laying up treasure on earth, all the while becoming
terminally vulnerable to Islam and other religions that still believed in God.

The corporation, by happenstance, was a chimera made of religion and
science—specifically, a severely compromised Christianity and an overwhelmingly assertive rationalism. And, even with the early subordination of religion
and the later super-ordination of something presumptuously and anachronistically
heralded as the "new" science, corporation model organization must be understood as a complicated dichotomy—a series of contrasts and comparisons,
all inherent in its dualistic ancestry.

For example, analysis by contrast would necessarily include the dissimilari-
ties in philosophy shown in Figure 3.1. Analysis by comparison, however,
might suggest at least some common practices, as shown in Figure 3.2. Yet,
the apparent similarities are deceptive. That the essential contradiction of
the corporation (and Western civilization) is ultimately insurmountable is
manifestly evident in the stark, unyielding contrasts, even within the comparisons, shown in Figure 3.3.

The uniqueness of the corporation is proved by the impossibility of finding
a word or phrase that accurately defines its sui generis composition. Even
analogy fails. Blending? It did not blend. Melding? It did not meld. Combination? In did not combine. Amalgamation, ironically, may be the English
term that best captures the dynamic interrelating of the critical attributes of
the corporation. The attributes are easy enough to identify, but their interrelationships are beyond understanding.

There are fourteen such features—seven each from religion and science—
all inherent, persistent, and perverse. It should come as no surprise that these
characteristics represent the sum total of theoretical possibilities of organization as corporation. Nor should it be surprising that the several variations
within and among them—typically differences of degree, not kind—are the
sum total of practical possibilities of the corporation as management. That is,
management is to the corporation what command is to religion and control
is to science. Command and control are only business of management.

What may be a bit surprising, however, is that these attributes, with only a
little fudging, substantially parallel the "principles" of management as stipulated by Henri Fayol in his critique (1916) of the French government's hapless
organizational bureaucracy (Table 3.1).

It was only logical, and for that reason inevitable, that rationalized management would become the modus operandi of the commercial corporation,
and rationalized administration of the public corporation-model organization. Although the first corporate charter in the new world (1675) made the

Figure 3.1

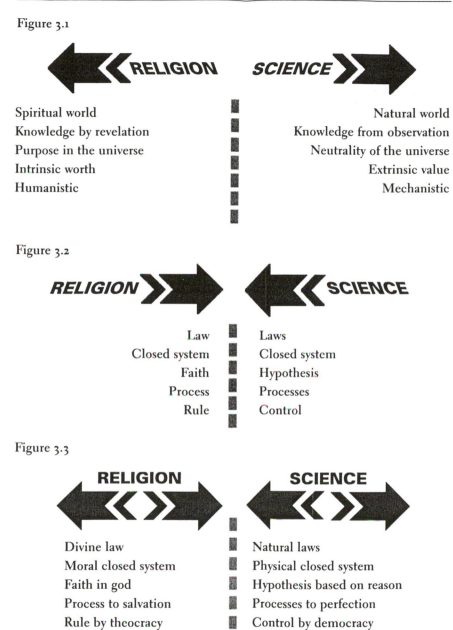

RELIGION

Spiritual world
Knowledge by revelation
Purpose in the universe
Intrinsic worth
Humanistic

SCIENCE

Natural world
Knowledge from observation
Neutrality of the universe
Extrinsic value
Mechanistic

Figure 3.2

RELIGION

Law
Closed system
Faith
Process
Rule

SCIENCE

Laws
Closed system
Hypothesis
Processes
Control

Figure 3.3

RELIGION

Divine law
Moral closed system
Faith in god
Process to salvation
Rule by theocracy

SCIENCE

Natural laws
Physical closed system
Hypothesis based on reason
Processes to perfection
Control by democracy

owners responsible for "managing, improving, ordering" the company, it was not until early in the twentieth century that the exigencies of size and complexity, both technological and human, converged to force the rationalization of organization. The result was the "science" of management, defined

Table 3.1
A Comparison of Fayol's Principles with Corporate Management

Fayol's Principles of Management	Features of the Corporation
• Division of work	• Isolation
• Authority	• Reason
• Discipline	• Obedience
• Unity of command	• Authority
• Unity of direction	• Predictability
• Interest of individual subordinate to group or general interest	• Hierarchy
• Fair wage	• Natural law
• Centralization–decentralization balance	• System
• Coordination of managers	• Mechanism
• Order	• Rank Order
• Equity (kindness and justice)	• Perfection
• Stability of tenure	• Position
• Initiative	• Collective
• *Esprit de corps*	• Community

and constructed after the fashion of all the other so-called sciences that spewed out when rationalism shattered the universe. So, while the modern corporation, legally and practically, had existed for over 200 years without the operational benefit of the applied techniques of the science of management, it was inevitable that the centuries-old concept and practice of managing things and people be exclusively appropriated by the corporation and, within that context, transformed into a scientific process. Some authors trace management all the way back to Moses and his delegation of authority to the twelve tribes. Others suggest that Socrates actually argued for management as a universal *art*. But those and other similar references are not more than the routine, necessary control exercised in various human endeavors. The word "management" was not used until early in the sixteenth century—and then as a rather generic term (often plural) having to do with the administration of business affairs. So it is perfectly understandable that "manage" was one of the responsibilities specified for the stockholders of the first corporation in the new world. But it was not until 1832 that Charles Babbage used the phrase "principles of management," thus inviting, actually requiring, the full development of those principles into a science. Interestingly, the word *manage* had at one time been professional jargon: In the twelfth century, it was a term particular to the breaking and training of horses. There is probably no connection whatsoever, but it is curious that management was defined throughout the twentieth century as "getting work done through people." Only in the 1990s did the American Management Associations add the preposition "with," in deference, no doubt, to the legislated hale fellow well met, politically correct collegiality of the times. Administration, the public sector derivative of management, which began to flourish in the 1930s, was formulated not as "principles" but as "proverbs." The basic idea was the same as management, only the emphasis was not on actually getting work done but on generating worklike activity sufficient to perpetuate the institution.

The effects of the inherent contradictions in the religion–science dichotomy, if they are to be understood fully, must be examined from two points of view. First, an analysis of the corporation's world—that is, the social order that exists within the corporation-model organization—will not only provide an understanding of the irreparable dysfunctionality of that system of organization but also suggest premonitions of the emerging new order. Second, an examination of the world of the corporation will not only clearly elucidate the intricate connection between the corporation-model organization and the larger society of Western civilization, especially its wealth production but also discover convincing evidence that the changing society has already rendered the corporation obsolete.

NOTES

1. Percy Bysshe Shelley, "Ozymandias," *Major British Writers*, ed. G. B. Harrison (New York: Harcourt, Brace and World, 1967), 681.

2. John Henry Cardinal Newman, *A Newman Treasury: Selections from the Prose Works of John Henry Cardinal Newman* (New York: Longmans, Green and Company, 1943), 79.

PART II

THE CORPORATION'S WORLD

CHAPTER 4

A Kingdom Divided

The old order changeth, yielding place to new,
And God fulfills Himself in many ways,
Lest one good custom should corrupt the world.
                                    Alfred Lord Tennyson[1]

The corporation's world was fundamentally conflicted by possibly the two most powerful forces that ever could be experienced by humanity. The conflict included, both in inquiry and answer, nothing less than the essential nature of the human being and, consequently, all aspects of human society. Ironically, the debate itself was of human origin. Through the struggle, over at least two centuries, the early concept of corporation as a single unified political body evolved into a unique dichotomized system of organization deemed suitable for every human enterprise, a system that reflected the inherent and irreconcilable schism in Western civilization itself.

Although in its modern construct it represents the triumph of rationalistic science, its infrastructure continues to reflect the basic tenets of Western religion. This dichotomy, implicit in the contemporary corporation-model organization, is the reason for its present dysfunctionality and imminent decline. This discussion will offer an analysis of each critical contradiction in an effort both to reveal its terminal condition and to discover clues as to the organization that is already displacing it.

It would be impossible ever to conduct a comprehensive analysis of the corporation. For one thing, the sheer complexity of the subject, historically and substantively, almost defies any logical arrangement of inquiry. Beyond that, the issues are fraught with imprecision and outright confusion that render final understanding virtually out of the question. One comes to realize quickly that both management and the corporate organization have always been catch-as-catch-can affairs.

About the best that can be done here is to examine, however cursorily, the fatal implications within the characteristics of the corporation-model organization. Yet even within this rather limited approach, which must necessarily deal only with the most salient issues, many other considerations, philosophical and practical, seem continually to insinuate themselves into the discussion. Beyond the sheer number of issues lies the question of depth and elaboration. Here again the subject threatens to push beyond the point of diminishing returns, so we must deliberately concentrate only on those implications with immediate practical significance in the context of this chapter.

The simplest approach is to take the seven attributes derived from religion, examine the definitions in the original context, and then analyze the perverse effect of rationalization on each. There is a twofold benefit in this task. First, historical accuracy is served, and the evolution of thought is always instructive, if not enticing. Actually, it is only in this way that the spectacular enantiodromia accomplished by rationalism can be truly appreciated. Furthermore, as a matter of strict analysis, this approach provides a full disclosure of the critical distinctions of mature rationalism as realized in organization. Earlier, it was sugested that the corporation model is characterized by fourteen features; a quick analysis reveals seven each from religion and science. When arranged as a point-by-point contrast, the contradiction is revealed rather emphatically. And a closer examination of each contradiction not only provides an understanding of the inestimable harm this system has inflicted on human beings but also bears credible evidence of a kingdom divided against itself. Neither the Church nor science could hold this civilization together.

Certainly, all these features are more or less universal. That is, they are found in almost all other forms of religion, if not all together then in various combinations and interpretations. But only in Christianity were they combined and interpreted in ways that ultimately define that which is Western.

Religion, Christianity	Science, Rationalism
• Authority	• Reason
• Hierarchy	• Natural law
• Rank order	• Predictability
• Position	• Perfection
• Obedience	• Mechanism
• Isolation	• System
• Community	• Collective

THE CORPORATION AND AUTHORITY

The idea of authority loomed over the world of the corporation like a giant cormorant over a dry sea. What was once, in its fullness, a reservoir of abundant life to all within its domain became a harsh wasteland where scavengers and predators vied for the dwindling survivors—all because authority lost, or renounced, its own source. Any authority that does not originate in divinity is always artificial—venal, abusive, deceitful, life threatening. It is difficult to generalize, but in the twentieth century the meaning of authority changed radically so that, as a rule, the more complex, the more profit-driven, and the more competitive the system, the greater the departure from the original.

Authority exists only in a context of values or, more precisely, within a value system. So in the Western tradition, as the context shifted from godly to godless, the nobility of legitimate authority gave way to the baseness of illegitimate power. Authority had always entailed two kinds of power: inherent—that is, arising from thoughtful experience at the limits of life—and imputed—that is, granted by calling or circumstance. Authority implicitly rejected the third kind of power, that which is seized, without apology, without remorse. Illegitimate power spurns all that authority professes.

Specifically, authority has four constituents, in more-or-less commensurate proportion: knowledge, responsibility, righteousness, and purpose. The first, knowledge, seemed always paramount. Christianity lauded Solomon as the paragon of transcendent knowledge (wisdom), and Plato vested authority most willingly in the philosopher-king. In fact, throughout the ages, every nonrationalistic culture has held in the highest esteem those who are seen as repositories of knowledge. The second, responsibility, was inescapable for those who ruled. "Mene, mene tekel upharsin" was written to a king by his angry boss. The message was that authority is to serve, not to be served. As for the third, righteousness, only those whose character was worthy of praise and emulation were worthy of ruling. Self-control was the requisite of controlling others. The fourth, purpose, was the essence of authority. In fact, it is impossible to think of authority without asking why; the only answer is advancement toward some worthy end. Purpose negated selfish ambition, aspired to the extraordinary, and served the mutual good for all who were embraced by that authority.

Any presumption of authority devoid of these virtues was tyranny, pure and simple, especially if the perverse rulers did not recognize it as such. That was the most heinous kind of usurpation. Ironically, ignorance is the logical conclusion of rationalism.

Rationalistic science swept away these obligatory virtues but clung tenaciously to the idea of domination. And why not? There is much to be said also for power, privilege, prestige, and position, other than alliteration and neat memory keying. It was just a matter of moral law, based on revelation or intuition, being repealed by rationalism and replaced by "natural laws," laws as interpreted by empirical science, and as postulated by rationalistic science. That was a pretty fancy move because at one time both systems of law were supposed to be the same. The significance of this shift was the critical difference between authoritative and authoritarian rule, between serving and being served, between leading and commanding.

The advertising graffiti of the modern age, the tutorial disquisitions, and the professional meanderings either blandly assumed or strove forcefully to prove a conclusion based on contradictory premises; specifically, that knowledge is not really a prerequisite of authority in a rationalistic context. Although much was made of the word, the meaning changed radically. It is typical of rationalism to deny by assertion and to assert by denial. So, within the context of the corporation model, knowledge, ironically, became the substance of things hoped for and the evidence of things not seen. Corporated "knowledge" could never be anything more than the accumulation of data-based whatnots, however sophisticated it may have seemed. But if words have any meaning at all, it is impossible for information ever to be sophisticated. It does not, and cannot, constitute knowledge. Certainly not wisdom. T. S. Eliot's question of the century has never been answered: "Where is the wisdom we lost in knowledge? Where is the knowledge we lost in information?"[2]

The only reply forthcoming in an age of information dizzy from its own excess was the grandiose motto of talk radio, ironically billboarded in Times Square (1995): "The greatest treasure is a wealth of information."[3]

Unbelievably, there was the adamant insistence that something called knowledge was an inherent quality of authoritariansim. And the more vulnerable the corporation became, the more insistently artificial knowledge was ascribed to authority. Consider this vacuous bit of ad agency–spun pandering as indicative of the corporation's shameless attempt to associate Zeus-like knowledge with those in positions of authority.

For a company's look—everything from its products and logo to its work space and billing statements—to successfully communicate a message, that message needs to be clear in the first place. Which means the CEO is the de facto head designer. Only the CEO can definitely answer questions like these: What business are we really in? What values shape our company and are important for customers and employees to know? As Hertz . . . would attest, you can't design anything well without understanding your company first.[4]

Yet in the corporation, responsibility often was supplanted by indulgence. Evidently, this was a little maneuver that rationalism picked up from the church (the idea of the sinecure). In all prescientific societies, and even now in most Eastern countries, it was expected that an equal measure of accountability be vested in all authority. Consequently, when something went wrong, the one possessing ultimate jurisdiction over the matter immediately assumed the blame and removed himself from authority (and sometimes the world) with great dispatch and little complaint. But in the modern Western organization, where nothing is more important than survival, authority was frequently divorced from responsibility. So when something went wrong the person ostensibly in charge would eloign himself from accountability ("distancing," as it is called) by blaming incompetent subordinates, hiding behind phalanxes of committees, diverting attention to side issues, shamelessly seeking sympathy for the heavy burden of command in the midst of uncontrollable circumstances, or pleading the weakness of the flesh. Incontinent repentance always commands sympathy if not forgiveness.

The ruler as narcissistic victim became the heroic ideal of a decadent civilization—and with good reason: Victimization was at the time the popular ersatz mentality. In fact, it was not uncommon for those in the highest positions of authority to be generously rewarded for failure (contract buyouts and golden parachutes)—consolation, no doubt, for suffering the irritation of having to put up with lesser mortals. Progressive successful failure became the preferred career track among chief executive officers.

But the most serious perversion of authority by the corporation was the complete abnegation of righteousness. In a godly world, authority was not license, nor was its prerogative assumed. Authority was the personification of moral force. And those whose lives exhibited such mettle were always with authority (authoritative) even if not in authority (authoritarian). Any society intent on preserving its own values will seek out, acknowledge, and pay homage to those who possess moral authority, however defined. This phenomenon has really little to do with organization per se, except that in that kind of society anyone else in a public or private office of authority is a pretender and lacks the character worthy of either honor (to be obeyed) or emulation (to be followed). Evidently, Shakespeare knew that kind of person:

> But man, proud man,
> Drest in a little brief authority,
> Most ignorant of what he's most assured,
> Plays such fanastic tricks before high heaven
> As make the angels weep.[5]

But rationalism made pretense reality. In the first place, the terms of honor were redefined. When science replaced righteousness with rightness, it changed authority from being to doing. And what an inversion! From that point onward, a person with artificial authority could promulgate laws while remaining lawless, exact tribute while revelling in extravagance, require strict discipline while engaging in profligacy, and rigidly control the lives of others while claiming unrestrained personal freedom. No honor here. And no shame. And no need. What in earlier times would have been judged malfeasance was intrinsic to the rationalistic construct of authority. In the corporation, any possibility of impropriety was obviated by the strict attachment of authority to office, regardless of the character of the person holding the office (as in, "Salute the uniform, not the person."). Authoritarianism thus became the corporation. If God had still been around, he probably would have damned it for this reason alone.

Second, the question of emulation raises the troublesome issue of leaders and leading—troublesome, that is, for the corporation organization and its nihilistic philosophy. The basic problem is a contradiction: Legitimate authority not only deserves to be followed but is, in fact, contingent upon being emulated. It is especially germane here to recall that authority originally presupposed knowledge, responsibility, righteousness, and purpose. At least two studies in North America have come to the same conclusion—that is, people still follow only those who are characterized by character, competence, commitment, and concern (in that order, as a matter of fact). They may choose or be forced to accept authoritarian rule, but in a truly authoritative relationship people choose to follow because the leader represents the personification of their own values. That should come as no surprise, since all human relationships are based on values. But when rationalism ridded the world of morality, it renounced natural leaders in any of its structures.

So, rationalism had to invent "leadership" as the amoral equivalent of authority. That accounts for questionable concepts such as this 1990s pronouncement by a former CEO turned dean of a business school: "High-performance companies are driven by their leaders."[6] Sorry. The unhappy fact is that leaders don't drive, and corporations don't have them! It also accounts for teasers such as this from Wharton School of Business (1995–96): "You have been given the responsibility to lead, but not the authority. This program explores the complex issues of ambiguous authority."[7]

There's a world of trouble all around. But implausibility did not deter those hell-bent on the fabrication of leadership as a science and especially as a commercial enterprise. As it might be expected, there were at least two constructs of this imaginary artifice—one based on the acquisition and application of certain skills, the other on the adherence to certain principles. In actual practice, there was a cavalier disregard for accuracy in categorical distinction. They were mixed and matched arbitrarily.

The skills approach assumed that leadership consisted of a set of variable and sometimes ill defined abilities, expressed always in behavioristic terms and that people—especially those with "aptitude" for leadership—could be identified, recruited, and trained for "leadership positions" within the corporation-model organization. One popular consulting firm even formulated a "leadership quotient" (LQ) test to sort out those especially gifted individuals who had the potential to be professional leaders. The result of subsequent leadership training ostensibly would be the creation of a cadre of leaders-at-large who would be ready for deployment to wherever people had a need to be led. The clear implication was that anyone so trained could, simply by plopping down a business card on any corporate boardroom table, cause others to fall in line behind ("Lafayette, we are here.").

Indicative of the generally accepted view of leadership was the Leadership Behavior Checklist used by 3M in 1992. There were ten categories, subdivided and graded on a scale of one to five (see Figure 4.1).

Judging from a rather extensive survey of all available publications and announcements in North America during the 1990s, every so-called leadership development curriculum of every university and every corporate or professional leadership-training program, however sincerely motivated and qualitatively cast in new-age lingo, was designed strictly to develop either the technical or the process expertise (always rational, linear, and objective) of those who had bravely chosen leadership as a career. Here again, considerable disappointment is at hand: The unhappy fact is that leading is not a matter of technique. Furthermore, no one chooses to be a leader. Leaders are chosen.

The second approach to leadership, strangely resembling the doctrinal cachet of religion, presumed to set forth principles of excellent, sometimes effective, conduct within the corporation-model organization. Based on expediency rather than morality, these more-or-less pragmatic rules were variously translated into discipline (as in "codes of conduct" and "professional ethics") and into ambition (as in "principles of leadership"). By the end of the twentieth century, secular doctrine completely replaced its sacred predecessor. In fact, in North America even mainstream religion greatly preferred rationalism over revelation. "Leadership" represented the profanation of authority.

The one author who held out the greatest promise of reinstating morality into authority was Stephen Covey. Unfortunately, admirable though the intention and the attempt, he did not deliver. In fact, even a generous analysis of his work soon reveals that his apocryphal gospel, an immensely popular synoptic rendition of terminal behaviorism, was actually bereft of morality. So, by his definition, "leadership" is little more than a collage of skills and "habits" disguised as "principles."[8] Actually, critical analysis is quite difficult, at best imprecise, owing to Covey's habits of casual ambiguity of language and desultory use of metaphor, to say nothing of his sometimes pernicious off-centered semantics. One knows not whether it is fish or foul. Covey represented the culmination of the rationalistic age.

There are two obvious, fundamental flaws in Covey's philosophy. First, his thinking was bound inextricably to a behavioristic world, a world of subtle linguistic shadings and malleable semantics. For example, central to his philosophy, he made much of the need for "principles" as the "center" of "leadership," and even went so far as to declare, "Principles, unlike values are objective and external [as opposed to values, which are] subjective and internal."[9] So far, so good. Unless, of course, principles are considered authoritarian and values are considered authoritative, as may indeed be the case. If so, then Covey tipped his hand early. But the insurmountable problem is that those principles supposedly are not based on any absolute morality or righteousness but are de-

Figure 4.1
Leadership Behavior Checklist

Leadership Behavior Checklist for (Organization): _____

Directions:
Rate the qualities of the organization's leadership behavior on the following checklist,
using a scale of 5 (high) to 1 (low).

Leading

1. Communicates, clarifies, and
   celebrates the vision

   5   4   3   2   1

2. Sets measurable goals for continuous
   improvement

   5   4   3   2   1

3. Gives recognition and rewards for
   meeting customer expectations

   5   4   3   2   1

4. Ensures availability of resources—
   time, materials, budget

   5   4   3   2   1

5. Sets an appropriate example for
   others to follow

   5   4   3   2   1

Guiding

6. Clarifies expectations and assures
   task understanding

   5   4   3   2   1

7. Creates a measurement system for
   monitoring performance

   5   4   3   2   1

8. Gives feedback on performance in
   meeting expectations

   5   4   3   2   1

9. Reinforces excellence and encourages
   higher performance

   5   4   3   2   1

10. Coaches rather than dictates the
    process of accomplishing objectives

    5   4   3   2   1

11. Asks questions about a situation
    before passing judgment

    5   4   3   2   1

12. Allows others to ask advice of
    management without making them
    feel incompetent

    5   4   3   2   1

Collaborating

13. Involves others in problem solving

    5   4   3   2   1

14. Cooperates with others and encourages
    cooperation rather than competition

    5   4   3   2   1

15. Recognizes and reinforces
    collaborative behavior

    5   4   3   2   1

Focus on Processes

16. Establishes clear standards and
    procedures

    5   4   3   2   1

17. Encourages the development of
    improved ways of doing things

    5   4   3   2   1

18. Provides the information needed to
    perform work

    5   4   3   2   1

rived from natural laws. It is significant that the plural form was used. This anach-
ronism was a clear admission that any distinction between natural law and moral
or spiritual law was to be out of the question. That is why his highest aim was to
develop people who were "effective" rather than "good." But morality is essentially the difference between behavior and character, habit and imperative, effectiveness and goodness, and leadership and leading.

Figure 4.1 (*continued*)

19. Ensures others have a clear understanding of goals, work flow, and expected outcomes

   5　4　3　2　1

Networking

20. Gets people to work together even if they are not direct reports

   5　4　3　2　1

21. Collaborates with other departments

   5　4　3　2　1

Diversity/Flexibility

22. Allows exceptions to the rules as required for meeting customer expectations

   5　4　3　2　1

23. Respects varying opinions and styles of completing work

   5　4　3　2　1

Openness/Sharing

24. Listens to others with an open mind

   5　4　3　2　1

25. Communicates own point of view willingly

   5　4　3　2　1

26. Respects varying opinions and differing styles of others

   5　4　3　2　1

27. Responds positively to feedback about own behavior

   5　4　3　2　1

Risk Taking

28. Is willing to take risks to reinforce the values of the organization

   5　4　3　2　1

29. Rewards the risk taking of others

   5　4　3　2　1

Involvement of Others

30. Establishes a working environment in which everyone feels involved and committed

   5　4　3　2　1

31. Involves others in planning to achieve performance goals

   5　4　3　2　1

32. Supports the working out of problems in teams

   5　4　3　2　1

People Assets

33. Views people as assets, not overhead

   5　4　3　2　1

34. Develops people through training and education

   5　4　3　2　1

35. Encourages shared decision making

   5　4　3　2　1

Source: Element One: Leadership for Quality Improvement. ©3M, 1982, used with permission.

It is instructive here to point out that "situational leadership" had become popular concurrently with "situational ethics." In the 1960s, John Fletcher proposed situationism as the rational middle ground between legalism (absolute laws) and antinomianism (no laws at all). He contended that there was and is one overarching law—*agape*—and that adherence to that norm required flexibility in the adaptation of behavior to various circumstances. The doctrine was thus basically pragmatic and relativistic ("Right" is only the expedient in behaving). It now seems clear that the only overarching law for situational leadership was productivity; for principle-centered leadership, it was effectiveness.

This is not idle academic bickering. Such thinking, especially when rendered by corporations in clumsy semantic impasto, was deceptive at least, destructive at most. Consider this excerpt from one of Whirlpool Corporation's publications: "Business with integrity. We will pursue our business with honor, fairness, and respect for both the individual and the public at large . . . ever mindful that there is no right way to do a wrong thing."[10] So much for being principle centered. The real question is whether it is possible to do the right thing in a wrong way.

In all honor, fairness, and respect, it should be pointed out that Covey himself acknowledged that his teachings were based on principles other than those of a moral (spiritual) universe; obviously he preferred his own to that of, say, Moses or Jesus ("The Seven Habits will help you avoid these Seven Deadly Sins [Gandhi's version]. And if you don't buy into the Seven Habits, try the Ten Commandments."[11]). It is fairly clear in which camp Covey pitched his tent; and it was not on Sinai or in the Galilean desert. Quite frankly, the seven cardinal virtues of the medieval world provide a more effective antidote to the "deadly sins," and a truer moral compass: Faith, hope, love, prudence, justice, fortitude, and temperance are attributes of character, not merely conditioned responses.

Second, Covey's world was the world of the corporation, and his mentality was a corporate mentality. For instance, his basic assumption was that leadership is practiced at four levels: personal, interpersonal, managerial, and organizational. All those levels were explained and exemplified in the context of the corporation-model structure. Even family relationships were presented as subservient to the corporation's welfare. Everything is seen from the corporation's point of view. In this way, Covey's teaching was seditious. He offered false hope to those who were trying to make the corporation work and, even more tragic, to those who were trying to work within it. Furthermore, like all other behaviorists, he believed that the "style" of "leadership" was a matter of the manager's choice: "Whenever a problem or opportunity arises, that requires the involvement of other people, the leader must make a choice. This essential leadership style choice is to decide on a power base— coercion, utility, or legitimacy. The choice will be limited by the character of the leader . . . and by her interactive skills, capacity, and history."[12]

Solomon was right: that which is crooked cannot be made straight. The assumption in such a statement is that the leader exists a priori, either because of cultivated leadership skills or vested position. How the leader chooses to deal with others is a matter of suiting style to circumstance. The line between accommodation and manipulation is never drawn.

Finally, the desecration of authority meant the repudiation of purpose as one of its constituents. The rejection is quite understandable. After all, the wealth-producing corporation could ill afford to make a big deal out of turning advantage into cash. In fact, corporations typically refused to come clean in their public presentations of mission. Or if they did, it was hedged beyond recognition. Consider the upside-down, inside-out hesitant declaration by Marriott Corporation (circa 1996): "We are committed to being the best lodging and contract service company in the world, by treating employees in ways that create extraordinary customer service and shareholder value." If honestly stated, it would read: "We are committed to creating extraordinary shareholder value." Quite frankly, deep down most people do not find avarice and greed particularly ennobling, especially when aimed at them. Wealth-consuming corporations, finding discretion the better part of valor, simply covered up their real purpose—revenue producing self-perpetuation—with a smokescreen of public interest claims.

The time was therefore ripe for the appearance of a new buzzword—vision. Some say Warren Bennis and Burt Nanus started the craze in 1985. If so, this was probably the seminal passage: "Vision is the commodity of leaders, and power is their currency."[13] This less-than-inspiring definition does not meet the criteria for vision listed three years later by Tom Peters. He insisted that vision be inspiring, clear, challenging, and detailed. Unfortunately, he had the right definition for the wrong word. *Vision* comes to English from the French, and that makes it immediately suspect—first, because of the enchanting symbolism inherent in the language itself and second, because it is the fancy argot most likely to impress plebians. *Eh bien, on fait ce qu'on peut.*

"Leadership" was apparently the only logical medium for "vision," if not its source, because all effusions about the subject started here. Some leadership experts were quite prescriptive: "Our message should be clear: Leaders are responsible for the creation of vision, and the vision provides the basic energy source for moving the organization toward the future."[14] Others accepted vision as a given for leadership: "Executives also must be taught to communicate effectively, since the most sophisticated vision is of no use unless it can be understood by others."[15]

Some proponents of "envisioning" or the "visionary model" actually deigned to quote Hebrew scripture, out of context, of course: "Where there is no vision, the people perish" (Proverbs 29: 11). Noted, with thanks. Now, here's another quote from the same author: "The way of the fool is right in his own eyes" (Proverbs 12: 15).

But the picture is clear enough. In a corporation, the chief has the vision and must somehow get others to share it; or if not share it, support it; or if not support it, accept it; or if not accept it, stay out of sight. It is significant that this point of view sees vision as something to be understood (intellectually), not visualized, not felt. How very different from the admonition by Antoine de Saint-Exupéry: If you want to build a ship, then don't drum up men to gather wood, give orders and divide the work. Rather teach them to yearn for the far and endless sea.[16]

René Pascal was right: "The heart has its reasons, which reason does not know."[17] Leadership, as defined by the turbid literature and counsel in the land of the blind, may require vision. There is no need to argue that, since meaning exists only in context; and those who invent a word have the right to define it. But in the context of legitimate authority, leading means something far more compelling. It is the personification of values. And that imperative makes all the difference in the world. Specifically, it is the difference between expectation and commitment; between *could be* and *is*; between destination and journey. Visions are passive, often clouded imaginings of possibility. Purpose is active, a clear declaration of certainty.

Visions cannot comprehend the entelechy of authority. But fortunately, that does not mean that ordinary human beings have lost their ability to discern the truth. Even when they do not know the words, they understand the meaning. The best evidence available, scientific and other, clearly indicates that even in the halcyon days of rationalism, people in any context or value system or circumstance, still intuitively knew what the corporation-model organization could not admit. In a moral universe, authority is not a matter of position; it is a matter of person. Authority is not a matter of rules; it is a matter of inspiration. Authority is not a matter of command; it is a matter of example.

NOTES

1. Alfred Lord Tennyson, "Morte d'Arthur," *The Norton Anthology of English Literature*, ed. M. H. Abrams (New York: W. W. Norton, 1968), 2: 840.

2. T. S. Eliot, "Choruses from 'The Rock,'" *The Complete Poems and Plays* (New York: Harcourt Brace, 1952), 96.

3. Bloomberg News Service.

4. *Syndesis*, advertisement, 1996–1997 (Hertz brochure).

5. William Shakespeare, *Measure for Measure*, II: ii, 118–123.

6. John Rau, "Nothing Succeeds like Training for Success," *Wall Street Journal*, September 12, 1994, p. A16.

7. "Wharton's Executive Education Programs," Wharton School of Business brochure, 1995–1996.

8. Stephen R. Covey, *Principle-Centered Leadership* (New York: Summit Books, 1990), 19.

9. Ibid.

10. Whirlpool Corporation, "One World, One Vision," 1994.

11. Covey, ibid., 93.

12. Ibid., 105.

13. Warren Bennis and Burt Nanus, *Leaders: Strategies for Taking Charge* (New York: HarperCollins, 1985), 17.

14. Noel M. Tichy and Mary Anne DeVanna, *The Transformational Leader* (New York: John Wiley and Sons, 1986), 146.

15. Rau, "Nothing Succeeds."

16. Antoine de Saint-Exupéry, *Airman's Odyssey* (New York: Harcourt, Brace & World, 1939), 413.

17. Blaise Pascal, *Thoughts*, sec. IV, 277, ed. W. F. Trotter (New York: P. F. Collier & Son, 1938), 98.

CHAPTER 5

The Corporation and Hierarchy

Rationalists, wearing square hats,
Think, in square rooms,
Looking at the floor,
Looking at the ceiling.
They confine themselves
To right-angled triangles.
If they tried rhomboids,
Cones, waving lines, ellipses —
As for example, the ellipse
of the half-moon —
Rationalists would wear sombreros.
Wallace Stevens[1]

Rationalism did not need cosmological evil to turn natural law against itself. The allure of hierarchy was far more irresistible than the forbidden fruit — and it came with the same promise: "You shall be as gods." The corporation model was a purloined design intended to serve the same ambition. As authority was corrupted, ecclesiastical order could be counterfeited with impunity. Whether the process was one of adaptation or transference is irrevelant, because the final result of either was the same: an unholy see.

It has already been pointed out that the hierarchical structure of society is universal and timeless, originating in the kinship pattern of family. What must be understood, however, is that the hierarchy is subject to cultural variations. In fact, a society's interpretation and exercise of the hierarchical system may be the fundamental distinguishing characteristic of that society. It may even be accurate to say that the interpretation constitutes the culture. Surprisingly, perhaps, anthropologists and ethicists (who make understanding culture their business) agree that nothing has meaning except in context. However, moralists will argue that meaning creates context. Whichever notion is accepted (most likely both are correct), the corporation-model organization represents a thoroughly rationalistic interpretation of the hierarchical system unique to Western culture.

Culture is about human relationships, individuals' commitments to each other and to the world around them, in as many dimensions and as expansive as the culture itself will allow. Thus, the broad range from simple to complex societies and the endless variations in temperament. The corporational hierarchy was about two specific kinds of relationships, those that pertain to value and those that have to do with values. One manifested itself in a mutation of patriarchy, the other in the permutation of ethical norms and moral imperatives.

The patriarchical structure was translated into the corporation-model organization in two dialectics—management style and gender. Management style was customarily defined as how and where in the system decisions were made and by whom. Although that definition may seem to suggest only technical, rational processes, in actuality management style ultimately involved every aspect of organization: specifically, authority, accountability, information, and power. So value overtones are immediately evident. There were many variations among the categorical schematics—usually depicted as continuums—proposed by management experts; but in every paradigm "authoritarian" was posited at one extreme. For example, two well-known versions suggested close parallels. One is the Kenneth Blanchard interpretation of "situational leadership," the other the standard presentation of management styles (see Figure 5.1).

What is significant about this concept is that it recognized two expressions of the authoritarian style: paternalistic and autocratic. These designations were familiar to both the language and the psychology of the corporation, albeit the jargon was often bandied about with casual disregard for accuracy

Figure 5.1
Leadership and Management Styles

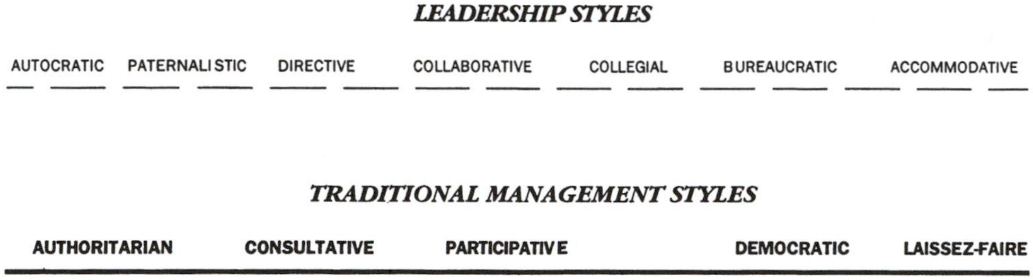

LEADERSHIP STYLES

AUTOCRATIC	PATERNALISTIC	DIRECTIVE	COLLABORATIVE	COLLEGIAL	BUREAUCRATIC	ACCOMMODATIVE

TRADITIONAL MANAGEMENT STYLES

AUTHORITARIAN	CONSULTATIVE	PARTICIPATIVE	DEMOCRATIC	LAISSEZ-FAIRE

in either meaning or application. Ostensibly, according to the lore and legend of the times, these styles were opposites within kind—one benevolent,
the other malevolent—or good guy–bad guy, in the popular idiom. But, in
actuality, they were as often as not one and the same. For example, it is impossible to conclude whether the following declaration represents comparison or contrast. "Straight talk. I'm straight with people, and I expect the same
from my children and my brokers."[2]

But it is possible to conclude very quickly and accurately that such pronouncements are indicative of an attitude that does not particularly value
people either as persons or as sources of genius. This statement, proceeding
directly from a chief executive officer, is characteristic of the authoritarian
style. In addition to being patronizing, it is unilateral, without provision for
appeal, eminently domained, and given to swagger.

In somewhat finer detail, and in the language of the corporation, the style
of management was predicated on ancient dimensional assumptions: all authority originates at the top of the organization, and ultimately returns there;
authority is delegated downward; and is diminished with every level so that
those at the bottom of the pyramid are not allowed to make any decisions
whatsoever. The same top-down flow was expected with regard to information. That not only proves the symmetry of the arrangement but also demonstrates its basic premise: Ignorant people should not be trusted to make
decisions. With the matter of accountability, however, a strange reversal takes
place: the direction of accountability is always upward, and that inverse pro-
portionality inevitably creates serious tension, if not uncontrollable stress.
The net effect is that accountability is exacted without control; the commensurate ability to control is granted without accountability. That is why all
systems given to this style, from small companies to nations, were characterized by fear and dependence. And, in fact, many deliberately cultivated these
vulnerabilities in order to achieve motivation and control of otherwise sloth-
ful and undisciplined workers.

However, perhaps because of a miscalculation of worker resolve, authoritarian management, forceful as it is, was resisted by opposite, sometimes equal,
forces—labor unions, for example. In fact, it was the authoritarian style that
gave birth to organized labor; it seems just another case of the universal dialectic at work in a specific socioeconomic circumstance. As a general rule, the
more authoritarian the style, the more powerful the resistance. It was power
versus authority, in more ways than one.

It was as much the obvious counterproductivity of this conflict as it was the
humanizing theories of management science in the early twentieth century
that led to the putative amelioration of the authoritarian style. It was a good
idea, but a good idea that did not work, because it could not work. For instance, with reference to the alleged styles, "laissez-faire" was in actuality the
antithesis of management; so it was out on a technicality. Democratic decision making made sense only in an autocratic context (such as government);

so it was rejected as a too obvious self-contradiction. And the consultative approach had a tendency to turn into a pernicious ruse called, "Guess what the boss wants."

The only style that offered any real hope was popularly known as "participatory." There were only two problems: no one ever knew for sure what it was; and the more corporations learned about it, the less they wanted to know. Authoritarian management was always the first, the last, and the only resort.

Much more subtle, if not more pervasive, than the corporation's application of rationalistic designs in the science of management and its purported styles, was its obsession with gender. One would expect the most telling aspect of any culture to be its language. In fact, it is probably true that language (or dialect) bears the culture (value system); furthermore, that order underlies essentiality at the most basic formations of language, such as the use of prepositions. But the thing about any language that speaks most directly to the value of human and other natural beings is the use (or nonuse) of gender.

The application of gender, whether sexually or symbolically, is the way of certain cultures to put everything in its place; in fact, gender is both the basic and ultimate declaration of relationships.

The corporation was masculine gender in terms of both sexuality and symbolism. Regarding sexuality, the very concept of hierarchy immediately invokes a system of "sacred" rule — a patriarchy that relegates all women on the planet to the duty of serving and pleasuring men. In Western civilization, that sexual subjection was based on the two specific tenets of the Judeo-Christian religion noted later in this study; that women were created second and sinned first. In a sense, the corporation represented the extension of male dominance within the traditional family into the larger, more impersonal social context of the workplace. In fact, so immutable were roles and relationships between the sexes that entire industries — their manufacturing processes, their operational controls, and even their economies — were based on the subordination of women. For example, in North America the garment business, the telecommunications industry, textile mills, public education, and the entire banking and insurance kabal have always been predicated on the overt exploitation of women as laborers. And despite all the so-called advancements in social equity, equal opportunity, and equalization of job worth that ostensibly occurred during the 1970s and 1980s, the corporation ultimately could not yield this point: exploitation of women means profitability.

Nor could it yield control. At the end of the twentieth century, the fundamental adverseness of the hierarchy toward women was just as much in evidence as it was in 546 BC — probably more so. The only proof needed for that assertion is the fact that in 1998, 60 percent of the workforce in North America were women, but only 3 to 5 percent of top management positions were held by them. Even the lack of statistical precision reeks of disdain beyond prejudice. It is truly amazing that as Western civilization, as a whole, through the provocation of a variety of democratizing, humanizing, rationalistic agendas, moved steadily, if slowly, toward equality of the sexes (typically, by the reluctant legislation of women's rights), the corporation model, although perhaps not the only male bastion of society, was the one most exclusively of, by, and for the male of the species. It should not be surprising, then, to discover that not since the ancient age of goddesses has any maternalistic society depicted itself as a hierarchy.

Regarding symbolism, it must be remembered that all languages (dialects), whether considered formations or constructs, are more or less complete systems of symbols, and that each language (or dialect) has its own distinctive, inherent nuances. Some are so distinctive they are incomprehensible to those not born to them. The language of the corporation knew no such subtlety. If understanding of the full implications of the corporation's vernacular was generally obscured, it was, ironically, because of the reverberating declaration of unyielding preference for all things masculine. Just as the corporation was genetically male, semantically it was, by any definition, masculine.

Reduced to its basic terms, morphology—the construct of the corporation's language—was uncompromisingly masculine. The suffixes alone declare the whole truth and nothing but the truth. Although the significance may be lost on modern-day English speakers (along with everything else), the original meanings are deeply imbedded in ordinary cultural practices. Consider, for example, just a few words indigenous to the corporation culture—"manager," "supervisor," "director," "controller." All these words are grammatically and innately masculine by virtue of the suffix "er" or "or." The feminine, of course, is "ess" or "ster" ("weaver"/"webster"). This intrinsic masculinity makes the late twentieth century politically correct contortions of the title "chairman" seem hopelessly pathetic. There is an impenetrable cloud of denial overshadowing the real issue. So what is the practical significance of all this academic trivia? Simply this: a female manager or supervisor or director or controller is a linguistic contradiction.

The metaphors of the corporation's language rigidly mark the boundaries of this exclusively male domain. The metaphors speak to what is in and what is out. There are two difficulties in pursuing this subject. First, metaphors are by their nature sometimes elusive; and, second, there is a danger of fouling the intended meaning by interpretation screened through unjustified or inaccurate presuppositions (such as stereotypes—"warriors" versus "villagers"). However, even with these sincere disclaimers, it is patently obvious that the metaphors of the corporation were distinctly masculine.

There were three categories of allusion: capture (those words having to do with foraging, hunting, and conquering); dominance (psychological, intellectual, and emotional); and permanence (endurance, staying power, and immortality). Such symbols are rampant in the literature of the corporation. Sufficiently illustrative is the language of a single article in Forbes.[3] Admittedly, the subject is an especially aggressive CEO, and the style may be a bit overwrought, but the symbolism was typical of the corporation's idiom.

August Busch III, the fourth generation of his family to head Anheuser-Busch Cos., Inc. hunts competitors the way he stalked the deer and moose whose heads stare from the walls of his rural Missouri ranch house. "The goal is dominance," he says. . . . Along the way, Busch brutally repulsed an attack on his market dominance by Philip Morris' formidable marketing machine.

"We are at war," Dennis Long, the president of the company wrote in an in-house newsletter in 1978.

"I have to win," admits the rarely interviewed Busch. Pounding his hand on the table. Bang! "This company is a winner, and I'm going to continue that track record."[4]

Relationships based on values are simpler than those proceeding from value. Definitively, they are objectifiable, direct, and practical. They immediately translate into priorities, principles, and standards. Analytically, the subject yields itself to almost point–counterpoint comparison–contrast. Technically, the matter of values is the clearest demonstration of what science did to religion when it was looking (even though religion took the credit). However, the actual substance of that demonstration does pose a bit of a problem. Basically, what science did was to obscure irrevocably the definitions to the point of reversal of meaning. Eventually no one, especially the intellectual, heard the slightest dissonance in the phrases "Christian ethics" and "corporate morality"; and dictionaries (whose normal reasoning is after the fact) used the terms "morality" and "ethics" to define each other. So if there is the tiniest difficulty with making precise distinctions between morality and ethics, it is for good reason.

Frankly, the only coherent way to approach any final judgment is through the use of stipulations as close as possible to the nominal definitions. This is neither arbitrary nor conniving: all words have a nominal definition historically, and real definitions are always the result of changeable general agreement. So stipulations of meaning are rather like a seawall, whose purpose is to retain as closely as possible the once natural shoreline against a wild and overbearing sea.

First, it is necessary to acknowledge that there are values based on human needs. Whether Abraham Maslow is the final authority on this subject may be debatable, but, validity aside for the moment, it is particularly significant that he found it most illustrative to arrange these needs (values) in a hierarchical order. These need-values, dealt with later in this essay, will not be explored here because they have to do with motivation, not relationships. That may be an ultrafine distinction, but it is a true one; otherwise there would be an explanation for the everyday inevitable conflicts between needs and convictions (or codes). The concern here is with the latter kind of values.

Second, there is the issue of whether these values themselves are subjective or objective. To this question, there is no easy answer—that is to say, no answer that would unite all inquirers in a rousing chorus of approval. But with due respect to all serious expositions on the subject, the only defensible

explanation is this: both. Specifically, values (of whatever kind) are subjective in interpretation and objective in both origin and application.

The values that determine relationships are of two persuasions: there are
those historically categorized as "morality," and those commonly referred to
as "ethics." This is where the stipulation begins. Morality is the basis of character; ethics, of conduct. By that definition, morality actually embraces ethics since character is expressed in action; and ethics ultimately require some
kind of moral context, even if it is an artificial one—that is, a standard, rather
than law.

Morality is based on the premise of the existence of absolute good and evil
(or right and wrong, in that context), and, furthermore, on the irreconcilable
opposition of two spiritual forces. The moral universe, hence the moral person, is characterized by congruence with moral "laws." These laws derive
from a source beyond the invention of humankind and are known by direct
revelation, as from God; or intuitive discovery, as by God. But morality is by
no means passive. The laws are undeniable imperatives, compelling practical action. It is in this way that character becomes conduct. Failure to follow
these laws results inevitably in condemnation and punishment by the presumed author of the legislation, who is also the judge. Justice is simple and
certain. At the risk of making much of a small thing, there is a hidden trap in
interpretation and application of moral laws. It occurs when the primary laws
are reduced to specific rules of conduct by decree, creed, or even practice. If
these rules and their attendant regulations are considered as equal in moral
force to the law itself, the result is an oppressive righteousness, which, ironically, is immoral by its own definition.

Ethics, on the other hand, are predicated on the assumption that there
exist within any culture—defining the culture—certain norms of human
behavior within a social context. These norms for society at large become
customs; for the community, mores; for the individual, code. Here the immediate concern is not with the issue of good versus evil but rather with fairness,
equity, and sometimes expediency. Whereas the laws of morality are quite
specific and ultimately absolute, ethical principles are pragmatic, constantly
forming themselves even within the same circumstance. That's why they are
described as "norms"; they represent the last normative behavior acceptable
by any respective group. Once the norms are established, however tentative,
deviation is punishable by penalty or exclusion. However, justice is negotiable and uncertain—and never satisfying.

Now, there is in this context a remarkable convergence of morality and
ethics in the question of absolute versus nonabsolute. It should not be surprising to find that this enigma, common to both, is answered exactly oppositely by each. The issues are neither academic nor theological. It is a practical,
everyday matter: What if one moral law conflicts with another? Is one to be
subordinated to the other? And are some ethical codes more sacrosanct than
others? What is truly marvelous about all this is that, in modern times, reli-

gion has sought after ratiocinative nonabsolutes, while science has searched for authoritative absolutes.

In the case of morality, both the Christian religion and Greek philosophy answered the question with a simple, "Yes, some laws are higher than others." When Jesus was challenged to identify the greatest commandment, he not only answered directly ("Love the Lord thy God with all thy heart, soul, and mind") but identified the second as well ("The second is like unto it. Thou shalt love thy neighbor as thyself"). Certainly, it is not surprising to find the last Platonist, an other-worldly scholar named Plotinus, arguing for the supremacy of some moral laws over others. Both appealed to a single highest law—Jesus, to love (*agape*); Plotinus, to moderation (*sophrosyne*). It was precisely this assertion of one overarching law—a law to which all others, although universal imperatives in their own right, were subject—that was the origin of "situationism," as it developed in mid-twentieth century. Actually, "situational ethics," the darling of the 1960s, was "situational morality," the supra law being love. But by that time the vocabulary, if not the philosophy, of religion had accepted the term "ethics" as a reasonable synonym for "morality." So many of the popular religious expositions and pronouncements dealing with ethics were in fact confused (and confusing) attempts to deal with what had been morality without using the word (For example, *Ethics: Alternatives and Issues*, by Norman I. Geisler [Grand Rapids, Mich.: Zondorvan, 1971]). In Haight–Ashbury, *agape* was easily replaced by *phileo* or *storge* and even more freely displaced by *eros*.

The modern corporation was inherently situational in its "morality." There was one supreme law—profit (or, in the case of wealth-consuming enterprises, self-perpetuation). All other values and all other relationships were subordinated to that imperative. The implication is obvious: the world is ruled by priority, with the importance of everything determined by its contribution to profit. Consequently, the world is sustained by the principle that the end justifies the means.

Ethics is a horse of a different color. Even in a moral universe, norms represent evolutionary practice: the contemporary scientific term, therefore, is "normative behavior." The point is that norms are not decreed, they are formed. Rather than being related to some almighty external supra law, ethics are relative only to each other. And the relativity is inversely proportional to the rigidity of the commonly accepted morality, if any. Hence, in an amoral universe there is a continuous process of defining right and wrong, not within the dictates of morality but as negotiated by general agreement within the context of actual give-and-take experience. That explains how there can be honor among thieves. Obviously, the practical effect of this dynamic is frequent and often seismic shifts in what is commonly acceptable in attitudes and behavior. Nothing in the world is subject to more radical change, within a shorter period of time, than the ethics of a rationalistic society. People with no appreciation of good and evil are rather fickle and very quick to negotiate.

When there are no supra law and no absolute scale of values, in every circumstance there is of compulsion, as well as practicality, an ordering of values from greatest to least—a hierarchy. Strangely enough, this exercise typically is pursued with the fanatical zeal and authoritarian pronouncements characteristic of the most didactic religions. As with religion, the concern is not with priority but with principle. The emphasis is on ways these principles are best negotiated. That is to say, the means justify the end.

In an amoral universe, all ethical norms proceed not from self-interest, but from selfishness. Self becomes the supra law, the altar upon which all other values may be sacrificed from time to time and the antistandard by which any conduct can be justified. The law of self becomes the artificial substitute for the moral context required by ethics. If that seems perverse, the practical consequences are even more so. This principle, paradoxically, most often proves to be an open invitation to dire settlements or outright surrender.

By the beginning of the twenty-first century, the hierarchy had become terminally fragile, because by then it was neither sacred nor a matter of rule. And the world was on the brink of discovering that it is impossible for bad people to do good.

NOTES

1. Wallace Stevens, "Six Significant Landscapes," *Wallace Stevens: Collected Poetry and Prose* (New York: Library of America, 1997), 60.
2. Wick Simmons, CEO, Prudential Securities, television commercial, 1996.
3. Seth Lubove, "Get'em Before They Get You," *Forbes*, July 31, 1995, 8.
4. Ibid.

CHAPTER 6

The Corporation of Rank Order and Position

Because you make the things of this world your goal,
which are diminished as each shares in them,
envy pumps hard the bellows for your sighs. . . .
As you can see, bad leadership has caused the
present state of evil in the world.

Dante[1]

In any organizational construct deriving from religion, authority is the foundation and hierarchy is the superstructure. Historically, that is especially true with regard to offsprings of Christianity (with its seven interlocking orders) and Hellenistic theology (with its innumerable emanations and eons). So, a system that is in effect a merger of the two was bound to be the ultimate in structure. And if the analogy works, rank becomes the infrastructure, providing the system's intrinsic connections among its parts, which nevertheless remain parts. Fundamental to the whole concept of rank is the assumption that these connections are based not on anything as pragmatic as what the parts actually do to benefit the whole system but on a faithful dedication to the notion of a superior–subordinate paradigm originating in the heavens and played out in every aspect of human society.

In principle, there was at work here nothing less than a divinely natural law. "God's in his heav'n; all's right with the world" suddenly takes on new, discomfitting, and discouraging meaning. Discomfitting because it is impossible to settle the issue of rank between only two respective components or principles in a given system unless every one is at the same time set in its right place relative to the others, from the least to the greatest. And so the task, at once both intimidating and tedious, is to arrange everything in the universe in a great chain of being. Discouraging, because inevitably there arises the nagging suspicion that the fix is in, beyond the individual's control. Here there is the prospect of the system being so rigid, so unyielding, that human efforts to bend it or overcome it are futile. One is best advised to find one's place in the scheme of things and accept it with praise and thanksgiving.

Within the authoritative–hierarchal construct, the rank of individuals proceeded quite nicely from circumstance—specifically, three circumstances: birth, grant, or virtue. One's class standing was determined by the societal position of one's parents. Rank among peers was described by the good grace of someone who outranked them all. Levels of honor were bestowed strictly according to the measure of one's tried and true character. For centuries, that was the order of human society throughout the world, although it does seem that "civilized" societies especially doted on rank and made much ado over the trappings thereof. In fact, the more rigid and thorough the ranking, the more civilized the society thought itself. But that was before the reordering of the universe by rationalism.

More than any other characteristic of the corporation model, rank order attests to the irreconcilable duality of corporation model. And the world that created it. And the world it created. Here, rationalism found itself caught in a contradiction of its own making. Its political philosophy, democracy, which extolled equality and personal freedom in government, was not the philosophy of the corporation. Although it is true that all democracies eventually took on the rule of rank, especially in their bureaucracies, the corporation model never made the slightest pretense to egalitarianism. It was built from the beginning on chain of command and, with the later application of scientific processes, developed an abundance of vertical control mechanisms. The result was the transmutation of the rank order of religion into its scientific equivalent—a reasonable facsimile without the moral attachments. That was probably the logical consequence of the scientizing of mostly proprietary (authoritarian) enterprises during the nineteenth century and therefore to be expected. But it is somewhat surprising to find a major consulting firm in organizational development as late as the 1990s still recommending arrangements from "top to bottom," in "order of importance within the structure of the organization," according to "some kind of rational order, on a scale." Moreover, and especially puzzling, the ultimate goal of the exercise was to determine the "distances between the ranks."[2] So much for the connections within the infrastructure. The truly horrifying news is that this firm claimed to have infected 4,000 client companies in thirty countries.

The obvious question is indicative of the basic contradiction: Why would rank order be anathema in the public mind of society—as in government, social class, and race—and be de rigueur in the organization structure of the corporation? The answer is both subtle and simple. Rationalism craftily changed the basis of rank. Religious systems of rank were predicated on circumstance, but rationalistic systems were based on condition—conditions that were strictly controlled by the corporation. The result was a rank order as arbitrary as it was fast and loose.

How it happened is as fascinating as what happened. As one would expect, there was a logical sequence involved—in more ways than one. First, the concept of "job" was invented. Actually, it was reinvented. The idea, as well as the word, is so old its origin is impossible to trace. From earliest recorded use of the word, *job* referred to a compact piece of some substance or a small definite piece of work such as a single cartload of something. How very handy the term to designate the sequential piecework of manufacturing! And how precisely the idea fit within the concept of rationalization of production. Although eventually stated in terms of work or worklike activity for individuals, job descriptions were cast according to rigorous scientific analyses of all the activities necessary for the processes of the enterprise. That was, as a matter of fact, organization as defined by the corporation model and management science. What is particularly significant is that these analyses and determinations were made independently of the person holding the job. Organizational development gurus were adamant that there was never to be any consideration of the job holder. When the activity was translated into a practical description of all the conditions comprising the job, it explicitly stated responsibilities, reporting relationships, authority, and necessary qualifications. The intent was not only to create a complete fixed structure in which all the parts fit exactly but also "to place all jobs in an organization in a sequence which represents the order and extent of their difficulty and importance within the organization."[3]

Second, obviously, jobs had to be assigned to somebody. It is, after all, a natural law that sooner or later somebody has to do something. With every job assignment there was the necessary implication of place within the scheme of things. The title of the job became the title of the job holder; the rank of the job the rank of the person performing it. So the transference of job level to superior–subordinate relationships among individuals was easy indeed, even logical. The truly insidious thing about this arrangement is this: Although a job represented only a small definite piece of work for the corporation, in an industrialized society it became the job holder's life. So, one's rank within the specific corporate system was extended into all personal and social relationships. The boss was always the boss—on and off the job.

Third, a new class system was established according to job type. Originating within the structure of the corporation, this order of rank permeated the broader society of the industrial age. It mattered greatly whether one's job was professional, executive, managerial, white collar, blue collar, laborer (skilled, semiskilled, or unskilled). Of course, economics followed more or less the order, but much more than comparative wealth was involved in this social arrangement: It was a matter of comparative worth. By the end of the century, as the decline of the corporation became evident, the idea of a job-type order threatened to project itself even into the society of the cyber age. As early as 1990, pundits, prophets, and secretaries of labor were describing an emerging four-tier socioeconomy based on "job" (even though jobs as defined by the corporation were rapidly becoming obsolete). The neo-order, it was predicted, would be made up of (from top to bottom) "symbolic-analytic" professionals, "in-person service" providers, "routine production" workers, and a few (5%) noncategorical workers.[4] Strange, at least from a nonrationalistic point of view, that rationalism succeeded in completely exenterating the original godly reason for rank order and replaced it with thoroughly demoralized rationale — demoralized in every sense of the word. That is, it was devoid of morality, given to ennui, and always on the verge of collapse.

Position was the avoirdupois of the corporation. As is the case with that system of weights and measures, its origin is somewhat dubious and its application often pointless. Even so, position was the standard by which all matters were assayed, the meter by which all stores were meted, and the scales by which balance was maintained.

There are many truly weird things in the language and literature of the corporation — some hilarious, some pathetic, some beyond description. Many pass understanding. But none is more flabbergasting than the unfailing, insistent, and inexplicable semantical leap — no matter who the author or what the purpose of the exposition — from "job" to "position." It was simple. It was dazzling. It was subtle, enticing. It promised what it had to in order to get the job done. And this leap actually occurred often within a single sentence. No rhyme. No reason. Consider this explanation, quite respected at the time, of the correct placement of "job analysis" as a step in a well-known project planning instructional exercise:

ORGANIZING

> Step (8) C.   Identify and analyze the various *job tasks* necessary to implement the project. Only by rigorous activities analysis can managers determine what has to be performed and how each *position* fits into the organization structure.[5]

Are we to conclude that job tasks automatically constituted positions? Or did the positions already exist in some kind of fixed organization structure so the job tasks could be somehow transferred to them? It would be bad enough if this confusion were merely a case of accumulated slipshod writing style (after all, no one has ever accused organizational development experts of being scholars). But the really bad news is that the gap was neither mistake nor trick. It simply did not exist. In the world of the corporation, job was synonymous with position. It had to be so, because only in this way could the corporation overcome the inconsistencies and problems arising from the rank ordering of jobs within the corporation and the corporate society and, at the same time, lend dignity to undignified work.

Position became the X factor. By it, all action was justified; by it, interest within disinterest was sustained; by it, permanence—a reality only within the corporation—was established. It was at once noun, verb, and adjective—avoirdupois.

Maybe "justified" is too strong a word, especially if it is inferred to carry any notion of righteousness or rectitude. No, here the meaning is rightness or correctness of each part and the integrity of the whole system. Nor is it a matter of justice, as defined in a legal context, but of adjudication (that is, testimony as to value) within the fixtures of the corporation model organization. The fundamental issue was the justification of rank, a principle to which the corporation was uncompromisingly committed. Dealing with that principle was critical, because if rank could be justified, so could anything else. Actually, there is a curious inversion of logic here. It is also true that, since anything can be rationalized, rank can be quickly an easily justified even in a democratic philosophy. So position was made both exemplar and exponent of rank.

As exemplar, position was as simple as as declaration and as complex as a fractal. By declaration all positions were established; their mere existence was proof of their rightness. It is; therefore, it should be, must be. Such an absolute state of being could be achieved only by the adamant detachment of organization from persons or, for that matter, any human consideration. Position was called forth strictly in terms of its place within the structure of the corporation, as pure an abstraction as ever there was. And place was always located within the geography of authority. It was especially critical that position not be connected to a person, as it had been in a godly world. The granting of position had been the last remnant of the kingly prerogative. Louis XIV (1643–1715) ruefully observed that position was the "dernier droit du roi." He thought enough of this sardonic pith to have it etched or cast on everything in France that did not move. But in the godless world, even though eventually position would be conditionally "assigned" to someone, and even though that person would presume conditionally to "fill" the position, it could not in any way be attributed to or depend upon a human source, certainly not a divine one. In this way, position served the nettlesome problem of rank in a democratic society: position made it hypothetically possible for every person to fill some position (especially with the legislated guarantee of equal opportunity) and thus achieve some personal rank or status. Western education, especially in the nineteenth and twentieth centuries, was designed to provide entry into the world of position; the object of all curricula was to get one. And friendly corporate headhunters routinely advised wayfaring pilgrims to seek a position, not a job.

As a fractal, position brought to the corporation the only magic it would ever know—the only magic it could stand. The basic design of the corporation was geometric. That design quickly became known as "traditional" organization because it was the template for the organizational charts of all Western enterprises. Or perhaps it was because the experts in organization theory early on pronounced the design "traditional," and all corporate enterprises, being much given to form and precedence, assumed it all to be so and fell in line—and staff. Whatever the case, the geometric design (the pyramid) was the corporation model's only organization. But there was a pattern within the pattern, so that no matter how imprecise or incomplete the total organization design, position always asserted itself as the ruling order. Witness, the very first act of any cohort within the corporation (say, a committee or task force or club) was to organize according to position. It was first nature for the corporated mentality. Even when the strictly geometrical design of the traditional organization became intellectually déclassé, as it did in the waning days of the corporation, and even when the design ostensibly was set aside in deference to the prevailing humanistic or naturalistic fad du jour, position still remained the very essence—the DNA—of the corporation model.

If position as exemplar established the order that was right and correct, then position as exponent adjudicated the value implicit within that order. No matter what the business of the enterprise and no matter what the basis for determining specific position, either organizationally or personally, position was the only true indicator of value. The measure of that value was three-fold: privilege, authority, and status. Never a grant, always an assignment; never a gift, always an office, position was constituted of some combination—not necessarily commensurate—of these three awards. The combinations always were arranged in a vertical (rank) order. Privilege meant two things: control over one's own time and activities (that is, to do as one pleases) and economic benefit, including various perquisites (that is, to have what one wants). Typically, authority was translated into jurisdiction over the privileges of others. If not exactly balanced with accountability, authority quickly became power of the third kind. And that raises again the troublesome prospect of excess authority within the corporation. There is an unnatural law at work here: The higher the authority, the less specific the expectations. In fact, that becomes another privilege—the freedom of unknowing. Status was the social blessing of the corporation. It was the tangible expression of unmerited favor, the objectification of value. Therefore, it was usually bestowed with much ostentation and ceremony.

Position was the only captivation of the corporation—the only hold it could ever have over the individuals it considered its resources. In this world, built as it was on the most fundamental conflict of interests, position was the only incentive that could entice through its blatant appeal to self-interest beyond economics. It is true that position almost always equated with financial remuneration—but only within the limits afforded by the corporation. Economic motivation, however, for all its mundane and emotional tug and push, was simply no match for the natural magnetism of all the glorious promise of position. Perhaps it is true that human beings are economic animals. Perhaps it is also true that they will do anything for money. But, above all, they are social, security conscious, and instinctively competitive. Nothing, absolutely nothing, could satisfy like position. So the corporation, devoid of human traits itself, craftily traded position for its own interest—which was always and only economic. At least, that's the way it was in wealth-producing enterprises. But by some strange application of the law of diminishing returns, in wealth-consuming corporations, where self-perpetuation was the primary interest of both the individual and the system, and where position was all there was, position actually accrued to the advantage of the system. The more the positions, and the more fixed, the more permanent the whole system. There was almost perfect coincidence of corporation and individual interests in position. Hence, the stifling, tedious bureaucracies of governments, churches, military organizations, and educational systems. Self-perpetuation was the lowest common denominator of the system and the person.

The attraction of position was not so much in the possession as in the prospect offered by each position—a higher position. Although every position was independently set and secured within the construct of the organization, no position was ever final. Positioning was the constant career move. It was realized through a very complicated process described as "promotion"—obviously, the idea being to move up, as on a ladder. Position was the allure of the corporation; promotion was the lure. It was irresistible to both ambition and dissatisfaction. That meant no one could escape its gravitational pull, for this one compelling reason: Promotion amounted to moving farther and farther away from the main business of the enterprise and being rewarded for the escape. This was the greatest promise of the corporation. For the ambitious (20%—Pareto's Law), the main business was a distraction; for the dissatisfied (80%—actual statistics), it was a burden. The prospect of promotion was the only force strong enough to move them both—always up, and eventually out.

Promotion was the great mystery of the corporation. No one ever figured it out. If someone did, there was no telling. All rationale for promotion was the corporation's secret. For a long time, rumor had it that promotion somehow was based on merit. But there were two very practical, if not philosophical, obstacles that rendered any so-called "performance-based" system virtually impossible. For one thing, the corporation, for all its insistence on objectivity and rationalization, was never able (or disposed) to develop any credible method of performance evaluation; job descriptions certainly provided no basis for assessment of actual activity (not to mention results), and there were simply too many subjective factors involved. As a matter of fact, in a strange twist of logic, no evaluation methodology ever devised by the corporation could assess real job performance; and in institutions, evaluation consisted of subjective marking of behavioral characteristics. That fact tended to make any evaluation into perfunctory, after-the-fact inconsequentiality, fabricated to support a foregone conclusion. For another thing, the corporation's structure could not tolerate promotion based on performance. That is to say, performance could never be the sole criterion for promotion. Such an equation would most assuredly destroy the corporation's rigid and limited rank order. In yet another strange twist of illogic, the corporation-model organization actually had to limit performance in order to maintain its balance. As a perverse but necessary correlative, some incentives of the corporation actually limited performance. For example, sales commissions had (salary schedule) caps. All extraordinary production was immediately and urgently normed down.

Finally, position always left the impression of permanence, even after it was gone. Apparently, it was the vain attempt of the corporation, the only artifact on the planet with the grant of eternal life to fulfill its own destiny. Besides that, it was the way the corporation offered everlasting life to those so possessed. Corporate titles appear in every obituary.

Permanence was an illusion, but the corporation had to sustain it as reality. For the corporation, that meant a perpetual dilemma: adjusting its reality to that which was real. Wealth-producing corporations responded in two ways. Some rather haughtily refused to budge, insisting that the rest of the world conform to them. But that did not work; the world, cold as it is, simply looked the other way while they became obsolete.

But the ones of enduring reputation were those that, ironically, dealt with the challenge by ceaselessly shifting positions. This activity was inexplicably described early as "reorganization," and late, in the desperate last days of the corporation-model organization as "restructuring." Although those terms may conjure up excited imaginings of radical departures, of fresh new creations and quickened energy, alas, reorganization, as it turned out, was nothing more than the corporation's way of warding off any substantive change; and restructuring was the reinforcement of old bulwarks. The intent of all this shuffling about was in effect to achieve and maintain stasis. It is no wonder then that the corporation became totally dysfunctional; for all its frenetically moving about of parts, it never really changed position.

Wealth-consuming organizations had an easier time of it. Since almost all were quasi-governmental entities or had otherwise terminally ingratiated themselves to government, they simply legislated permanence, position by position. For example, by the end of the century it was common for state law to require that all governmental jurisdictions (such as school districts) be uniformly constructed of prescribed positions, each with its own detailed description, including not only responsibilities and authority but also the requirements for the certification of permanent holders of the positions. These organizations were eventually buried intact—vertically. And that position was the only permanence ever achieved by the corporation-model organization.

NOTES

1. Dante Alighieri, *The Divine Comedy*, vol. 2: *Purgatory*, trans. Mark Musa (New York: Penguin Books, 1981), 162.

2. Alvin O. Bellak, "The Hay Guide Chart® Profile Method of Job Evaluation" (New York: Hay Group, n.d.), 4.

3. Ibid., 5.

4. Robert Reich, *The Work of Nations* (New York: Random House, 1992), 174.

5. *Project Planning* (Plymouth, Mich.: Human Synergistics International, 1989), 2.

CHAPTER 7

The Corporation and Obedience

You know, my friends, with what a brave Carouse
I made a Second Marriage in my house;
divorced old barren Reason from my bed,
and took the daughter of the Vine to Spouse.

Edward Fitzgerald[1]

Any way one looks at it, obedience is the perpetual nether side of authority. That side is either dark and stormy or bright and shining depending on the planetary phase of the authority. Whether serving is absorbed or disbursed by that authority is the ultimate test not only of good and bad but also of legitimacy. It may also be the difference between service and servitude.

The implications of this compound, sometimes elusive duality are universal and, one supposes, eternal. Obviously, there is far more involved here than the systemized command-control relationships within the corporation model, although that system is indeed thoroughly infused by the principles at work in the dynamic of authority-obedience.

In a godly world, the world that existed before (without) rationalistic science, authority was considered good. It was sometimes onerous, sometimes abusive, sometimes ridiculous, but it was good nevertheless. With legitimate authority like that, obedience was usually easy or at least acceptable; it was both intuitive and logical. There was the blessed assurance that obedience was the right thing to do morally and also the right thing to do for the well-being of me and everybody else. It was the divine order of God's will and dominion.

No alternative anyone could imagine provided more or better. Even though theocracies and monarchies seem always to thrive on red-line intensity—typically either because of some grand cause they have undertaken or else because of some trifle blown to majestic proportions—and thus frequently have a turbulent time of it, they never compromise the expectation of obedience.

Even so, within godly authority there was also, almost as a correlative, the fundamental assumption of service—and not just from the standpoint of those subject to human authority. It was also held that those in authority were themselves servants of both a higher order and those pledged to obey them: "Let every person be in subjection to the governing authorities. For there is no authority except from God, and those which exist are established by God" (Romans 13: 1).

In the Western tradition, kings and queens, as well as their minions, took this seriously as authentication: "Elizabeth II, by the grace of God the United Kingdom of Great Britain and Northern Ireland and of her other realms and territories Queen, head of the commonwealth defender of the faith." Any monarch who acknowledged the supremacy, even the existence, of any other deity put his or her claim to the throne at considerable risk. The Church, if not popular opinion, would see to that. In a godly world, only the godless reject authority. But, as what may be the ultimate example of the exception proving the rule, illegitimate authority, whether in claim or conduct, was resisted and often overthrown. If weak, it could easily turn into farce:

"We, Seth, Emperor of Azania, Chief of the Chiefs of Sakuyu, Lord of Wanda and Tyrant of the Seas, Bachelor of the Arts of Oxford University, being in this twenty-fourth year of life, summoned by the wisdom of Almighty God and the unanimous voice of our people to the throne of our ancestors, do hereby proclaim. . . ." Seth paused in this dictation and gazed out across the harbour where in the fresh breeze of early morning the last dhow was setting sail for the open sea. "Rats," he said; "Stinking curs. They are running away."[2]

But if that authority was powerful enough to force servitude, ultimately it was resisted. The more perverse the authority, the quicker and greater the resistance until rebellion broke out and, by mass usurpation, cancelled the grant of authority or, by counterforce, abolished it altogether in the name of either godly rule (historically early) or individual freedom (historically later).

In an ungodly world, the looking glass effect quickly takes over, and everything gets inverted—doubly so. What can be analyzed clearly is not always clearly perceived. It is a world of certain uncertainty. But this is sure: Godly authority of any expression is rejected on general principle. The tables of stone are continually smashed at the feet of the graven image, and everyone dances, in a ring, defiance. It is not that disobedience is natural; it is that obedience is unnatural. The great irony, of course, is that all rationalistic constructs of human organization were themselves based on preemptive au-

thority, which is, more accurately, either a reasonable facsimile or an ingenious counterfeit of godly order. Here again there occurred the typical inverse. In effect, rather than yielding obedience to God and absolutes, human
beings chose to adhere to the rule of other human beings, who were supposed to be easier masters—more reasonable, more generous—who promised liberty and justice for all.

Response to the authority was far more complicated than the two simple
options presented by godly authority—that is, obedience or disobedience (acceptance or rejection). With rationalistic authority there were three possible responses, each with unsettled interpretation. Two were variations on obedience
and disobedience. The third, an invention of rationalism—rationalization.

First, there was obedience. In this instance, the language shifted significantly to "compliance," which, unlike obedience, may be willing or unwill-
ingly, conscious or unconscious. Compliance requires no moral dimension.
It was precisely this response upon which the corporation-model organization depended and, as we shall see, the response it was overdesigned to in-
duce. In fact, it eventually came about that aggressive compliance was
confused with achievement.

Second, as a matter of opposites, there was disobedience, or in this world,
"noncompliance." Although this reaction, as we shall see presently, was the
greatest possible threat to the corporation, sometimes noncompliance—especially within a broader context of, say, oppressive regimes—was seen by
people mostly of liberal persuasion to be rather noble. "Civil disobedience"
became the mantra of heroes until it was trivialized by political opportunists
in the 1960s. Here again we see a dramatic example of the amazing dichotomy
in Western civilization: That which was acceptable, even admired, in society at
large was forcefully repudiated within the confines of the corporation. Such noncompliance, often theatrically acted out, was usually either predicated on the
self-indulgent morality of some counterrationalistic cause or perpetrated in a
sanctimonious individual crusade or, hypothetically, enacted en masse.

It is a curious fact of history that there has never been a massive revolt
against a rationalistic system of authority. Angry protests, yes, but not revolt.
The fall of the Soviet Union in the late twentieth century was as close as it
gets. However, that debacle was not a tearing down but a breaking up, a collapse, surely the foreboding of the end of all authoritarian-rationalistic systems. There are no revolutions anymore because they are unnecessary.

The third response, the invention of rationalism and implicit in the word
itself, was negotiation. Everything in a godless world could be rationalized—
everything, that is, except authority. Always before, absolutes were inherent
in authority. To accept one was to accept the other; to reject one was to reject
the other. Rationalism simply separated the two and placed anything for-
merly derived from absolute imperatives on the bargaining table. Authority
of the rationalistic kind served notice early that it would compromise anything for the sake of its own preservation.

This was an entirely new idea and full of great promise. For one thing, it held out the prospect of universal liberty, freedom, and justice for all. No one had ever presumed to negotiate with godly authority—the means and the methods, perhaps, even the timing of blessings and curses—but not its judgment. That was absolute, even when rejected. All rebels knew they were rebellious. But rationalism offered its own judgment about matters pertaining to authority and obedience, and that proved in the end to be no judgment at all. Judgment requires absolutes.

The ultimate result of negotiation as a response to authority was actually twofold; and both responses were paradoxes, either of which could be credited with (or blamed for) the final undoing of rationalism. First, when there are no absolutes, no justifiable demands or constraints, no overriding values, no actual purpose, then everything is negotiated to the lowest common denominator. The exact level of that denominator is decided by the barganing, but two things always remain constant: It will be the lowest, and it will be the basest.

Second, and perhaps even more perverse, is rationalism's pretense of yielding authority along with negotiated obedience. It was a dangerous game, all right, and one that rationalism finally lost; but for a long time it manipulated the unauthorized players masterfully. Throughout the history of Western civilization, the advantage always belonged to those in authority—not to the powerful, to those in authority. That was, in fact, the fundamental premise of all Western organization. But that ideal was conceived in a godly universe where authority was once considered the domain of the gods or, later, the goodness of God. If that arrangement rings of injustice in the ears of those given to idealize modern democracy, it is only because they refuse to hear the echos of injustice in rationalistic processes that promised equitable treatment of people and fair settlement of all matters pertaining to personal well-being, and, then, when those without authority began making demands of their own, took it all back, simply and only because the processes were intrinsically biased in favor of those with authority. In the rationalistic world, authority is subject to no one, or no thing. Perhaps the most cynical ruse perpetrated by the corporation, and later by government, was something termed "empowerment." A lie within a lie, it was as if power were external to the individual—and that the only ultimate source of that "power" was authority. Some honest seekers of self-control actually believed they were empowered and traipsed about, happy and satisfied, at the ends of their tethers. In the final analysis, all those without authority found it impossible to negotiate their way out of controlled dependency. They had no bargaining chips. In fact, they had nothing except what those in authority gave them or threw away.

The demands of Godly authority were forthright, all-assuming, nonapologetic: They issued as commands—originally ten, with both prerogative and righteousness implicit. Before the advent of rationalism, and in diminishing proportion afterward, divine commands were duly appropriated into laws, rules, and regulations: laws to ensure the proper governance of the state; rules to prescribe acceptable conduct of the individual; regulations to order society. In each case, it quickly became evident even to the most casual observer that authority, as interpreted by human beings, had a natural propensity to enlarge itself through division and multiplication simultaneously. So, long before human reason was brought to bear upon the task, citizens of all Western nations were thoroughly commandeered.

This circumstance presented a serendipitous coincidence for rationalism. Not only could it mutate the concept of authority into an intellectual construct of nonabsolute absolutism, but it could at the same time overcome the one critical weakness of the old authoritarian system, that is, the lack of control mechanisms and devices. Rationalism discovered early in the twentieth century, much to its everlasting delight, that it could achieve complete and unfailing control over all organizational activity through an intricate web of precepts, procedures, processes, and protocols, all bobbined up by policies.

The discovery of policies, along with the happy realization of their natural susceptibility to infinite rationalistic application, was the greatest thing that ever happened to the corporation-model organization. And happen it did. Nothing this perfect could have been imagined—much less invented. Policies, as implemented within rationalized organization, had five distinct features, which taken together made policies so indispensable that in the final stage of the corporation model, they were all that remained of the system.

First, the word "policy" itself was special, conveying at once both the aura of state approbation and assurance of the common good. *Politéia* in any form exuded respectability, even credibility. It spoke not only of organized or established forms of government or administration but also, even more specifically, of those courses of action adopted by such entities that would be advantageous to all involved. When the corporation graciously appropriated the term for its own singular use, even the most minuscule operational detail was deserving of individed attention and much pomp and circumstance. There were no unimportant policies. In fact, all policies were created equal.

Second, policies represented the final separation of the corporation from divine authority. From this point on, God was totally out of it. Rationalism had created its own opposite, parallel universe. The Hebraic–Christian religion had held that God twice created the world by his Word, and by that Word, the *logos*, kept that world and its universe together. Likewise rationalism verbalized its world into existence, fettled everything into place, and held it there—rigidly. No divine assistance was required.

This rigidity was actualized in two simultaneous expressions, one dependent upon the other: bureaucracy and the corporated human being. Erich Fromm in one of his compassionate tirades hit the mark:

In a bureaucratically organized and centralized industrialism, tastes are manipulated so that people consume maximally and in predictable and profitable directions. Their intelligence and character became standardized by the ever increasing role of tests which select the mediocre and the unadventurous in preference to the original and daring. Indeed, the bureaucratic–industrial civilization which has been victorious in Europe and North America has created a new type of man; he can be described as the organization man, as the automation man.[3]

While it is true this assessment reflects an extraordinarily dark view of industrialization, there is nevertheless something quite frightening at least about the possibility of such degradation.

Third, policies allowed rationalized organization, especially the institution, to obscure the distinction between governance and administration (or management). In fact, the more rationalized, the more obscure. It was simply a matter of prodigious quantity. Earlier it was noted that authority always expands itself; but nothing on earth is as proliferate as policies. For example, the representative of a well-known household appliance manufacturing company, in responding to a question about the number of their policies, admitted: "We could not possibly ever guess at how many policies we have. Nobody in the entire organization could answer that question unless they develop some type of committee to research it."[4]

In like fashion, a metropolitan school board spokesperson reported that state board policies covered their policies; and that, specifically, eight "articles" had to be localized. The result: "Each article has *volumes* of policies—too many to guess." It is sadly obvious that in this kind of micropolicied world nothing is sacred and everything is sacred. The only thing differentiating policies is the time it takes to look them up.

Fourth, policies meant that objectification could be defined and utilized as it suited corporations. Quoting company policy was the most expedient (and legal) way of dealing with issues or persons about whom the company has already made up its subjective mind. Policies made abuse civil, even polite. For example, one national retail chain instituted what it called a "20–40–60 policy." After twenty years on the job; after forty years of age; after $60,000 annual compensation, employees are no longer profitable and, therefore, are terminated. In general, policies as objectification served the corporation remarkably well in the last half of the twentieth century, when government intrusion was at its height. A well-crafted policy could cover a multitude of sin. And governments, looking in the wrong place as usual, never understood that policy is actually the last practice.

Fifth, and most significant, policies pushed anyone they chose beyond choice. And they chose everyone. That was the difference between obedience and compliance, a distinction essential to a rationalistic system. Obedience presupposes, even requires, the possibility of disobedience. Compliance, on the other hand, urgently seeks to eliminate any possibility of noncompliance. Obedience—even that forced by harsh, oppressive authority (as in slavery or totalitarianism)—recognizes the dignity in the refusal to obey. Even though it may punish and destroy the disobedient, there is still a fundamental respect for the uniquely human quality of choice. It is free moral agency in its basic form. Obedience simply says, "Thou shalt not steal." Compliance surrounds the individual with instructions and restraints calculated not merely to foreclose all opportunity, but to remove the very idea of stealing. Ultimate control of organizational processes is achieved by controlling each individual. The corollary loss of emotion and imagination was considered an added benefit. Eventually, to use the quaint phrase of Joseph Heller, an intrepid observer who was caught up in policies as no one else ever was, everyone was "disappeared" into the impossibility of anything else. And all the demeaning expectations and obligations usually associated with obedience were also disappeared into eradication of motivation and creativity. Finally, whatever life had existed within the corporation was disappeared into the lifelessness of compliance.

It is reasonable to surmise that if the corporation had possessed a mind, policies would have been a death wish.

NOTES

1. Edward Fitzgerald, "The Rabaiyat of Omar Khayyam," *Victorian Poetry: Clough to Kipling*, ed. Author J. Carr (New York: Holt, Rinehart and Winston, 1959), 281.

2. Evelyn Waugh, *Black Mischief* (New York: Dell, 1960), 193.

3. Erich Fromm, *The Heart of Man* (New York: Harper and Row, 1964), 57.

4. This and the following quotations are responses to a telephone survey conducted April 24–28, 1995.

CHAPTER 8

The Corporation and Isolation

Knowing not a human being there
Jude began to be impressed with the isolation of his own
personality, as with a self-spectore, the sensation being
of one who walked but could not make himself seen or heard.
Thomas Hardy[1]

Isolation is the necessary condition of salvation. That is the secret of a godly universe. While they may not be forthcoming in their admission of it, all religions and all other expressions of godly order acknowledge the essentiality of isolation in all their doctrines and practices having to do with the redemption of human beings, whether in the present world or the world to come. In Eastern religions, it is the intensity of isolation that lifts one into a state of purity, worthy of unity with the life force of the universe. Universally, salvation, however conceived, is never a group experience. Destruction may be en masse, but not salvation. Both Greco-Roman and Christian religions are replete with stories and threats of wholesale destruction, the most horrific of which is the Christian eschatological version of the earth's final destruction by fire. But there is no instance or promise of collective salvation before, during, or after that conflagration, rapture to the contrary notwithstanding.

While there are many, often substantial, variations on the theme of salvation, the archetypal motif proceeds from the state of awareness (by the individual) of being utterly and hopelessly lost—that is, having no meaning, no purpose, no control—to some specific act of contrition, repentance or abnegation (usually involving suffering or sacrifice) in response to divine grace or some other redemptive power; finally, to the state and assurance of being completely and eternally saved. Typically, especially in the Western Christian tradition, there are two interpretations of salvation, each requiring the unmitigated isolation of the person as the condition of both the propitiative saving action and the continuing dynamic of being saved. The Greek word commonly used by Christian writers is *soterion*. The word simply means "health and welfare" and, from all indications, is intended to describe the very best existence that a human being can experience—practically in the actual world—and that was the ultimate meaning of redemption. It was never meant to suggest that salvation was reserved for some eternal afterlife, somewhere in the ethereal realms. Neither did it imply that one should expect to live without pain, grief, and turmoil in the present world, but simply that all these adverse things, however real, could be overcome by a new, ever-present reality. Peace is to be found only in the middle of a storm.

The idea of sanctification, moreover, is quite expressly a process or condition not only emanating from isolation but also resulting from its glorification. Here is an amazing coincidence of Hellenistic philosophy and Christian theology. Aristotle called the experience *katharisma*; Saint Paul referred to it as *hagiasmos*. It is somewhat puzzling that even though psychologists such as Jung (through symbol) and Fraser (through pattern), as well as critics such as R. B. Sharpe, have pointed out the Hebraic–Christian ritual inherent in *katharsis*, no Christian apologist has seen fit to suggest any historical or spiritual connection between the "proper purgation" (Aristotle's phrase) wrought by vicarious identification with the tragic hero and the "cleansing" propitiated by a substitutionary atoning sacrifice. The death of Agamemnon, the passion of Jesus, the dementia of Lear—each after its own fashion—evokes a descent into self possible only in spiritual isolation. Isolation is the place of both birth and death, which, in all mythology, occur simultaneously.

Yet both *katharisma* and *hagiasmos* are more than processes of purification. They are the state of ultimate human being, literally "set apart" from all other persons for a unique, eternal purpose. And it is significant that the Greek word *aionios*, used by both Hellenistic and Christian authors, carries much more emphasis on the quality of earthly life (that is, happiness), than on everlasting existence (that is, time only).

It is precisely this isolation that puts the being in human and the human in being. Only here can the person discover and realize those innate divine properties that ultimately bring the person as close to the nature of God as is humanly possible. In other words, this is where the human meets the divine. But it is also where the divine meets the human. It is worth recalling that in the Christian myth isolation also brings God as close to the nature of human beings as divinely possible. This perhaps explains the many deliberate escapes by Jesus to extended periods of solitude in the wilderness and to his God-forsaken psalm from the cross ("Eloi, eloi, lama sabachthani"). Within the person, constituting the person, the divine nature is manifested in three states of being: specifically, *wholeness* (self-possession), *sovereignty* (self-control), and *connectedness* (self-justification).

As for the first, *wholeness* is much more than the three composite parts of the person as acknowledged by both Hellenistic and Christian authorities (*psyche*, *soma*, and *pneuma*). That analysis is true, all right—fundamentally, undeniably. But the wholeness of the human being is not merely a matter of aggregated or disaggregated parts, whatever the kind or quality. It is, rather, a matter of critical attributes sufficient to constitute a being not only identifiable from all others but also unique among all others. That is to say, the possession of self.

Self-possession implies that the person by nature can, and eventually must, ask and answer three questions that pertain only to self: Who am I? Why am I? and Where am I? These questions are meaningless outside the context of self. The first may be as profoundly simple as a name or it may be as simply profound as introspection in extending solitude—a communion not with self, but among self—extraordinarily serious sustained thought about the ordinary. The second raises the issue of purpose, whether it exists at all and whether it is by or for the individual human being. The third speaks to the fundamental nature of human existence, the reality in which the person lives and whether the person is subject or object, cause or effect, coming or going.

The *sovereignty* of person is actually more than self-control, even in the fullest expression of that term. The concept transcends both autonomy and discipline. But these powers are not diminished in any way or to the slightest degree. Rather, both are inherent in sovereignty. Autonomy bestows self-rule upon the person by granting the prerogative, even the obligation, of choice. And sovereignty without actual self-determination would be but a sham or illusion. The centrality of this idea in the development of Western civilization will be examined later at some length from the point of view of both individual freedom and democratic governance. Discipline confers the rule of self to the person by subjecting all thoughts, emotions, and action to the will of the person. This is the meaning of *paros*—literally, "meekness"—humility raised to heroic proportions. This idea also runs through the annals of the Western experience as a constant reminder of the divine nature of human beings. It is not only the power that moves the person to be and to do but also the only force capable of overcoming the baser instincts of the person's other nature. Hubris, therefore, is impossible.

But the sovereignty of the person is far more than all that. Here the issue is establishing a moral being of such presence in the universe that the person can declare with God, "I am." Whether for good or evil is beside the point. In this domain it is not the definition, or even the actuality, of good or evil that is significant. In fact, the question is irrelevant. The only issue is the absolute supremacy of the person before all other forces and beings in the cosmos. Does this mean that moral being has nothing to do with good and evil? Quite to the contrary, it is moral being that factors morality. Without it, morality—

whether of episode or disposition—would be both a logical and moral impossibility. The truly grand significance of this is that it is only through the sovereignty of the individual that good and evil are admitted into the universe. Temptation is neither more nor less than the intersection of all good and all evil. While temptation occurs strictly in personal isolation, its pronouncement reverberates beyond self-control or control of one's world—or, in its fullest expression, to the creation of one's own world.

Of *connectedness*, to say that it is more than the linkage of human beings to others or to other things is not to diminish the basic idea in terms of either philosophical import or historical consequence. Western civilization is essentially about the discovery and formation of connections. No one ever gave more thought to this than the Greeks; the very idea was an obsession. Their legacy is a myriad glossary conceptualizing virtually every connection possible between, among, and, perhaps, within human beings. And most of their terms have made their way not only into the modern Western languages but also into the Western psyche. All contemporary political, social, and ethical theory, if not practice, originates here. Politically there was the idea of the state (*politeia*); socially the notion of community (*koinon*, advanced later by Rousseau as the "social contract"); and ethically the distinctly human possibility of being true to self and to others (*ethos*).

Any version of Western history, even constructionistic or revisionistic, will bear witness to the fact that Western civilization, more than any other human society, took connectedness to its ultimate, artificially forcing it over and beyond natural orders, eventually pushing it beyond all tolerance into disconnectedness. But that extravagance or misappropriation did not in any way invalidate what seems to be a natural human imperative—that is, to be connected to others.

Christianity, likewise, at least in its primitive form, was fundamentally about connections—here as a testament ostensibly fulfilling the Hebraic traditions and prophecies of Law (of both God and Moses). All human connections lay along two axes—vertical (with God) and horizontal (with others). For example, it was a matter of routine exegesis that the ten commandments divide logically into these two categories. Jesus affirmed the idea when he pronounced the "greatest" commandment and its corollary. "You shall love the Lord thy God with all your heart, soul, and might. And the second is like unto it: You shall love your neighbor as yourself." In fact, he even insisted that one's relationship with God was dependent on one's relationship with others.

If the Greeks intellectualized connectedness and sought to institutionalize it, Christianity treated connectedness as an intensely personal matter, involving the total person—physical, mental, and spiritual. Certainly, there was the acknowledged connection with the state ("honor the king") and with others ("live peacefully with all men"), and even a special intimate interdependence within the koinonia, the exclusive fellowship of the Church. But the overwhelming emphasis in Christianity was the connection of persons to each other. Kinship was more than metaphor. Human beings were brothers, sisters, fathers, and mothers to one another inasmuch as they were all children of God. Being the keeper of one's brother was never a commandment; it was a given.

Although any version of history, secular or ecclesiastical, sooner or later will be forced to admit that the institutionalized Church, perhaps the Christian religion itself, eventually lost—and, in some cases, disparaged—this concept, that does not mean that the idea is any less compelling. Connectedness is not merely about linkages—it is not a matter of many, but of one. The implicit issue is the justification of the person—each person. Being justified is the ultimate need in being human. It is the absolute certification of worth. And, not unexpectedly, both Hellenism and Christianity wrestled mightily with the idea. One begins to wonder how a basic human need became so esoteric or so simple an idea such a multidimensional philosophical problem. This is the truth: everything with consciousness must be set right; in fact, sometimes this irrepressible urge is the only evidence of consciousness. Plants grow toward the sun. Babies fear falling. Dying people ask the time. Only conscience complicates justification.

The two traditions came to this complication in exactly opposite ways. In Hellenistic thought, justification was to be found in both vengeance and virtue; that is, either in righting a wrong (the recipient side of justice) or in righting oneself (the incipient side of justice). Force and reason were joined as the means to each. Justification took as many forms as conditions; and the definition, hence the experience, was eventful and fleeting. So, justification became the uncontrollable and insatiable addiction that drove all the pursuits and pursuers defined in the Western canon as "noble" or "ideal"—from the avenger to the savior, often as one.

Christianity, on the other hand, took one simple definition and proceeded religiously to render it incomprehensible, much less satisfying. Of all the esoteric metaphysical spiritual notions posed by Christian theologians, justification is the only one impossible to understand. Its basic promise is clear enough; that is, the alignment of each person with God's moral laws. But the definition is always put forth in strictly legalistic terms—the nature and need for righteousness, of being right. So the whole issue becomes hopelessly confused by the relentless, meticulous interplay between law and grace. Saint Paul's paranoid disquisition about this legal tangle may be fairly strong evidence that mental instability is more likely than justification. The human mind cannot be twisted through so many contortions and still remain intact (Romans 7). The upshot is that one can never be sure whether he or she is justified. There is no evidence. No proof. Just sheer exhaustion. But the defense can never rest. One can never be confident of one's place, purpose, or worth. Seeking justification, human beings find in modern Christianity only the confusion of endless argument.

In a strange sort of way, the failure of both traditions to offer any assurance of justification actually brings us to the only real justification anyone can experience. It is not the justification to others, by others, or for others. It is, rather, the justification of, by, and for oneself. Eventually, every person discovers that the only justification is self-justification. That is why connectedness is a matter of one.

It is a remarkable irony that individual uniqueness is realized through connection: But uniformity is the consequence of disconnection. Maybe this is the reason Sartre declared, "Hell is other people."

The hope and means of personal justification, of discovering meaning and purpose in one's life, were (are) without question the most promising aspects of religion. This is where everyone signs up. Here again, the fix is in—or, more precisely, within—the scientific additive. Rationalism and its godchild, the corporation, transformed isolation into the necessary condition of alienation. That was the secret of a godless universe—a secret all people knew but would not admit—even to themselves. Lost is unutterable. It would be unfair to suggest that alienation was the intent of rationalistic constructs, but it is both fair and accurate to observe that alienation was and is the only possible consequence of the infraction of godly order. Alienation was implicit in the design of the constructs, so in actuality the result was, more often that not, personal annihilation. Rationalism laid claim to isolation in two ways, either of which alone would have been sufficient for the effectual cancellation of the person. In both cases, the grinding force was the friction between any alleged system and its components, the whole versus the parts. One was the obsessive creation of atomistic systems of production; the other was the atomizing of ideas. The first, physical, concocted meaninglessness by unlimited fragmented complexity. That was depersonalization. The second, spiritual, destroyed meaning by reducing all concepts pertaining to the human being to absurd imponderables. That was dehumanization. Depersonalization rendered both self-possession and self-control impossible; eventually, even the ideas were lost. Dehumanization destroyed any hope of justification.

Depersonalization was built into the corporation model. It was implicit in the concept from its mechanistic efficiencies to its parallel naturalistic theories of human behavior, both analytical to the exclusion of synthesis. Actually, natural law may be at work here: The more rationalized a system, the more depersonalized it is.

There is no need to recount the atrocities committed by the corporation system against the person. Social critics of all stripes—artists, activists, judges, historians, even, from time to time, journalists—have been a constant, if baffled, voice of reason. They are usually highly articulate; often beyond reproach, without guile. But the corporation was beyond reason, unimpressed by and unattached to either society or truth. It was simply not in the makeup of a system based on the twin incubi of profit and production to consider the person anything more than a necessary expense to be minimized, a "vital machine" to be maximized, and a "human resource" to be capitalized. The first rendered the person expendable; the second a mathematical equation; the third a basic commodity. Neither depersonalization nor dehumanization

Figure 8.1

occurred because of any special interest in the person, but purely out of disregard. The corporation was devoid of both philosophy and feeling. Consider the real message in an advertisement like the one shown in Figure 8.1.

This kind of impersonalization became standard operating procedure. In fact, any human contact was considered so unusual it required special attention as a management issue. The reason was obviously the fact that the corporation-model organization was based on analysis—the breaking down of the thing into separate parts. According to Harvard psychiatrist Edward M. Hollowell, any kind of personal contact must be dealt with as "the human moment." The unusual experience he describes as "an authentic psychological encounter when two people share the same space."

When Henry Ford cranked up his assembly line in 1916, he was merely putting into effect on a grand scale the primary tenet of rationalized production—that is, the processed division of labor. His goal was the generation of profit by manufacturing (already an anachronistic term since little was actually done by hand) an affordable car using the most efficient processes possible. And it worked. His "army" of workers were either so indoctrinated or so desperate for money that they allowed every part of their lives to be controlled by the militaristic regimen imposed by the abusive, dictatorial Mr. Ford. These industrialized slaves made him one of the richest men in the world. Whether a different system would have produced the same results at that time and place is impossible to know; but the unprecedented drama yielded several heretofore undiscovered exigencies about human beings and their systems even before Ford Motor Company caved in to the unions in 1941.

First, there is a natural human aversion to efficiency of any kind. Second, the point of resistance—and, in this case, also of diminishing returns—in process efficiency is boredom, not, as it had been thought, the lack of "work ethic." Third, boredom is overcome not by engineering compensation within efficiencies but by different kinds of compensation outside the process. Specifically, it yields to force, financial reward, and a sense of wholeness or completion (the assembly line worker would actually see—and own—a finished product). The last was the best idea. Force produced only temporary results. Money did not always provide incentive. It would become painfully obvious that it is impossible to pay someone enough to do something he or she does not like doing.

NOTE

1. Thomas Hardy, *Jude the Obscure* (Boston: Houghton Mifflin, 1965), 64.

CHAPTER 9

The Corporation's Isolation
and Depersonalization

We can no longer deny that the dark stirrings of the unconsciousness are
effective powers—that psychic forces exist which cannot, for the present
at least, be fitted in with our rational world order.

C. J. Jung[1]

But to the matter of *wholeness*: That simple idea would become one of the
four most critical questions of the twentieth century. What is the nature of
systems? Not surprisingly, rationalism's first answer, an answer formulated
long before the assembly line, was one word—components. That is, pieces of
something, made to specifications, that are precisely interchangeable within
kind, but always and ever a part. All human enterprises eventually atrophy,
decline, and pass away according to the attitudes established at their outset.
So it was with the idea of components. What was conceptually inextricable
in systems persisted in complexity; and, worse, the dies that cast all things
mechanical seemed also to recast all things human.

The line became the metaphor of industrialization. Anything that can be
said of the line—more accurately, the line segment—could also be said of
the modern corporation. To the degree that specific corporations emulated
the features of process, uniformity, and precision, they contributed to the
depersonalization that characterized not only systems of productions but also
all Western organization throughout the twentieth century. Process limited
the person to "functioning"; uniformity guaranteed conformity of thinking

and behavior; precision meant submission. By mid-century, every aspect of society had been completely blanched of anything human and a new race evolved. "Homo mechanicus," Fromm called them; assembly required, but not expected. Self-possession became an oxymoron.

The unhappy leap from human to machine occurred with the development of the factory model. Here, labor was parted out on the factory floor, not by sequence but by activity. Whereas sequential work could hardly be completely segmented, work activity, especially "piece work," was discreet by definition. This separation was only exacerbated by shifts in economic systems from manufacturing to service and from service to information. There was no visible project as such, so any concept of the whole was impossible to imagine. Each work activity stood virtually alone as if it were its own independent enterprise. This explains why in the 1990s, after decades of trying to deal with the impossibilities of coordination and communication, the corporation gave up the attempt altogether and declared these obstacles to be advantages. At the end of the century, some of the most avant garde organizational theories advocated that systems, all supercharged by technology, be constituted of individuals who pursued their own "projects," more or less coordinated with the projects of others, but often incommunicado.

By its two fundamental features—departmentalization and specialization—the factory model eradicated any subjective sense of wholeness and, consequently, any sense of self. Of course, neither of these aspects was unfamiliar to the means of production in prerationalized economies. Farmers of all climes understood and practiced division of labor long before Frederick Taylor. They routinely parceled their crops, herds, and labor into calculated bets against the seasons. It was an exercise in prudence as well as control. And specialization is as old as arts and crafts. But the one was all within a specific context, generally under the purview of one individual, so there was immediate awareness about the status and significance of any component. In like manner, components were fully integrated and balanced, if not in fact, then in the mind of at least one person. The other was the ultimate in personalization: An artifact always bore the mark of its maker—not merely as a signature but through the transubstantiation of personality that occurs only in creation.

Departmentalism was not merely a convenience of control: It was the practical, albeit unconscious, resolution of the nagging nineteenth-century enigma about the nature of systems—whether they are atomistic or organismic. The corporation's reconsidered if not reconstituted answer, since by now postulation had replaced observation, was "both." Surely, by now that kind of ambiguous whiplash duplicity comes as no surprise.

The very word "department" declares irreconcilable division. If "part" implies—requires—"whole," then "department" expresses a basic duality—essentially, two entities linked as whole to part and part to whole, as if the thing is defined by its opposite. If all this sounds like so much doublespeak, consider the difference between a sculpture and a bicycle and then ask, "Which is more like the human being?" or "Which is the preferred design of human systems?" The inevitable tension between the two identities can result only in a structural dichotomy. Some management professionals of the dialectic school and bipolar intellect actually recommended deliberately accentuating the strain between the corporation system and its departments — "healthy," they said. Some routinely drew distinct lines of demarcation — "loose–tight," they said. And some went so far as to encourage competition between them — "improvement," they said. All this eventually led to system breakup and then to system breakdown. The technical terms for the breakup was "decentralization," or "site-based management." The technical term for the breakdown would be "downsizing."

The word "department" made the subject of the debate not production mechanisms but governance, with all the implicit questions and answers about authority. The questions were never answered because they were never addressed forthrightly. The answers were never questioned. In fact, as corporated systems became more complete and more culturally rationalized, the possibility of a solution became ever more remote. Although much touted as a progressive management tactic, decentralization, when it was introduced by General Motors in the 1920s, was simply a matter of command following control. And so it was for the duration of the corporation model. Over the years, decentralization seemed to take two forms. It was either a last desperate attempt to force old-fashioned centralized control on the whole system or unconditional surrender in the face of the overwhelming atomistic energy of the time. If the latter, then the much debated question of whether the corporation fragmented itself out of existence or another force took over is answered.

While departmentalization and decentralization were system issues and often more artificial than actual, the very idea of these divisions had the effect of marooning castaways in various square islands of an organizational chart, separated by nontransversible lines (some dotted) from all the other square islands. For the individual, the results were disorientation and immobility. Surely, even Alfred Sloan would have been lost.

Specialization separated the isolates completely by shutting down communication. All specialities developed their own language to the degree that any meaningful exchange of information with others — to say nothing of understanding — was all but impossible. Jargon resists interpretation. Specialization, it seems, means knowing more and more about less and less, until one knows everything about virtually nothing — but cannot explain it. That is the ultimate rationalistic isolation. No self can live here — no body, no soul, no spirit.

In these two ways — departmentalism and specialization — the factory system successfully purged the corporation-model organization of anything related to personality and reduced the person to insignificance — both inside and outside the workplace. Inside, it meant a world inhabited by vital machines—exactly as the originators of the system had imagined and engineered. Outside, in the broader social arena, the factory mentality most assuredly was responsible for the "classic" depersonalization that permeated all of Western civilization by the 1950s.

The history of the relationship between human beings and machines is an amazing story of role reversal. It happened in stages—almost evolutionary, but the end was a far cry from Spencer's equilibration. Or maybe it was not.

Phase I. Early basic machines (levers, screws, pulleys, and the like) worked for human beings. Machines were uncomplicated devices for getting work done; they were extensions of the person.

Phase II. Complex machines (machines made up of machines) began to integrate humans into the machinery. While size was most often overwhelming from a personal perspective, it was only a condition of depersonalization. Complexity was the closest science ever came to art. The effect was that human beings became parts of machines. It was difficult to tell them apart. Even the terra cotta warriors of Xian have individual faces. As we have seen already, definitions are shaky at best, and certainly not to be trusted with one's full weight. However, it is more than coincidence that the common definition of "machine" (a device for "getting work done") was identical to the common definition of "management" ("getting work done through people"). In practical application, both were judged by the same two measures, efficiency and mechanical advantage. By the time something termed "management by objectives and self-control" became the rage among those attempting to salvage the corporation-model organization, the machinery was out of control. And by the time their fancy lightly turned to "teaming" and other modishly warm synergistic daisy chains (circa 1975), it was too late. Anything pertaining to the person had long since been removed as a necessary part of the corporation or, for that matter, any human activity.

Phase III. With automation, control shifted from human being to machine. Far more than the question of who, or what, has the switch, automation eventually changed every aspect of human life on the planet. But two are especially important; one very practical, the other no less real and far more devastating. First, in terms of economics, machines not only replaced human workers but also became formidable competitors for resources of all kinds. Even the tax codes favored investment in machinery over people. And distributive governments tolerated no limits in expenditures for vast mechanical infrastructures. Second, and specifically to the point of this discussion, automation changed the human psyche, at least for several generations, from an attitude of dominion over all God's creation to one of subservience to the creations of science. It was a gradual process, imperceptible at the beginning. But little by little, and by surprisingly easy transition, machines actually began to regulate human behavior—potentially, all human activity. The result was that control over human life was given over to machines. Or was it taken by them? Not merely in the routine activities of various enterprises, but in the design of those enterprises. It was as if human beings felt compelled, for some reason, to insure that the maximum mechanical capability was always achieved. (And everyone thought the Luddites were extremists.) For almost 150 years in the United States, public education, for all the soaring rhetoric about citizenship and personal fulfillment, prepared students to use machines as a career. By the 1980s, education had become a mindless process for manufacturing servomechanisms. The nature of the product is always the nature of production.

Phase IV. Information systems were the brainchild of automation. The concept is fairly simple: Control over or within any process necessitated "feedback." That is, information from the output of the process is used to modify its own activity. It is a long way from a simple thermostat to a megacorporation, but the principle is the same: Information is control. (If there is an unexpected coincidence in principle with authoritarian management here, consider the impossibility of decentralizing management without decentralizing information.) The way was called "cybernetics" (after *kyberno*, which means "to steer") by Norbert Weiner who introduced it as a science, albeit a questionable one, in 1948. Based on statistics and the laws of probability, it attempted to deal with the continuous adaptation of a system to external requirements, usually in the form of a specific intent—such as hitting a target with a .50 caliber machine gun. Originally an approach involving communication and control systems in living organisms, machines, and even sociopolitical organization, cybernetics redeployed into discreet sciences such as communication theory, control theory (which became a major movement in education), computation theory, and psychology ("psycho-cybernetics"), but the term "cybernetics" was quickly and forever appropriated by the science of the computer, especially in artificial intelligence. Computers were the instrument of information and, therefore, of control. With these technological marvels, not only could every existing human activity—real or imagined—be programmed but exotic new systems could be hypothesized. Since there was absolutely no human enterprise, experience, or fantasy that could not be translated into digital code, sheaved, bundled, committed randomly to "cyberspace," and retrieved at some given time and place, there was a mad race by technoentrepreneurs to exploit a marketplace without any boundaries or rules.

The Internet and the World Wide Web have been touted by the scions of the information industry as the twenty-first century equivalents of the printing press, suggesting a comparable revolutionary impact on human society and portending another quantum leap in the progress of civilization. Somehow, for all the press, the comparison fails. But the comparison does raise the possibility of a contrast; that is, the difference between knowledge and information. In the first place, the Internet is at best only a technical tour de force of the basic principle of reproducing human ideas in symbolic language and making the compositions universally available. The question before the Net is simple: What is available here that is not already available in another form? That is to say, what does it do by way of increasing knowledge, bettering the human condition, relieving suffering, fortifying aspiration? In the second place, the Net may be a classic example of pushing a really good thing so far that it becomes something else entirely. There is a fundamental difference between the printing press and the Net. Maybe it is a matter of intent. The printing press was an invention of necessity, arising out of the passion for knowledge and personal liberty. Gutenberg really believed his first publication would advance both noble purposes and dedicated the craft forever to these twin ideals. The printer's craft thus became the vehicle of all revolutions since, revolutions fueled by the dream of personal freedom and of societies conducive to the peace and prosperity of all individuals. It gave that power to every person. The net occurred simply because of possibility—technical and commercial. The result was the unlimited expansion of information and linkages—all totally out of context and, therefore, meaningless. As an implication of the range and scope of this situation, Pope John Paul II, in his encyclical "Faith and Reason" (1998) issued this stern warning: "In this maelstrom of data and facts in which we live and which seem to comprise the very fabric of life, many people wonder whether it still makes sense to ask about meaning."[2]

The much publicized "age of information" (circa 1970–2000) was above all else an unprecedented commercial success. The only event in human history even vaguely resembling all the hype and hysteria, and then more metaphysically than actual, was the California gold rush of the late 1840s. But like all comparisons, this one is imperfect. In the information business, at least by classical definitions, there is no possibility of really creating wealth. That's why the trafficking was in information, spun out of thin air, with all the substance thereof. But that fact seemed to escape the attention of corporate executives who spent billions of dollars to chase something hyped as "cutting-edge" technology—which promised both efficiency and effectiveness—only to reduce productivity and quality. It was not uncommon for companies, service and manufacturing alike, to reduce their sales and marketing forces and reinvest the "savings" in the latest technological gimmicks. The insurance industry was probably the most charmed. More than one major company severely reduced its budget for marketing in order to invest in management information systems.

It was not until after the great splurge in technology between 1992 and 1998 that productivity analysts began to realize that technology was actually having an adverse effect. Except for computer companies themselves (only 1% of the U.S. economy) productivity, most especially in manufacturing, had surprisingly declined. In fact, the productivity analysis began to speak of the point of diminishing returns in the application of technology.[3] Some manufacturers, such as Delphi Automotive Systems, began to deroboticize in order to improve both productivity and quality.

Perhaps the most debilitating effect of technology on human beings was the loss of locus of control and its corollary creativity. Technology defined its own reality, a reality based on the assumption that human beings can be narrowly compressed into response mechanisms. Originality and creativity were programmed out of human capability by computer programs predicated strictly on objective response. It was the ultimate in behavioristic programming, the ultimate conditioning. Technology proved at last to be a deterrent to thought, to imagination, and a distraction from substance of any kind. Technology could not satisfy the soul.

Whatever else can be said about this hullabaloo, one thing is certain: Information was not only control, it was *in* control. The result was the complete removal of the person from what once had been human activity.

Phase V. Antiinformation (anticontrol) systems were the inevitable consequences of two natural laws: Computer technology compounds itself at a rate greater than the speed of thought, thereby causing a permanent state of obsolescence; and all computerized systems eventually reach a point of disintegration, that point being positively correlated to complexity (which, by the way, is the fundamental issue of human control). Regarding the first, by the mid-1990s computer networks had transformed all existing human activity into a totally new reality—more accurately, a new group of realities—ultimately involving all economic, social, political, and personal orders. Virtually all existing systems of Western civilization were displaced by information "networks." Dot Com became an overnight global celebrity. And it all happened fast. In a blinding flash. The phenomenon would be termed, by at least one romantic scientist, "punctuated equilibrium," after the unexpectedly surprising quirk in natural evolution by the same name.

Some people, some human systems, never regained control. Improvement was not enough. "Reform," always grounded in the past, was irrelevant, delusional backwash in the cyber-tide. It may be difficult to fully comprehend, but in terms of basic orientation and world view, there was more difference between a Westerner born in 1930 and one born in 1990 than there was between a person born in 3500 BC and one born in 1900. Three of the top ten books on the *New York Times* best-seller list in June 1996 were guides to simplifying one's life, and the common theme was much more than merely surviving the fin de siècle madness. Again, Pope John Paul II offers this dire assessment: "The increasing fragmentation of knowledge makes the search for meaning difficult and often fruitless. If this technology is not ordered to something greater than a merely Utilitarian end, then it could soon prove inhuman and even become the potential destroyer of the human race."[4]

There is actually a natural law pertaining to information: That is, information always destroys order. And the first corollary is that the greater the abundance of information and the greater the rigidity of the system—whether by force or sheer intractability—the more catastrophic the breakdown. What this means is that, contrary to the wisdom of the current age, control does not result in order. And when information *is* control, disorder follows as night follows day. There is no need to pine over quantum mysteries about order in chaos and other such foolish "new age" notions; if there is a sensation of disorder, a cognition of disorder, then disorder is real.

The second corollary is that people never learn because they cannot unlearn. It is impossible to reflect on the madding, superhuman attempt to link all people together out there in the big sky without recalling an earlier, similar, albeit less technologically sophisticated, episode of ambition overleaping itself. Allegory, fable, or myth, the ancient tower of Babel fiasco (Genesis 11: 1–9) bears an uncanny resemblance to the latest celestial misadventure.

Now, just to raise the remote possibility that the information superhighway begins and ends at the tower of Babel, consider the two outcomes in the original story: dispersion and confusion of language. Regarding the second, never in history has there been as much demand for and use of cryptography as in the years since the popularization of the Net. What had once been an esoteric art, unappreciated except in times of war, suddenly became a booming business as corporation systems scurried to protect their vital interests from those who otherwise would purloin their language and their property. It was a system at war within itself and with itself. Regarding the first, dispersion, the end of the modern version of the story was "atomized isolation." That was the phrase the pundits, prophets, and scribes used to describe the age. No other words could have captured as well the profound alienation of both the individual human being and the collective society. But the actuality was beyond words.

For more than two thousand years, Western philosophy had extolled the virtues of being human. Its twin visions had been brought into focus by a remarkable, unique image of the god–man, seen not as a set of critical attributes belonging to the person but as transcendent, eternal verities by which each person could discover the full meaning of human being. Ideal but not abstractions, practical but not artifices, reliable but not mechanical, these truths could be validated through demonstration in every aspect of human life. Beyond that, they represented the ultimate states of being. Together, they became absolute referents of humanity. That is to say, hereby shall we know what it means to be ordinarily extraordinarily human. Plato and the Greeks provided four of the cardinal virtues: justice, prudence, temperance, and fortitude. Saint Paul and the Christians, three more: faith, hope, and love.

These principles are virtually unassailable. There was no other system, no other vision of the human being, and no experience or argument that could make them either better or worse. They endured as the touchstones of individual character and social order for two thousand years. Even dehumanization did not dare challenge these eternal verities. It merely rationalized them out of existence and, in so doing, destroyed the only referents of humanity. Prudence, temperance, and fortitude were the first to go—in one swoop—

because, obviously, there was no hard evidence that these virtues were real; they were not subject to scientific observation, could not be objectified (except as they existed in human conduct, an observation that constituted a logical fallacy). Prudence might as well be cowardice; temperance, apathy; fortitude, stupidity. There was considerable evidence of all these perversions. Faith was swept away in the tide of reason; hope was dashed forever by naturalism; love disappeared into the conditions of behaviorism. Justice was the last to go.

NOTES

1. C. J. Jung, "Modern Man in Search of a Soul," *Alienation: The Culture of Modern Man*, vol. 2, ed. Gerald Sykes (New York: George Braziller, 1964), 1002.

2. Pope John Paul II, "Faith and Reason" (13th Encyclical), *USA Today*, October 16, 1998, p. 10A.

3. "How Real is the New Economy?" *The Economist*, July 24, 1999, p. 17.

4. John Paul II, "Faith and Reason."

CHAPTER 10

The Corporation and Communion

It was the truths that made the people grotesques. The old man had quite an elaborate theory concerning the matter. It was his notion that the moment one of the people took one of the truths to himself, called it his truth, and tried to live his life by it, he became a grotesque and the truth he embraced became a falsehood.

Sherwood Anderson[1]

Communion is the ultimate act of faith. This one principle, in a rare instance of metaphor turned literal, is the magic that for centuries held together all the other tenets of Western civilization and, in so doing, made that society—those societies—unique in all the world, for all time. That is not to say that other societies, past and present, are not built on some idea of community. They are. More to the point, all societies are essentially demonstrations of and commitments to basic beliefs (or disbeliefs) about divinity, human beings, and the relationships between and among them. It is true that the more rationalistic or naturalistic the society, the less the actual presence of community, tending ultimately toward absence. Yet the need for communion is why, contrary to the pronouncements and wishes of modern science, human societies will be always inherently various and distinctive. But none of the many other variations bears much resemblance to the Western interpretation.

The uniqueness of the Western idea of community lies in a double singularity: one, in its substance—that is, its philosophical assumptions and its practical expression of those assumptions—and two, its formation—that is, the way the concept developed. In the first, the magic principle of communion itself is transformed into an even higher ideal. Faith is defined not as creed, doctrine, or apology but as the unswerving confidence in the goodness of others. Consequently, the act of faith is more than ceremony or ritual, confession or purpose. It is, rather, the uncompromising dedication to the welfare of others. No other society—no other civilization—has ever made such a declaration, and certainly no other has made the attempt. This is the solidarity of the West: "No man is an island, entire of itself; every man is piece of the continent, a part of the main; if a clod be washed away by the sea, Europe is the less, as well as if a promontory were, as well as if a manor of thy friends or of thine own were; any man's death diminishes me, because I am involved in mankind."[2] Community, therefore, becomes not a matter of convenience or necessity arising from social, economic, geographical, environmental or any other physical consideration. Nor is it of philosophical origin, nor of rationalistic intent. It is strictly of the human spirit. Western community is a spiritual place. It is the place of the plural "I" and the singular "we." The place where every person is "one of us." Only a fool would suggest that this ideal was, or ever could be, perfectly realized. Only a skeptic would dismiss it as an illusion. And only a cynic would deny that the idea is always there, at once both the society's most fundamental assumption and its highest aspiration.

Communion carries the force of moral imperative. The fragility of trust lies in the fact that trust is found only in trusting. But therein also lies its power. Its loss is unthinkable. "The real significance of crime," according to Joseph Conrad, is in its being "a breach of faith with the community of mankind."[3]

Second, the way in which the Western idea of community developed is unparalleled in both historical process and actual result. The clearest indication of the essential nature of this concept to Western civilization, and the only explanation of its ubiquitous persistence throughout the world, is that it represents a coincidence, not merely a convergence, of the three traditions of faith that constituted that civilization. All other aspects of this civilization were derived from blending, mixing, often synthesizing the critical attributes of the three strands—Judaism, Hellenism, and Christianity. But in the case of community, it is virtually impossible to distinguish among them. In fact, with allowance for the respective particulars about the person of God, any one of those traditions could easily stand for the others. For example, *quhal* for *communitas*; *communitas* for *ekklesia*. And it is reassuring that *synagogue* (literally, to "lead together"), also the meeting place of the earliest Christians, is Greek. Language is not only culture; it links cultures to one another—and the linkage is fundamentally a matter of religious faith. Significantly, the word *religion* means "to bind together." But the coincidence is far more than language or incidental analogs of beliefs and practices. Western community has four facets. On each, the constituent traditions are in complete congruence: *kind, values, oneness, commonality*. And on each the traditions are uncompromisingly resolute.

But, modern science destroyed the original meaning of community by skill-fully, and with a new instrument, recutting those facets to reflect a very differ-ent reality—alleged by the crafty craftspersons to be greatly superior to the natural, certified as the real truth. The light of each surface was refracted inward, creating a very murky effect quite opposite the brilliant myriad of truth; it became a blurred melange of "truths." This is truly an amazing thing: The notion of community, implying a communion that can be realized only within the larger context of diversity, is thus transmogrified into the idea of collectivism, which is a contrivance—an artifice—that purports either to meld or to bind together irreconcilable disparities.

Throughout the twentieth century, collectivism was the underlying phi-losophy of all "progressive" or "liberal" social, political, even economic ini-tiatives and, in most cases, their ultimate objective. By the end of the century, science had succeeded in constructing fully rationalized alter-communities, obviously more delusion than illusion. Yet, the original ideas about commu-nity thrived in natural formations, outside and within the constructs.

First, the idea of *kind* is inherent in Godly order. In fact, it is impossible to imagine any order without kind. Confusion is the only alternative. In Jewish and Christian theology, the universal order of life is declared by the founding father: "Then God said, "Let the earth bring forth living creatures after their kind: cattle and creeping things and beasts of the earth after their kind" (Gen-esis 1: 24). This after the creation of a world ordered by kind: "Let the earth sprout vegetation, plants, yielding seed, and fruit trees bearing fruit after their kind, with seed in them, on the earth" (Genesis 1: 11).

Here were potentially incalculable kinds. Even today there are still thou-sands of known species yet to be classified and perhaps more than that still to be discovered. The word "species" raises an issue that at least needs to be acknowledged here, not simply as a point of fairness, but because of what is says about our understanding of kind. The fact is we do not understand it precisely. Plato offered a quite emphatic conundrum "All absolute natures or kinds are known severally by the absolute idea of knowledge." Aristotle got the basic concept right with the distinction between "genus" and "species," but he himself was muddled as to the specific lines of demarcation or the significance thereof. The scholastics, Christian successors to the Aristotelian order, were consumed by this burning question in their various "determinings"; and for a long time they set the intellectual world ablaze.

The issue still has not been resolved. The practical strain of scholasticism that became dominant and that, no doubt, provided the main channel for much of our contemporary thinking—"moderate realists," as its proponents were termed—held that humanity is something outside the perception, but exists only in individual living human beings and is differentiated in each one. The other view (held by the "ultra-realists"), strictly Platonistic, con-tended that there was one ideal of humanity, fully realized in each person. There is remarkable coincidence of moderate realism and modern idealism;

they meet in the realm of the conceptual. In fact, the problem seems to be the conceptualization, that is, the superimposition of human intellectual constructs on the natural universe.

Differentiation by kind is natural. There is no artifice, no imposed system, no distorting lens. This is a real disclosure: Knowing the kind of something means allowing each thing to reveal itself as it will, without interference, without the distorting screen of predisposition or the constrictive mold of prescription. All living things revert to kind. Human beings are no exception, even though the definition of "kind" has been made explosively complex by the nimble finagling of rationalism. Quite possibly, rationalism's most specious allegation is that human beings are a single species—the human "race." The matter was once quite simple: Christian scripture uses the word "mankind" to refer to all humanity. Technically, the word means having the image of man as opposed to that of gods or animals. Science, on the other hand, coined the self-congratulatory compound *Homo sapiens*—literally, "wise man." Indeed, it takes one to know one.

Both authorities, however, acknowledge and demonstrate that the "kind" on which community is based is a much more specific differentiation; that is, different kinds of people. Most historians agree that the reason the Roman empire became so vast and endured so long was its strategy of recognizing and preserving—within certain limits—the identities of the various kinds of people under its dominion. Communities were used as controlling devices, abetting social order, tax collection, road construction, and allegiance to Caesar. Contrariwise, Jewish history is a continuing war with all other kinds of people. It seems that being God's chosen race evokes universal outrage and resentment. Although the Apostle Paul, in a rare moment of consanguinity, declared that "there is neither Jew nor Greek" in Christ, the spiritual negation affirms the physical distinction. In modern times, quite ironically, science—contrary to its own major premise—offers proof of many kinds of human beings, just as there are many kinds of, say, fish—from stumpknockers to humpbacks. Evolution, whether theory or fact, is nothing more or less than an array of kinds without the factor of time. Lately, it is becoming increasingly difficult to maintain a convincing argument for the transmutation of species. For example, the best research concludes that the Neanderthal man, still pictured in many twentieth-century encyclopedias as a critical link in the evolutionary chain, was, rather, a free-standing dead-end Homo. That being the case, the questions of better and worse, advanced and primitive, superior and inferior become moot. Of course, no one would ever consider the possibility of devolution.

The natural formation of human communities based on kind has been the basic assumption of all societies—the very essence of all societies—if not of all civilizations. In fact, the side-by-side use of "society" and "civilization" in this context raises some disturbing possibilities. It is possible for a society to be uncivilized. It is possible for a society to be uncivilized and not be aware of it. It is possible for a society to be uncivilized and not care. After all, the hallmarks of civilization are determined by those societies that deem themselves civilized. Like all artifactual systems, civility is defined by those who invent it. I am, therefore I think. But community is self-defining.

When the seventeenth-century Europeans declared the first nations of North America, Africa, and Polynesia uncivilized—or when twentieth-century anthropologists, poking around in the sub-Saharan for old bones and junk, "find" the slightest trace of ancient living things and hustle to anoint it as "prehistoric," and fabricate a whole society around it (complete with working 3-D models of the world 500 million years ago)—including vehement denials of claims made by other story-board imaginists regarding the details of that same world, there is a general celebration of superiority throughout the civilized world. Modern dictionaries, usually the staid repositories of unabridged truth, join in the euphoria; civilization, according to them, means "highly developed—intellectually, socially, and culturally."

That definition is itself a splendid example of rationalism's annoying habit of staking dubious claim to certain words in order to establish divergent or deviate realities as truth. Intellectual honesty, social grace, and cultural respect, however, demand that civilized persons seriously reconsider their view of those who act like them.

Communities lie somewhere between humankind and the individual. The once faddish idea of a "global community"—a.k.a. "global village"—was either a metaphor pushed beyond the limits of the imagination into fantasy or a shrewdly enticing phrase leading to a distributive, egalitarian agenda. It simply cannot happen, owing, ironically enough, to a universal phenomenon that can be described only as "natural selection." That is, human beings naturally choose others like themselves in an attempt to create a meaningful, life-giving context. That choice is based on physical, mental, and spiritual sameness.

Margaret Wheatley and other meteoric new-age luminaries found the natural grouping of, say, birds and animals perplexing, if not inexplicable. Following the first rule of rationalism—that is, when science fails, resort to mysticism—she proposed that all these groups are held together as groups by a "strange attractor." But she did know what the attractor might be. How absolutely delicious the mysteries of the natural world. And how marvelous it is, indeed, that the strange attractor is nothing more or less than sameness. Such magnetism, inherent within kind, means that the possibilities for the formations of communities are infinite—from playground fights to aquarian conspiracies—transcending time and space, synchronistically existing on the same location. Any unnatural structuring is but weariness of the flesh, aggravation of the mind, and vexation of the spirit—surely to be resisted to the last conscious thought.

The second aspect of community is same *values*. While seeing oneself reflected is fundamental, that delightful speculum does not a community make. The essence of community is feeling oneself refracted. And that feeling moves the conversation far into the interior. It would be logical to suggest that this feeling is the consequence of mutual allegiance to a certain set of values reduced to creed, code, or standards. But that is not the whole truth. To be sure, such commonly held principles may represent intellectual agreement paraded as "consensus," or they may be real emotional commitments — if not moral convictions, then certainly pledges of honor. But no creed or code or standard can substitute for values beyond commitment to principles; that is, commitment to each other because of principles. It's this simple: there are countless examples of groups who earnestly subscribe to well-wrought, finely tuned paradigms and yet are bitterly divided by heartfelt passion. Commitment to one another is a far cry from commitment to principles. The only measure is forgiveness.

It goes without saying that community is relative. Obviously, some are more so than others; yet all — from club to cult — are by definition community. Of course, even the most rigid of them have some degree of elasticity because if they become brittle they break up into smaller and smaller pieces. And everything about modern civilization seems to be aimed at particalization. The only critical absolute is a common core of values that transcends anything that would otherwise separate. Values based on need, however temporary, can constitute the common core of community. That is true in catastrophes, especially natural disasters, in which people are suddenly thrown together by the need to survive. The community exists only as long as the immediate threat. As the mutual anxiety diminishes, individuals drift back to their previous occupations. But the values of community are those deep, abiding convictions that never go away and cannot be taken away. Only those values have the power of binding people together.

It is precisely here that modern rationalism attacks even the idea of community — that is, by attempting to drive a wedge between values and loyalty. The assumption that these two imperatives can be separated is alone sufficient to destroy the basic principle of community; and the assumption that there is an ultimate, if not inherent conflict between the two and that one must be chosen over the other — that, in effect, is anticommunity. The solution, according to Henry Louis Gates, Jr., is immanently logical: Learn "to talk about right and wrong without recourse to abstract principles."[4] After all, as he says, "The old codes . . . gave way to the cool calculus of moral rationalism." So, in any corporate, social, or political circumstance, one is advised to develop only weak ties with other people: "In an age of 'weak ties,' of free agency triumphant, the virtues of adhesion can seem as fragile as the ozone layer." There is no such thing as personal responsibility in a collective. There is a real irony at work here. Each community is unique, one of a kind, distinctive.

But all collectives are alike. The only thing that must hold is the restraining device — the form, the container, the corporation. There is no center. The common core of values of community is replaced by external control that ranges from overt force to blunt sociopolitical intrusions, from corporate charters to municipal boundaries, from cell blocks to public school class-rooms—basically, any collection of disperate human beings, in any number, in any place or every place, that can be compressed into a system other than themselves, whether conscious or unconscious.

For three reasons, community is the only context in which individual identity can be realized. First, collectives do not admit individualism, certainly not individual uniqueness or specialty. Conformity is required. Melting pots are encouraged. Everything is normed. Second, there is the matter of freedom. The beginning of collective is the end of personal freedom. There is no choice, because there are no options. All questions have been answered. Third, there is question of motivation. The collective has a life force outside the person. There is no reason for the individual to initiate my action or to resist. Discontent is the last motive.

When distinctions are obscured, both the idea and the experience are lost. That is evidently what happened to *oneness*. It was lost, or hidden, in "unity," the only approximation a rationalistic view of human society could accept or understand. Oneness was a central doctrine of Christianity; but "unity" became the watchword of rationalism—secular and religious. It makes a world of difference whether human beings in the plural are seen as sheaves bound together by a cord or as the same stuff requiring no binding. The issues here are both the nature of the substance—whether one or many—and the bond—whether internal or external, natural or artificial.

For example, "E pluribus unum," the majestic motto that adorns U.S. currency—right alongside "In God we trust"—was certainly taken out of context and, worse still, completely reinterpreted—either through disregard of Latin or an intent to deceive. As for context, when Virgil penned the line (if, indeed, it was he), he was simply, yet seriously, describing how to make a salad (the poem is titled "Moretum"); and this phrase deals with the recipe for a stupendous cheese and garlic paste. "*E pluribus unus*," in context, means "Out of many comes a single color." Nothing stately here or grand; nothing political or philosophic. Just a damn fine salad.

The misinterpretation and misapplication of a neat Latin phrase, however beguiling, could not make one out of many. There is no doubt that the motto adopted in 1782 was intended to refer to the conjoined states in North America as a single political unity and, in historical perspective, place a heavy emphasis on inclining the U.S. Constitution toward nationalism. There was no intent whatever to allude to an obvious singularity—a nation of immigrants made up of every tribe and tongue—all bound together by a single mechanism—something called "the United States of America." How greatly different the cheese and garlic paste. It is an essence, not a compound.

Oneness is the opposite of unity—just as the number one is the opposite of all other numbers. And every number divided by itself is one. There is an especially disappointing irony in the fact that scientists and mathematicians never seemed to be able to make the leap from abstract numbers to practical humanity. That seems to be an age-old problem; even Plato observed that he had hardly ever known a mathematician who was capable of reasoning. Collectives, after all, are nothing more than mathematical equations.

The rationalistic perversions of community, however, were easy to understand but impossible to realize in practical experience. There were three: the lingering myth of diversity within community, the constructivist allegation that communities are "built," and the materialistic assertion that human beings are the building blocks, hewn and hammered into place.[5]

First, there is no such thing as "diverse community." The phrase itself is an oxymoron. Even the word "diverse" assumes a referent, a base. The modern scientific definition of community—the one accepted by all social scientists, and their kind—as a heterogeneous grouping of any number of living things (plants, animals, microorganisms, human beings) based on interdependent "functions" as well as complementary features and unitary completeness (i.e., an ecosystem), is a galling demonstration of confiscating an idea by backing into a definition. Metaphor is made the primary meaning; the original meaning becomes metaphor. The genuine becomes the imitation; the imitation is somehow the genuine. The double dealing of meaning is sacred in the lore of science.

Second, and obviously a corollary of the assumption of diversity, was the truly strange notion that community can be built—more accurately, that communities can be built. It may seem inconceivable that such an idea could have been so easily channelled into mainstream thinking, unchallenged and unproved. But "community building" became a regular enterprise in post-1970s America.

Community building— intellectual, political, commercial—was the test for rationalism. All its precepts and promises converged in this one activity. And every system predicated on rationalistic philosophy was brought to the moment of truth. The truth is that while inordinate energy and resources were being dedicated to constructing unnatural facsimiles of community, real communities were forming throughout Western civilization with enough energy of their own to completely upheave all constructs. Natural law in action.

Third, the final indignity of rationalism was the subjection of human beings to constructs. Whether the loss of soul was a prerequisite or consequence is moot. The fact is that the human being is sacrificed to the system. Community became a descent into oblivion. The conditions are always the same: (1) The scientific idea of community assumed the unquestioned a priori existence of an organization that could be turned into a community, by hook or crook. All so-called "members" were required to conform to preset structures and regulations; "community," it was said, "will emerge only when the attitude of the individual members allows for it."[6] The pressure was on the person to comply. (2) The severity of the decline increased beyond the point of retrieval with the necessary suspension of personal preconceptions and the readiness to "flow" with the possibilities that arise through "connection building." That was the attitude adjustment required for entry into this makeshift union. It was suggested, "There is no firm set of formula rules that can tell us when to hold on and when to let go."[7] (3) Meaninglessness occurred with the detachment from any certain context. Rather, all members must be willing to adapt to the "unfolding social reality of the situation"; that is, "Trust in oneself to 'ride' with the situation in a skilled way."[8] (4) Finally, there must be the corporate abandonment of individuality; specifically, static notions of who we are must be checked at the door.

Corporated, rationalized "communities," whether in theory or practice, moved science as far as possible from actual human experience. Unity, however conceived or attempted, does not community make—for one simple reason: Community is not made; it is.

The fourth aspect of community is *commonality*. It is the beginning and the end of community—at once both its fundamental nature and its fullest expression. And that is the reason modern Western civilization could not realize community. The idea was there, all right, as an insistent reminder—at times tantalizing, at times accusatory, sometimes repulsive, but always provocative—of the essence of community. What makes the idea so intriguing is the fact that most of the constituent traditions of Western civilization are grounded in community. Yet few ever expected to actually achieve it—at least not in this world. Plato taught it in *The Republic*—advocating the mutuality of everything, including spouses; but he characteristically pulled back just before actuality. In *The Laws*, Plato advocates complete communism, extended to the whole state, as ideal; but, for practical purposes, he abandoned the idea, even for rulers. Socrates went further, at least in theory. He stipulated that in order to insure the greatest unity in the state, there must be no private property, including women and children. The mantra: "Friends have all things in common." The Jewish Essenes, however, actually achieved a rather severe version of commune. And the early disciples of Jesus practiced the purest form of communism imaginable (Acts 4: 32–35)—a fact which the Church, with the exception of symbolic monastic orders, has conveniently ignored or, in the case of mainstream Protestantism, explained away.

Sir Thomas More offered the ultimate solution to community in 1576. In *Utopia* he gave both name and impetus to a whole genre of literary excursions, to say nothing of a rash of social experiments. Scholars will forevermore argue about the stylistic mode of this work and therefore of More's personal philosophy; but it would be impossible to say just how influential this book has been over the centuries. This much is certain: There are uncanny similarities between More's "Nowhere" and every attempt at communal society since. Not surprisingly, that was especially evident in all socialistic agendas and reform movements during nineteenth- and twentieth-century England and America. Most remarkable is the fact that the great reform in China included practices exactly like those in More's world (for example, the abolition of private property and the rotation of all citizens for farm duty).

The most significant idea advanced by More was not about human relationships within a community per se but about the size of any given community. Heretofore, it had been a common-sense assumption that community was of necessity limited by size. The Greeks had held that a small city was the largest possible democratic state; Aristotle fixed a maximum population for the *polis*. The Jewish synagogues were family based; likewise, the Christian congregations were extended households. More himself was impressed—probably inspired—by monastic communities. But in *Utopia*, community is nationalized. Well, almost. Fifty-four cities are each intricately organized as communes, all connected in one social–economic system. And that was the assumption of all Western democracies from their beginning—community had no limits. Complexity was not even a consideration. National communities—world communities—were not only possible but desirable. With that assumption, collectives were the only possibility.

Only one tragedy greater than the loss of community could have befallen Western civilization: That was the transmogrification of the idea into its opposite. The loss was not merely the uniqueness of the culture, which ultimately was compromised out of existence, but the desecration of the very highest ideals of humanity, ideals that the world would be likely never to see again. The bitter irony is that the erstwhile paragon of faith self-destructed, willfully trading the promise of its birthright for a lie of its own making. By the close of the twentieth century it was painfully obvious that if community was to survive as a human experience it would be in a context other than Western society. That was the ultimate legacy of the corporation.

NOTES

1. Sherwood Anderson, "The Book of the Grotesque," *Winesburgh, Ohio* (New York: Viking Press, 1964), 25.

2. John Donne, "Devotions upon Emergent Occasions," *The Norton Anthology of English Literature*, ed. M. H. Abrams (New York: W. W. Norton, 1968), 1: 915.

3. Joseph Conrad, *Lord Jim* (New York: Holt, Rhinehart and Winston, 1957), 135.

4. Henry Louis Gates, Jr., "The End of Loyalty," *The New Yorker*, March 9, 1998, p. 34.

5. Paul Maltessich and Barbara Monsey, *Community Building: What Makes It Work* (St. Paul, Minn.: Amherst H. Wilder Foundation, 1997), 57–59.

6. *The Process-Centered School: Sustaining a Renaissance Community*, ed. Arthur L. Costa and Rosemarie M. Liebmann (Thousand Oaks, Calif.: Corwin Press, 1997), 42.

7. Ibid.

8. Ibid.

CHAPTER 11

The Corporation and the Science of Management

It is the peculiar payne of us . . . to manege wyth reason, especially
rough horses.

Castiglione's Courtyer[1]

For almost all of the twentieth century, the corporation-model organization
earnestly attempted to right itself. It desperately sought solutions to the many
problems that had arisen from its own internal contradictions and been intensified both by the increasing complexity of economic circumstances and production techniques and by the dramatic changes occurring in society—many of which
it had itself created. True to form, it turned to science for its salvation. Between
1911 and 1926, an entire new science was invented, one intended specifically to
deal with the human and technical conundrums inherent in modern organization. Management was supposed to be the remedy for "getting work done"
through people. Unfortunately, it did not live up to its promise. Rather, for
the remainder of the century, management became the problem.

The history of Western organization is the history of the corporation; the
history of the corporation is the history of management; the history of management is the history of Western organization. If that seems to be doublespeak,
it is only because of the ironic imprecision in any language having to do with
modern organization. It does help, however, to realize that virtually no attention has been given the corporation model per se and that historically everything that pertains to management has been considered part and parcel of
the broader rubric of organizational theory. For this reason, it is possible, and
perhaps instructive, to approach the subject from both points of view—spe-

cifically, as a study of management philosophy and as a study of organizational theory. While there is the imminent risk in this endeavor that pedantry will discourage learning, a quick synopsis of each approach promises to yield a sometimes sympathetic understanding of the corporation's pathology. Unfortunately, there are no big ideas here, nothing to excite the imagination.

The story of management has been told so often, always with the easy variations of the oral tradition, that by now most historians will recount the same basic narrative. For example, Jay M. Shafritz and J. Steven Ott have provided the most readable and thorough account in their *Classics of Organization Theory*.[2] Probably the most succinct and user-friendly version is that presented in several media by Kenneth Blanchard. What is amazing is that his informally frank treatment of the subject, as objective as it is, did not incite instant revolution by those trapped in the world of the corporation. The most likely explanation for the general catatonia is that by the time of his revealing analysis, corporated people had been conditioned beyond response. Or maybe they simply did not realize they had a choice.

According to Blanchard, four great consecutive waves of management swept over and through the corporation establishment during roughly a seventy-year span. The waves imagery is intriguing; and although easily carried beyond the tolerance of metaphor, there are some meaningful tropish implications in swirling currents, blackwash, undertow, side channels, maelstroms, flotsam, and jetsam. Actually, "waves" may be overly dramatic, if not hyperbolic. Whoever said "history is biography" was right: Every wave was nothing more than the wake of somebody who presumed to know how things work and, even more brazen, dared to tell. Every movement in management not only has a name, it is attached to a name.

For example, the first wave to sweep over the corporation was propelled by the observation and conclusions of Frederick Winslow Taylor and company (*The Principles of Scientific Management*, 1911). In a rationalistic world, it seemed not only acceptable but entirely expected that all his so-called "research" was fabricated. What really mattered was the postulation. "Classical" management was so for three reasons. First, it was the first coherent management system, bringing rationalized order to erstwhile seat-of-the-pants boondoggles aimed at "breaking and training" people. Second, it effectively combined the duality of ancestry—science and religion—by insisting on perfectable mechanistic processes and workers and demanding rigidly hierarchical categories of rank and responsibility. Third, it never went away.

The duality of classical management was the epitome of the age. On one side, it was purely rationalistic—this was termed "scientific" management; on the other, it was a rationalistic version of Christian order—called "administrative" management. One consisted of "principles," the other of "proverbs." Scientific management was concerned strictly with the mechanisms of production processes. Human beings were considered part of the machinery— their work, like that of other machines, reducible to time and motion.

There is always a mystical parallel between product and process. The process is implicit in the product; the product implicit in the process. In the industrialized world, where the product was judged by its adherence to design specifications, so also was the process. Scientific management was based on the assumption that it is possible to achieve perfection in the product and, likewise, that there is one best way to produce it. Furthermore, products made of interchangeable parts (the key to mass production) require processes of similarily matched components. Even before Taylor's work, Babbage had attempted to achieve absolute efficiency in production through the division of labor and precise job design. So the purpose of management was to invent and enforce that one best way and to bring the functions of everyone into conformity with the design. Industrial engineering was always a behavioral science. Inexplicably, and somewhat contrary to Blanchard's interpretation, this basic assumption about process and the corollary purpose of management remained constant throughout the twentieth century—long after the end of the industrialized economy.

"Administrative" management was simply the transference of the principles of mechanics to human institutions already dominated by authoritarian rule. That explains why Fayol's principles are dualistic. Administrative management was as qualitative as any rationalistic construct of a dedicated social order could be but only because the subject ultimately forced attention on human qualities. Accordingly, administrative theory was enunciated in softer terms—most illustrative, "proverbs" rather than "principles"—but it was, nevertheless, scientific through and through. "The first task of administrative theory is to develop a set of concepts that will permit the description in terms relevant to the theory, of administrative situations. These concepts, to be scientifically useful, must be operational; that is, their meanings must correspond to empirically observable facts or situations."[3]

The scientific philosophy of management comprised four assumptions: (1) that human beings are economic animals, (2) that all human organization is predicated on rank and chain of command, (3) that, in organizations of production, managers are a special class, set apart from other workers, and that organization efficiency requires specialization and division of labor, and (4) that the purpose of management is to build and maintain a high-performance human machine ("well-oiled," as it were) through six control-command activities (five specified by Fayol; the last added by committee): planning, organizing, staffing, directing, controlling, and evaluating. An administrative version by Luther Gulick and Lyndall Urwick (c. 1937) at first appears significantly less authoritarian (planning, organizing, staffing, directing, *coordinating*, *reporting*, and *budgeting*), but in actuality it was more so, elevating control and evaluation to levels even above the manager. These "functions" in one form or another, became the modern definitions of management and eventually, as each developed into unending disputatious complexity, the sum total of that profession. All management (administrative) theory and prac-

tice—including all related books, courses, curricula, workshops, articles, and
paternoster sermons on the mount—were but variegated re-presentations.
Any discussion or study of management began and ended with these principles. And there was never anything new.

The second wave—actually originated by Robert Owen (a socialist) in the
early nineteenth century and championed by Elton Mayo in the 1930s—
while often termed "social" was in actuality "behavioristic" management. The
adjective is the clue. Although it would eventually experiment with every
hypothesis that behaviorism could deduce, behavioristic management was
fundamentally a rationalistic construct of six assumptions, each implicit with
appropriate scientific responses, that together constituted a complete philosophy of getting work done through people. The first was that workers were
"vital machines"—a term used by Owen in 1813—and necessarily had to be
treated differently from nonliving machines. Even so, their work, like that of
all machines, had to be processed, uniformed, and made precise ("structured"
became the operative term) for the sake of efficiency if not effectiveness.
Actually, the phrase "vital machine parts" might have more accurately described the assumption, because each worker was considered only a component of a larger mechanism and so was susceptible to wear, breakdown, and
replacement.

But the second assumption acknowledged that human beings were distinct from their mechanical counterparts. It was on this assumption that the
behavioristic philosophy was based. Specifically, it held that humans are rational
beings; therefore, they are both self-serving and purposeful. These are the recur-
ring essential themes of behavioristic management. It is rather amazing that even
into the 1980s the life insurance industry in North America marketed its wares
on the premise that people were motivated by certain self-interests, in this
order: profit, pride, pleasure, caution, utility, love, and ambition.

The third assumption was closely related. It was that workers could be
motivated (conditioned, as it turned out) to greater productivity. The fourth
was complementary: that the cause of all human response is external to the
person and is realized as either reward or punishment, promise or threat. The
fifth assumption was a boon to wealth-producing enterprises. It was the happy
discovery (allegedly proved by experiments such as the Western Electric case,
1924–1932) that economic incentive was not the paramount motivator of workers. The experimenters concluded, prematurely as it turned out, that the cause
of increases in productivity was change—any kind of change—and spent the
rest of the century trying to make it work for them. Sixth, it was acknowledged that any work group was in fact a social system (or "unit," as the boffins
were wont to call it), possessing its own energy, controlling its own tempo and
sometimes its own direction; therefore, motivation of the individual was best
accomplished in a group setting and had something to do with relationships.

The adaptive reaction to these assumptions was, of course, intervention in
the form of intense concentration on the human factor—"human relations,"

as it was termed—to the degree that, before long, the response emerged as a "movement," characterized by personal incentives, touchy-feely affirmation of self-worth, and a ploy of participation in matters allegedly important to the business.

It was supposed at the time, and long after, that the human relations approach to management stood in stark contrast to the old-line scientific management. Usually, the two are presented as opposite extremes. In actuality, there was no real difference. Human relations à la behaviorism was merely the scientizing of the social factors involved in group work and would always be nothing more than a management contrivance with productivity in mind.

The third wave was a veritable tsunami. It was not so much the heft of its substance as the force of its overpowering swell that created a tide capable of lifting all vessels into a whole new universe. As Shakespeare observed, "There is a tide in the affairs of men, which, taken at the flood, leads on to fortune." And so it was with "management science." In this case, finding the responsible parties is well-nigh impossible because there were so many who influenced this kind of thinking, although the ageless Peter Drucker usually is given credit by his legion of disciples and worshippers from afar. And it is true that his landmark book, *The Practice of Management* (1954), codified management forevermore, became the sacred text for management by objectives, and was followed religiously by corporate executives until the end. And why not? It played the siren's song: "The Manager is the dynamic, life-giving element in every business. Without his leadership the 'resources of production' would remain resources and never become production."[4]

However, Drucker was merely articulating the collective wisdom and practice of the time. He was only a reporter, not a theoretician. But the idea of management science caught on quickly, especially in business schools. And when the idea was combined with the idealism and technology of the 1960s, the result was indefatigable presumption.

Accepting the principles of both the classical and behavioristic philosophies, management science logically and predictably developed in its own dichotomous fashion. It was both quantitative and qualitative, with each strangely seeking to produce the other. This was the first time that the idea of a double obverse was seriously articulated in North America. Frederick Engels, in the early nineteenth century, had theorized only one transubstantiation— quantitative to qualitative—and was bashed for being abstruse, if not beyond the pale. But the modern *physike* unabashedly worked not only this way but the other way as well. This presumed "profound knowledge" was sufficient to inform all management theories of the remainder of the century, especially that of W. Edwards Deming. His Total Quality Management (TQM)—a truly odd apples-and-oranges fourteen-point mixture of operational research methodologies and "participatory" management dictums—quite by historical accident, would become the last great attempt of the corporation model to preserve itself. Ironically, when judged by its own standards, TQM proved to be mostly hype and hoopla. And even when companies faked the whole she-bang and lied about its effectiveness, the federal government gave them "quality" awards. Universal standards can never be more than minimum.

The purely quantitative current, harking back to the earlier scientific management of Babbage and Taylor, was based on mathematical analysis and so was much given to statistics of every conceivable stripe. That meant an endless array of statistical analyses pertaining to every aspect of the process, uniformity, and precision of production mechanisms. Only now, the data were also about the human machine as an inherent part of that mechanism. There is little doubt that this obsessive rush to analysis was the harbinger of the "age of information" and the world of insatiable, obsolescing business machines. There was nothing that could not be classified, sorted, micromeasured, standardized, normed, disaggregated, plotted, and stored in databases, so there was no decision, strategic or tactical, that could not be "data driven"—the mantra of scientific management. And if that were not enough, the data could be interpreted according to any inquiry past or present, so historical patterns could be discovered or even reconstructed and future trends or possibilities predicted. Newton redux.

It did not take much calculation to appreciate the unlimited potential presented by this ceaseless, obedient rash of information. In a totally unexpected turn of events, quantitative analysis became a ready instrument for fabricating optional realities—past and future (after all, the present can never be context). The past was selectively formatted into case studies designed for infinite second-guessing, chiefly by anal-rententive professors whose experience consisted solely of second-guessing case studies. Game playing quickly became the forte of academic business. It added pizzazz to otherwise dreary anthropologies of profit and loss.

Even so, historical case studies were not as titillating as computer models of the future. These hummers could come alive and, with the mere press of a key, could be anything the creator willed. From exercises as simple as programming a retail store for maximum return per square foot to projects as complicated as establishing global labor-intensive manufacturing–marketing–distribution systems for controlled products, there was simply no end to "what if?" Modeling in any other world would have been a godsend. But here no faith was required: With scenarios, all things were possible—even fantasy.

Without question, the most auspicious result of quantitative analysis was its inevitable discovery of systems. One can only imagine the astonishment of management yobs when they realized that everything is connected to everything else and that nothing has any significance except in the context of these connections—however seen, however interpreted. Complex computer models did it. They required much more than simple analysis of each part, because no action can occur in isolation. The model demanded that all the parts had to work together in a total fit and fix, albeit often in coincidental subsystems, also interconnected with the whole. It is important to note here, however, that there was, by assumption, an essential difference between the whole system and its parts—a difference that inevitably produced a variety of tensions within the system. The tension was seen as an indicator of vitality. This assumption would later prove to be old skins for new wine. Systems did not work as expected by the industrial mentality; there was an essentiality that simply could not be comprehended by traditional models.

"Systems thinking," as it was later termed, was predicated on two basic assumptions—holism and interrelationships. Although the potentiality of the concept would not be realized until after the popularization of quantum theory (starting in 1986), systems thinking probably was the single most powerful influence on organization in the twentieth century. Not only did a systems approach give new meaning to the "effectiveness" and "efficiency" of mechanisms, it of necessity acknowledged the human component as a distinctive part of the whole construct. For the first time, mechanistic systems could be neither built nor operated without the consideration of a correlative social system (however behavioristic in interpretation); and numerical relationships could not be authenticated until human interrelationships were factored in.

With the advent of systems thinking, action within the corporation model took on the four aspects shown in Figure 11.1. This matrix was the only thing about the corporation model that had universal application to human organization, most probably because these elements were the characteristics of all human action long before the corporation model came into existence. That's why they would endure long after the demise of the corporation.

It is difficult to say whether the fourth movement was a wave or a waiver. There seems to be an all-too-easy transition from relationships to relativity; so if the "contingency" philosophy of management seems a bit loose, it is for good reason. This great surge is always described by the name of Fred E. Fiedler, the indisputable champion of behavioral relativism, even though Herbert Simon introduced the concept in "The Proverbs of Administration" (1946). The basic idea, ostensibly the antithesis of classical management, is that there is no one right way in production mechanisms and processes. Rather, the appropriate response is always determined by the situation, and even though there may be many similarities among situations, each is unique.

Figure 11.1

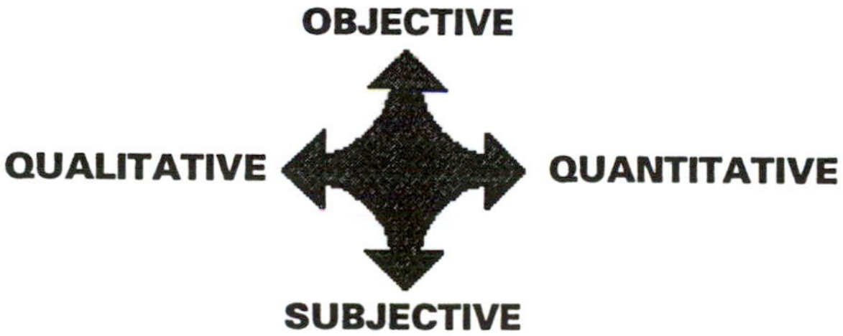

OBJECTIVE

QUALITATIVE   QUANTITATIVE

SUBJECTIVE

Therefore, in any specific instance, the way to proceed in decision making is to analyze all factors involved by utilizing whatever traditional approach is suitable—be it scientific, behavioristic, quantitative, or a combination thereof. For example, a production problem might require a time-and-motion study; a personnel difficulty might be best dealt with by behavioristic methods, and a marketing plan might be best developed by mathematical extrapolation. Furthermore, this kind of management must be multidisciplinary, combining knowledge from as many fields as practical. This was termed "situational management." Peter Drucker reported on this also. What is not completely clear is whether this flexibility was the happy result of enlightened, liberated thinking—faith in humanity and all that—or simply controlled panic in the face of malfunctioning systems and rebellious people spasmodically emboldened to defy the existing order of things.

NOTES

1. Castiglione's Courtyer, trans. Thomas Hoby, *The Compact Edition of the Oxford English Dictionary* (London: Oxford University Press, 1971).

2. Jay M. Shafritz and J. Steven Ott, *Classics of Organization Theory* (Belmont, Calif.: Wadsworth, 1996).

3. Herbert A. Simon, "The Proverbs of Administration," *Public Administration Review*, Winter 1946, pp. 53–67.

4. Peter Drucker, *The Practice of Management* (New York: Harper and Row, 1954), 3.

CHAPTER 12

═══════════════

Old Skins and New Wine

Nor do men put new wine in old wine-skins; otherwise the skins burst, and the wine pours out, and the wine skins are ruined.

Matthew 9: 17

Whatever the reason, the lingering effect of situational management was a twofold anomaly: "leadership" as a science, and management as "participatory." The corporation would never be the same. With regard to the first, the emergence of "leadership" as both activity and position having something to do with management is curious indeed. Even more inexplicable is the persistence during the next forty years of situational definitions—in every instance requiring giant semantic leaps of faith. For example, sometimes it seemed that "leadership" and "management" were more or less synonymous. Fred E. Fiedler suggested as much; and James Cribbin, a little known but major perpetrator of incalculable confusion, acknowledging Fiedler as the head shaman, proclaimed, "All leadership is situational," and went on to do the world the favor of succinctly rendering four "non-productive" and three "productive" (albeit nonabsolute) leadership styles of the "manager–leader."[1] Dauntless, he ventured on to identify the nine factors that "have an important bearing on the choice of a leadership style"—all from the point of view of the manager. It is safe to say that imprecise language was the basic idiom of situational leadership. Even more gratuitous is the notion that leadership is stylish, to be selected at the discretion of the manager who would aspire to lead.

Then Warren Bennis declared management and leadership not only different but also contrasting activities. The real problem with this analysis is that, logically, contrast is possible only with things of the same class. According to his often-parroted distinction, "Managers do things right; leaders do the right things." That seemed to settle the issue, especially for those who intended to do neither. In the late 1970s, Abraham Zaleznik provided a more expansive contrast of managers and leaders. He characterized managers as individuals who maintain the balance of operations, relate to others according to their role, remain detached and impersonal, totally identified with corporation. Leaders, on the other hand, create new approaches, relate to others in a personal way, take risks, and are not constricted by corporate limits. Still later, something called "transformational leadership" became the rage, evidently borne of desperation as traditional corporate systems began to crumble: The elaborate hope seemed to call for an overarching semantical power sufficient to glaze the familiar with the slick goo of innovation.

In the final stage of the corporation-model organization, there was an unprecedented explosion of leadership philosophies—"transactional–transformational leadership," "cultural leadership," "the tao of leadership," "leadership and the new science," "the leadership secrets of Attila the Hun," "leadership jazz," and so on. However, none of these attempts was able to escape the enervating context of "situational management." Leadership by this definition was always fundamentally rationalistic (notwithstanding the spurious claim that it was an art), confined to a corporation model ("leadership" customarily referred to upper-echelon managers as a group), and manipulative (subject to continuous negotiation of style). It is not exaggeration to suggest that the cumulative effect of this abject misunderstanding of leading—specifically, its confusion with management science—reflected the disorientation of society in general. Only one person dared tell the truth. John W. Gardner, to his everlasting credit, admitted, "More than four decades of objective research have not produced clear answers . . . about leadership."[2]

By the 1990s, Western civilization was openly acknowledging a "leadership crisis" of catastrophic proportions, and there were no solutions. For instance, lamenting the mediocrity of political leaders at the turn of the century, William Rees-Mogg, the distinguished journalist, observed, "The simultaneous collapse in the quality of world leadership must be more than a coincidence."[3] Indeed. Corporation-model organizations, whether wealth producing or wealth consuming, ultimately can neither produce nor tolerate authentic leaders. Neither can their societies.

As for the second anomalous effect, situational management provided optimal conditions for the development of a "participatory" approach to decision making, and sometime accountability, that had been the fondest longing of the human relations advocates. Proponents of situational management, for example, had identified at least three management (they would say "leadership") styles that to some degree tolerated, if not invited, participation: "collaborative," "collegial," and "democratic." Participatory management, however, was eventually identified as something other—just what was never clear, but always both passionately sanguine and deceitfully manipulative.

Participatory management, like "situational leadership," was a relativistic concept and was thus variously practiced. By 1990, definition was moot, since it had become clear that the term was only a cynical rhetorical device—a prime example of MBJPA (management by jerking people around). That explains why it was about this time that participatory management was easily swallowed up by a blatantly cynical ploy called "empowerment," a politically correct form of suppression. Empowerment firmly ensconced those in authority because it certified that they were the source of power for those so favored. Without them, the "empowered" would be powerless.

Ironically, the fundamental assumptions behind participatory management were valid. For example, a real double benefit may be achieved if those who are closest to a task are involved in decision making about the task. The results are twofold: better decisions, and more support for the decisions. The best decision with most support was the best of all possible scenarios. Unfortunately, the corporation-model organization simply could not live with that assumption, or without it.

The ramifications of the idea of participatory management presented a real threat to traditional organization. It seemed to make vague inclusionary promises that the corporation could not understand and could never keep. It was an open invitation for preposterous running amok. It should come as no surprise in all this confusion that the reductio ad absurdum was the invention of the phrase "participatory leadership." No wonder the president of a large chemical company declared in a private conversation with me, "Participatory management for us was like dancing with a bear. You know, you ask the bear to dance, but the bear tells you when the dance is over."

Another, an executive of a well-known insurance company, confessed in a round-table discussion with her business peers, "We have been trying to implement participatory management for 35 years; and, so far, we have not been able to make it work."

What was it about this basically good idea that made it impossible to implement? There is only one answer: the corporation-model mentality, manifested in two ways. First, there were almost as many interpretations as organizations and authors. Some versions were virtually tyrannical, with microrules restricting and regulating participation and complicated report forms. But some were basically laissez-faire, with participants held together only by time and space. The approaches to participation were variously dubbed "quality circles," "vertical teams," "cross-functional teams," "high-performance teams," and any number of other teaming or group designations. The decision-making methods ranged from mathematical derivatives such as delphi matrices to spiritual meanderings such as Hoshin and Ouija boards. Practicality ended somewhere in the vicinity of scientific harmonic convergence.

Second, there were barriers within the structure of the corporation-model organization that could not be overcome. Although the fundamental assumptions underlying the idea of participative management really did have tremendous potential (the decisions made by groups closest to the action were demonstrably better than decisions made any other way), that was true only if certain assumptions were actual. The synthesis of that which was discovered in practice and material found in the literature on the subject produced five assumptions (principles) behind the concept of "participatory management." They are presented here in the old language of the corporation:

1. The person doing the job is the expert.
2. That which is strategic must be validated by the operational; that which is operational must have strategic context for meaning.
3. Authority, accountability, and information are commensurate.
4. Decisions are made at the lowest level possible.
5. Group decisions are made by "consensus."

Then something that seemed quite shocking at the time became abundantly clear: None of these principles can be realized in the traditional corporation structure. In fact, everything about the corporation is adverse to them. Furthermore, management can never be participatory, since it is essentially and only authoritarian and rationalistic. Simply stated, "participatory management" was an oxymoron. Like all other hypothesized variations of management (called "styles"), it never existed except as a desperate attempt to fool workers into believing that the rigid authoritarian rank-order inherent in the corporation structure had been suspended. If the five principles were ever to be realized, it would occur outside management and outside the corporation model. And each would have to be reconceptualized.

Since the history of management is the history of organization, especially the North American version, it is not surprising that twentieth-century organization theory roughly parallels the progressive development of management. There were four philosophies of management and four models of organization (or organizational behavior, as it is usually termed). It is immediately obvious that management and organization are inextricable, so speculation about which is the major and which is the minor is foolish indeed. It would have been a reasonable hypothesis to suggest that management was a scientific distillation of the principles of the Christian religion applied to social order, and organizational models the various applications of "natural" laws (and theories) to individual behavior; but from the earliest forms of each, "classical" management and "classical" organization, they are substantively intertwined. Other than this pervasive mutuality, it is also dramatically apparent that the four periods (models) of organization structure represent not merely philosophical and historical stages but are, in effect, the accumulation of quasi-intellectual outcroppings. From that vantage, it is clear that management also is residual. The last corporations were monolithic morains. Only the melting could reveal just how thoroughly indiscriminate the collection of trash and treasure had been.

In the final analysis, neither management philosophy nor organizational theory was sufficient fully to disclose the perverse implications of the corporation-model organization or to resolve the intrinsic contradictions, certainly not to justify the corporation's deleterious effects on humanity. In fact, both were tangential, often diversionary, because of either motive or blindness. The real significance of the corporation model was twofold: first, its dramatic embodiment of the fundamental Western values regarding social order and individual behavior (because of the lack of any other plausible explanation of reality), and second, its inherent self-destructiveness (because of its own contradictory postulates).

In the first instance, the corporation was marked by three absolute necessities: the disregard for life, the denial of morality, and the assertion of its own supremacy. In the second instance, it was distinguished by its compound contradiction: its religion-based precepts were antithetical, sometimes ridiculously so, to its scientific pronouncements; and its laws were incompatible, sometimes ludicrously so, with the very natural law it purported to represent. And both were out of kilter with a moral universe.

The cutting edge of the corporation was always felt most intensely by these people whose existence lay only within the organized contradiction. Surely, most of them knew instinctively that something was wrong, but no one seemed to know what, even though everyone kept trying to fix it. Probably no one would have admitted that the real trouble was the world they had created or allowed to be created around them—a world beyond redemption.

The corporation had created its own world, its own kingdom, by displacing, through the manifold agency of rationalistic science, both the Church and monarchy as the right and righteous organization of Western society. As such, it imposed absolute rule over all under its domination and rendered them dependent on its largess for their general and personal welfare. It was a godless kingdom—the ultimate contradiction.

NOTES

1. James Cribben, *Effective Managerial Leadership* (New York: American Management Association, 1972), 105–123.

2. John W. Gardner, "Leaders and Followers," *Liberal Education*, March–April 1987, p. 14.

3. William Rees-Mogg, "World Leaders in Mediocrity," *The London Times*, 20 March 1995, p. 16.

PART III

THE WORLD OF
THE CORPORATION—
ITS RELIGION

CHAPTER 13

The Making of Gods

If you want to be a God of the Information Age, you might have to toss
out your jammies.

Kevin Maney[1]

Lately, it has become intellectually camp to blame the dysfunctionality of
contemporary organization on Isaac Newton and his damned scientific empiricism. The part about dysfunctionality is quite true (every organization in
North America—for that matter, all those of Western civilization—is terminally dysfunctional—corporate, government, economic, social, religious,
educational); what is not totally correct, however, is the allegation that Newton caused it all. How and why we arrived at our state of affairs is an intriguing, albeit sometimes sorrowful, tale of human perambulation—some would
say aberration—over a period of roughly thirty-five hundred years on three
continents. We should not be surprised to find that it takes a little time and
effort to fully understand what we so astoundingly have done to ourselves
through organization. But it is well worth that investment, not just for curiosity's
sake but because without some knowledge of this history there is little hope
that we shall ever understand fully the dominant contemporary organizational model and, therefore, virtually no possibility that we shall emerge from
the current madding state of affairs into organizations fit for human beings.
As a matter of fact, adolescent impatience and the frantic rush to fix things by
lately arrived experts schooled in the fanciful theories of the day but ignorant
of either philosophical or historical context are precisely the reasons why we

keep perpetuating our anxiety—and our folly. Furthermore, only a comprehensive examination of the historical development of Western organization
can reveal both the evolving aspects of society and the changing nature of
human affiliation that are necessary fully to understand the adverse features
of the modern corporation. Only then can we begin to understand the system of affiliation that is replacing it.

As pointed out earlier, there are two major influences on modern organization, and the second has a variation substantial enough to merit separate
consideration: they are religion and science (and scientism). Although each
influence thoroughly dominated its own millennium, captivating every aspect of society and creating the society's dominant organization, the cumulative effect of all this is realized in the modern corporation. That is not to say
there was perfect historical coincidence of philosophy and time. Religion
was paramount long before 4 BC or even 4004 BC; rational science did not
emerge until the seventeenth century. Nor is it to suggest that the influences
have been mutually exclusive. Religion obviously persists in its pervasive influence over every aspect of Western civilization. And some science, legitimate even by modern standards, was already fairly sophisticated, albeit strictly
practical in its manifestation, as early as 3500 BC in various parts of the globe.

If our contemporary world is small, then the world of the ancients must
have been incredibly large. They lived in three dimensions, all right, but not
as seen today. For even the most intelligent of them (and there is no real
indication that innate human intelligence has since become greater or lesser),
their world consisted of where I am, where I have been, and where I have
heard about. Beyond that, there was another world, the supernatural, filled
with inexplicable forces at once both terrible and beautiful, that held sway, in
concert or in contest, over the terrestrial plane and all those dwelling therein.
That world and its deities were divided fairly evenly between forces benevolent, forces malevolent, and forces ambivalent. Eventually, the good clustered in places like Nirvana or Heaven and the bad in the netherworld of
Hell. Up was good; down was bad.

As these forces were identified by geographical place, natural element, or
imputed disposition, they were personified (given names); and developed quite
fascinating personal and family histories—all behaving much like the humans who had created them. Some had split personalities, alternately curs-
ing and blessing; others underwent permanent personality changes, for better
or worse. Sooner or later almost all became deities, acknowledged as both
rulers, to be obeyed and lords, to be worshiped. On the one hand, they were
accorded authority over mere mortals—to give and to take away; on the other
hand, they were attributed knowledge transcending human ken—to declare
the truth, the whole truth, and nothing but the truth. Superstition or religion, the net effect was the same.

There is a great curiosity about all this, in that for the longest time, perhaps
even until the present hour, there raged a considerable debate about the number

of gods. Ultimately, about all the brouhaha proved is that ignorance has unlimited capacity for fear and ineluctable propensity to denigration. Chiefly, the controversy centered on the question of whether there were many gods or one.

The very earliest humans, according to all the evidence we can gather, saw
gods in just about everything around them. In fact, in an effort to insure that they
were constantly in touch with deities and also, presumably, for the practical necessity of telling them apart, these first representatives of the species *Homo sapiens* began the custom—later both popular and profitable—of symbolically
representing the gods made with the human mind with little things made with
human hands—talismans, totems, idols, and the like. Security and convenience
were thus merged into symbols of obedience and adoration. That was the official
beginning of religion.

Quite understandably, these early folk took to placing the icons on or near
things of value for both protection and sanctification. And, before long, by
easy transference, the icon actually began to impute value to anything it
touched or was affixed unto, especially media of exchange, agreements, promises, and proclamations. Another striking development was the early recognition of the inherent magnetism of gods toward things, even colors, of intrinsic
value—the rare, the pure, the beautiful. So there was an overwhelming tendency for precious metal to accumulate in the treasuries of gods. This is the
one and only indisputable economic axiom.

All this seemed to work in the best interest of everyone for a long time—
centuries perhaps. It all began to fall apart only when the gods began requiring their own residences on earth—usually, temples. The only requirement a
god had, other than a prime location, was that his (or her) headquarters be
bigger and more elaborate than all the others.

But back to the issue at hand—the number of gods. The ancient Greeks,
the people who originated this thing we call Western civilization, were such
ardent polytheists that they actually caused overpopulation in the supernatural world—to say nothing of oversubscribed temple real estate—and had to
kill some off. Even as late as the first century AD, about the time one would
think that all gods had either revealed themselves or been flushed out (as in
the Pantheon) by clamoring mortals filled with unspeakable fear and certain
knowledge of their own abject worthlessness, the Athenians, just to make
sure, erected a faceless monument on deity row in honor of the "unknown"
god. This, by the way, was quite significant for an ancillary reason: It is the only
admission on record that the Greeks did not know everything. Long before that,
at least by four centuries, the Hebrews, who by all reports insisted that there was
but one god and routinely went to war to prove it, most often, and, quite dis-
creetly, used a plural form of address (*elohim*) in conversations with and about
him. This prudent hedging of bets at least reduced the number to three. The
number did not become one until human beings became god.

Whoever the first man–god, it became obvious very quickly that he was on
to something, and others, similarly possessed, began asserting their godly sta-

tus. The trick, of course, was establishing and maintaining the authoritative connection with the most popular supernatural being of the time. Early kings used conjurors, witches, wise men, and prophets to make the connection; the caesars immediately deified themselves; the European rulers asserted divine right. Legend has it that most of these sovereigns were the actual descendants of Jesus Christ through Mary Magdalene who escaped with her three sons to Spain after the crucifixion. It would be interesting to guess the origin of this legend.

George Washington chose the title "high mightiness." American presidents since then adjure, "So help me God." Rulers of all ages and all climes were and are characterized by identification as or with deity. They all took on the image and likeness of gods—worthy of obedience and worship—rulers and lords. To emphasize the point, they affected godly titles such as "majesty," "highness," "excellency," "vicar of god," "chief executive officer," "chief" of whatever, "supreme commander," "president." Gods they were all, and eventually the only gods that mattered.

NOTE

1. Kevin Maney, *USA Today*, December 7, 1993.

CHAPTER 14

The Making of Kings

Render unto Caesar the things that are Caesar's.

Matthew 22: 21

Kings could not exist in a godless society. If it were possible, the only other way they could arise would be through the fundamental natural group—the family. Anthropologists can deal with that question. The fact is that in Western civilization the question is moot since the foundation and pattern of the family were based strictly on some concept of deity. It does, however, admit the inextricable connection, no doubt causative, between the development of families and the development of organizations with kings. The amazing thing is that for almost two millennia no one has questioned this connection in terms of its appropriateness or desirability.

It was evidently not just by dint of biology or effective domestic negotiation that the family very early took on its universal single form as a patriarchy. It was because of belief in, and doubtlessly fear of, a divine power. It appears that all religions, even the very earliest, simplest expressions, had this one thing in common: The man was considered the superior. Specific to the Western tradition, the Hebrew scriptures declared that the woman was twice subordinate with cause: She was created from the man to be his "helpmate," and she sinned first and convinced the man to follow suit. That is why husbands were made "rulers" over their wives; the woman was to be protected— and watched. Later, Christianity affirmed this rank by asserting that the husband was head of the wife as Christ is head of the Church. The Greco-

Roman traditions, and certainly those of early European tribes and nations, likewise subordinated women, albeit with many variations on the theme. The basis of the early Roman Commonwealth was *patria potestas*, the father's power. But the Roman mother was originally a position of honor: She took her full part of life, albeit still subject to her husband at home and to men in general. It was not until the influence of the Greeks crept in that women were thoroughly debased. The Greek version of the subordination of women had, for a long time, made two applications of the idea: Wives were secluded— completely; courtesans were advanced in social, political, cultural, and religious activities. The classiest courtesans, the most powerful, were the *hetairai*, but even they were ultimately subject to their patrons. It is impossible to know the exact status of women in remote rural communities, but there is no doubt that as urbanization occurred, women (and children as well) were never more than chattel, usually no more than slaves, subject to all kinds of denigration and abuse. Even in those rare instances where matriarchy seemed the order, in actuality, the head of the family was the oldest brother of the matriarch's mother. This avuncular arrangement survives even today among some Native North Americans.

But family structure was more than just a matter simply of order. It was a matter of rank, not just by family role but by gender, prowess, birth order, and seniority. For example, concepts such as paterfamilias and primogeniture existed before written history. When the family expanded from its natural group to a social organization, the same rank ordering persisted in ever-increasing elaboration and permanence. As families became joint families or extended families, rank became rigid, ardent, and social. Male seniority became ultimate status, and elders were granted, or assumed, power as either rulers or judges and were accorded the commensurate authority and honor.

Joint families combined to form clans, probably the simplest social unit, and the god-order of the natural family became the accepted arrangement of the clan. It is not without reason that this arrangement was described as a hierarchy. At this point, paradoxically enough, the confusion about right and might began. Heretofore, right was the source of might; but from this time onward, might, as often as not, would be interpreted as evidence of right.

By the time tribes were formed from the unification of clans, the basic organization design of society was cast—a rank ordering of virtually everyone and everything pertaining to him or her. There were three implications of this design: position, stratification, and symbolism.

Regarding the creation of positions, the family order, although based on rank, was intimate and relational. The rank order of the tribe was the beginning of a structure that was impersonal and positional. That is not to suggest that the tribal honchos set out to depersonalize and stratify their organizations, but such was the ultimate result. Actually, a rigid organization was necessary under the circumstances, merely for the purposes of control, communication, and defense. As customs became codes and traditions laws, as religious order for the transmission of information became systems, and as military activity became a science, the design of every organization became, compatibly, the hierarchy. Soon organization became an end itself, established without any consideration of its relationship to any specific purpose beyond itself.

As far as we know, it was the Lydians—a prosperous, industrious, and perhaps overorganized little kingdom, in what is now Turkey—who actually created the organizational chart (c. 546 BC) that today is prevalent throughout Western civilization. "Traditional" organization is 2,600 years old; and for exactly that long, position has been more important than person and order more important than efficacy. Even more significant is the fact that this organizational chart was based on one person controlling another person for no reason other than rank. Ultimately, rank became a prized commodity to be bargained for, seized, and protected; and patronage became both a prerequisite and a privilege of rank. This meant, obviously, that everybody—even the ruler—was controlled by someone else.

It is easy to see the correlation between the rank order of the organization and the stratification of the whole of society. A good case could be made that the dedication to organization actually shaped society itself. The master–slave relationship had existed at least since the days of the extended family, with slaves being considered a part of the household. And conquered peoples were commonly enslaved by victorious kings for public works. But the class system was a relatively late development of the socialized patriarchal organization.

Historians say that the class (caste) system began in India about 700 BC; however, the famous code of Hammurabi, dated circa 1950 BC, reflects a rigid class system already in place among the Babylonians. In the Western tradition, there was a slow and uneven process of social stratification beginning even earlier, with the classes—based mostly on birth and occupation—from time to time variously identified but always separate, and from time to time more or less fixed—often enforced as a matter of law. In fact, the earliest democracy (594 BC), in the city–state of Athens, began as an attempt by Solon to establish an egalitarian social order primarily because the ability to amass wealth by the lower-class pursuits of trade, commerce, and craftsmanship had already begun to equalize society, at least in economic status. But the class system was already so engrained in society that the aspiration of egalitarianism soon acceded to representative democracy—with a congress, a president, and a supreme court with nine members. It was indeed an ominous portend: Never would any democracy be more than a matter of limited, diluted, and sometime sham participation in choice within and among hierarchical systems.

Some historians possibly oversimplify the matter of class by suggesting only three: nobility, clergy, and peasants. Eventually, these classes became rather permanently fixed, as in "three estates" later officially recognized within the French government. Try as we might, it is difficult to find in Western history any specific social ordering that did not, or does not, conform to at least those three distinctions. The only notable exception would be the merchant class, which ultimately, as cities formed, became the bourgeoisie, often ridiculed by the very aristocrats who joined them in profit-making ventures. Money, it seems, is the only thing connecting the classes at all. However, it has never had the ability to reconcile them, nor to eradicate class distinctions. The only thing that could at least obscure the distinction was education. It has always been the greatest leveling influence on society. That explains why the clergy persisted as a special rank long after their close association with deity was forsaken.

The rank-ordered arrangement of organization, and of society itself, required the extensive use of symbols, obviously to communicate, overtly or covertly, the position of the person or group. The symbols of organization were of four types: visual, linguistic, spatial, and tangible. It is instructive to note that the visual symbols such as insignia, seals, and logos made much of natural things—specifically fauna and flora, celestial bodies, and exotic colors. Eagles have always been emblematic of rank—stars even more so. Oak clusters and olive trees are also big. The colors scarlet, purple, and gold rule the day. That all these symbols are "primaries," or "best of class," is an indication of just how ingrained the notion of rank order was even in the earliest societies. The amazing thing is that the significance of these symbols is as old as organization. The distinction of rank within specific organizations, and especially within society at large, soon became symbolized by dress itself. In fact, in some societies, rank-ordered clothing was dictated by law.

As for the symbolism of language, it seems that from time immemorial speech has indicated class. It is the most permanent impression of status, because it literally speaks of all the privilege or burden of class—birth, learning, occupation, concept of reality. Spoken language has always been the most unforgiving—even the cruelest symbol. The Greeks had the audacity to brand everyone else in the world "barbarians"—because foreign accented tongues sounded like so much "bar-bar" to their delicate, qualitatively attuned ears. There have always been three universal laws regarding language as a symbol of rank—the law of altitude (the more artificial the language, the higher the rank), the law of geography (the closer language is to the equator, the lower the class of those who speak it), and the law of ethereality (the more esoteric the language, the more sophisticated those who use it).

It has already been pointed out that the gods have always seemed enamored of space, especially when cast in comparative terms. So it is not surprising to find space, by both size and location, especially symbolic of rank. By size, the space required by someone of rank is historically at least 1.5 times that of the next-lower subordinate. This ratio was established in the grain distribution centers of Egypt in the sixth century BC and has not varied an iota since. The ratio holds fast until the very so-called top levels of the organization are reached, where space is subject to no bounds whatsoever. Of course, since the top or best of anything is superior by definition, physical position

within a given edifice occupied by a human organization of necessity correlates with rank within the group. Likewise, the relationship among personal
spaces has always required special attention; so special, in fact, that elaborate
protocols for every imaginable social circumstance are developed to prevent
gauche intrusion into the wrong space—that is, to keep everyone else in his or
her place. Any violation of these rules of location and distance is disgraceful.

Finally, there is the symbolism of touch. One of the most remarkable things
about Western organization is that such a subtle thing as touch could become perhaps the surest indication of rank. Except in the cases of service
(cleaning or coiffing), touching another is always a sign of at least equality.
Subordinates simply do not touch superiors. Touching is always a privilege of
the higher rank, political correctness notwithstanding. Even in the touch
associated with customary greetings, the person of superior rank or class ini-
tiates the contact.

So complete was the organization of the tribe that all that was needed to
form an ethnarchy was for many tribes of the same basic religious perspective
to show up at the same place at the same time. Many things might bring
them together—natural disasters, wars, migration, or geopolitical alliances
variously concocted; but the one thing that held them together—the ultimate nationalizing factor—was a common language; for herein resided all
the nuances of faith, order, knowledge, and relationship. Race and geography, contrary to popular notions, were secondary and tertiary considerations.

What is truly remarkable about the early development of organization is
that long before the beginning of the first millennium, as Western civilization reckons time, "sacred rule" was the essence of patriarchal and monar-
chical orders in societies all around the world. Throughout history, it became
the inherent design of all other "rules" of every prefix. There is something
implicit in this fact that speaks to the universality of the hierarchical organization today. It is here, and only here, that East meets West. And it is here that
all forms of modern organization find their common ancestor.

CHAPTER 15

The Making of the
God–King Organization

> Christ intends business executives. He teaches these are ten talent men.
> His plan is that in the human economy the few are to lead, the many to
> follow. There are to be rulers and ruled.
>
> John J. Eagan and Robert E. Speer[1]

It is virtually impossible to get an accurate fix on the beginning of the first millennium. While that may seem an insignificant problem—pedantic at best—it may actually prove to be a quite important matter, not only to those who crave precision in the reckoning of time but also to those who seek to understand the systems human beings are wont to create for themselves. The current calendar places the birth of Christ in 4 BC; it seems even Bishop Ussher, like Johannes Kepler, fails the accuracy test with regard to chronology. But the villian really was Dionysius Exiguus who invented the BC–AD distinction in the fifth century. One of the basic problems here is that the Romans had no concept of zero, so no one still can say for sure whether a decimal year, say 1990, is the end of a decade or the beginning of another. It is an even more frustrating enigma at the turn of millennia. Those purists who must have clear breaks will not find any satisfaction here.

For the purpose of this study, the first millennium began in 27 BC. In that year, the Roman senate, moving deliberately to fill the position vacated by Julius Caesar's untidy departure seventeen years earlier, declared that Octavian thenceforth would be "Augustus Caesar." Significantly, "Augustus" was an appellation traditionally reserved for gods; and in fact, Augustus was later deified. Probably because of some basic personality disorder or genetic defect, he refused to be called "lord" by his subjects and was quick to dispatch anyone who thus dared to grovel — thereby proving his lordship. He was also capable of this splendid irony with regard to other human systems: When he wanted to put off indefinitely some unpleasant task or person, he would schedule the encounter according to the Greek "kalends," which, of course, did not exist.

Since there has always been so much confusion over the calendar and no one seems to know for sure how to rectify it, it is helpful to mark the early stages of intellectual development by major events such as the reigns of kings. Augustus is important, in part, because by the time of his reign the Greek domination of Western civilization had ended. It is truly remarkable that from the death of Alexander the Great in 353 BC until the ascent of Augustus, the Greeks had ruled the world by force of mere intellect. The Romans would rule by force of arms. But the important thing here is that the religious influences that were so thoroughly to shape human organization in Western civilization had taken on two overwhelming, often contradictory, historical and philosophical identities. During Augustus' reign (ending AD 14), there was born the progenitor of yet another faith that would ultimately merge the ideas and energies of the two into one irresistible, supernatural concept of organization.

First, it was the ancient Jewish god who would endure as the basic character of organization — a god absolute and resolute, unchanging, jealous, roaring out of Zion, demanding obedience and exacting justice as the transcendent creator and ruler of the universe. Second, there was the philosophy of the Greeks — more accurately of Plato, and to a lesser degree Aristotle — with its bifurcated insistence on an ideal world beyond this shadowland (an ideal every person could experience firsthand through pantheistic associations in every aspect of life) coupled with an unrelenting fascination with the way things really work — the reality no one could deny. The Jewish religion would provide the basic concept of godly order; the Greek philosophy (not a religion in the strictest sense, but only when it lacked ritual and ceremony) would provide the idea of a rational system and, consequently, the validating proof of reality. The Platonic system consisted of the two salient nostrums that would hold even until this day as the fundamental tenets of Western organization: the great chain of being and the concept of perfection. The Aristotelian method of proof would become the plumbline of Western civilization: that is, reason — transformed into rationalism.

It is critically important here to note that both religious–philosophical forces — Judaism and Hellenism — centered on the personal responsibility and well-being of the individual, despite order, rank, or class. The Ten Commandments are cast as instructions to a person: ("Thou shalt not kill"), and Plato sought justice for the individual through personal and social ethics. Aristotle taught the person how to use the senses to think one's way to being. The Jewish religion promised individual salvation through purification by atonement;[2] Hellenism preached personal freedom through the full exercise of one's own powers, and infinite learning through the exercise of mind and body. What is especially sig-

nificant, however, is that both considered the interests of the individual ultimately subordinate to those of the larger social organization. This subordination was not a response to authoritarian control but provided a context for the
meaning and purpose of life. It is a paradox that individual fulfillment, even
one's identity, depends upon living and moving within a society.

These two philosophical currents would not flow directly nor intact into
the mainstream of organization development, even though each historically
would preserve its discrete attributes. Sometimes they took such disparate
courses that they not only moved to poles opposite each other but also strained
identification with their own original forms—for example, the Jewish Kabbala,
and the mystery religions' blending of Neoplatonism with Zoroastrianism.
But ultimately they would converge into a single channel—Christianity. That
religion would stand alone as the single greatest influence on the development of organization in the West for at least 1,600 years. It is little wonder that
its ubiquity persists even until now.

It is the philosophical confluence of Jewish and Hellenistic thought, rather
than history, that is important here: justice served by atonement; order restored by redemption from sin; perfection (i.e., *teleios*) achieved through grace;
faith proved by reason; strictness of conscience versus spontaneity of thought
and action. It is especially noteworthy that the apostles John and Paul appealed to the philosophy of Plato and the Greeks to argue their claim that
Christianity was the fulfillment of the law of Moses and the logical extension
of Hellenistic thought—revealed in the verifiable person of Jesus. For example, John, writing at the end of the first century in opposition to the
Gnostics, seized upon their very Neoplatonic notion of emanations and eons
to describe how a transcendent God became immanent: "In the beginning
was the Word, and the Word was with God, and the Word was God. . . . And
the Word became flesh and dwelt among us" (John 1: 1, 14). Earlier, Paul, in
his letter ostensibly to the Christians living in a hilltop enclave near Ephesus,
had offered an extensive argument for seven great orders by rank: cosmological, historical, spiritual, ecclesiastical, governmental, familial, and personal.
Even more to the point of Plato's chain of being, he alleges that man is "just
a little lower than the angels" (Romans 8: 38, 39) and even suggests a specific
rank order among the angels. Dionysius, a fourth century Franciscan, would
work all this out in startling detail. All this from a Roman citizen who had a
Ph.D. in Mosaic law, quoted Greek poets in their own dialects, and spread
the gospel by advancing the workings of nature as proof of his faith's reason-
ableness. Sometimes, to prove his point, he even alleged that human nature
was a source of revelation consistent with his own doctrine: "When the Gen-
tiles, which have not the law, do by nature the things contained in the law,
these . . . are a law unto themselves" (Romans 2: 14).

In fact, it has been suggested by some, probably more fanciful than scientific, that Paul actually wrote the first description of what in modern times
would be called the corporation:

For the body is not one member, but many. If the foot shall say, Because I am not the hand, I am not of the body; is it therefore not of the body? And if the ear shall say, Because I am not the eye, I am not of the body; is it therefore not of the body? If the whole body were an eye, where were the hearing? If the whole were hearing, where were the smelling? And if they were all one member, where were the body? But now are they many members, yet but one body. And the eye cannot say unto the hand, I have no need of thee: nor again the head to the feet, I have no need of you. (I Corinthians 12: 14–17; 19–21)

Paul then, as if by way of contradiction, went on to ordain a rigid rank order in the organization of the body. "Now you are the body of Christ, and members in particular. And God hath set some in the church, first apostles, secondarily prophets, thirdly teachers, after that miracles, then gifts of healings, helps, governments, diversities of tongues" (I Corinthians 12: 27, 28).

Suffice it to say that by the time the church finally chose Rome as its western headquarters in AD 150, the basic character of Western organization was permanently established in all aspects of society. It is almost ironic that both the Church and the Roman government, bitter enemies who each considered the other atheistic, were expressions of the same organization and order in conflict with itself, a simple case of two realities. But in the end the Church won out, not necessarily because its theology was superior but because its economics was sounder. How strange it is that enemies always take on the likenesses of each other. And so it was an easy matter for the Roman Church to assume the seat vacated by the Roman government. It is not merely an academic curiosity that by the time of its declining—even as early as AD 200— the Roman civilization, in every aspect, was characterized by theistic, authoritarian, rank-ordered, hierarchical organization. That civilization eventually would provide the model for the development of everything Western— language, literature, law, government, military, chronology, religion, society, science, and an attitude and tradition of superiority that led to cruelty and abuse of even its own.

What is truly meaningful is that all expressions of this type of organization, whether ecclesiastical, civil or military, were aimed at conquering territory, restraining behavior, and collecting wealth. War was the result of three simple imperatives: rule or be ruled; more is never enough; domination is the only security. They had not yet learned to fight over ideas. The restraining was accomplished by fear and sometimes hope—and hope was always the lesser of two evils. Survival was sufficient motivation for surrender. As for wealth, this type organization was never intended to produce goods or to benefit the individual within the system. It was rather a device aimed at acquiring treasure, land, and resources for the aggrandizement and satisfaction of the rulers. All roads still lead to Rome.

As for the historical development of Western organization during the first millennium, one should not surmise that the actual blending of Judaism and

Hellenism in Christianity occurred as smoothly or as quickly as the easy intellectual compatibility might suggest. Quite the contrary, as all the currents
of Western civilization sloshed around three continents, these mighty forces
relentlessly chased each other hither and yon in a sometime frightful display
of evil that often belied their own professions of good. When things finally
settled into a comparatively gentle ebb and flow, it was Christianity, specifically the Church of Rome, that had survived. Some would argue it survived
by default; others because of its inherent power.

The crossing of the Rhine by the Franks in AD 200 very early tilted the odds
in favor of Christianity. It marked the beginning of the end of the Roman
Empire. But it is very clear that Christianity's adaptability, its capacity for
absorption, and its inclusive world view set it apart from the rigid exclusivity
of Judaism and the esotericism of Hellenism and gave it vitality that the others lacked. So it is not surprising that in AD 313, as the Roman Empire deteriorated, Constantine established Christianity as the successor authority. As an
example of Christianity's rapid spread, one of the Frankish kings, Clovis, was
a practicing Christian, free of any heresy as a matter of fact, when he invaded
Roman territory in AD 486. Actually, that should come as no surprise either,
since most religious historians believe that Christianity in its very pristine
form had been taken by the apostles and other evangelists throughout the
civilized world by the middle of the first century. By the time of Clovis, its
influence was manifestly evident in all aspects of Frankish society.

So powerful was the force of Christianity that throughout the so-called
Dark Ages (AD 400–800) as the once serene Roman Empire disintegrated
into civil and political chaos and as virtually every existing sign and symbol of
Western civilization was destroyed, the church persisted as the one single
lifeline of Western civilization. Even when seriously challenged by the Germanic tribes during the period from 500–700, it had the vitality to constantly
reassert itself as the dominant force on the continent. It is quite likely that
without this presence, the robust civilizations of Byzantium and of North
Africa, which were in their prime stages of development, would have covered the remnants of Western civilization and it would have become just
another collection of archeological curiosities. When Pope Leo III declared
Charlemagne "Emperor of the Roman Empire" in 800, Western civilization
took on a new life—new in kind as well as in time. It meant, first, that a new
world order was permanently established; second, that the Roman Catholic
Church had supplanted the Roman empire; and, third, that the Church was
assured a perpetual source of income. All revenues lead to Rome.

No one is exactly sure about the origin of feudalism. There is evidence that
it was practiced in China as early as the second century BC, and most historians agree that the Romans resorted to some form of it in the first century AD to
quell the innate aggressiveness of the Germanic tribes as the conquest of
their homelands moved apace. If the latter is true, then the Church would
have found it a rather serendipitous, even blessed, means of forwarding its

own purpose. It is likely that this is the reason feudalism became the dominant organization of the Frankish kingdoms by the end of the fourth century.

Whatever its origin, it is a fact, little appreciated in modern times, that feudalism was the order of Western civilization for most of the first millennium — dominating both the so-called Dark Ages and the Middle Ages (800–1300). Historically and substantively, it was the fullest expression of the hierarchical rank-ordered concept of the world and human society as presumed and prescribed by the Christian religion. It not only constituted a complete human ecosystem but also embraced every aspect of human life, collective and individual. So all encompassing was it that some scholars see it as an overlay of several systems rather than a single system with a multiplicity of expressions.

For example, one could argue that it was a purely religious system. In fact, the idea could be reasonably advanced that it was a system of religion — thoroughly sacred in all its parts, it derived its very existence from the authority of the Church and in turn paid tribute for the privilege. The basic idea has its roots deep within the history of the Christian religion: It is actually reminiscent of the short-lived reciprocal arrangement worked out in the Garden of Eden. Even when Henry VIII successfully challenged the Roman Church's authority, he merely robbed Peter to pay Paul. The Church of England was a mirror image of what had been rejected — only with some loss of innocence. This rather symbiotic relationship would prevail through the centuries in self-professed democratic nations, even after the Reformation overwrought the separation of Church and state. All secular democracies still pay tribute to religion in the form of economic advantage. Whether as deference in honor, as payment for refuge, or as a bribe for noninterference, it is a vestige of feudalism, and the net effect is the same as in the Middle Ages.

Feudalism could be seen also as a social system, since it was based on strict class and rank within the community and did, indeed, cast permanently the social order of Europe and America far beyond the reach of revolutions or the din of dubious outrage over human inequality. But most historians refer to the feudalism as a political system because it apparently, first and foremost, provided an inescapable order of civil rule—law and order. Here again, its influence seems never to wane. All English law and most legal systems of other Western countries are predicated on the elaborate legal code developed during the Middle Ages. Even modern officers of the law maintain their medieval titles.

More than anything else, however, feudalism was an economic system. The first clue is in the root *feud* which translates "fee." One could make a good case, especially in retrospect of a thousand years, that it was in fact a "fee-for-service" economic system. But it was much more. Feudalism is the first instance of organization for the purpose of wealth production—in this case, wealth derived from the land. It was not wealth in a strict commercial sense, perhaps—although trade did occur among fiefs—but wealth to be accrued or consumed by those affiliated with the fief.

Logically, it was the essence of simplicity, combining for the first time two economic schemes meant for each other: franchising, with the prerogative of livelihood flowing downward; and the pyramid, with the benefit of net-gain revenue flowing upward. Quite literally, it was a marriage made in heaven. Specifically, within the lord's domain, sanctioned by the Church, vassals were granted the authority to rule fiefs; within the walls of each fief, there labored serfs, peasants, and craftsmen—all at the good grace of the vassal. Everyone in the fief paid fealty to the vassal and was obliged either to take up arms in the vassal's defense or agree to socage (*pro patria*); the vassal paid fealty to the lord and was pledged to raising an army from time to time to serve the lord's purposes. Everyone paid fealty to the Church. Eventually the fiefs joined to create one large crusading army for the Church as it went about to subjugate or kill unregenerate heathens—by definition, anyone who had the gall not to ante up for his or her unmerited salvation. At least an ancillary purpose of the crusades was to expand the quite lucrative feudalistic system that served everyone so well (*pro Deus; pro patria et Deus*).

But there is another consideration here that makes feudalism much more than just a matter of historical curiosity and, for that matter, more than history. No one can deny that it was the organization of the first millennium, but not many recognized that—in spirit, form, and practice—it was the essence of Western organization, even as late as the twentieth century.

Consider simple chronology: Probably because of the power of the Magna Carta, signed in 1215 by a reluctant King John, the feudal system was not officially abolished in England until 1660 (fifty-three years after the arrival of economic refugees at Plymouth Rock and twenty-eight years before the "Bloodless Revolution" in the English Parliament) or in Scotland until the middle of the eighteenth century (about the time of the Federalist Papers) or in France until the Revolution of 1789 (thirteen years after the Declaration of Independence by the United States). If feudalism did not substantially influence these landmark developments in Western civilization, it was not for lack of opportunity. Furthermore, in no case was the abolition of feudalism seriously enforced; it was always a more-or-less civil rights apology, lip-synched to cute slogans like "liberty, equality, fraternity," and "all men are created equal"—all to appease the masses who seem always to believe what authority declares. In fact, feudalism was alive and well in Germany until 1944 almost in its pristine form.

The expansive duration of the feudal system is virtually incalculable. Not only has it persisted for, lo, these many centuries, but it is also the immediate source of modern Western organization—including governments. That it is both the origin and the type of any and all expressions of Western organization is abundantly clear—from monarchy to the welfare state, from colony to sovereign nation, from plantation to factory, from assembly line to board room, from share-cropping to employee ownership, from obligatory military service to perpetual property taxes, from distinctions as mundane as management and labor. All these, old and new, are just so many variations of a single theme—the god–king organization.

NOTES

1. John J. Eagan and Robert E. Speer, *John J. Eagan—A Memoir* (Birmingham: American Cast Iron Pipe, 1921), 124–125.

2. One of the best treatments of this subject can be found in Manfred Davidmann, *Struggle for Freedom: The Social Cause-and-Effect Relationship* (© M.D., 1995, mdavidmann@solbaram.org). He argues that the Torah actually created religious and societal order to bring about individual freedom, personal well-being, and satisfying lives.

PART IV

THE WORLD OF
THE CORPORATION—
ITS SCIENCE

CHAPTER 16

The Myths of Western Civilization

Here is a place that is no place and here is no place that is a place.
Calvin C. Hernton[1]

Human experiences are defined only in retrospect, that is, when the prospect of loss intensifies value. So it was with Western civilization. As long as there were no boundaries, only frontiers, and as long as there were no limits, only possibilities, and as long as there was no question about right and wrong, only sheer assertion as sufficient morality, the energy of the thing itself created an overwhelming reality of the present that needed no defining and a dynamic vitality that resisted any point-in-time definition. But between 1965 and 1975, four occurrences in North America marked the beginning of the search for the past: the civil rights movement, the estrangement of academia, the loss of credibility by government, and the rise of Japan to economic prominence. Western civilization would never be able to reconstitute itself, but that did not keep it from trying.

It was not just the usual riff-raffish fringe groups that seem always to spring up at the first sign of social and political change—reactionaries, as they are called. By the end of the twentieth century, the fate of the entire concept of Western civilization had become the most serious concern of Western civilization. This quest turned inward, producing such remorseful treatises as *The Closing of the American Mind, The Western Canon*, and *The Book of Virtues* and evoking all kinds of moralistic lamentation about the rampant variations of Western civilization, from Russia to Argentina, and the impossibility of recapturing a single definition, as if it ever existed. In winter the dawn comes late.

However limited its tenure and however confused its definition, Western civilization proffered five critical assertions. Although they are only assumptions, taken separately or together, they are unique to the Western experience; and even though all are based on both ungodly and unnatural presuppositions, they constitute the great myth once appropriated as the world's greatest civilization:

1. Intuition and reason are severable; and reason is always superior.
2. Human beings and their artifacts are perfectible and deserve to be perfected.
3. All people have the right to democracy, defined as majority rule.
4. Patronage is apt penance for wealth.
5. All people can be made to live together in peace.

What is truly ironic, defying all faith and reason, is that a myth sustained by both religion and science is the greatest paradox of all. When myth becomes reality, everything else is nonsense.

The first assumption is encompassed in the philosophy of rationalism, the second in the most recent version of humanism, the third in the idealized democracy of the modern age, the fourth in capitalism, so-called, and the fifth in the science of behaviorism.

These assertions, in effect, constituted the forces shaping the society of Western civilization. While it is not necessary, according to reason, to make precise logical correlations between these characteristic assertions and the general aspects of society, it is possible to logically construct a sensible arrangement. There may be other variations, but Figure 16.1 demonstrates the simplest way to categorize and relate the factors.

Furthermore, anyone who knows twentieth-century theory and practice regarding organization and management will immediately recognize how thoroughly pervasive these forces were in the practical operations of any corporation-model organization. Specifically, the mantras of management were "data-driven," "research-based," "rational decision making." The corporation-model organization worshipped at the altar of "continuous improvement," "best practices," and "benchmarks"—all holding forth the promise of perfectibility in a material world. The modern corporation attempted democratic practices by adopting "participatory management," "shared decision making," and "teaming." The primary resource in the production of wealth was "capital"; human beings were considered to be competitive economic animals. Finally, the corporation-model organization was structured by "rank" and "class," and all human motivation was based on conditioned response to external stimuli—reward and punishment.

Taken together, these adamant assertions created not only the myths of the civilization but also, inevitably, the myths of the corporation-model organization. In this immediate context, the person suffered the most deleterious consequences of a fictive world.

Figure 16.1

ASPECTS OF SOCIETY	ASSERTIONS OF WESTERN CIVILIZATION
REALITY *KNOWLEDGE*	**RATIONALISM**
FAITH *RELATIONSHIP*	**HUMANISM**
GOVERNANCE *CONTROL*	**DEMOCRACY**
ECONOMY *WEALTH*	**CAPITALISM**
SYSTEM *ORDER*	**BEHAVIORISM**

NOTE

1. Calvin C. Hernton, "Madhouse," from *I Am the Darker Brother: An Anthology of Modern Poems by African Americans*, ed. Arnold Adoff (New York: Aladdin Paperbacks, 1997), 13.

CHAPTER 17

The Assertion of Reason

But it does move.

Galileo[1]

Paradox is an absolute feature of science. That phenomenon immediately separates it from religion. Although both are alternately from time to time the yin and yang of the argument over the relationship between fact and faith, inquiry and assertion, presumption and assumption, one proceeds from the infinite to the finite, the other from the finite to the infinite. And while neither may settle anything (as William James said, "We have to live today by what truth we can get today, and be ready tomorrow to call it falsehood"),[2] science by its very definition, in modern times at least, is forced to accept tentativeness as a way of life, a hazard of the trade so to speak. The term "modern" here refers to the past four hundred years of Western civilization in the full knowledge that Cicero also declared his times modern. But present times are perhaps uniquely modern in the sense that the intrinsic uncertainty of science does not prevent the occasional by-god pronouncement of absolute truth—a wonderful latter-day convergence of religion and science. This all came about because of something that happened in the seventeenth century.

The definition of science is always a matter of historical context. Who is to say exactly when the human race began contemplating what is now called science? For that matter, who is to say what science is? The Latin word simply means "to know," clearly locating the activity somewhere within the human mind. It is important here to remember that Aristotle had earlier made a distinction between two kinds of knowledge (*gnosis*): *episteme*, derived from *theoria*, and *phronesis*, implicit in doing, acting, performing. *Episteme* was understanding acquired by contemplative observation of the world; *phronesis* was the intuitive cognition of a higher meaning implicit in one's own action. (Plutarch defined *phronesis* as practical knowledge, Cicero as the knowledge of the things to be sought and the things that need to be avoided, Plato as the discernment of what should be done and what should not be done. In all instances, it was the most practical kind of knowledge.) Beyond knowledge as such, there was *sophia*, translated almost always as wisdom — that is, the understanding of the universal implications of what one knows through both *episteme* and *phronesis*. Actually, the only reason Aristotle was such a great philosopher and able to make such fine distinctions is that he lived in a simple world. Were he alive today, he would no doubt be considered eccentric or insane. Even though in the twentieth century Einstein would attempt to downplay the mystery of science by allowing it to be only "the refinement of ordinary thinking," it's still the highest expression of the human mind — the intellect, the soul.

Reduced to its earliest, simplest expression, science (or perhaps more accurately pre-science) comes very close to the superstition it later derided — conjuring, astrology, alchemy, and the like. The similarity is mostly in the search — for the power to comprehend, for the mysteries of the natural universe, and for the alkahest for all human problems and the panacea for all human ills. In that sense, the definition of science is constant. In fact, early science forever established the ultimate validation criterion for all science to come — a simple question: Is it life giving? The simplest, earliest forms of Western science were practical applications of universal principles that still baffle contemporary minds: For example, the Egyptian pyramids, the hanging gardens of Babylon, the Temple of Diana at Ephesus, the statue of Zeus at Olympia, King Mausoleos' mausoleum at Haliearnascus, the Colossus at Rhodes, and the Lighthouse at Alexandria. To these seven wonders add the shadowy Stonehenge astronomical clock, the copper sewers of fourth-century Crete, the unerring navigation of ancient mariners, and the healing power of aboriginal remedies.

Early science was not all superstition or arts and crafts. There was much understanding of what today would be called modern science. Just how much more the early scientists knew about the universe and their place in it we can never be sure. That it was not enough to sustain them and their world seems rather obvious, but perhaps they discovered eons ago what contemporary scientist sometimes fail to acknowledge: That is, there is a limit to what science can do to better the human condition.

Whatever intellectual treasures they had mined from the universe, except for some of those variously cast in stone, were strewn carelessly about or covered over by the savaging of the Dark Ages and the reclamation of nature. The island of Delos is a profoundly sad place. As the Western world disintegrated into chaos, four human conditions seemed to mock the very promise of science: ignorance, war, plague, and famine swept away any notion of a friendly world. It is not surprising that during the Middle Ages the Church, ever the archenemy of science, would seize upon these desperate circumstances — mostly of its own making — to extol the *soteria* (literally, "health and welfare") of the afterlife. Medieval theology was simply a formula for adapting to or escaping from the harsh realities of the world in order to prepare one's soul for a glorious future life. That was obviously an easy sell, because nothing could have been worse than the there and then. It is no wonder that anything offering the slightest hope in that world would be considered enlightening. ("Deliver me from Ghosties, and Goules, long-leggity Beastes, and things that go bump in the night.")[3]

By the end of the Middle Ages, science had been reduced to arithmetic, music, geometry, and astronomy — the quadrivium of the medieval university's masters degree curriculum. The science that had survived was basically Aristotelian which meant that although deriving from the supernatural it was a passionless declaration of reality solely as it can be deduced through the physical senses — an *episteme* that is absolute and immutable. Whatever meaning one was to find in life was available only in this context. It is curious indeed that the Aristotelian view of the world and the Church's gospel of a world corrupted and condemned by sin perfectly coincided. The net effect of each, and so much more so when allied, was acceptance of the way things are. The locus of control was always outside the human. It is almost as if superstition, religion, and science had conspired to reduce human beings to victims of some inescapable, unapproachable power.

Aristotle was very clear about the essentiality of sense of doom to tragedy. "Since, therefore, it is the business of the tragic poet to give that pleasure which arises from pity and terror, through imitation, it is evident that he ought to produce that effect by the circumstances of the action itself."[4]

Since that pronouncement and further definition of tragedy has involved a protagonist who commands our earnest good will and is impelled in a given world by a purpose or undertaking of certain seriousness or magnitude; by that very purpose or undertaking, subject to that same world, necessarily meets with grave spiritual or physical suffering. Three traditions of tragedy have persisted in Western literature, and all portray the human being as victim: the tragic flaw, as victim of virtue to excess; the fall from high estate, as victim of the wheel of fortune; and the ideal hero who, although without hope, is dauntless before the wyrd or fate. The first is of Greek origin, the second Franco-Italian, and the third Anglo-Saxon. It is significant indeed that all three concepts were fully developed by the year 1000.

During all the doom and gloom, other forces were stirring that would eventually converge into a new science, a new reality, and a new attitude toward religion — utter contempt. There were four such forces — each as commercial as it was intellectual. Each in its own special way would have had a lasting effect on

Western organization, but together, over a period of five hundred years they would combine to change forever the very concept of organization.

The organization of the first millennium, the hierarchy, was so firmly entrenched that it would endure throughout the second millennium. However, there would be one great difference. The first order was one strictly of control by divine and human authority—command. That meant that it was subject to the will or whim of super forces, be they gods or men; but it was lacking the control that is possible only within a system—a design that held all things together by invoking the "laws" of nature. Equally important to the new organization was the way the design was apprehended—not by revelation or decree but by rational processes of the human mind. But, so deep were the intellectual roots in the past it would not be until the seventeenth century that empiricism would emerge as the "new science," springing, as it were, from new roots. And it would be the eighteenth century before it expanded into totally human, totally intellectual rationalism.

It is not amiss to refer to the four developments as "forces" because, indeed, they had the effect of moving human beings toward a radically new perspective of the world. The first, albeit not necessarily in chronological order, was the English language itself. For all the beauty of Greek and all the stateliness of Latin, neither had the capacity to fully express the scope, complexity, and precision of the new science. They simply ceased to expand, Greek ultimately reaching a maximum of only 10,000 words, and both were the languages of an atavistic universe. Greek was paganistic; Latin ex *cathedra*. Both were history.

English, quite oppositely, became a robust linguistic sponge, swelling with every infusion of idea and culture, eventually containing some 350,000 terms of various concepts. It was a very different tongue from the Anglo-Saxon language—a harsh Germanic language brought to Britain from north central Germany during the fifth century. The usual processes of language development had produced "*englisc*"—basically the Northumbrian and Mercian dialect. When the culture center moved to West Saxony, all the earlier Mercian literature was copied into the West Saxon dialect, thus producing, if not a kind of standard language, at least the mainstream idiom, now called Old English, by the year 1000. And then something happened—something to ensure that English, by its very nature open to the universe, would become, in fact, universal—something that neither Greek nor Latin could be. The event was the Norman invasion.

William the Conqueror, so-called because of his victory at Hastings in 1066, did much more than simply expand the French economy; he constructed a permanent cultural bridge between the European continent and the tiny island. Across this bridge would flow all the best that was thought, said, and done in European culture. Conversely, that nation and its language eventually would dominate the entire world, and during the latter half of the second millennium would itself serve as a bridge to a new world unfettered by the shackles of the old, a virtual blank slate for the free and full exercise of every implication of the new science. Latin died hard. In the first part of the sixteenth century, evidently because he had detected the shifting center of the linguistic world, Erasmus proposed that Latin be established as a kind of early Esperanto—a universal language unifying all intellectual discourse. But even he, the continent's single most influential person during that century, could not constrain the energy of new thinking and expression of the new language.

It should not be surprising that it was two Englishmen who introduced the new science into Western thought. What may be a mild surprise is that they wrote in Latin—Sir Francis Bacon because he thought English, even in the seventeenth century, would not survive, although it had been accepted as the nation's common language for over two hundred years; and Isaac Newton, evidently because he thought Latin was the scholarly thing to do—as indeed it was right up until the mid-twentieth century. In fact, one of the most significant "rational" works—that of Giambattista Vico—was not translated into English until the 1940s. However, it was all always explained in English.

The second force was the new math. And this was the unlikeliest connection of all. Roman numerals, while they look imposing on stone and are a delight to behold otherwise, simply did not lend themselves to quick calculations, fractions, or abstract ideas. If the secrets of the universe were to be understood, there had to be a more manageable system for expressing its mysteries, and, more exactly, its laws. Enter Fibonacci, known to his family (Benaccio) as Leonardo. When he returned to his home town of Pisa with his father, who had been on a lengthy assignment in the North African City of Bugia, he brought with him the benefit of his years of schooling by the Muslims.

As it turned out, the best thing he had learned was the Arabic system of numerals; and in 1202 he published *Liber Abaci*, introducing Arabic numbers to the Western world. Algebra (literally, *al-jabr*—"to connect pieces") and all derivative mathematical science had arrived on the Western front. No one could predict it at the time of course, but this system of numbers was the key that broke the code of the universe. It was the grand decipher. Without this system, Galileo would not have been able to reconceptualize the order of the cosmos; and Newton's *Philosophiae Naturalis Principia Mathematica*, the basis of the new science, would never have been possible.

He was called Fibonacci by everyone other than his family; the name means "blockhead." The reason is that while musing about the love life of rabbits, he created a crazy puzzle no one since has been able to explain, even though everyone keeps trying. It had to do with the ubiquitous secret of all living things—the "golden mean." But so far, no one knows what it means.

The third force behind the new science was, surprisingly, the rediscovery of Plato. In fact, this quite possibly was the most significant influence. At least one critic thinks so: "The safest general characterization of the European philosophical tradition is that it consists of a series of footnotes to Plato."[5] Given the sorry state of affairs resulting from the Aristotelian world view and the doctrine of the Church, this came as a great relief, at least for the people who knew about it. And beyond that, it created a limitless vista from the human perspective. In fact, that is what the proponents of this perspective were called—humanists; and the effect they wielded on Western civilization is now celebrated as the Renaissance.

Renaissance humanism, developed first in the fourteenth and fifteenth centuries, was marked by a passion for rediscovering and studying ancient literature. Implicit in that literature was the Platonic view of the human being as a glorious creature, capable of infinite individual development, set in a world that was not to be deplored but explored and enjoyed. In the "classical" works, the humanists found justification for the exultation of human nature and built thereon a completely new idealistic gospel of human progress. Breaking sharply with the early medieval attitudes that subordinated the human to the supernatural and divine, the humanist asserted the uncompromisable dignity of all that is human. In contrast to the earlier Christian doctrine, they stressed the virtue of enjoying the present life in its fullness, rather than using it as miserable preparation for a future life.

The break was cleaner and more adversarial on the continent, even though Erasmus held the two sides together for a short time by emphasizing their common concepts: unity of the universe, supernaturalism, pacifism, and Latin as the universal tongue. The English philosophers, much as the scholastics had done in the twelfth and thirteenth centuries, would attempt to blend the best of classical culture with Christianity. Some philosophers even formed a school of "supernatural rationalism." Both Isaac Newton and John Locke joined. Yet, all the while, philosophers such as Pierre Bayle, writing in the late seventeenth century, were already declaring that religion and science were irreconcilable. Nevertheless, the very attempt to blend them created a lasting division within the Western tradition, and, even more troublesome, a dichotomy—a contradiction in all the English and American constructs arising from the new science. This is a contradiction unresolved to this day—a dilemma that was the root cause of the decline and fall of Western institutions.

The influence of the humanists was profound and enduring. Even though the Renaissance was chiefly a literary and cultural rebirth, the implications of the humanistic philosophy were broad indeed, sufficient, in fact, to form the philosophical basis of the new science in all its interpretations and applications. Trying to pinpoint the dates of the Renaissance is a futile exercise. Suffice it to say that the rebirth occurred variously over a period of four hundred years from 1300 to 1700 with a few glimmers of light as far back as the twelfth century. For us, the important thing is not the when, not even the where, but the what.

The fourth force, quite simply, was the westward movement of commerce and the corresponding radical change not only in location of wealth but also in definition, philosophies, and attitudes regarding the nature and control of it. In 1492, the plates of the world's commercial surface shifted; and in 1498, when Vasco da Gama actually did reach India by sailing around Africa, the whole earth quaked. The resulting tidal wave meant that the Mediterranean would no longer be the center of world commerce. The merchants of Venice, who heretofore had held a virtual monopoly on trade from India via western Asia, were faced with the dismal prospect of bankrupt obsolesence.

At the opening of the sixteenth century, the Venetian Republic ruled as large a population as England at the time. Its fleet was supreme at sea; its bankers handled most of the precious metals of Europe that went to pay for the goods of the Orient. It had a system of merchant ambassadors, or agents, reporting from cities in Europe regarding market conditions and political conditions. The doges ruled, at the pleasure of the wealthiest citizens, in strict splendor, not just over their subjects but over vast treasures of every conceivable kind. What they lacked in taste (kindly, the debut of the eclectic style), they made up for in extravagance. The proudest days of Venice were during the last half of the fifteenth century—just before its fall.

As the center of commerce dispersed into many centers along the Atlantic, there correspondingly occurred another, equally significant shift culturally and philosophically. Simply stated, the ties with the Orient were severed not just in an economic sense but also in those matters that pertain to the question of meaning in and of human existence. Heretofore, there was considerable exchange of ideas, Eastern and Western, and some actually grew in affinity despite the bitter conflicts in religions; but when the trading stopped, so did the intellectual discourse. What could have been a beautiful marriage ended in separation. Sir Francis Bacon's *Novum Organum* (1625) was the divorce decree.

With regard to wealth—the basic commodity of commerce, one supposes—two things occurred. First, as sea trade increased the amount and variety of goods available and reduced the time required to deliver them, wealth began to be defined in common terms—not merely as precious metals or stones or other virtu, natural or crafted, from exotic lands. Economists will have to decide whether that occurred because the stuff of wealth actually became more accessible, or because there was a fundamental rethinking of what constitutes wealth. I suspect the latter to be the case. That is why the rationalistic economist Adam Smith, writing in the eighteenth century, defined wealth in such practical terms.

Second, the question of the control of wealth inevitably arose and was eventually debated in very new ways. Wealth was no longer a state affair. The new science would adamantly declare the inalienable individual rights of humans—including the right to economic wherewithal. Whether it was to be earned or granted is a part of the question as yet unanswered even though, for four centuries, revolutions and world wars have been waged to justly settle accounts.

So when Bacon published his pivotal work, it was both from and within a context thoroughly prepared to give science a new meaning. It was also a bridge between two worlds; but once that bridge was crossed, there was no going back. Before long, the bridge disappeared from the intellectual landscape altogether, and in its place, there was only a formidable chasm. Bacon called his essay simply and appropriately *Novum Organum*, the new instrument. But the title itself was not a tribute to Aristotle; it was calculated to signal a radical departure from the Aristolian world view.

An instrument to be used for what purposes? Bacon's ambitious answer: to discover the will of God for humankind, thus achieving the knowledge necessary for fullness of life and optimal development. The discovery of that divine will, he insisted, could be made only by the application of "the scientific method." It could not be intuited, as in superstition; it was not apprehended merely through the senses, as suggested by Aristotle; it was not a matter of revelation, as taught by the Christian religion. It preceded from the objective universe itself, and was there as the ultimate and permanent expression of God—save for men and women themselves. Furthermore, they themselves had sufficient reason to both understand and control their world. The very idea is charged with powerful optimism, an optimism sufficient to drive simultaneously four revolutions during the next four hundred years— scientific, political, economic, and social.

The world and all in it were, in Bacon's thinking, created by God; that world was essentially a *cosmos*, existing strictly for the benefit of humans. That world was purely objective and by carefully directed and sustained observation could be totally comprehended by the human mind and eventually turned to such advantage of humans being that they could actually "take command over natural things." The new science was the real gospel, the authenticated "good news." Rationalism would become to science what Christianity had been to religion.

This is not to say, however, that Bacon in any way intended to diminish faith in a divine, benevolent creator of the universe. Quite to the contrary, it was his intent to gain universal access to him. As Bacon himself described his intent, playing on a phrase from Jesus himself: "Access to the kingdom of man, which is founded upon the sciences, may resemble that to the kingdom of Heaven, where no admission is conceded, except to children."[6] And to that simplicity he was genuinely devoted, warning almost prophetically of the dangers of rationalism as portrayed in three types of persons; specifically, the "sophistical" (those philosophers who make a great deal out of little things and little out of many things), the empirical (the purely rationalistic scientist such as those on the continent), and the superstitious (those who would seek to scientize religion). He was right on all three counts.

The new science would transform the world in several dramatic ways. Just about the time Galileo, looking at the stars through his new telescope, confirmed what Copernicus had argued—that the sun, not the earth, is the center of the physical universe, Bacon asserted that the source of knowledge was not God, but humans. That meant the burden of proof for all of humankind's questions and answers lay strictly in its own hands—or minds. Furthermore, it meant a permanent separation of the rational from the intuitive, the objective from the subjective, and the almost desperate declaration of the superiority of the rational and the objective. Eventually, that led to the dumbfounded confusion of the natural order of things with human artifacts—or was it the other way around? When God was removed from the universe, anything became possible; so, when everything became impossible, there was no solution. One can only wonder what our reality would be today if the thinkers of the seventeenth century had chosen to see the world through other lenses.

This "new instrument," in short, meant that human organization had come into its own. From this point onward, it would become just as much an artifact as, say, Roman aquaducts. The difference was that it would be a rational construct, subject to all the complexities and contradictions that only a system of the mind can produce. But first, last, and always, it was an artifact. The critical attributes of that artifact were logical, necessary products of rational thinking. They would define organization in terms of systemization. In fact, they were one and the same.

Rationalism, however, did not exist in the rarefied atmosphere of philosophical discourse or in the hallowed halls of academic citadels. It was rather an unprecedented vibrant force, rivaled only by the force of the high Renaissance and fueled by its spirit of invention and discovery, however redefined. Only this time the primary agent of change would be the genius of human beings themselves. Eventually, rationalism pervaded every aspect of Western civilization, transforming everything it touched in ways heretofore unimaginable. It was as if the whole world had been anxiously awaiting its enlightenment.

No one has understood better than Evelyn Waugh the profound significance of this historical shift on all aspects of Western society: "The vast exuberance of the Renaissance had been canalized. . . . The course of . . . history lay plain ahead: Competitive nationalism, competitive industrialism, competitive imperialism, the looms and coal mines and counting houses, the joint-stock companies and cantonments; the power and the weakness of great possessions."[7]

Four aspects of society were particularly affected by the new science. Together they determined the characteristics of the modern corporation more than any other influence. The societal aspects were economy, faith, governance, and control. Specifically, rationalism transformed the previous forms of thought and expression into the modern forms of capitalism, democracy, humanism, and behaviorism. The first two were the creations of the eighteenth century. Humanism, in its current definition, emerged in the nineteenth century; and behaviorism was born and flourished in the first half of the twentieth century.

The corporation-model organization absorbed all these influences. Through its alleged free-market competition, capitalism dictated in large part both the purpose and the dynamic of the organization. Democracy, while adverse to the fundamental disposition of the corporation, ultimately was poorly imitated in the organization of the corporation. Humanism transformed the corporation's moral tenor, moving it from the human to the materialistic. And behaviorism became the basic assumption of human motivation through the science of management.

NOTES

1. Galileo, in an aside after admitting heresy, 1633.

2. William James, *Pragmatism: A New Name for Some Old Ways of Thinking* (New York: Longmans, Green and Co., 1948), 223.

3. An old Cornish prayer.

4. Aristotle, *Poetics*, ed. Ernest Rhys (London: J. M. Dent and Sons, Ltd., 1947), 27.

5. Alfred North Whitehead, *Process and Reality* (New York: Macmillan, 1929), 63.

6. Francis Bacon, *The Physical and Metaphysical Works of Lord Bacon*, ed. Joseph Devey (London: George Bell and Sons, 1901), 405.

7. Evelyn Waugh, *Edmund Campion: Jesuit and Martyr* (Garden City, N.Y.: Doubleday, 1956), 15.

CHAPTER 18

The Assertion of Humanism

And the Lord God said, "Behold the man has become like one of Us, to know good and evil; and now, lest he put forth his hand, and take also of the tree of life, and eat, and live forever"; therefore . . . he drove the man out; and he placed at the east of the Garden of Eden cherubim and a flaming sword which turned every way to keep the way to the tree of life.

Genesis 3: 22–24

At first it may seem a somewhat farfetched notion to suggest that humanism is in any way substantively related to the corporation-model organization. But that impression quickly disappears upon considering the profound implications that this philosophy has had and continues to have on corporation-model systems. There are at least three critical connections so intricately forged that one wonders whether either the philosophy or the organization could have existed without the other. First, humanism confirmed the basic rationale of the corporation; that is, materialistic wealth is the ultimate good for human beings and the only reason for organized enterprise. The corporation's only purpose is the creation of that wealth. Second, it preached the doctrine of human potential, if not universally, then certainly for those few individuals who by dint of circumstance and personal prowess could achieve extraordinary things. They, in fact, could control not only their own lives but, more or less, the lives of others. Even the great humanist John Stuart Mill admitted that there would always be the masses. Third, and precisely to the point, if individuals could achieve perfection, then human systems could also be made perfect by the understanding and application of the science and mathematics of the new science.

Historically, those connections were made over most of two centuries. Early nineteenth-century humanism, after wrestling with moral and ethical possibilities, finally came to the conclusion, although rather obliquely, that materialism was the only path to the greatest good in human life. In its intermediate form, it advanced, probably as a response to naturalism, the doctrine of unlimited human potential, a philosophy that dominated all aspects of Western society through world wars, economic depressions, and political upheaval. That assurance motivated almost all free enterprise in contemporary society. Finally, the idea of perfection came to corporation-model organizations late in the twentieth century as the so-called "quality" movement, characteristically maintaining that continuous improvement in the processes of production would ultimately ensure perfection in the product.

As enticing as all this may be, to blandly accept those postulates is to completely ignore the nature of systems in general and of human systems in specific, and to run the risk of serious frustration and disappointment in all the arenas of human endeavor. There were profound implications in the philosophy of humanism, implications that created entirely new criteria for defining the nature and quality of human life, individually or corporately.

It seems that humans always have been driven by the idea of human perfection. It is in their hearts if not in their genes. By now, it is a cliché that the new science made a lot of old ideas possible. In no instance was this truer than with the idea of human perfection. Perfection, indeed! That old Platonic notion, which for a millennium and a half had lain dormant under the dark cover of Aristotelian philosophy, suddenly sprang to life in the light of a new day. Human perfection, which had once been only fantasy at worst, speculation at best, now became an objective reality demonstrable with virtuosity sufficient to impress even the most hidebound Aristotelian. It was especially an intellectual windfall to those Aristotelians of the clergy who had been put somewhat on the defensive over the issue of continually postponed salvation.

What was lacking all along was context, means, and definition. The new science, especially the Newtonian version, provided all three. Curiously enough, in the search for perfection, definition is of necessity the last consideration, because until perfection is achieved no one knows what it is.

Implicit in the new science — in its fundamental logical construct, as well as its practical application and historical development — was a certain progression, if not process. The context of perfection was determined by discovery; the means to perfection, by invention; the definition, by postulation. This became the permanent motif of the new science — observation, imitation, designing.

The power of discovery came as a shock, even to Newton. It is more than just an insignificant footnote to intellectual history that he actually did not set out to create a whole new context for the human experience. He was attempting to shore up the existing one. Newton's *Philosophiae Naturalis Principia Mathematica* was intended to prove that the ordered character of the universe had its origin in God. Newton's mission was doomed from the start. If he actually proved the existence of God by empirical evidence, then the whole idea of faith goes up in fact; if he did not prove the existence of God, then any faith is foolishness—either way, religion becomes intellectual self-deception. His first discovery was all right; that is, that the universe is a gigantic mechanism, all its parts working in uniform, predictable ways—these he called "laws." This was the triumph of applied mathematics, which in one basic generalization—that is, the law of gravity—explained all the processes in the universe. His second discovery was still all right because it was consistent with the writings of the Apostle Paul and some early Church theologians; that is, the universe is, in fact, the revelation of God, without any need of personal revelation through Christ or written text inspired by the Holy Spirit—certainly not by joyless clerics. Furthermore, human beings, by virtue of their ability to reason, could understand it all.

But his third discovery was more Platonic than Newton would want to admit; and it had repercussions that would cause him to shudder: The universe no longer had any need of God—as creator maybe, as sustainer no. The creation being a fact, the only question was how to keep things going. The answer: there was within the universe a self-sustaining, self-regenerating energy; and there was within the human mind "sufficient reason" to make the best of it—or to suffer the worst of it. The very idea got all thinking people off their butts and into the fray. But wait. There still remained to be settled the terms of the engagement.

The idea of a totally ordered, Godless universe had been foreshadowed centuries earlier in Plato's "Great Chain of Being." Thinking about the chain in strictly vertical images is the mistake of a severely narrow mind. In fact, the chain idea had gained so much intellectual respectability that it had become, more than a century earlier, the motif of the renowned Elizabethan world picture. Far from rendering the concept immaterial, Newton's *Philosophiae Naturalis Principia Mathematica* attested to its soundness and substance. In religion, concepts such as the nine orders of angels and the three planes of existence were confirmed; but the new knowledge would concern itself not so much with the conflict of good and evil as with the separation of mind and matter. In science, the "obligatory hierarchy" of ranks among plants and animals was confirmed; the new issue was evolution of the species. In economics, the rigid specification of the wealth of labor by class was confirmed. However, the emerging order was nothing other than dialectic materialism. In the social realm, the caste system was confirmed; the new declension became the rendered judgment on various cultures. In politics, rule of law was confirmed; the new question was who gets to write the laws. In physics, the atomic makeup of the world was confirmed; the question now became what of organicism.

There were three principles of Plato's "Great Chain of Being": plenitude, gradation, and completeness. (Incidentally, these are still the hallmarks of the corporation-model organization.) Newton, probably without intending to, reinforced all of them. The meaning of this affirmation was wide ranging, indeed. The context, the natural universe, provided by the new science, was specifically characterized by uniformity (plenitude would mean an infinite array of things in like groups), process (in a living world of gradation, nothing is static), and precision (all things must fit together exactly). It would be in those terms that human beings would seek perfection, whether individually or as societies or in the means of production. The search would not be in the moralistic context of religion—not even in the idealistic world of Hellenistic philosophy—but in the objective reality of empiricism. The way to perfection lay within the intellect. No longer would human beings be victimized by the wild and adverse forces of nature or by a brazenly puissant church. They could actually control their own lives by the exercise of their own reason to first understand immutable natural laws and then create their own world. It is not without reason that proficiency in these "skills" is still referred to as "mastery."

Before Newton's *Philosophiae Naturalis Principia Mathematica*, René Descartes had written the twenty-one rules for the direction of the mind (he had intended thirty-six). Upon third thought, he reduced them to four: Accept as true only what is apprehended so clearly and distinctly that no one can doubt it; break up each problem into as many parts as it will yield and tackle these in turn; observe an order in the inquiry passing from the simple to the complex; and make sure of covering whole ground. Above all, he cautioned that one should doubt everything but his or her own existence. It is rather amazing, even to a rational mind, that these rules survived through the twentieth century as the cardinal academic principles of "critical thinking," as the accepted model for problem solving, as the fundamental design of all production activity, as the intrinsic principles of organization, and as the basic philosophy of a rational universe.

At the second level of engagement, the human mind could begin actually to direct the natural order of things. The secret to that was inherent in the natural order itself—predictability. Once humans got hold of that idea, they could actually outrun their own experience: Adhering always to the laws of mathematics, they could now set out from observable data (evidence), extrapolate (since time was no longer a barrier to knowledge, backwards and forward) to the limit of their ability to understand, and return to observable data (proof). By this process of reason, they could actually exercise control over both time and natural events by their choice of timing in the application of universal imperatives to control the quality of their lives. When translated into the means of production, it meant that constantly improving the quantitative measures of the process would increase the quality of the product. On a higher plane, intellectually they could simply start with a supposition (a hypothesis), experiment to their minds' content, and then draw a conclusion proved manifestly true by the reliable testimony of natural laws and the practical evidence, usually of workability.

It is also rather amazing, even to a rational mind, that this "scientific method" became the essential measure of science as late as the twenty-first century. The scientific method was the fulcrum that lifted humanity out of the darkness of despair into the bright new world of its own creation. In fact, the only thing it could not do was determine when, or if, conclusions became knowledge or whether the product was really worthwhile. If anything, therefore, it intensified the search for meaning, ever increasing the need for some trustworthy context.

The third level of engagement would approach the question earnestly and with some degree of real success. The universe consisted of more than abstract laws, and the human mind was capable of more than thinking critically. Descartes alleged, and Newton proved, that the natural world existed in a state of discontinuity: Each thing breaks up into a series of atomic particles with no connection among them; that is, essentially without form and void. Only when the human mind begins to brood over this vast expanse of the universe can anything of meaning be constructed. In that sense, human beings, with innate free will, are able to create the world continually—taking over where God had been left off. Humans become the authors and finishers of their world. Descartes would say it most succinctly: *Cogito, ergo sum.* John Milton had been somewhat more poetic and philosophical: "The mind is its own place, and in itself/Can make a Heaven of Hell, a Hell of Heaven."[1] Strangely enough, it was not until the discovery of the subatomic world that human beings would come fully to understand their own cosmic identity.

In a truly remarkable, even unexpected, way the imagination became the prime mover in the invention of artifacts designed and continuously improved to give maximum meaning and purpose to life and thereby contribute to something called human "progress." It is worth noting here that the very concept of progress would be impossible without the linear view of things human, including history, provided by rationalism. What was once mere process, now (upon the strength of reason) becomes progress in historical terms, and continuous improvement in personal development and practical enterprises. "New" and "improved" become synonyms.

But progress toward what? Why, human perfection, of course—what else? Possibility thinking had arrived. As the fulsome adage had it, "Whatever the human mind could conceive, human beings could achieve"—all through artful interaction with the laws of nature. It is not without reason that in the seventeenth century the word *technique*, heretofore an expression of art, became almost solely a term applied to science. When, in the nineteenth century, it was eventually separated, cleansed of intuition, revelation, or morality, and made purely quantitative, it became technology. Nor is it without reason that during the same century, the word *science*, always before universally applied to all kinds of learning, was redefined strictly as in the "new" science. This was the triumph of rationalism: that the mind believe nothing in the name of religion, anything in the name of science.

The very word "technology" is testimony to the cold ambition of modern science. It actually suggests a knowledge detached from knowledge. It is instructive to note that Aristotle took great pains to distinguish *techne* from both *episteme* and *phronesis*. According to him, *poiesis* is the process of artifactual production that consists of neither theory nor action. That which guides this artifactual production he termed *techne*. What is important is that the activity produces an object that lies beyond the dynamics of the activity itself. Whatever etymological connection there may be in the various cognates (and that is not meant to imply that the modern word "technology" has the same meaning as *techne*), at least the association reveals three authentic characteristics of technology: It is always determined by its object, existing only in application; it is subject to manipulation and control; and, it is always servant, never master.

Finally, the definition of perfection would be postulated strictly in personal terms within a material universe. Moral perfection in a spiritual universe was no longer even a question. It is curious indeed that the new scientists, then and now, seem never to consider the logical or, for that matter, even the grammatical requirements of something (or someone) being good, before it (he or she) can be better. The reason the new scientists had to take the notion of a moral universe off the table early is that they could not deal logically with the possibility of perfect evil or, to use their language, perfect wrong. So they dutifully pressed on, seeking human perfection along one of the only two avenues remaining: humanism and materialism, both the offspring of rationalism; and some keep looking for the intersection. One avenue, humanism, would eventually lead to political and social revolutions throughout Western civilization; the other, rationalism, to economic revolutions. Successful politics was the promise of the greatest good for the greatest number of people.

Humanism would not reach its cumulative definition of human perfection until the mid-twentieth century. By then, as one might expect, it was the "new humanism," as originally fostered a century before by Matthew Arnold of sweetness-and-light fame. Its tenets, which had become almost a part of popular culture, were approximately these: Human perfection is achievable and desirable; high standards demand the "cultivation" of every part of the human being; all the parts must be developed harmoniously and discriminatingly (holistically, as it were); being concerned with the norm of humanity, it is interested only in the universal and permanent, not in temporary codes and conduct of conventional society; and the idea is to identify the paragon of excellence in any human endeavor.

It was the next stipulation that would do humanism in. It declared that the fundamental quality of human existence was not natural but ethical and that the ultimate ethical principle is that of self-control, tantamount to self-respect (or specifically, "liberation from other constraints and subjection to inner law"). That sounded too much like moralism to be accepted by the new scientists. Ironically, it was they who had raised the question originally and provided the means of discovery and invention; but even though the scientific method had been exercised honestly and judiciously in reaching this definition of perfection, the conclusion was intellectually unacceptable. The thing had turned on itself and devoured itself, tail first.

The only option remaining for the achievement of human perfection was materialism. In personal terms, it meant having, or hoping to have, always a better life, typically defined by increasing one's possessions, comfort, and convenience or by "self-improvement" through the acquisition of skills, knowledge, and abilities or by physical beauty calculated to impress and physical acumen adequate for sustained longevity—all that was once and for all expressed as "the pursuit of happiness." Eventually, materialism makes the finer things of life—those that satisfy the spirit—either unattractive or unaffordable.

The assertion of human, and consequently system, perfectibility obviously could not be confined to the merely philosophical. There were, in fact, three necessary practical implications of such magnitude that each was bound to create upheaval, even revolution, within Western civilization. First, the idea of human perfection required that all people start at zero: a common start meant equality of all people. Second, the idea of the human elevated individual self-interest over other considerations; rights would supersede responsibility. Third, there is no such thing as absolute, final truth: Human perfectibility is impossible by any external moral (spiritual) standard. Only thoroughly rationalized systems could embrace any one of these ideas.

NOTE

1. John Milton, *Paradise Lost*, I: 254–255, *The Norton Anthology of English Literature*, ed. M. H. Abrams (New York: W. W. Norton, 1926), 920.

CHAPTER 19

The Assertion of Democracy

If we take the term in the strict sense, there has never been a real democracy, and there never will be.

Jean Jacques Rousseau[1]

The corporation interpretation and application of democracy exactly paralleled that of the fledging governments purportedly ruled by the people. In both instances, the rights and privileges of democratic principles were limited to only a few. That is to say, the capitalists and the entrepreneurs proclaimed individual and collective freedom for themselves but denied it to those laboring within the system. This practice was a faithful imitation of the political arrangement that enfranchised only those of wealth or inherited status. It is not surprising to find that the corporation-model organization had no more success with the idea than government. The problem really is the idea. But it does demonstrate how rationalism could take an ancient, abandoned concept and resuscitate it through a new rationalism that held human beings (some of them, at least) to be the center of the universe — the be all and end all.

Democracy is a state of mind. From all indications, it always has been and always will be. This is so for three reasons. First, it is purely an intellectual fabrication, so much so that it actually seems to violate rationalism's patented insistence on logic and empirical methods. Second, in practice it always exists in a kind of amorphousness, its only certainty being the constant strange declaration of negotiable absolutes. Third, its acceptance, for that matter its definition, is dependent strictly on the perception of individuals within a group that they are somehow better off than the rest of the group.

As a fabrication, this kind of governance certainly was not born of the new science. However, the old idea would not have amounted to much without it. But rather than simply making an old idea possible, rationalism proposed brand new possibilities—all based on the principle of the sovereignty of the human being over all matters pertaining to the human being. In the classical democracies, with rare exception, rule by the people was by design either so severely confined that the attempt virtually amounted to laboratory-controlled experiments or so restricted in application that it was little more than a gentleman's agreement among peers to leave each other alone and ignore everyone else. It was both clique and claque.

The new science, as expressed in cultural rationalism, could accept nothing less than the universality of human reason and the commonality of human beings. And why not? As the order of the universe shifted in fits and starts from earth centered to solar centered, there was a corresponding (some would say inverse) shift in the locus of control in human affairs—specifically, from the divine to the human. "Man" became the center of the universe. As Alexander Pope pontificated, "The proper study of mankind is man."[2] The use of the word "man" in this context is revealing for a couple of reasons. On the one hand, it spoke of commonality; but on the other, of a commonality among the males of the species. When the proponents of democracy shouted "fraternity," they meant it.

The androcentric emphasis quickly established, in a thundering (sometimes bombastic) crescendo, three theoretical postulates upon which all modern democracy would be based: equality of all people, universal natural rights, and the supremacy of the individual. Equality translates self-governance; rights translate self-indulgence; supremacy of the individual translates self-righteousness. These three principles and the implications thereof would forever permeate Western democracy and confound the corporation-model organization. Far from academic categorization, this triad is nowhere more explicit than in the Declaration of Independence of the American colonies—itself a testament to the influence of deism at the time: specifically, that all men are created equal, and that they are endowed with certain inalienable rights, and that they are free to enjoy their own lives and liberty and to pursue their own happiness. The only problem with that soaring rhetoric is that no one has ever been able to explain precisely what it means.

There was another quite curious thing about the concept of democracy spawned by rational thinking. It was itself not rational—at least not by the scientific definition. The hallmark of the new science, taking its cue from Aristotle, was its insistence on careful observation and analysis of nature and the logical deduction of fixed laws by which human beings could order their world and gain some assurance of permanence. However, democracy is unnatural; it simply does not exist in nature—anywhere, anytime. It is not without reason the various kinds of life groups on the planet have always been referred to as "kingdoms." The very idea of democracy is not based on scientific observation but on observing with a rationalistic bias—not upon that which is observed but upon the observer. The idea of democracy was never the result of discovery and imitation of the laws of nature but the imposition of human reason over natural law by the creation of an intellectual artifice.

Admittedly, one has to be fleet of syllogism and have a high tolerance for nonsequitur even to follow that kind of thinking, much less to accept it. The rationalists skipped happily over their first rule of observation and the second of imitation and went straight to postulation. But reduced to its essence, democracy simply meant that humans, through their own intellectual prowess, had not only separated themselves from nature but actually risen above it.

And that leads to yet another difference between the ancient notions of democracy and those of modern times. Try as they might, the early advocates of democracy could not get past the problem of some kind of divine authority. In fact, the persistent argument that there is no authority without divine origin has never been refuted. Denied, yes, but not invalidated. The crux of the matter is this: Whether revealed in natural or supernatural ways, the assumption of deity automatically precludes any possibility of individual or collective self-governance. A popular myth of twentieth-century America is that democracy and Christianity are Siamese siblings connected at the head. But democracy, if it can exist at all, can exist only in a godless world. It is either a cynical sham or an act of abject ignorance to suggest that God is favorably disposed to a democratic form of government. It is a safe assumption that all gods prefer theocracy. The Christian religion is based unequivocally on Christ ("the anointed") as king.

The new science opened the door to democracy as a legitimate form of governance not only by removing God from the world but also by eliminating even the need for divine intervention in human affairs. Ordinary human beings—for indeed they all are—became both designers and builders; and democracy as a system of governance became the ultimate fabrication. It is amusing to note that, just as the religionists used to refer to nature to prove divine order in the universe, rationalists pandered to the true believers by continuing to make intentionally oblique references to deity as a part of nature. Consider the cynical implications in the phrase "nature and nature's God." These three factors—the concept of commonality, the assertion of human reason over natural orders, and the negation of deity—combined to make democracy strictly a phenomenon of Western civilization. In the corporation, all three factors took on a decidedly authoritarian slant.

With regard to the matter of practice, democracy is mostly like mercury—no one can pin it down; its form and substance continue to be a work in progress. It is truly one of the marvels of history, especially the empirical–rationalistic age, that there has never been a universally accepted definition, no single model or formula, of democracy. It always seems to consist more of promise than of realization, more of hope than of experience. One could make a really strong case that the United States represents the fullest expression so far, perhaps the fullest possible, of a democratic system of government. If that is true, it is for good reason. American democracy was considered an experiment from the outset. It had virtually no precedent, no guide, no guarantee. There is a strong possibility that ad lib is the way of democracy. Furthermore, it was developed de novo, in pristine circumstances as it were. No existing system had to be displaced. The only hindrances were the experiences and mentality of even those who had presumed to conduct this experiment. For example, President Washington was almost made "king" Washington, "his high mightiness." The New World was democratic long before its separation from European monarchies simply by virtue of the collective disposition that held to the supremacy of the individual. Yet the meaning of democracy, even the United States, has seldom been the same two years running. Somehow, that does little to inspire confidence in either self-rule or rationalistic science.

The trouble seems to lie in the three postulates of democracy mentioned before; namely, equality, rights, and the individual. One of the new possibilities presented by rationalism is that none of these matters can ever be settled. However, the essential compulsion of rationalism is that we keep trying.

With regard to the first, equality, Plato was doubtlessly having a great good time when he declared, with tongue in both cheeks, that democracy is "an agreeable form of anarchy with plenty of variety and an equality of a peculiar kind for equals and unequals alike."[3] If you listen carefully, you can still hear him chuckling. But no one else has ever better captured the serious enigma in the idea of human equality. And no one seems to know what to do with it. For example, Christianity historically has agreed that all people are equal but only "in the eyes of God"—whatever that is supposed to mean. One thing it definitely did not mean was that all people deserve equal treatment; one has to curry the favor of God or be damned. Aristocracy assumed that all people of a certain class were equal; but because they were bred to be the best, they incurred both the privilege and the burden of governing others. Oligarchy assumed that all people were equal but some were more equal than others. Even dyed-in-the-wool rationalists, when pushed to the wall, as in the drafting of (say) a democratic constitution, could but argue that all people were born (or "created," by the interpretation of Christian rationalism) equal; equality is innate but not inherent. After that, ambiguity sets in. But the tacit assumption was that the subsequent status of everyone was up for grabs, depending on any number of variable factors, including balance sheets and social behavior. So the very idea of human equality is, at best, a dubious problem that requires constant solving.

One way to simplify the question is to remember that the whole idea of equality seems to have been conceived strictly within the context of governance; so that means, at least originally, it was confined to matters legal and political. That is, everyone was supposed to enjoy the same status with regard both to influence over the direction of society and to privilege within the society. That definition of equality is understandable as well as appealing. However, there was one requirement: one first had to be admitted into the group or larger society that purported to be democratic. Since equality was thus a matter of a common grant, or enfranchisement, it is accurate to say that democracy more often than not chose (chooses) its participants rather than letting the participants choose democracy. Witness the continuing expansion of democracy in Western countries as previous nonequals are granted legal and political equality. It is a long way from the Magna Carta to the Voting Rights Act of 1964. Even the United States Constitution originally set in place a very limited democracy; it was not until Lincoln's Gettysburg Address that equality began to take on universal meaning.

There is strong evidence that the constant expansion of democracy occurred within government systems not because of any basic altruism within either democracy or its proponents but because inevitably, simply as a logical conclusion of the assumptions of rationalism, equality was made a matter of justice. Not fairness, but justice. Without the morality of divine authority, the only recourse for order is the fabrication of human systems of justice, however untrustworthy.

And all this worked swimmingly well, erratically perhaps, but well enough to be seriously pursued — that is, as long as equality was only a matter of legal and political status. But another kind of expansion began, not of political status but of the idea of human equality itself. Democratic enthusiasts learned slowly, and much to their chagrin, that it is one thing for individuals to be equal before law, quite another to be equal to each other. Aristotle had warned of this eventuality: "Democracy arises out of the notion that those who are equal in any respect are equal in all respects; because men are equally free, they claim to be absolutely equal."[4]

Really serious trouble arose when, in the early-twentieth century, the conversation shifted to social democracy and then, by mid-century, to "economic democracy." The genie was out of the bottle. Equality and democracy would forevermore be defined by the reference of individuals to each other. All had three wishes: to be treated like everyone else, to be as good as anyone else, to have as much as anyone else. Herein lies the fatal double-whammy flaw of democracy. First, democratizing, defined by equality, began a constant wearing away of actual inequality to the lowest common denominator — a deliberate, selfish descent into mediocrity. Eventually, mediocracy would be preferred to "meritocracy" because the very act of excelling raised some people above others. Excellence thus becomes a pipe dream. Second, Plato warned that democracies would cease to exist when their citizens realized they could vote simply for themselves anything they wanted or wanted to be. We can now pinpoint the exact time of the demise: just as soon as "equal" meant "same," democracy lost not only its plausibility but, even worse, its credibility.

Nevertheless, for all its implicit inconsistencies and contradictions, from the mid-nineteenth century through the twentieth, in every aspect of society, public and private, the assertion of equality was the one preoccupation, sometimes appearing as an obsession, of Western civilization, especially of the United States—at least until all the unenfranchised hordes began demanding their right to full participation. The idea was at once both conscience and incubus of every aspect of society. After all this time and turmoil, the only thing that is known for sure about this issue is that it is unresolvable. About the best anyone can do is admit that the only way democracy can exist is for each person within the system to be able to somehow sustain this one belief: I am equal to everyone else; but everyone else is not equal to me.

Now to the matter of rights. The discovery of human rights as the dictate of nothing less than natural law was a tremendous relief. For at least six thousand years, and especially during the reign of the Church, people in the Western world had not found law very friendly. Religious law had bound them to obedience and constant penance ("Whatever is not of duty is sin"). Civil law had bound them to servitude and poverty. Both had sent them off to war. The very idea of universal birthrights was tantamount, even superior, to the Gospel. And no earthly authority could withstand its promise. It is no wonder, for example, that when Voltaire returned to the continent after attending the funeral of Newton, his overwhelming passion for the doctrine of his late hero quickly turned to fervent evangelism, inspiring the masses, a whole nation, to claim what was rightfully theirs. The idea itself was revolutionary; in fact, all revolutions are based on the assumption of human rights. Whenever and wherever human rights are preached, all existing governments, including contemporary democracies, are greatly at risk.

It is not stretching the metaphor to describe either the message or the effect of rights in religious terms. It has been noted that the idea of equality became possible only in a godless world. The absence of a god, however, produces an unnatural circumstance, that is, a universe without any moral center. The difference between Christian communism (as practiced in the early Church) and democratic egalitariaism (as pursued in the United States) is that in one each person is committed to everyone else (service), while in the other each is committed to self (rights). What was needed was a simple, sure reference point from which a complete system could be formed. The idea of human rights became the reference point, and constitutions of governance became the system. As with the word "laws," the use of the word "rights" in itself cast prerogatives in a quasi-moralistic context, quite simply, because by implication the absence or denial is wrong. Human rights, however variously defined, were the closest thing to moral imperatives that society or the individual in a rationalistic world would know. Rights replaced righteousness.

Fundamentally, three kinds of rights were perceived: the right to be, the right to do, and the right to have. And all three boldly argued a new source of salvation—that is, "I have the right to help myself." The interpretations of that phrase would dichotomize Western democracies forever. Even so, it is no wonder that the spread of democracy, especially in the nineteenth and twentieth centuries and especially by the United States, was pursued with missionary zeal. The idea was to bring American democracy to cultures and societies all over the world—often by force—whether or not they wanted it or were able to sustain it. There is an easy transition from the euphoria of achieving and defending democracy by arms to the exhilaration of militarily imposing it on others. Quite often all this worldwide crusade activity was occurring while the evangelists themselves were withholding the rights of people within their own systems. Zealots are born of hypocrisy. Nor did they ever imagine the possibility of lately "freed" people voting for totalitarianism.

The basic problem with human rights is threefold: how and by whom are they defined, how and by whom are they guaranteed, and how and by whom are they directed? Rousseau and his motley disciples argued that natural law, as it was perceived, was sufficient as the source and arbiter of human rights. He opposed any artificial codifying of natural law, which could easily be followed, into laws of governance, which of necessity had to be enforced. Obviously, Rousseau did not prevail, primarily because of the overwhelming rationalistic compulsion to leave nothing to chance. Strangely, natural law was either too ambiguous or too uncertain for them. There might have been another slight motivation as well: Simply following natural law allows for no human intervention—and even natural law is subject to interpretation for advantage, especially if it is parsed out in natural laws.

Thus there ensued, as stock in trade of democracy, the endless development and redevelopment of rules and regulations designed to spell out, in increasingly minute detail, exactly what each right meant and, with even more specificity, how those rights are to be realized by anybody when everybody has the same rights simultaneously in the same place. But try as they might, so far the legalists have not been able to imagine all possible human conditions or promulgate laws appropriate to every possible circumstance. As a result, in contemporary democracies previous judgment or practice has had to assume the force of law. Ironically, specificity usually creates confusion; so logic dictates that when we can no longer figure things out rationally, we just do what we did before—and what we are doing now. Sometimes this is called precedence; sometimes common law. And it describes only the substantive part of legal systems in democracies. Even more complicated are the processes by which the laws are enforced. The more democratic a legal system, the more tangled it is; rights have a way of compounding themselves endlessly, so that finality of process is rendered unlikely. When the rights of everyone involved are duly considered in a legal conflict, a conclusion is impossible. A criminal is likely to be rewarded; a victim is likely to be punished.

About the only thing the whole experiment with human rights has taught us is that the more rights people have, the more laws they need. Reality inversion is a phenomenon endemic to the rationalistic world.

NOTES

1. Jean Jacques Rousseau, *The Social Contract and the Discourses*, trans. G.D.H. Cole (New York: Alfred A. Knopf, 1993), 237.

2. Alexander Pope, "Essay on Man," epistle II, *The Norton Anthology of English Literature*, ed. M. H. Abrams (New York: W. W. Norton, 1962), 1476.

3. Plato, *The Republic*, trans. Francis MacDonald Conford (London: Oxford University Press, 1941), 283.

4. Aristotle, *Politics*, trans. Benjamin Jowett, in *Great Books of the Western World*, ed. Mortimer J. Adler (Chicago: Encyclopaedia Britannica, 1952), 502.

CHAPTER 20

Democracy and Organization

First of all, they are free. Liberty and free speech are rife everywhere; anyone is allowed to do what he likes.

Plato[1]

Although the corporation-model organization, at least in its original conceptualization, did not admit the principles of democracy into its system, it was ultimately forced to deal with the matter when the science of management forced the issue, acknowledging it as indeed a management style. This application also was incompatible with the basic disposition of the corporation. Nevertheless, there are valuable lessons to be learned from the inherent conditions of democracy both as an explanation of the failure of this type of governance within modern corporation-model systems, especially in the public sector, and as an early indication of emerging systems of organization.

The dangers of presuming to adapt democratic processes to authoritarian systems became evident very early in public versions of the corporation-model organization. Although in most instances instigated with honest intent to honor the principle of representation for all involved, the inherent contradiction was insurmountable; and the intent turned to promises that could not be kept.

THE CONDITION OF DEMOCRACY

It helps neither government nor the corporation that democracy is a continuing saga, written by a random collection of tyros, each of whom surreptitiously has also assumed the role of protagonist and thus is intent on providing a different ending. Like all good fiction, democracy exists only as long as the authors themselves are willing to suspend their own disbelief. It has often been noted by those who profess democracy that as a system it requires three conditions for survival: a climate that establishes and maintains the expectation, an agreement on fundamentals with regard to how it will work, and a will to continue the arrangement. The first translates into language as, more or less, the symbol of context. The second translates into judgment about certain assumptions. The third translates into the question of personal commitment.

The first condition is a climate of ambiguity. Any meaning of democracy is obscured by the terminology itself, so much so in fact that connotation quite easily becomes denotation, not as a matter of the natural, historical development of language, but within a single paragraph with or without conscious intent. Democracy is a compound word (not prefix–suffix) and is therefore quite inexact even in its nominal definition. In a context of ambiguity, everyone creates his or her own meanings. It is not surprising, then, that real definitions of democracy freely range in precision from didacticism to nuance. The two words "people" and "rule" were originally combined, we think, to capture the concept of people ruling themselves. We can only conclude that the Greeks chose this word rather than "autocracy" (literally "self-rule") simply because democracy is a collective noun. They probably knew what they meant. But the devil is in English prepositions.

For example, in a political sense, Abraham Lincoln was either attempting to articulate the broadest application possible of the contemporary interpretation of the term or he, intentionally or unintentionally, added two new dimensions to the idea. Neither the Greeks nor the framers of the United States Constitution would have used the prepositions "of" or "for." Both are prepositions of detachment that implicitly proclaim government as a thing apart from the people—a subtle but dramatic change in the original idea of government "by" the people. As a matter of fact, most serious historians now concede that Lincoln in his Gettysburg Address rewrote the Constitution. A single well-turned phrase turned an entire nation. Any democracy depends on a context of ambiguity—both of language and thought—on a people willing to live with, even insisting upon, imprecise distinctions and vague meanings, all in the hope of negotiating the best advantage for themselves. It is here that finesse becomes doublespeak; elaboration, condesension; argument and persuasion, propaganda.

When the fertile ambiguity of language is combined with the distance of a representative system of governance, as typical in Western societies, the whole notion becomes confused beyond any understanding or agreement. And that is the essential character of democracy. Furthermore, the very nature of representation poses serious problems. It is worth remembering that "democracy," after all, proposes, even presupposes, rule—rule of people by people. Representative government establishes a group or a class of rulers who themselves may be unclear as to the significance of democracy or, being human, may be tempted by the power that lies within the ambiguity of language or the remoteness from those they represent to pursue their own agendas—to the point where it becomes impossible to tell the Yahoos from the Houyhnhnms. It is here that authority first gives way to power. Authority demands precise language and accountability; power thrives on the obsfucation of both. Tyranny can be exercised by an individual, a group, or the majority. So no matter whether a consequence of misconception or manipulation, of deception or delusion, the sad net effect is that laws are placed in the hands of outlaws; knaves rule the righteous; and slaves think themselves free.

The second condition is unchallenged assumptions. Assumption is the basis for all forms of governance, political or corporate. Even systems based on scientific rationalism are so conceived and so dedicated. Therefore, it comes as a shock to many, if it comes at all, that democracy is based on assumptions that are unnatural as well as irrational. That apparent paradox is explained by the observation that by the time the proponents of scientific rationalism got around to creating political systems they had gone beyond merely reporting how things work and begun to postulate how they should work. Most people, either impressed by clever scientific language or willing to be fooled, could not or would not discern the difference.

There are five such assumptions within democracy. The first is that all people know what is best for them. Self interest, it is alleged, is either a correlative or a source of this knowledge which, in the ultimate democratic system, is undeniable and unchallengeable. Even the great democrat Tom Jefferson admitted trouble with this assumption. He defined knowledge strictly in terms of the "eternal verities"—the knowledge that frees. In fact, the test separating data and information from knoweldge was freedom toward the exercise of one's full powers. He insisted that the only way genuine knowledge could be assured among the masses was development, through education and other cultural experiences, of an "enlightened" citizenry. He realized that a society's system of education defines its moral character far more than its practice of religion or its establishment of government.

Two hundred years later, however, national leaders in the United States assert that "even the most ignorant people know what is best for them. Jefferson would have found it inconceivable that anyone would use the words "ignorant" and "best" in the same sentence. Indeed, that kind of blighted optimism overlooks one of Jefferson's more cryptic observations to the effect that if you pool ignorance, you get pooled ignorance. Any form of governance must be judged by the kind of people in whom authority is placed. Plato noted, "With a magnificent indifference to the sort of life a man has led before he enters politics, it will promote to honor anyone who calls himself the people's friend."[2] Unfortunately, democracy has always been the form of governance most likely to make rulers of those who are intellectually deficient and morally bereft. For this reason, democracy is also the form of government most likely to self-destruct.

The second assumption is that the majority is always right—not in the moral sense of right makes might but in the rationalistic sense that might makes right. Majority rule is the rule of democracy. That means, obviously, that democratic processes are not intended to make—and cannot make—decisions that benefit the whole group. Furthermore, it is a logical impossibility that all people have equal rights when the majority rules. In the final stages of democracy, even proportional representation—a concept that promised to more accurately reflect the interests and attitudes of the various segments of a society—was abandoned and condemned so as to create "mandates" not upon minorities but upon the majority. From this assumption emerged the philosophy and practice of the two-party system of politics that dominated American and British democracies. The object of each party was the imposition of its will on the other. Democracy was ever the choice of bullies. As long as there are minorities, there can be no true democracy.

The third assumption logically follows; that is, *E pluribus unum* to the contrary notwithstanding, division is always preferable to unity in governance. Whether the terms are "shadow government," "backbenchers," or "liberals" and "conservatives," the net effect is the same: In every democracy, there is always a significant percentage of the population (up to 49.9%) disenfranchised by the very process they believe to represent their best interest. Democracy is always characterized by winners and losers. The house is always divided, and that is a desirable circumstance in the dualistic universe of rationalism. It, however, is the antithesis of the principle of mutuality uncompromisingly put forth by the Hebraic–Christian tradition. Furthermore, when winning is pursued at all cost, the first thing spent is moral conviction. That is why a democratic system is an easy choice for those who have already made the initial investment.

Thus, the fourth assumption: finality in anything that pertains to governance is both impossible and undesirable: impossible because absolutes do not exist in the pursuit of incrementalized improvement and undesirable because of the eternal prospect of power. In the first instance, democratic solutions ultimately settle nothing but continue to provide even more complicated, unsolvable problems, until the contraption inevitably collapses under the weight of its own ambition. This is why democracy is the choice of pettifoggers. In the second instance, democratic processes are calculated to cause the consolidation of special interest factions and to avoid or negotiate conflicts, not to solve problems between them, in an attempt to create control above the legal machinery of a process that would otherwise be dangerously free. As any psephologist knows, voting does not always mean choice; and choice does not always mean democracy. Voting becomes only a temporary stay against anarchy. For this reason, democracy is the system of choice among fleeing felons and others temperamentally opposed to law.

The fifth assumption of democracy is that authority and responsibility are severable. While democratic systems are eager to advance the authority ostensibly derived from the people, there is an unfortunate circumstance that makes the authority absolute; that is, it simply will not admit accountability. Those in authority are exempt from responsibility because of the unimaginable complicity of events and systems surrounding them; everything can be explained away. And those who place them in authority insist on doing so in secret; the secret ballot has always been for those who lacked the courage of their conviction. It is tit for tat between the scamps and the scavengers. The upshot of this irresponsibility is that whenever something goes wrong with democracy, it is quite difficult to fix or, for that matter, to detect. Even more frightening is what the separation of accountability from authority does to power. There are three kinds of power: that which arises within the person, that which is derived from others, and that which is seized. Authority without commensurate responsibility is seized power, and if tolerated, it quickly becomes tyrannical and then corrupt. That is why democracy is the choice of despots, perverts, and those who are overrighteous much.

The existence of democracy, however perceived by those who attempt to practice it, is contingent upon suspended judgment of these five assumptions. The mere challenge of any one of them destroys the faith in the fundamentals required to sustain this collective illusion. So the third condition of sustaining a democracy, the willingness to continue the arrangement, is satisfied not by commitment to anything as noble as principles or as altruistic as mutual benefit but by commitment strictly to one's own personal interest, regardless of the interests of others. Continuing the agreement rests solely on the confidence of each person that he or she is not just better off individually because of participation in a collective system but better off than anyone else, even at the lowest level of human existence. Only then will he or she agree in advance to live with whatever the ballot yields.

The very idea of democracy proved eventually to be the single most powerful influence in and on Western civilization and correspondingly, on the corporation. It represented the height of their development and the fundamental cause of their inevitable demise. The idea would prove to be a force so powerful yet so impractical that, when force-fitted into the old hierarchical system, it would create such an internal conflict that the corporation-model organization was bound from the start to self-destruction.

DEMOCRACY AND THE INDIVIDUAL

Democracy, as an idea if not in practice, is critically important to an understanding of the pathology of the corporation-model organization, especially in its broader societal application. It is here, more than any other aspect of society, that one find the most dramatic example of the contradiction inherent in the corporation. Quite simply, the corporation seems to flourish only in a democratic state. Yet, oddly, each is the exact opposite of the other; it is a case of authoritarianism and democracy not merely coexisting but actually thriving off each other, as if some sort of unnatural symbiosis had been discovered.

Furthermore, in addition to the conflicting philosophical dispositions, there is a fundamental difference in the views and treatment of human beings. Democracy exalts the individual while at the same time promising equalization. The corporation has little regard for individuals, consigning them to a rigid scale of value referred to as rank. The majority of the population is near the bottom. The question is how it is possible for citizens of Western civilization to live in political democracy and yet be virtual slaves to a corporate system, both economically and socially.

It is not that the management philosophies of the nineteenth and twentieth centuries did not recognize this contradiction; in fact, most reflected the struggle, and many attempted to deal with it. But, unfortunately, none was able to resolve the dilemma. A completely different system was the only answer.

The conflict between the two orders (and an early clue as to the kind of organization that would eventually displace the corporation-model organization) is most evident in the promise of democracy to honor the supremacy of the individual.

Fundamentally, democracy is the romancing of the individual. It adores, pursues, entices, and possesses, not with love but with liberty. The romance is consummated according to the status intended for and afforded to the person: Specifically, there are three states—individuality, individualism, and individualness. I use a differentiating conjunction because each state represents the virtual exclusion of the others, practically if not philosophically. In fact, the first may be said to be personal, the second social, the third spiritual. It is not merely a matter of emphasis; it is a matter of definition. If there is procession in these dimensions, it is from the person as subject to the person as object to the person as an abstraction. Democracy is defined by which of these three states is pursued and achieved, and to what degree. That explains much about the historical development of Western democracy, as well as the variations that exist among democracies at any given time.

INDIVIDUALITY

Individuality is everything that constitutes the person—physical, mental, and spiritual. If there is any one thing that sets democracy apart from other forms of governance, it is the recognition of the distinctiveness of each person and the promulgation of the full development thereof. All early attempts at democracy focused on this idea as the central theme, so much so that the whole purpose of democracy originally seems to have been the realization of the unique potentiality of each individual. This was, and still could be, the definition of liberty. For example, Aristotle defined freedom as "the unrestricted exercise of one's full powers." Almost nineteen hundred years later, Wilhelm von Humboldt declared, "The end of man, or that which is prescribed by the eternal or inevitable dictates of reason . . . is the highest and most harmonious development of his powers to a complete and consistent whole."[3] Democracy is so essentially individuality that the idea echoes in all forms of modern democracy. Herein lies its spontaneity, its creativity, and its promise. And herein lies its power. It was this simple idea that during the eighteenth century brought down great monarchies in Europe. And it threatens every democracy in the twenty-first century.

In anything so dynamic, so vital, two questions immediately arise: (1) Is the source of energy reliable?; and (2) does it want discipline or direction? When these questions are individualized, the issues become the capacity and motivation of each human being. And that discussion, no matter how the questions are resolved, presents the ominous possibility that individualization in a social context—the essence of democracy—will result in a wilderness of conflict, completely choking off any hope of an orderly society—in a word, anarchy. But here the trail is well marked, even though there is no path. Many explorers have arrived at this intersection before, but none has provided a better survey and left better directions than John Stuart Mill.

In his famous treatise *On Liberty*, written in 1859, he speaks as only a Christian rationalist could to each of these intertwined issues. In fact, so intent is he on blending Christianity with rationalism that at one juncture we find him attempting to reconcile Calvin with Plato. It never occurred to him, or to many others of his persuasion, that there was any limit to a person's capacity for development. Hope always attends the untried. But there is a healthy infusion of practicality in his argument. He admits that although there will always be geniuses and ordinary people (the "masses") the only real difference is not in gifts and talents but strictly a matter of individual choice. And that is the obligation of society to the person—to ensure both the freedom of choice and a variety of experiences sufficient for the realization of his or her potential. That's why Mill chooses to describe human development always as self-development. The most amazing insight provided by his discourse, and the point completely ignored by all the latter-day gurus of the "human-potential" movement, is that individuality is one thing and one thing only—uniqueness.

Uniqueness simply means that comparison is not possible. Neither is competition. Nor is human development vertical, along a single axis, quantitative; it is, rather, multidirectional, involving an endless array of kinds—qualitative. According to Mill, each person can develop only in his or her own individual mode: "It is not by wearing down into uniformity all that is individual is in themselves, but by cultivating it and calling it forth."[4] To quote Ralph Waldo Emerson quoting the Oracle at Delphi, "To thine own self be true." That is why there can be no limitation.

Also, Mill acknowledges that the inherent primary, if not the only, motivating force in each individual is self-interest or, as he phrased it, "desires and strong impulses."[5] Once that is understood, nothing else needs to be known about human motivation. That self-interest is more than sufficient "energy" both to move a person toward his or her own aspirations and to establish a person as the best and only architect of his or her life. Having declared as a simple truth what all people know but few will admit, Mill not unexpectedly produces a simple but passionate rationalistic process for taking control of one's own life:

He who lets the world, or his own portion of it, choose his plan of life for him, has no need of any other faculty than the ape-like one of imitation. He who chooses his plan for himself, employes all his faculties. He must use observation to see, reasoning and judgment to foresee, activity to gather materials for decision, discrimination to decide, and when he has decided, firmness and self-control to hold to his deliberate decision.[6]

Third, Mill is adamant about the principle upon which the relationship between the individual and society must be based. There are only two. The first principle, simply stated, maintains that the person is sovereign over all things that pertain to himself or herself alone; absolute independence is a human right. The second principle requires a bit more elaboration:

The sole end for which mankind are warranted, individually or collectively, in interfering with the liberty of action of any of their number, is self-protection.

That the only purpose for which power can be rightfully exercised over any member of a civilized community, against his will, is to prevent harm to others. His own good, either physical or moral, is not a sufficient warrant.

He cannot rightfully be compelled to do or forbear because it will be better for him to do so, because it will make him happier, because, in the opinions of others, to do so would be wise, or even right.[7]

However, this policy of nonintervention should not be taken to mean that there is no reciprocal or mutually beneficial connection between the individual and the larger society. Quite the opposite is the case. The reasoning goes, if society leaves the person to his or her own devices, within the constraints of the rights and interests of others, and allows for choice and a variety of experiences toward full development of individual originality, the whole society will benefit as a natural consequence. The only hitch, if there is one in this glorious scheme, is that the burden of proof is always on the individual.

INDIVIDUALISM

Individualism is to government what individuality is to society. And that means that it is necessarily, first and last, a political matter, involving the relationship between the individual and what has come to be known as the state. Individualism holds that the person, not the state (and certainly not God), is the ultimate political authority, because only the person can determine, through reason, what is right and wrong, thus becoming a moral authority higher than the legal authority of any political artifice such as government. In fact the state's only authority is granted to it by individuals acting collectively—that is, its authority is derived from the people.

That premise has become the sine qua non of Western democracies. Because government is subject to individuals, they can change it, resist it, disobey it, drop out of it, or destroy it if it ever becomes an establishment. Thomas Jefferson, perhaps the epitome of individualism remarked that "The tree of liberty must be refurbished from time to time with the blood of patriots and tyrants."[8] That's the makings of revolution. In fact, all democracies are born of revolution and must be nurtured and sustained in the same fashion. Since all government, including even that which purports to be democratic, is inevitably either repressive or oppressive—because of stagnation or political will—the purest form of democracy is a state of continuous revolution. As Stanislaw Lem pined, if we only knew the tune they played before the walls of Jericho!

It would be helpful in this discussion to remember its historical development and hence its constituent qualities; otherwise, individualism becomes nothing more than self-indulgence run amok. The pure doctrine of individualism, while based on self-interest, did not advocate selfishness and would not tolerate the abuse of others. These the views of Plato and Aristotle are in agreement with those of the rationalists. The classical argument for the superiority of the state was based not on the need for external authoritative control but rather on the necessity for moral discipline. Those who made this argument knew that any release of the energy of individualism requires a commensurate force of constraint by government. As an existing government attempts to expand divisibility, merely by doing so it creates the tension of equal and opposite pull toward unifying control. In a truly free society, that force can only be morality. In practice, that has become something of a problem for modern democracies—since all are predicated on rationalism—that is, human reason and experience rather than acceptance of absolutes; so typically these democracies tend to direct the behavior of each person through a swarm of continuing updates on acceptable conduct. Authoritarian government crushes individualism by force; democracy strangles it with regulations.

Without question, it is John Locke's philosophy that has dominated the political systems of at least England, France, and the United States for the past three hundred years. Essentially, he believed that all men possess certain natural rights—chief among which were life, liberty, and property. Rulers derived their authority from the consent of the people and hold that authority only as long as they rule justly. It is not an overstatement to suggest that the United States is a direct result, perhaps even the embodiment, of Locke's political liberalism. The source of its power was the fusion of Western thought without subordinating the substance to methodology. His philosophy of individualism is not only the basis of the U.S. Constitution and the government system, it was the driving force behind the American revolution, westward expansion, the Civil War, two world wars, and the protest movement of the Vietnam era. The entire history of the United States is a declaration of independence for the individual. From Tom Paine's civil disobedience, to Whitman's maudlin sentimentality about everything in America, to the near-defiant attitude of those who pushed westward for the first time (that's when individualism became rugged), to the Edisons, Bells, and Duryeas who persisted because of who they were, and to each of those who died in some unknown place in the defense of what they thought was liberty—all this and much more is the legacy of individualism.

INDIVIDUALNESS

The third dimension of the individual, individualness, represents either the consummation of democracy or its complete demise. In the Newtonic world, there are three variations on the theme of individual. Individuality argues that the highest form of human fulfillment is becoming; this is classicism. Individualism finds its culmination in doing; this is romanticism. Individualness declares that the only meaning and purpose in life is being; this is existentialism. The latter is at once both isolative and introspective, emphasizing the distinctiveness of each person to the exclusion of any need or notion of connectedness with others. It is the individual raised to cosmological proportions and is, therefore, a kind of spiritual quest.

The isolation of the individual was a given in the dominant European philosophy of the mid- to late-nineteenth century. The only question was whether it resulted in salvation or alienation. The dominant philosophy of the age, determinism in some form or another, had just about everybody who thought at all thinking that the universe was a hostile place and that all the forces of nature were massed against the lonely, struggling individual whose doom was already sealed.

Søren Kierkegaard concluded that the end of human life is mere existence—nothing more, nothing less. The basic tenents of his philosophy are consistent with, if not the same as, individuality and individualism: human beings are unique: They are part of a natural universe; but only they, among other living things, can reflect and make free decisions. Kierkegaard pushes the individual further: Each person must discover the meaning and purpose of his or her own life; and that requires a life of meditation and single-minded commitment to one's own projects. "Projects" is the correct word because existentialism is essentially spiritual alchemy.

Fully developed by the mid-twentieth century, existentialism, particularly as interpreted by Karl Jaspers and Martin Heidegger, acknowledged the longing of the individual to transcend nature and society in search of God—but, of course, not the God of the Hebraic–Christian tradition. Even so, theistic existentialists would suggest that the pursuit of the divine by each individual is the only source of human bonding in a societal context. The introspective character of individualness comes from rationalism's obsession with psychoanalysis.

The instant Locke, leading with his trump, slapped rasa on the tabula, he set off a mad rush of free thinking wannabees, each trying to figure out the parts and inner workings of the individual. Grammatically speaking, sentences no longer contained direct objects—they all stopped with indirect objects. Life became not what we do but what happens to us. During the past three centuries, the solutions have ranged from the crazy to the pathetic, making for a yammering cacophany of endless and confused debate. For example, the bitter argument over heredity versus environment was settled only by the advent of television.

Without question, the single greatest influence on the subject of human nature, the philosophy that has permeated every aspect of Western life in the twentieth century, is that of Sigmund Freud. His analytical approach to the human psyche not only wove rational science imperceptibly into the fabric of existence but gave life a defining texture otherwise lacking. He spun out a triple braid that could be integrated into the tapestry of being by the least experienced apprentice. Oversimplification is probably not possible, since by now his theory has become folklore: The id was the instinctive, natural part of the person; the ego, the mental; the superego, the spiritual. (This is beginning to sound like Greek—soma, psyche, pneuma.) Freud's philosophy gained quick and universal popularity, some would suggest because it could all be easily explained by good sex. And that explanation, it seems, is the basic flaw in the doctrine of individualness.

Nevertheless, individualness had become the dominant psychology of the United States by the end of the twentieth century because of two overpowering and adverse influences on the individual. One was the deluge of information, so called, being spewed from every pore in the regurgitative universe. It is surprising that too much information has the same effect as none at all—hysterical confusion. The curse of living in North America in the late 1990s was being always surrounded by frantically-moving, formless clusters of people, all of whom sounded like Kermit the Frog, prattling on and on about their databases and modems—showing theirs and wanting to see yours.

The second influence was the sudden rise and torrential currents in the flood of cultures all over the globe—especially in the free societies of the West. It was a cataclysm that threatened to sweep away the moorings of tradition, obliterate all recognizable historical or geographical signs of place, and destroy the individual identity that was predicated on the traditional values of the established culture. Because of its very nature, ironically, the most vulnerable of all was the culture of freedom, what had been Western civilization.

Within the broader Western society, the diverse cultures each consolidated its own, became unusually rigid and defensive, and seized every lapse in the cultures around it to leverage the whole society to its advantage. Hypersensitivity and rent-seeking made consensus a thing of the past. In a final irony, government became a club with which to beat upon others. The elimination of the person is an unavoidable consequence of social diversity. The pursuit of some kind of personal authentication, again the only avenue to meaning, led to the inside. The happy ones learned to be alone without feeling lonely and to find in solitude more meaning than the world around them could provide. Government and governance became, for them, an inconsequential farce played by fools and knaves on dark and rickety stages in an empty theater. Society—social organization of any kind—became irrelevant.

Since the overwhelming body of both natural and historical evidence proves the impossibility of the existence of democracy—either in philosophical concept or in practical construct—one must conclude that anywhere it is alleged to exist it is purely and simply a matter of perception and, therefore, either an illusion or a charade. The only consistent feature in the various interpretations is the blatant promise of the simultaneous advantage of each person over all the others. No other form of governance can make that statement, or would dare to do so. For example, in a monarchy, everyone else is better off; under communism, no one is better off than anyone else; under fascism, everyone is worse off. As a matter of fact, these distinctions are not heady political philosophy or well-crafted government mechanisms but conclusive proof of the kind of governance actually present. Now we know why both Plato and Aristotle argued that democracy is impossible.

NOTES

1. Plato, *The Rupublic*, trans. Francis MacDonald Conford (London: Oxford University Press, 1941), 282.

2. Ibid., 283.

3. John Stuart Mill, *On Liberty* (London: Longmans, Green and Company, 1887), 33.

4. Ibid., 36.

5. Ibid., 33.

6. Ibid., 34.

7. Ibid., 36.

8. Thomas Jefferson, Letter to William S. Smith, November 13, 1787, *Thomas Jefferson* (New York: Literary Classics of the United States, 1984), 911.

CHAPTER 21

The Making of Capitalism

> We can see at once that a society cannot hold wealth in honour and at the same time establish a proper self control in its citizens.
>
> Plato[1]

Capitalism did not spring fully developed from the mind of rationalistic science; that is to say, it did not simply appear suddenly as a complete, mature socioeconomic system. It was, however, the only logical economic conclusion in a dualistic, rationalistic universe. It was rationalism that engendered it, identified it, systematized it, and justified it.

First, the engendering. As the wave of individual liberty swept over Western civilization during the eighteenth century, it created at once both the expectation of and the necessity for individual economic freedom. That duality within itself is Hegelian; that is, the realization of individual economic freedom (any freedom, for that matter) is always in the fusion of expectation and necessity. In practical and historical terms, liberty meant that people, who for centuries had been locked in state-controlled economies, suddenly, with the prospect of personal freedom, discovered that economic freedom and political freedom are inextricably connected. Exactly what the connection is remains a matter of lingering debate. In fact, it is the one issue that defines "liberalism" and "conservatism"—the liberals believing that the two freedoms are mutually interdependent but severable, the conservatives declaring them the same thing. However that question is answered, it must deal eventually with the fundamental issue—the capability of both the individual and the *polis* to sustain themselves economically and the relationship between the two. Ulti-mately, it is this relationship that is the premise of all human organization.

It is not surprising, then, that in the Western world there was a striking similarity between the reformation of political systems and the shaping of economic systems. Democracy was the means by which political rule was transformed from monarches to elected rulers — but the net effect was that the individual was still ruled and the governance was still patriarchical. The only real change was that a few individuals were allowed to vote. And people were quite happy with that — ecstatic, as a matter of fact. They continue to celebrate it regularly, even to this day. So why would we expect anything other than that in the economic reformation?

Here, as with political reform, there was the ostensible intent to place the production and control of wealth in the hands of individuals, but there was simply neither the popular capacity nor the common will to do more than replicate the former system. The net effect was that authority-controlled eco-nomic systems became capital-controlled economies. The only difference for the individual, other than the capitalists themselves, was that now he or she, while still working for someone else, could acquire and spend money. Neverthe-less, the world changed irretrievably the day the question "What do you do?" was answered by a reference to one's employment and the question "What do you make?" was answered with a sum. It was the same day. Almost before anyone realized what was happening, capital became the commodity of personal free-dom. Probably more than anything else, this is the legacy of rationalism.

Second, the defining. Rationalism provided the nominal as well as the real definition of capitalism, even before it had a name, by establishing both its logical classification and its critical attributes. The classification was the con-text of a materialistic universe. Capitalism could never have arisen in a spiri-tual world. Newton's empiricism was an attempt to prove how natural laws work (God with us); rationalism was the attempt to explain how the forces of nature might work best for human beings who were, in fact, a part of the natural order of things (God once removed). Modern materialism, the cul-mination of empiricism and rationalism, attempted to explain everything in the universe, including both the individual and the collective action of hu-man beings, in purely physical terms without any reference at all to the su-pernatural or even the intellectual (God nonexistent). Human life thus became what natural conditions made it. In this kind of world, the innate self-interest of each person means one thing and one thing only: the struggle to accumulate enough material to satisfy personal needs and aspirations. Whereas humanism had first declared that the *summum bonum* was achiev-ing human perfection based on the best said, thought, and done by human beings and then finally admitted that the only perfection in a godless uni-verse was to be found in the material world, materialism declared up front that the best life a person could expect was one filled with material things and then — when "enough" proved to be a one-word oxymoron — admitted that survival was about the best a person could do. Capitalism was the natural convergence of humanism and materialism.

That was the context. The critical attributes of capitalism, however, would evolve only as two fundamental relationships were resolved: the relationship between human beings and the natural world in the production of material goods and the relationship between (not among) human beings in the control and use of those goods. This compound dualism is the essence of all economic systems. While none of these issues can ever be settled with precision, simply because all the relationships exist in a state of dynamic tension, it is the purported settlement among them that gives the names to the various economic systems—capitalism and socialism being the alleged polar opposites of the nineteenth and twentieth centuries.

Ironically, "evolution" is probably the most accurate term to describe the development of capitalism. The very earliest economic relationships contain many of its elements, and historians have long noted that the prefiguring of capitalism is the agrarian and artisan economies of ancient Egypt, Babylon, Carthage, Greece, and Rome. But it was only in the latter part of the Middle Ages that the rudiments of capitalism began to appear as a privatized version of mercantilism—an economic system based on nationalized commerce among and within cities, states, and countries. In the sixteenth and seventeenth centuries, most of the trading companies in England were chartered collective entrepreneurial enterprises undertaken by any number of stockholders invested for gain or loss in the venture, or, as they often proved, adventure.

However, it was not until the production of goods was "rationalized" that capitalism could exist as an economic system. That rationalization, which occurred between 1770 and 1840, is commonly known as the Industrial Revolution. The revolution essentially meant that, in the production of goods, human relationships with nature were brought into line with the application of scientific knowledge (technology), even though relationships between individuals and social institutions conspicuously lagged behind.

It is ironic that the originators of capitalism never used the term or even heard it. The word was coined in the late nineteenth century by opponents of individual economic freedom and was originally used rather perjoratively to describe those who invested wealth in the pursuit of more wealth ("capitalists"). The Scottish economist Adam Smith, in An Inquiry into the Nature and Causes of the Wealth of Nations (1776), simply used the popular rationalistic terms to discuss the emerging system. A libertarian of the first water, he wrote of the natural order of liberty as the only principle needed to liberate the productive forces of human beings from the shackles of governmental authority. His theory, based on the existence of a natural harmony in economic matters, advocated the acceptance of natural laws of economics without the interference of artifactual impositions. This doctrine is known today as laissez-faire economics. The natural order consisted of more than the mechanics of economics. He assumed that all economic activities would be subject to the natural laws of ethics that comport fairness rather than legal codes that exact justice.

The implication of this basic assumption obviously is that capitalism is more than an economic system; it constitutes a way of life, referred to by some historians as "capitalist civilization." It is important to note here that, in its purest form, capitalism has four critical attributes: private ownership of all the means of production, a free market, competition, and profit. These imperatives, albeit variously interpreted, would dictate the organization of Western civilization for almost three centuries.

Third, the systemizing. As production was rationalized, so was capitalism. In fact, capitalism is merely a rationalistic construct with the four critical attributes constituting its four dimensions. The first order of business was systematizing the private ownership of the property of production. The whole idea of capitalism was to conjoin the production of wealth (goods and products) and the control of wealth in the hands of the same individual(s). That idea was the first and last consideration of capitalism. At the outset, the only way such conjunction seemed possible was to unify work and ownership — a revolutionary idea for a civilization still predominently feudalistic in both its mentality and its economic practices. But the idea had been made compellingly logical by Locke, who reasoned that the ownership of property was not something to be granted by governmental authority or inherited by birth but earned by individual effort and initiative.

When the enterprise is small and the technology simple, capitalism seems to approximate both natural and ethical order. It was in that form that capitalism flourished in Europe and especially in the American colonies during the seventeenth and eighteenth centuries. Individual farmers, artisans, merchants, and artists were all owner–producers, and they controlled whatever revenue they produced. Their aim was to generate "income," commensurate with need and effort. Typically, they had neither the ambition nor the opportunity to create wealth. On a larger scale, but also fairly simple, were the trading companies. The differences were that these were joint efforts and were aimed at increasing the wealth of the investors. Two such notable companies were the Treasurer and Company of Adventurers and Planters of the City of London for the First Colony of Virginia, a joint-stock enterprise that authorized the voyage of the Mayflower, and the Hudson Bay Company (1670), which is still in existence.

The corporation model was to organization what industrialization was to production. The metaphor itself was not exactly new. The idea of an organization with collective ownership and with a life longer than any person can be traced as far back as the Ancient Greeks and Romans. For instance, the *collegium* and *universitas* included trading groups. As early as 1245 the Church, in an effort more clearly to articulate the concept, used the term *corpus* to suggest that individuals could incorporate themselves in a body, with many parts acting as one entity. Actually, the word was an easy, if not logical, choice:

The Church had always proclaimed itself as the body of Christ and tried to practice the concept in its own monasteries. But the commercial corporation was the first organization designed strictly for the production of material wealth. That was and is still its only purpose.

The first corporation in the New World was chartered on 8 January 1675. On that date, the New York Fishing Company was ordained by the Governor and Council of New York, acting for the Duke of York, for the purpose of "settling a fishery in these parts." The language of the charter is noteworthy in that it contains every structural aspect of the corporation model that is still prevalent over three hundred years later. It begins: "The Governor desiring and reserving by all fitting meanes in its power to promote and encourage cod fish fishing in these parts, and finding upon enquiry, and the best information and advise that the most probable meanes to effect it is by a company and joynt stock, both by the advice of his Councell allow and authorize the same."[2]

Shares of capital stock were £10 each. So much for the ownership of the means of production. But the charter goes on to establish the specific architecture of the company and (by necessary inference, even though the word is not used), the corporation: "that upon the 9th of February, every member of the said company, or his sufficient deputy, shall meet together at New Yorke to consent and by the plurality of votes make all orders, rules, and officers, and so from time to time, and take all accounts for the managing, improving, and ordering all things relating to said company and joynt stock of above, for the said fishery."[3]

It is said that old habits are hard to break, and it is clear that the corporation was little more than a replication of the feudal system. There are only two significant differences. First, the ownership of production was transferred from the king to private capitalists. Second, there was a specific delineation of control mechanisms—"orders," "rules," and "officers"—all aimed at "managing," "improving," and "ordering." In fact, the language of the first paragraph, the preamble, is the language of command; the language of the second paragraph that of control. But there is something to be learned here other than the origin and character of the corporation: That is, private property exists only by the good grace of government, which therefore remains the grand patron in every case. Private property is always a privilege, never a right.

There are two very critical considerations of this arrangement, each presenting a fascinating implicit dichotomy. First, the capitalistic corporation did not, and could not, fully realize the idea of unifying the production of wealth with the control of wealth. The labor of those who worked in the organization for fee, wage, or salary was generally without benefit of either ownership or control or share of the proceeds. And the larger the organization, the less significant any individual worker. Second, the system of fundamental government patronage meant that as corporations become more complex economically, legally, and socially, government and corporations would become so interrelated that by the end of the twentieth century they would be virtually indistinguishable and would often actually exchange roles—with government attempting to produce wealth and corporations attempting to control its distribution. It is worth recalling here that the political freedom and the economic freedom of the individual may be the same.

The rationalization of free markets was undertaken with the bare-faced assumption that natural systems require systemization. Thus, there would appear ultimately the unlikely prospect of controlling free enterprise. Even though this end could have been predicted, capitalism did not begin that way. Adam Smith, the champion of the free market, reasoned that trade and commerce were merely a part of the natural order of things and that nature was therefore quite sufficient within itself to sustain order in the commercial activities of human beings. He counselled laissez-faire because he knew from experience the inherent tendency of government to impose artificial rules and regulations to direct or enhance natural forces. And he believed that no matter how well intended the interference might be, or how logical, any attempt whatsoever to meddle with the processes and interactions of natural laws would always result in uncontrollable, expansive disruption—always adverse, usually perverse.

NOTES

1. Plato, *The Republic*, trans. Francis MacDonald Conford (London: Oxford University Press, 1941), 280.

2. New York Fishing Company Charter, New York State Library, A1894, vol. 24: 67B.

3. Ibid.

CHAPTER 22

Capitalism and the Corporation

Since capitalist enterprise, by its very achievements, tends to automatize progress, we conclude that it tends to make itself superfluous — to break to pieces under the pressure of its own success.

Joseph Alois Schumpeter[1]

Pure capitalism, as defined by rationalistic science, can have only one real system. And it is a simple one: supply and demand; or more accurately, demand and supply. This natural dualism within the economic universe is the dynamic stasis of capitalism. No concept ever suffers from simplification; but it is seldom the purpose of science to reduce the pain inherent in any idea. So the idea of free market has always been a challenge for rationalism because freedom of any kind requires not the creation of a system but the construction of a nonsystem or, perhaps more precisely, an antisystem. Smith's theory was simple if not naive: If producers had freedom of occupation and enterprise and were left alone to produce and if users were left alone to use, there would always be an inexorable propensity toward perfect market balance. It must be remembered that the context of his supposition was the agricultural economy of Scotland in the eighteenth century.

But what if the balance is seen as a process? And what if an attempt is made by government or capitalists to control either the products in question or the rate and exchange of production and use? The question becomes one of cause and effect. The great debate over which is which fueled the bitter animosity between demand economies and consumer economies during the nineteenth and twentieth centuries. From all indications, Smith intended to suggest that there was a simple quid-pro-quo interaction between production of goods and use of goods. It was more a matter of inherent relationship—of mutual (Hegelian) definition. Rather than supply stimulating demand or demand creating supply, the idea was the honest acknowledgment that all the supply in the world is merely inventory until someone is willing to purchase it; and demand is only need or want until there is availability and accessibility.

Actually, the free market was a practice not altogether uncommon in earlier economies dominated by land and labor. In an agrarian economy, the primary resource is land, and the agent of transformation in the production of wealth is labor. That which is produced is used up, thus creating a constant demand–supply situation even in commodity futures. In this system, bartering (on a small scale) and trading (on a larger scale) were, in effect, demonstrations of supply and demand in action. But something happens when the primary resource is capital and the transforming agent is rationalized process. The natural order is upset on both counts.

Capital is simply wealth deployed for the purpose of creating more wealth. Assets, on the other hand, represent wealth accumulated and stored. Obviously, the first problem is that there can never be enough wealth produced. This is the original vicious cycle. In agrarian language, somehow the barn seems to grow larger than the largest crop. The demand always exceeds the supply. The demand is for more capital to produce more wealth. No natural law here. The second problem is that when a society commits itself to capital as the wellspring of life on the planet, it puts itself in the precarious situation of having created, and locked itself into, a totally unnatural life-support system that, perversely, requires its life to sustain. No natural law here, either. So it seems the real issue in this matter of the free market system is not government interference but the inescapable captivation of capitalism.

In discussing the systemization of competition, one is tempted merely to reduce it to one word—war. (According to Karl von Clausewitz, "Rather than comparing [war] to art we could more accurately compare it to commerce, which is also a conflict of human interests and activities."[2]) But that would be fair to neither the art of warfare nor military science. They have a nobility, a sense of honor, and even a beauty not to be found in capitalistic competition. Furthermore, war has been described as brief episodes of confused, terrifying life-and-death combat separated by long intervals of boredom. Competition is exactly the opposite: sustained intense struggle over long periods of time, interrupted by occasions of tedium. Capitalism is competition. Without competition, the notion of private ownership is an enigmatic question, and the idea of free market is an inexplicable answer.

There is a curious last paragraph in the charter of the New York Fishing Company. It reads almost like an afterthought: "that this Company bee not understood anywayes to debarre or hinder other Person or Persons, from fishing by themselves, or in Companyes, as they see fit."[3] It is unclear whether this proviso represents mere beneficence of the governor, encouragement for similar commercial exploits, or the prophecy that sooner or later other enterprises would arise purporting to supply the same goods, products, or services to the same customers. If the last possibility was the intent, then this was the original definition of competition in a capitalistic context. It is the context, however, that requires elaboration.

Capitalistic competition as a system is based on four principles: marketplace, variableness of value, mass advantage, and survival of the fittest. Regarding the first, the assumption is that there is an economic dynamic beyond the basic natural law of supply and demand. Also, it exists even outside the bounds of the omnipotent state, which attempts to dictate every aspect of the production and consumption of goods; and furthermore, it transcends everyday custom and usage, which is, for the most part, oblivious to controls of any kind.

The marketplace, whether geographically or intellectually situated, is the continuous chatter that attempts to settle the conflict (a deal) between producers and consumers. There is no way to limit the cacophony and usually no way to tell who is talking and who is listening. Yet, the whole act of competing revolves around something referred to as "market share." "Market" means that the kind and size of the marketplace can be known by analyzing and aggregating its various segments; and "share" implies the possibility of winning or capturing all, or most of, at least one segment. The former is ascertained either by primordial wild-ass guessing (premanagement), prediction (in-vitro management), or scientific research (postmanagement). All are equally reliable. Market dominance is achieved by throwing everything into it. And that, as a matter of fact, raises the only consistent feature of the marketplace: it absorbs in direct proportion to what it dispenses. Stated simply, it takes exactly what it gives. That is the only settlement: Such a paradox should not be unexpected in a dualistic universe of equals and opposites.

Settlement is possible only when value is variable. So, variableness of value is the second principle of capitalistic competition. The choice of the word "value" rather than "worth" is deliberate, for one simple reason: There can be value without worth but no worth without value. This is the axiom of the marketplace. Fixed values, if that were possible, would mean fixed prices; fixed prices remove even the prospect of competition because the marketplace is destroyed. So strong is the variability of value that when governments or corporations attempt, for whatever reason, to fix prices, the marketplace fades to black.

Five forces energize the value of any given good, product, or service at any given time; and the convergence of these forces yields of the value of the good, product, or service. First, there is the force of need, whether basic and continuous or driven by events or circumstances and therefore temporary. Second is the very compulsion of desire, fundamentally an emotional compulsion that demands satisfaction. Third, there is the circumstance of scarcity that establishes a positive correlation between availability and value. Fourth is the power of discrimination according to quality, an undefinable certainty totally dependent on comparison and thus subject to the variability of changing lenses. Finally, there is the tension of with–without contrast, typically an exercise by which preference is decided in advance and value is validated in retrospect.

The principle of mass advantage is the dubious yet irresistible promise of capitalistic competition. Just as surely as philosophical rationalism gave rise to materialism, cultural rationalism led to consumerism. The basic assumption is that all persons have an individual and collective right to unrestricted choice of the best possible goods and products and that this kind of mass consumption, both quantitatively and qualitatively, is possible only with mass production or, perhaps more accurately, production by the masses. That is to say, everyone must be free, either alone or in concert with others, to engage in any enterprise, subject to all the inherent risks and rewards. Of course, this circumstance could mean a tendency toward an overabundance of poor-quality goods at high prices. Because there is ultimately a necessary equalization of production and consumption and because there is relative equality in bargaining power within and between producers and consumers, that does not happen.

In effect, there is the same tension between producers and consumers that is found in competition. In the mid-twentieth century, John Kenneth Galbraith wrote about something he referred to as "countervailing power" on the demand side of the equation when the purchasing clout of suppliers becomes a factor. But the real countervailing power is the natural give and take between producers and users. So the actual result is fewer and fewer producers and more and better products at comparatively low prices. It is just another triumph of the law of equal and opposite actions.

The fourth principle of competition is survival, and for good reason. The marketplace is dispassionate and unforgiving. Those intrepid souls who enter the fray as producers do so strictly at their own risk. Once there, they must continue to meet or exceed the constantly increasing demands of a volatile environment or they will cease to exist: the only two options are grow or die. It is interesting to note that just about the time that the marketplace idea was catching on, Charles Darwin was developing his theory of natural selection— the survival of the fittest. As a matter of fact, that phrase has real meaning in a market economy. Survival is about the most one can hope for because the market itself is never satisfied with either quantity or quality; so "fittest" describes those whose entrepreneurial inventions best fit the demands at a specific time and place. And it also emphasizes the fact that scarcity is the primal condition of competition. Capitalism is the only economic system that thrives on scarcity; therefore, if capitalists do not find scarcity, they create it.

This imperative means that stasis is impossible. Production enterprises are continually either diminishing or developing, with more always diminishing than developing. So the many soon are reduced to the few, but the fewer and fewer wax stronger and stronger, ultimately to the point of being able to dominate the marketplace by controlling all the other factors of competition. This is monopoly.

In practical terms, there is no difference between the control of the economy by monopoly (de facto power) and the control of the economy by the government (de jure authority). The irony of the situation is that the principle of survival, if left to run its own course, inevitably destroys the marketplace, either by eliminating producers or by turning them into surrogate governments.

The working of the same dynamic both destroys production enterprises and creates monopolies. The effect on people is the same in either case. Actually, there are four such effects; and, not surprisingly, all are contrary to the original intent of capitalism. First, human beings, whether those within the enterprise itself or consumers, are considered and treated as resources; that is, as something that must be used up in the struggle to ensure the survival of the enterprise. Second, there is an inevitable separation of producers and users, especially in terms of credible pricing and availability. In fact, as the gap widens, it is typically filled by other nonproducer, nonconsumer enterprises known as suppliers, who rely on volume buying and selling to guarantee their own survival. Third, whether the production enterprise grows toward monopoly, the individual's freedom of occupation is compromised, often to the point of no freedom at all. Any assertive effort by those within the enterprise—say, as in collective action (unions)—usually succeeds only in making the system even more intractable, a rigidity without any relevance to the requirements of the production enterprise (featherbedding). Fourth, there is an inverse pressure between internal production necessities and external production controls: Specifically, once individual producers (workers) become a third party, they are caught between regressive incentives and progressive restraints.

The conclusion of the matter of competition is simple: An actual competition-based economy is impossible because it either self-destructs or is taken over by external regulatory authority such as a government. That seems only fair; any system based on destroying others always destroys itself. Historically speaking, that would have already happened in Western capitalistic societies (and, in fact, probably has) were it not for the intervention of democratic government which, acting strictly in its own best interest, publicly presumes to protect the losers and constrain the winners and privately conspires to fund its own mischief. Thus, the whole concept of free-market competition is rendered academic, and the practice is farce.

The genius of rationalization is at its creative best in the systemization of profit. As with all the other artifacts of the modern world, rationalism did not invent the idea of profit; but it took rationalism to make profit a real business. The practice of profit is, of course, very old. Even the earliest trade and commerce was intended to do more than merely break even. All the private expeditions undertaken from the Middle Ages through the nineteenth century were aimed at generating profit. A whole merchant class grew up around the single principle of profit; but with the rise of capitalism and the consequential creation of organizations whose only purpose was the creation of wealth, an entirely new system, if not definition, of profit was born.

The corporation model requires that the collective production of individuals be of considerably less value to them than it is to the ultimate users of their goods and products. Essentially, workers agree to sell their production to the corporation at a price far below market value. Within this margin, the corporation finds the wherewithal to finance its own future exploits and reward its investors. This system is a paradigm of practicality if for no other reason than the condition that none of the individual producers employed in the corporation's activities could have ever been as productive (hence, never as individually profitable — in terms of wages and salaries) as he or she could be within the corporation. And it is precisely balanced; in the world of numbers, there is never any gain without the exactly corresponding loss.

It is this balance that the commercial corporation must be able to control if it is to survive. From this perspective, it is the organization itself caught at the pressure point — attempting, on the one hand, to be competitive in the marketplace and, on the other, necessarily having to minimize the cost of production. It is a jabberwocky snicker-snack. Profit requires bringing to the marketplace the highest quality goods at the lowest price; at the same time, profit requires maximum efficiency in the forces of production, efficiency that is potentially contrary to both high quality and current market value. Because of this dire circumstance, corporations have no choice but to consider those people employed in its purpose as resources to be used up — not as sources to be developed, and never as producers to be rewarded according to individual merit but as components paid strictly within the parameters of the corporation's own financial priorities. Those employed within the corporation must somehow maintain their own value-producing capability, or they are quickly scuttled because they are no longer profitable to the corporation.

The capitalistic system of profit raises two issues that, although fundamental to the concept itself, have yet to be seriously addressed, much less resolved. Either threatens to destroy capitalism. They are the dependence of individual producers on the corporation-model organization for their personal economic well-being, and the accounting of profit to non-wealth-producing (that is, only revenue-generating services) enterprises. The result of the first is entropy — unless cut short by abandonment; the result of the second is eventual economic implosion. So it seems that the whole capitalistic system, like profit, depends on an impossibly fine margin.

Finally, rationalism provided the justification of capitalism. It did so not by justifying all aspects of capitalism but by justifying only one — profit. That was the only logical approach. Private ownership of the means of production, free markets, and competition simply do not resonate with the moral implications of profit. In fact, those features of capitalism are not within themselves moral issues, other than, perhaps, private ownership. It was also the only fair approach. As the swashbuckling corporate pursuit of profit ran rampant in the nineteenth century, the lingering influence of the Christian religion — although decimated by hundreds of factions — demanded, from habit or genuine conviction, that consciences somehow be assuaged. After all, unfair advantage in commercial activities (usury, for example) had been once considered a sin.

The rationalistic solution was marvelous, indeed—and two-sided, a veritable trompe l'oeil: Turn science into religion and religion into science. From the left came Herbert Spencer (British) and his acolytes, declaring the justice of profit as being consistent with natural order. And from the right came William Graham Sumner (American) and his disciples, proclaiming the natural virtue of profit. When they had done, profit never looked so good. Conscience, as well as the world, was cleansed. Pillage, loot, and plunder became evils of the heathenistic past. David Hume had already noted (early in the eighteenth century), with some admiration, that avarice is the "spur" of industry. But it took a while for the general public to appreciate the nobility inherent in greed.

Spencer was a civil engineer who through his unlikely simultaneous study of hydrotechnics and Malthusian population theory developed the idea of evolution. According to Spencer, "Evolution is the progressive integration of matter accompanied by dissipation of motion; and dissolution is the disorganization of matter accompanied by the acceleration of motion."[4] Mark him as a monist in substance, a dualist in kind. Because of something he called "the persistence of force," any kind of homogeneity in the universe is impossible, since the different effects of that force cause differences to arise within any and all things. For that reason, it is natural for more and more complex systems to evolve continuously into progressively higher orders. As that progression occurs, naturally the simpler systems would be sloughed off. This natural selection within human society resulted in something he termed "survival of the fittest."[5] By that term he meant the calculated adaptation of an organism to the forces of nature. On second thought, mark him as a monist in substance, a pluralist in kind. It was only through the persistence of force that the human race had progressed from the earliest primitive states because only the best of each generation had survived.

It is somewhat ironic that Spencer, while confining his theory to human beings, left open the door for Charles Darwin to systemize the spectacular, and earth-shaking, universal application of the theory of evolution. Spencer was an inveterate optimist. Ebullient and personable, he was the personification of the gospel he preached. He believed, much like the humanists before him, that human perfection is possible—if not in all individuals, then most assuredly in human society. Surprisingly, according to him, evolution had a final state ("Evolution has an impassable limit")[6] which he called "equilibration" or equilibrium. This means that an organism ends in death. However, human society, because of human will and intelligence, finally achieves a stable, harmonious state. "Evolution can end only in the establishment of the greatest perfection and most complete happiness."[7] Utopia is no longer fantasy; it is science.

The preface to his *Data of Ethics* bore evidence of the ethical concern he would later very succinctly confess: "My ultimate purpose . . . has been that of finding for the principles of right and wrong in conduct at large, a scientific basis."[8] In his essay *Social Statics* he called for a return to the natural rights of each person and proclaimed that doctrine as the only ethical standard. But, further, he maintained that fundamental to all ethics is that "adaptation" of the human character to the conditions of life. The root of all evil is "non-adaptation of constitution to conditions."[9] Those who do not or cannot adapt—the unfit—will be eliminated by natural process. "The whole effort of nature is to get rid of such, to clear the world of them, and make room for better."[10] The egalitarian implications of democracy, and the ambition of Jeremy Bentham to bring the greatest good to the greatest number of people, amounted to invidious condescension to the unequal and the unfit—an affront to logic and contrary to natural law.

Spencer's appeal was far greater in America than in England—and for good reason. America needed him to justify the abusive exploitation, uncontrolled competition, and economic discrimination that characterized the postbellum industrial era in a nation still struggling with its own conscience. Spencer reconciled the opposites with one word. When it came to the troubling question of the day, the question of the conflict between science and religion, Spencer gave an inspired answer; that is, science is always subordinated to the "unknowable."

That sounded enough like God for the likes of John D. Rockefeller and Andrew Carnegie who, suffering under the guilt of wealth and greatly offended by the cynical have-not accusation that every great fortune is built on an equally great crime, were anxious to become converts—yea, even evangelists—for the gospel of wealth. And preach they did. It is providential that Rockefeller's memorable "American Beauty Rose" speech was delivered to a Sunday school class: "The growth of a large business is merely a survival of the fittest. . . . The American Beauty rose can be produced in the splendor and fragrance which bring cheer to its beholder only by sacrificing the early buds which grow up around it. This is not an evil tendency in business. It is merely the working out of a law of nature and a law of God."[11] And a doting Carnegie effused in his autobiography this lachrymose panegeric to esurience:

I remember that light came as in a flood and all was clear. Not only had I got rid of theology and the supernatural, but I had found the truth of evolution. "All is well since all grows better," became my motto, my true source of comfort. Man was not created with an instinct for his own degradation, but from the lower he had risen to the higher forms. Nor is there any conceivable end to his march to perfection. His face is turned to the light; he stands in the sun and looks upward.[12]

But for all Spencer's saving grace, it was William Graham Sumner, a preacher, who ultimately established the scientific ethic of capitalism. Sumner graduated from Yale in 1857, two years before Darwin's *Origin of Species* appeared. Given by both upbringing and his university curriculum to the serious and vigorous study of theology, he seemed drawn inexorably into the heated social debates of the later part of the nineteenth century. In his *Study of Sociology*—he invented the term as well as the science—he boldly attempted a synthesis of the three traditions of Western culture: Christian morality, laissez-fare economics, and Spencer's doctrine of survival of the fittest; according to most critics and industrialists, he succeeded as well as anyone could. His doctrine assumed that the industrious, temperate, frugal family man of the Puritan work ethic was the same as the strong or the "fittest" in the struggle for existence (which struggle he acknowledged as a fact of life). Overlying that assumption was the acceptance of laissez-faire economics as a kind of determinism that was at once both naturalistic and Calvinistic.

There was no greater Christian apologist for capitalism than Sumner—for that matter, no greater apologist of any persuasion. He assumed unequivocally the inherent morality of capitalism, in terms of both individual achievement and social advancement. Human progress is moral progress, and moral progress is essentially the development of the economic universe. "Let every man be sober, industrious, prudent and wise and bring up his children to be likewise, and poverty will be abolished in a few generations,"[13] he prophesied. The greatest asset in the universal struggle for survival is the production of capital because capital is the only source of the progressive development of civilization. This accumulation of wealth is tangible evidence of being God's elect. Millionaires are the bloom of a competitive civilization:

The millionaires are a product of natural selection, acting on the whole body of men to pick out those who can meet the requirement of certain work to be done. . . . It is because they are thus selected that wealth—both their own and that entrusted to them—aggregates under their hands. . . . They may fairly be regarded as the naturally selected agents of society for certain work. They get high wages and live in luxury, but the bargain is a good one for society. There is the intensest competition for their place and occupation. This assures us that all who are competent for this function will be employed in it, so that the cost of it will be reduced to the lowest terms.[14]

Furthermore, according to Sumner, social advance depends on hereditary wealth, accumulated by families over generations. Any attack on hereditary wealth would eventually turn out to be an attack on the family and would, if pressed, reduce men to "swine." Only if the fittest are allowed continuously to increase their wealth does the whole society benefit—not from noblesse oblige or from moral obligation but as a natural consequence of wealth in the hands of capitalists. Successful capitalists are the servants of human progress, and to serve rightfully they must trample under foot the weak, the ignorant, the defenseless, and the unfit. In fact, the expeditious elimination of these unfortunates is God's will. Any regret over their loss or suffering is pure sentimentality. Any attempt at elementary or charitable assistance is a waste of energy and contrary to natural (God's) law. The moral contradiction inherent within capitalism was sometimes rather pathetically revealed. Somehow, there is an implicit sadness in the following contrast of value:

Paradise	State of Tennessee
	Charter of Incorporation
Papa, won't you take me back to Muhlenburg County	Be it known, that W. R. Cole, E. R. Lindsey, Edward T. Sanford, Bolton Smith, and George Tillman are hereby constituted a body politic and corporate by the name and style of
Down by the green river where paradise lay.	
I'm sorry, my son, but you're too late in asking,	
Mr. Peabody's coal trucks have hauled it away.	"George Peabody Colleges for Teachers"

Paradise

*Papa, won't you take me back to
   Muhlenburg County*

*Down by the green river where paradise
lay.*

*I'm sorry, my son, but you're too late in
asking,*

*Mr. Peabody's coal trucks have hauled it
away.*

John Prine
© RCA 1972

State of Tennessee
Charter of Incorporation

Be it known, that W. R. Cole, E. R. Lindsey, Edward T. Sanford, Bolton Smith, and George Tillman are hereby constituted a body politic and corporate by the name and style of

"George Peabody Colleges
for Teachers"

for the purpose of establishing, conducting, and maintaining in the State a college or educational institution for the higher education of teachers.

State of Tennessee
Davidson County
30th September, 1909

It is quite understandable then that by the end of the nineteenth century, at least in the United States, profit and wealth were proclaimed in mainstream churches as not only naturally right within themselves, but undeniable indicators of righteousness. In fact, Protestantism was willingly adopted as the spiritual godfather of capitalism and became its greatest benefactor and one of its greatest beneficiaries. Thus, the church's ancient battle with evil was won by evolution. There is no place for evil in a rationalistic universe.

It should be noted here, for the sake of historical accuracy, that the amalgamation of Spencer's idea of survival of the fittest and Sumner's doctrine of the virtue of profit created an economic ethic uniquely characteristic of North America. The phrase "Protestant capitalism" may be redundant, but that ethic and its correlate, the famous "work ethic," by sheer force of greed and the natural seductiveness of materialism, not to mention the base yearnings of human nature, soon became the object of envy or scorn in all the other versions of Western civilization, especially in countries where neither the politics (nondemocratic) nor the religion (non-Protestant) would allow that ethic to flourish.

The people of Western civilization, especially those of North America, ought to take great comfort in the knowledge that there is at least one thing upon which their religion and their science agree.

NOTES

1. Joseph Alois Schumpeter, *Capitalism, Socialism, and Democracy* (New York: Harper and Row, 1942), 134.

2. Karl von Clausewitz, *On War*, ed. Michael Howard and Peter Paret (Princeton, N.J.: Princeton University Press, 1976), 149.

3. New York Fishing Company Charter, New York State Library, A1894, 24: 67B.

4. Herbert Spencer, *First Principle* (New York: D. Appleton, 1864), 407.

5. Herbert Spencer, "A Theory of Population Deduced from the General Law of Animal Fertility," *Westminster Review* 57 (1852): 499–500.

6. Spencer, *First Principle*, 496.

7. Ibid., 530.

8. Herbert Spencer, *Data of Ethics* (Kila, Mont.: Kessinger Publishing, 1998), 1: 31.

9. Herbert Spencer, *Social Statics* (New York: D. Appleton, 1864), 79–80.

10. Ibid.

11. William J. Ghent, *Our Benevolent Feudalism* (New York: Macmillan, 1902), 29.

12. Andrew Carnegie, *Autobiography of Andrew Carnegie* (Boston: privately printed, 1920), 327.

13. William Graham Sumner, *The Challenge of Facts and Other Essays* (New Haven: Yale University Press, 1914), 109.

14. William Graham Sumner, *Essays of William Graham Sumner* (New Haven: Yale University Press, 1934), 68.

CHAPTER 23

The Assertion of Behaviorism

And that . . . is the secret of happiness and virtue—liking what you've got to do. All conditioning aims at that: making people like their inescapable social destiny.

Aldous Huxley[1]

Behaviorism might accurately be described as the culmination of rationalism. It was the ultimate expression of the philosophy that three hundred years earlier had declared human reason the new organum of science. As it became the dominant mentality of Western civilization, eventually pervading every aspect of that society, it, more than any other single influence determined the nature of human organization in general and the corporation in particular, not from a purely abstract point of view about system design but as the practical necessity of accommodating the diminished human being that the philosophy itself had produced.

It is difficult to tell whether the corporation-model organization simply responded pragmatically to the practical exigencies accompanying limited human capacity or actually promulgated the conditioning. The answer, most likely, is that it did both. But one thing is certain: It did nothing to encourage the development of the innate power of human beings. On the contrary, it capitalized on their incapacity. Even the education and training, indigenous to the society at large, that ostensibly was designed to serve the interests of the corporation-model organization, conformed the human to the restrictions of artifactual systems.

Everything about the internal workings of the corporation—from its organizational design, to its production methodologies and measures, to its authoritarian way of getting work done through people, to its concept of "human resources," to its understanding of motivation and reward—everything was an unapologetic manifestation of the principles of behavioral science. That is why it is critical in this larger discussion of the decline of the corporation-model organization to consider fully the implications of the assumptions made by this philosophy.

Behaviorism is the science of creating people in their own image. Far more than a school of thought having to do with the discipline of psychology, behaviorism represents a world view or, more precisely, a view of humanity. An absolute declaration of the human condition, it contained its own epistemology and ontology. As such, it is the ultimate paradox of rationalism. Bacon's *Novum Organum* had rapturously touted human reason as the instrument by which human beings could take command of the world around them and thus enter the kingdom of God. Behaviorism, the historical if not logical progeny of rationalism, declared the mind of little or no importance in the organism's desperate attempt to survive by adapting to the natural and social forces of a godless world. Humanism promised the perfectibility of the human being, even if in materialistic terms; behaviorism advanced the concept of continuous evolution of higher orders as determined by their ability to adjust to a progressively more complex environment. Democracy declared the individual the end of society; behaviorism decreed social structure the end of the individual. Capitalism assumed humans to be economic animals; behaviorism was predicated on their inherent animalism.

Some schools claim that the basic tenets of behaviorism are foreshadowed in the objectivism of Greece before Socrates. That may well be. After all, science is the art of making old ideas real. But the modern philosophy (some would say program) emerged only with the advent of Spencer's doctrine of survival of the fittest. But it was Charles Darwin who would become the Melchizedek of behaviorism. He ascended to this unique priestly office by taking Spencer's fundamental idea of survival through adaptation and adapting it so it could fit all the possible experiences, conditions, and circumstances of living things. The title of his revolutionary book is a thesis in itself: *On the Origin of Species by Means of Natural Selection, or The Preservation of Favored Races in the Struggle for Life.* Although Darwin, as a naturalist, was content in this work to concentrate on biological phenomena in the animal kingdom (there is only one allusion to human evolution), he did, in fact, establish the case for what would later be popularly known as "biological determinism"; and that philosophy would presently become the single-source explanation for all things pertaining to being human. His evidence and proofs were so compelling that this philosophy ultimately either engendered or captured all modern human sciences. It alone provided the logical underpinnings and validation for the work of Thomas B. Watson (the first behaviorist),

Ivan Pavlov (the inventor of conditioning), and Sigmund Freud (the guru of psychoanalysis).

By 1940, behaviorism was the unrivaled dominant intellectual force in Western culture, not only pervading and infusing every human science but also ruling all political, cultural, educational, and even religious expressions of civilization and providing the rationale for all facets of human organization, from the design of the system to the treatment of the individual. Any idea to the contrary was considered, paradoxically enough, either antiintellectual or culturally unsophisticated. Bacon's *Novum Organum* had finally had its way with humanity, and, in the process, human beings had become more or less. While it is true that behaviorism did not become a coherent influence until after the corporation model was fully developed, it became the corporation's one and only psychology. Correspondingly, it remained the dominant influence on Western civilization until the twenty-first century.

Although behaviorism was the result, historically and logically, of the evolution of rational philosophy over a period of almost three hundred years, when it emerged, with psychology, as a full-blown system in the early twentieth century (c. 1912), it was radically counter to the lingering popular Christian–Platonic notions of the nature of human beings, humankind's place in the universe, and each individual's hope in an ideal world. Behaviorism, like all other human sciences, could exist only in a godless universe. This confrontation was the final stage of the war implicit in the dualism of the universe, and faith was no match for empiricism. In fact, behaviorism would prove to be science's doomsday device against the axis powers of Christianity and Hellenism.

As often with warfare, it is impossible to know for sure whether it was a masterful diversionary strategy, brilliantly developed and executed by the cunning of science, or just the typical myopic misapprehension and hysterical confusion of religion that gave behaviorism an unconditional victory. But this much is for sure: The forces of Western religion, united as never before, mobilized to fight a war of words over the idea of natural evolution of the human being. After several skirmishes of blood-curdling beöts, hurled insults, and chilling invectives, a major battle—the famous Scopes trial (1925)—was decisively carried by science. But the victory, either mercifully or calculatingly, was not pressed, nor was peace made. So, the conflict continued, with the hostilities devolving into frenzied episodes of Tourette-like paroxysms over strange intellectual mutations such as "creation science," and other issues such as separation of church and state, abortion, and values-based public education. All the while, the real war had been over ideas; and science had long since captured the mind and heart of the Western world—and its organization.

The conflict between religion and behaviorism is best understood in terms of contrast. There are six categories of opposing assumptions—assumptions that once accepted quickly become rigid principles governing all human conduct and all human enterprise. These categories, here rather finely drawn, are of course closely interrelated; but each makes its own profound assertion about what it means to be human. The categorical contrasts, arranged in ascending order, are

- conditioning versus conscience
- stimulus versus thought
- objective versus subjective
- need versus conviction
- physical versus metaphysical
- survival versus purpose

The first three deal with the fundamental nature of the person; the fourth concerns the nature of reality for the human being; and the last two address the ultimate capacity of the person. Each was an assault on human beings.

NOTE

1. Aldous Huxley, *Brave New World* (New York: Harper and Row, 1946), 17.

CHAPTER 24

Behaviorism and
the Nature of the Person

Man is amazing, but he is not a masterpiece. . . . Perhaps the artist was a
little mad. Eh? What do you think? Sometimes it seems to me that man
is come from where he is not wanted, where there is no place for him;
for if not, why should he want all the place.

Joseph Conrad[1]

The modern corporation-model organization, especially after 1940, generally
held a rather limited view of the human being. Fundamentally, it assumed
that motivation was accomplished only by appeals to basic physical and economic needs. It was almost as if the speculations of an earlier generation had
been validated by a respectable science. Human beings were indeed both
"economic animals" and "vital machines." As late as the 1990s, convention
programs of the American Society of Training Directors still featured discussions about worker motivation that were based strictly on the premise that
people are primarily moved by either hope or fear, reward or punishment—
provoked by external stimuli.

SURVIVAL VERSUS PURPOSE

The idea of survival of the fittest not only was a fundamental assumption of
rationalistic science, it also became the signature of behaviorism. All of
behaviorism's other characteristics bear the impression of this principle. For
it is true that the objective of life always establishes the parameters of living.
There are three such parameters implicit in the doctrine of survival of the

fittest, and each can be stated to a single word—adaptation, validation, and limitation. Taken together, they constitute a complete psychology.

Adaptation, as the operative word of survival of the fittest, implies that the locus of control is always outside the human being, that the ultimate terms of survival are dictated by mechanistic natural forces, and that success in living—even life itself—is achieved by discovering the way the world works and becoming a part of the works. At best, humans are reactive, anxious beings prone to expect little and complain much. The practical implications of this philosophy are severe, ranging from a personal attitude of "I go where I'm pushed," to collective acquiescence in the face of unfavorable circumstances, to violence as a natural adpative response. No matter what happens, the person becomes a victim of circumstance, even of his or her own past or present natural urges. There is no cause other than condition. Conditions determine the action of the person; the person does not control conditions. The net effect is that the only hope is in luck, fate, chance, and magic. In fact, the mindset is such that victimization becomes a self-fulfilling prophecy. If any initiative is ever attempted, it is always without any sense of responsibility; and irresponsibility renders self-respect no more possible for a human than for an amoeba. Neither creature can be self-made. The opposite of adaptation is creation. Adaptation may require creativity, but creation is quite another matter. Creation is much more than ingenuity; it assumes that purpose, control, and responsibility are all within the aegis of the person. Unfortunately, none of these powers can be verified by empirical evidence, so for the rationalist they do not exist.

Validation results from the various attempts to survive that actually work—typically, those tactics that suceed for the individual at a specific time and place. Historical accumulation of experience is of little consequence as a guide to success but serves only as laboratory record from which human behavior can be predicted on the basis of precedence—analytically or scientifically. The only thing that matters is the organism's immediate adaptive response to current conditions. This philosophy is the basis of pragmatism and its more sophisticated correlative, the "scientific method." Practically, it is more than a mere expedient; it is raised to an ethic. Survival becomes the means as well as the end of life. Therefore, the old question of whether the end justifies the means is moot. The opposite of empirical validation is morality—principles of living as human beings—principles that presuppose the supremacy of the spiritual universe over things natural, and of right and wrong as absolutes built into the cosmos.

Limitation is inherent in fitting. Even though the superlative is always used ("fittest") and even though the advancement of the species is insured by the constant competition among them, the height of aspiration is necessarily determined by external measures. No matter how fit the organism, the most it can do is survive. Even if survival is defined in terms of continually increasing standards of living, there is always a corresponding elevation in the demands on the human being merely to stay alive. Success means coping. Distress is the way of life. The opposite of limitation is the will—the capacity to imagine, commit, and do. If there is will, there is no limit other than the will itself. Herein lies the most serious vulnerability of human beings—the capability of willing themselves into extinction.

PHYSICAL VERSUS METAPHYSICAL

The separation of the two was either a plausible misunderstanding or editorial license. To this day, it is not clear whether Aristotle's publisher intended "meta-physical" to be instruction to the printer or the title of the work. But it is a matter of fact that this term was used first to mark the difference between the author's first essay, titled "Physics" and the one that followed, which was called by Aristotle "The First Philosophy." The former treatise dealt with external nature as apprehended by the physical sciences; the latter with philosophical abstractions such as causality, being, God, potentiality and actuality, and reason. Whatever the original intent of the notation, the word was almost immediately lit upon by career thinkers as the most apt designation of that vast, lawless sphere of human imagination known as philosophy—vast, because conceivably it touches every human experience; lawless, because it knows no restraint (wisdom has also attracted its share of whores); imagination, because it is the mind's own doing and undoing.

The mind is the domain of the metaphysical, a world that lies somewhere between two realities—one purely physical, the other purely spiritual. And those who travel here must eventually choose one or the other as a destination. But those energetic, restless souls who reside here have neither itinerary nor secundment; direction is unimportant, and settlement is impossible. And the residents have surely been a marvelous race. To them is owed most of what is known in the modern world. For example, their number includes the notorious scholastics of the Middle Ages. Scholasticism, which flourished in the thirteenth century, according to the Church historian George P. Fisher, was "the application of reason to theology . . . to systematize and prove existing traditional beliefs."[2] It was philosophers such as Thomas Acquinas, Albertus Magnus, Duns Scotus, and William of Occam who dared to use deductive logic, especially syllogism, to justify the ways of God to man. Replete with laborious, often tendentious argument and persuasion, their works, and especially their reasoned defense of faith, provided the impetus and basis for the likes of Bacon and Newton, even though their approach would shift to dependence on inductive reasoning. It is a testament to the scholastics that the goddess of reason is today ensconced in Notre Dame Cathedral.

There was also a curious group of poets, who, although misnamed by John Dryden as "metaphysical," provide something of an oasis in what could otherwise become a vast desert of turgid argument. John Donne and his disciples—divergent thinkers all—twisted language and logic, played with ambiguities and paradoxes, and constructed fanciful conceits as if in some game of riddles.

And, of course, there were the empiricists and rationalists of the seventeenth and eighteenth century — Bacon, Newton, Locke, Descartes, Mill, Hegel — and all the rest who, as we well know by now, established the principles and created the context for all modern philosophy. But there is bound to be trouble lurking when every sentence ends with "and." The problem is that philosophy, by its very definition, is expansive, unpredictable. The very next thought may contradict the one just attested. Furthermore, anyone can be a philosopher — this is one vocation in which there is no noticeable difference between the amateur and the professional. Before the advent of public education, thinking was open to just about anyone with an idea. Of course, educational systems, especially bastions of "higher learning," struggled mightily to quarantine the outbreak of inquiry and invention that swept over Western civilization at the end of the nineteenth century and to inoculate the entire population to make them immune to any and all kinds of thinking. One must congratulate them on their stunning accomplishment: By the 1930s, thinking had become the rarest of all afflictions. There was a brief epidemic of thought-like activity in the 1960s, but it proved to be only a nervous reaction to an overdose of an expired prescription. Since it was its own antidote, the fever subsided quickly.

However, the fact remains that before public education could develop and administer the antithought vaccine — labeled "curriculum" — the damage had already been done. People had been infected by thinking of the worst varieties. While the etiology is uncertain, it is clear that early in the twentieth century the entire population had succumbed to one of two virulent mutant viruses — one ethereal, the other terrestrial. The ethereal strain was represented best by German theology or, on second thought, perhaps by American cheap imitation of Teutonic evanescence. A particularly devastating strain, the virus destroyed brain cells by vaporizing them. Consider this horrifying fit of ineffectual vacuuism from "Prolegomenon to a Theory of Religion," by Gerald James Larson, about whom little else is known:

Within the context of these considerations, let me now proceed to suggest a definition of religion and to offer as well two corollary definitions that grow out of the basal definition. I suggest the following: Religion is a "complete system of human communication" (or a "form of life") showing in primarily "commissive," "behabitive," and "exercitive" modes how a community comports itself when it encounters an "untranscendable negation of . . . possibilities."[3]

It is safe to say that the basal definition itself negates the possibility of transcending the two corollary definitions, so there is no real need to define them. Fortunately, this kind of affliction was suffered by relatively few unfortunate souls who had some sort of genetic predilection to nonsense. Their malady, although incurable, was, thank God, successfully confined to seminaries and seems to have had no noticeable effect on the rest of the population, although traces of it were detected in the pop psychology of the 1970s.

But the other strand infected almost everyone in Western civilization, rendering him or her catatonic. Behaviorism was the renegade deviant of rationalism. It not only attacked people; it destroyed also its own progenitor; and it did it by assuming the characteristics of its victim. In an unbelievable demonstration of pure chutzpah, it reasoned that there is no such thing as reason. Without question, this is the alltime greatest coup of rationalism, however perverted. It succeeded only because of the inherent human tendency to ascribe profundity to anything that is incomprehensible.

Essentially, behaviorism asserted that the mind is the efferent neurochemical part of human physiology that directs the body's response to external conditions. Since mental being is intangible, it was not considered a matter suitable for study by natural science; it was simply the residue of the medieval concept of the soul. One's emotions, thought powers, memory, habits—all were seen as the biological means by which a person meets the exigencies of daily living. Accordingly, emotion is a muscular and glandular activity; memory is the ability to recall and use; imagination is judged by its expression in conduct and is assumed to be only a nascent kind of vocal or gestural reaction; personality is the total of one's habits of behavior.

With this physicalization of the mind, behaviorism falls prey to its own disingenuity, because the process of making its case it becomes little more than a secular religion itself (scientism). The very thing it opposes is the only thing it proposes. There is the authoritative source, pronouncing even the contrary of its own pronouncement; there is the closed system that demands verification only by its own definitives; and there is the immaculate condescension or smug antagonism toward those not of the faith. In this way, honest rationalistic inquiry is forced into a strait between the sacred and secular versions of religion; ultimately, it must declare at least one of them false.

NEED VERSUS CONVICTION

This category is the most subtle of the lot, but it may well be the most decisive. The subject is human motivation—what moves people, why they behave the way they do, and whether the common denominator among them is the lowest or the highest. There is no middle ground. The significance of this question, as well as the answer, lies not in the sequacious analysis of human behavior but in the justification for that behavior. That all people are motivated primarily by self-interest is acknowledged by both religion and rationalistic science. But they are at loggerheads over what self-interest means—those on both sides sometimes quarreling among themselves. The debate is essentially over values or, perhaps, value systems—values being those imperatives that irresistibly call forth action. And there are only two possible kinds: values based on physical need and values based on conviction—what are called by other schools of modern psychology and religion external motivation (reward and punishment) and internal motivation (spiritual satisfaction). To complicate the matter further, the two kinds may not be mutually exclusive. In fact, it is their coexistence that seems to often to create unbearable dilemmas for the individual. For example, do I steal bread or let my family starve? Do I seek to appease tyranny or risk my life in resistance? The resolution to such conflicts comes only by unequivocally refusing one of the options or by eliminating both.

Behaviorism holds that the question itself is moot; and the idea of decision merely self-imposed anxiety suffered by those still given to an atavistic concept of soul. In fact, the word "need" would be rejected by behaviorists if there were intended any implicit suggestion of motivation other than instinctive survival response. The impulse to survive is the only driving force in human behavior; so meeting that need is the only human response. Further, behaviorism defines need strictly within the context of a physical being attempting to get along in a materialistic universe, a being whose mind is little more than the magnetic calibrator in the skull of a wild goose.

Obviously, there is no place here for anything like conviction, certainly nothing like moral imperative; the closest thing to it is the urgent, perhaps desperate, confidence in oneself to behave appropriately, a confidence gained through experience or physical prowess. Paradoxically, conviction necessarily places confidence in something outside the person—something seen as absolute, something transcendent. So the needs typically of concern to behaviorists are those that deal with physical satisfaction, physical security, and physical stability. Behaviorists assume that people live mostly along the alimentary canal; so they are visited there regularly by advertisements promising to meet those cravings and urges.

That these basic needs exist is undeniable; even the most radical spiritualist would agree. As a matter of note, of the forty miracles Jesus of Nazareth is said to have performed, all but one was predicated on someone's immediate physical need (the blasting of the fig tree was probably just the petulance of a nice guy having a bad day).

But there are two fairly serious implications to ending the discussion of need with the physical. First, behaviorism is not equipped to deal with the sometime distinction between needs and wants: for all practical purposes, in a behavioristic world, they are the same. Any perceived difference is semantics. The ultimate effect in human disposition is that satisfaction becomes gratification; security avarice; and stability complacency. And the most devout behaviorist will admit that these are less than desirable traits but can offer no excuse or solution.

Second, behaviorism, by limiting human need to the physical, negates the possibility of any mental or spiritual component of the human makeup. Classical wisdom, as well as early Christianity, accepted the tripartite nature of humans: body, soul (mind), and spirit. Behaviorism compressed the mind into a total physical package and ignored the mental and spiritual. That's why conviction fell out of the question. Even the most adamant humanist would agree. When Abraham Maslow, in the middle of the twentieth century, attempted to explain human motivation in terms expressly contrary to behaviorism or psychoanalysis, he was bound by common sense to place those categories of physical need in the first three levels of his famous hierarchy. Contrary to popular interpretation, he did not mean to suggest that these needs were somehow progressively forgotten as one climbs the pyramid; rather, the so-called levels should be taken together as an interdependent system, all existing simultaneously, each within the others. People who are starving also need self-actualization.

When conviction is removed as a motivating force, several attributes, thought rather highly of at other times and in other places, become the mere infatuations of a defective mind; and those characteristics otherwise deemed indicators of the nobility that sets human beings apart from other animals are lost. For example, honor becomes only a fictional plot device because real honor requires a capacity for shame. Humility disappears because it is based on an appreciation of the innate worth of other people. Virtue becomes artificial because it is defined by good. Love for others becomes impossible because it is the outward expression of love for oneself. And peace of mind becomes a tormenting wish because it can come only from transcending intellectual understanding and attainment of a state within the human spirit— unseen, unprovable, and unwordable.

The behavior of human beings can be contrived, but it cannot be faked. Whether approached from the view of psychoanalysis (mind over body) or behaviorism (body all over) or humanistic psychology (the complex progressive interaction of both), human behavior—whether compliance or achievement, whether reactive or active, whether internal or external—cannot be inconsistent with, nor can it exceed, the motivation that prompts it. And that is the reason this category of contrasts is the most decisive. It is the answer by which people create themselves in their own images—or some others.

NOTES

1. Joseph Conrad, *Lord Jim* (New York: Holt, Rinehart and Winston, 1957), 179.

2. George P. Fisher, *History of Christian Doctrine* (New York: Charles Scribner's Sons, 1908), 213.

3. Gerald James Larson, "Prolegomenon to a Theory of Religion," *Journal of the America Academy of Religion* (65, Fall 1997): 655–665.

CHAPTER 25

Behaviorism and the Nature of Human Reality

She says, "I am content when wakened birds,
Before they fly, test the reality
Of misty fields, by their sweet questionings;
But when the birds are gone, and their warm fields
Return no more, where, then, is paradise?"

Wallace Stevens[1]

It is not an overstatement to suggest that the greatest loss suffered by systems organized according to the corporation model was the abnegation of human potential. Seeking to guarantee maximum production at minimum cost, commercial enterprises invariably reduced human beings to objective specifications and measured them by mathematical standards. In so doing, time after time, they discouraged personal initiative and prevented truly extraordinary performance. Especially in bureaucratic institutions, depersonalization precluded any effort or achievement above the minimum requirement.

This category of contrasts may be the most significant of all because of its far-reaching practical implications. The crux of the matter may be in the reflexive: The objective may be subjective; but can the subjective be objective? If that seems a foolish question, it is only because of the presupposition that the objective actually exists. Behaviorism insists that, with any subject, the only reality is that which can be measured, demonstrated, or observed — within the context of that reality. Anything else is not worthy of consideration, being either fiction, figment, or fantasy. Insistence on scientific verification, as a matter of reference, is the basic tenet of empiricism, and the underlying assumption of rationalism. When this philosophy is applied to human behavior, it means that in any given activity the interest is not in the experience of the human being (that is mere speculation) but in understanding the action–reaction of the subject to certain stimuli, often as a clue to the action–reaction that can be anticipated from other stimuli or as an explanation of relationships among subjects. The only items of interest all along are the stimuli.

That kind of understanding is, no doubt, essential to the process of adaptation, to various human interactions, and, quite possibly, to the definition of self. But there is a curious paradox here: that objectification of human behavior has never been content to stop with analysis or even interpretation. Objectification demands judgment. It seems that the word itself—"objective"—is judgmental. It is impossible to render human behavior in objective terms without objectifying the person. And it is impossible, from the behaviorist's standpoint, to separate judgment of behavior from judgment of the person. There is simply no basis in behavioral science for that distinction. Implicit in objectification is the use of data not only to analyze and evaluate but also to subsequently control behavior.

Behaviorism maintains that everything from metabolism to orgasm can and should be statistically described; it can be normed; it can be standardized; it can be turned into critical attributes and common denominations that invite comparison and contrast. Phrases such as "percentiles" (ranking), "best practice," "benchmarks," "standards," and "standard deviation" quickly spring from cant jargon to mentality. Uniformatization sets in. Individuals are judged by how well they measure up, and everyone is expected to be above average, which tends to decline. Objective moves from adjective to noun. Far from simply an insurmountable mathematical challenge, the purpose of objectification easily turns from clinical experimentation to detection and correction of any deviation or aberration, thence to restoring the abnormal person to acceptability among his or her peers or to stipulating a new peer group by declaring the abnormal normal. It is a cold-blooded, presumptuous effort to establish order in a hot-blooded, disorderly subject.

Speaking of comparison and contrast, there is a curious parallel between the objectivism of behavioral science and the objectivism of religion. One might even surmise that there is a connection between that similarity and the introduction of pop psychology into much of late twentieth-century Christian doctrine. Objectification was what the Mosaic law was all about: It defined righteousness strictly in terms of action–reaction (works). Jesus was also adamant about the use of objectification in judging others: "By their fruits shall you know them." And Paul even tried to objectify love (quite possibly, that is why he lived alone).

There are two differences between Christianity and behaviorism. The first is the matter of source—one is based on divine revelation (the question is always in the answer); the other is a group-think subjective interpretation of tendentious empirical evidence (the answer is always in the question). One deals with overcoming sin; the other with being physically fit, intellectually astute, socially acceptable, and politically correct. Still, neither modern Christianity nor behaviorism finds any inconsistency in the idea of bad people doing good things; and both hold that character, like competence, is demonstrated, not possessed. The second point of difference is the matter of exclusivity. Christianity excludes by discriminating against those who do not act in strict compliance with its code of conduct. In fact, it is customary for religion to regard some people as better than others on the basis of their behavior or even of their physical appearance. Behaviorism is indiscriminate, granting grace to all except those who do not have faith in its basic tenets. Disbelievers are condemned to eternal scorn.

There are three critical issues here, all questions: the self, relationships, and aesthetics. Regarding the first, whether religious or scientific, objectification always diminishes the self. Religion's definition of the person as a soul seems wonderfully extravagant until it is realized that serious strictures accompany grace. The soul is captive not only to the ritual and ceremony of the institution but also to the continuous judgment of others belonging to the order. The status, even the worth, of the person depends at any given time on perceived compliance with expectations regarding conduct. Behaviorism goes even further in the diminution of the person by reducing the whole of one's being to observable behavior. The person is defined as personality. Personality comprises a portfolio of descriptions that cluster exhibited behaviors into "types." Significantly, the instruments used to determine the type of a given individual are commonly referred to as "tests" (typically, forced choice) as if they could be passed or failed. Much more than the relatively simple distinctions made by psychoanalysis, and at least in appearance more sophisticated than the crude morph-typing of early physiology, the typology of behaviorism is complicated to the point of contrivance, often depending on obscurity for clarification, and certainly not beholden to any known rule of logical classification. As a matter of fact, sometimes it is difficult to distinguish science from superstition or folk wisdom.

The more scientific of the encoding instruments, those based on validated observation and analysis of human behavior, offered the practical benefit of deft, if rigid, charting, plotting, and percenting of every person into at least one of several predictable patterns of response to everything in the world. For example, the most influential of the typesets, the Myers–Briggs Type Indicator (c. 1943), along with its many slavish derivatives, was for most of the twentieth century the undisputed source of who, or what, people were. It was based on Carl Jung's theory of type according to four dominant functions: sensing, intuition, thinking, and feeling. Although this system was impossible to validate outside the Jungian universe, Isabel Briggs Myers paired these as dichotomized indices of personality types, called up another Jungian polarity (introversion and extroversion) and refined another (judgment–perception) to create a matrix of sixteen types. All are bipolar, discontinuous types, and all are assumed to be genuine dichotomies with true zero points. There is neither ambiguity nor uncertainty. Nothing is left to the imagination.

For the better part of five decades, businesses were staffed, schools designed, and military occupational specialties assigned on the basis of this system. The obvious benefits of this kind of typecasting are precision in career and job placement and profound self-knowledge, if not fulfillment, as a human being. Placement is as certain as matching terminology or numbers, and self-actualization is as sure as fitting the identified mold. Convenient as well as impressive, this kind of categorical imperative had such popular appeal that it quickly took on commercial value, and a whole covey of typographical systems grew up—typologies ranging from nouveau astrology that deployed people psychoscientifically around the horoscope according to their position vis-à-vis celestial bodies; to color charts that distributed people around the calendar according to their "season"; to various matrices that positioned people based on things like decision making, people versus task orientation, passivity and aggressiveness (or inverse combinations of the two); and whether they were right or left brained or ambicerebral. The unlikely result of all this typographic frenzy was that personality became a high-fashion consumer product, popular with the seminar crowd, *Readers' Digest* subscribers, and home shoppers.

Regarding the second, the objectification of the person rules out any possibility of relationships, presuming rather to describe the goings-on between and among human beings as "interaction." It is ironically appropriate that there has never been any attempt scientifically to collate these interactions into a single, logically consistent compendium. But, practically speaking, even though these interactions are played out in several venues—community, economic, political, legal, religious—they occur only in two arenas, personal and social. In every case, the objectified human being appears somewhat less than a fully developed subject primarily because here again the only concern is behavior rather than the person as a being. For example, personal interactions occur at three levels of intensity—incidental, regular, and sustained—representing a progression from coincidence to curiosity to commitment; correspondingly, they depend upon proximity, magnetism, and chemistry. The incidental renders humans just that—incidents. Their random existence is one of ceaselessly balling about, colliding, banking off each other into remote corners, then careening back, whizzing by each other at breakneck speed, or striking each other glancing blows, looking for all the world as if the centrifugal and centripetal dynamic of the activity might eventually force some kind of fusion or fission. But any semblance of permanence is momentary and still a random collection of individual objects. And no one has a cue to what comes next. All they know is that nobody is ever where he or she is supposed to be, and that there is always someone in the way.

Interaction with others is more accurately described as "reaction"—much like the response of the human organism to any other external stimulus. Connectedness with others amounts to a series of random or intentional contacts, lately termed "touching base" or "interfacing"—there is a constant fundamental process here—an instinctive detecting, sensing, and adjusting of one's own posture while always maintaining uppermost the awareness of and concern for personal well-being, along with the readiness to preserve it if at all possible.

The net result is that civility is possible only when superficiality is not compromised. And individual identity is possible only through the negation of the person and, in lieu thereof, the assumption of roles. The idea of roles was a boon to the business of personal interaction. The typing of personality was, for all its intrigue and fascination, a bit academic, perhaps clinical. But roles—ah, that's where the action was. In the give and take, parry and thrust of a democratic society, there was considerable popular appeal to this practical classification of the masses. Life became a drama to be enacted on a stage—comedies, tragedies, farces—all acted by a cast of a thousand character types.

The metaphor of role, if indeed it were a metaphor, was eminently practical. It could be applied not only to any number of discreet personal actions within interaction but also to the individual's more-or-less characteristic persona. In the first case, for example, along about mid-century, several paradigms appeared claiming to delineate all the roles that an individual might play in group interaction. It was conventional wisdom that there were three basic categories: building, blocking, and maintenance roles such as the "initiator," the "aggressor," and the "gatekeeper."

More significant and as an example of the second case, the roles could be assumed rather permanently either from habit or from the persuasive expectations of others. But far beyond that simple taxonomy, in the second half of the century a veritable industry sprang up around roles. One of the early offerings was "transactional analysis" (parent, child, adult roles). A later offering was "Enneagram," a pseudo-Greek revival amalgam of pop psychology and new age drift that assigned people to one of nine feature roles, with an occasional walk-on part now and then. The prospect of owning a role was irresistible to people who otherwise had no identities. And so they rushed to sort them out, fondly to acquire one for themselves.

The various options, for convenience in merchandising, were customarily represented as "role models" or, in the context of action, "role modeling." These models took on two forms: actual real-life people who seemed attractive enough to elicit imitation if not envy and composite nonlife fabrications designed (much as Greek sculpture) to suit the most imaginative portrayal of life. It was a fascinating thing, indeed, this role making and role playing. It had all kinds of social significance. For example, we soon realized that, within any dominant group, erstwhile individuals have a tendency to take on the likeness of the person most influential at the time, evidenced conspicuously by fashion of dress or speech. In recessive groups, which typically do not have examples deemed worthy of emulating, individuals in the quest of validation have a tendency to construct their own fictional images, typically reflecting traits of the dominant group. This tactic was especially popular among advertising agencies as they attempted to interject minorities into mainstream society.

The objectification of the person does not stop with the translation of personal relationships into interactions among dramatis personae. In fact, it may be more accurate to say that objectification does not begin there. There is another dimension of relationships—social—that is at once neither merely the accumulation of ever-so-many personal interactions neatly arranged in scientifically identified groupings nor the inconsequential analysis of those interactive phenomena into anthropological insignificance. On the contrary, societal objectification always proceeds from the conceptual, not from the practical. It is always intended to have an effect—usually to bring about either stability or reform or progress without a societal context—through the judgment and control of the masters of that society. In all instances, it is diametrically opposed to any kind of subjective approach to socialization. Subjectification is based on feelings, not ideas; and the driving force is internal, not external. Rationalism, therefore, considers subjectivity terminally dangerous in a well-ordered society. It was for that reason that Western society came to be made up of constructs rather than formations—of laws rather than values, of artifacts rather than persons.

The question was how to extend the objectification of the person into a social context. The answer was astoundingly simple—rather than objectifying the individual, objectify the personal. By this one maneuver, everything that in other worlds would be considered subjective—feelings, affection, favoritism, simple likes and dislikes, and personal opinions—was dismissed as scientifically irrelevant. Held in special disregard, even contempt, were any purely personal value judgments with regard to other people or their conduct. The basic idea was that the person could be "socialized," through group therapy, sensitivity training, and cultural dialogue, toward understanding of others, nonjudgmental tolerance, and a benign attitude of equality in all things. The shift of language was radical: Feeling became sensing; caring became care-giving; trust became reliability; love became respect; and giving became sharing. Ethics was just another foreign word. The behaviorists soon discovered that understanding, as often as not, results in even more intolerance and that equality exists only in institutions—where people do not count.

The institution is, without doubt, the epitome of the objectification of society. As such, it is both the basic organizational component and the essential character of the modern Western world. Sooner or later, all artifactual systems have to become institutions or disappear. For that reason, the institution is the greatest invention of rationalistic science. That is not to say, of course, that there were no institutionalized systems long before the Enlightenment—the Church and the British monarchy being among the most notable examples. But the early forms were generally acknowledged to be systems in the final state of passing, a memorial, as it were, to what had once been vital. (To this day, by custom and sometimes by law, people are institutionalized only after they are dead.) It was not until the genius of rationalism was brought to bear on the creation of social artifacts that institutions were built by design, the design always based not just on precedent but on history as well. Beyond that, there were several obligatory features of modern institutions: They were held to be more important than people, even the people in them; they existed for one purpose and one purpose only, self-perpetuation; they found their only substance in by-laws and rules and regulations and policies, each aimed at closing the universe a bit more and depersonalizing the human being; and they invariably sustained themselves by the wealth of others.

But the apotheosis of objectification, and thus of science, was the emergence of a race of people who, although beholding beauty, had no eyes. Aesthetics was not new to rationalism or, for that matter, to empiricism. But science was new to aesthetics. The ironic fact is that the new science from its very beginning was predicated on the phenomenon of *aisthetikos*, on the experience of "sense perception." Why Bacon and the later empiricists did not seize upon this mot juste is something of a curiosity. Both Aristotle and Plato were familiar with the idea and its dominant, even decisive, role in the definition of reality. As a matter of fact, *aisthetikos* was and is the central question in all Western philosophy. All schools of thought, all forms of art, and all systems of reality are simply variations on this theme.

However, it was not until the middle of the eighteenth century—over a century after *Novum Organum*—and on the continent rather than in the British Isles that aesthetics emerged, first as a branch of philosophy. In an almost inconceivable two-volume unfinished treatise, *Aesthetica Acroamatica*, Alexander Gottlieb Baumgarten coined the word to describe the concept that, eventually, as a complete philosophy, dominated Western notions of beauty and art. Although virtually unknown by his own contemporaries, he was the intellectual mentor of many more celebrated scions of the Western world, including pivotal thinkers like Kant, Schiller, and Goethe. It was through the rugged and sometimes tedious debate waged by these writers that aesthetics developed in the nineteenth century as a separate system of philosophy. As a matter of fact, Kant wrote the definitive works on aesthetics, *Critique of Pure Reason* and *Critique of Judgment*. He saw aesthetics as the way to bridge the gap between empiricism (inductive) and rationalism (deductive) and pushed the philosophy just about as far as it can go, metaphysically. And then a remarkable thing happened: Aesthetics became a science, right along with all the other splintered disciplines engineered by behaviorism. The "science of aesthetics" appears to be an oxymoron.

When aesthetics entered the world of science or—perhaps, more accurately—when science invaded the world of aesthetics, the world changed utterly because human beings were transformed from subjects to objects. What had been impressions became expressions; what had been expressions became impressions. When Aristotle theorized on the nature and qualities of art, the emphasis was always on human experience in the defining moment.

The highest form of art, therefore, was tragedy—a heads-on collision of forces that would evoke fear and pity. And the ultimate test of the genuineness and the achievement of any artistic endeavor was *katharsis*, the cleansing of the human spirit. When Plato contemplated the real possibility of ideal beauty, it was with the aspiration of achieving the fullest expression of humanity or, as the later romantic poets would interpret it, an earnest longing to possess.

The judgments that these oracles pronounced on art and beauty, however analytical, were based on the process by which, and the degree to which, the person was involved in his or her own discovery of self, others, and the world. Of paramount importance in this process, critical attributes of art or beauty so identified were never assumed or intended to be rules. Art, thus, was the highest form of human communication—soul to soul—and beauty the most divine expression of the spirit. Even during the extended darkness of the Middle Ages when the Church presumed to be the sole source of art and beauty and both were dominated by Papal attitude and Church doctrine, the experience of the individual observer and participant was the primary concern of the artist. During the Renaissance, even though honest vitality often poured over into the extravagance of tacky variants, such as Mannerism, art and beauty were ebullient celebrations of life in all its many dimensions, not slavish imitations of atavistic creeds.

The significance of all this is that even when beauty and art were purely subjective matters both could be analyzed, systemized, codified, and criticized; in fact, all these endeavors became significant intellectual enterprises long before the advent of science. So it was not as if the application of rationalism to aesthetics invented justification and judgment. The difference was this: Subjectivity seeks to understand; objectivity presumes to dictate. One is a matter of spirituality, the other of utility. One frees, the other binds—another triumph of construct over formation. The immediate effect is that the very useful distinction Baumgarten made between theories of beauty and art is obliterated, and the two are fused into a single didactic. The basic questions for aesthetics had always been, "How do human beings know what is beautiful?" "Is it a reasoned assessment or an emotional response?" "Is there any relationship of art to morality or goodness?" Rationalistic science could accept only that which is reasonable and scientific—in a word, objective.

The transformation was gradual, sometimes subtle; but by the middle of the twentieth century it was complete. Aristotle understood objectivity probably better than the new critics. In fact, he recognized two aspects of objectivity—that which can be comported as the critical attributes sufficient to define a genre or quality of genre, and that which describes the "aesthetic distance" between the participants (creator or beholder) and the art itself. Without the tension of detachment, tragedy and comedy degenerate into melodrama and farce. We know why, for example, Sophocles has Oedipus' eyes put out off stage.

In the nineteenth century, John Keats introduced the delightful phrase "negative capability," which he used first to describe Shakespeare's extraordinary ability to withhold his own emotions, thereby achieving a sublime universality. In modern criticism, the idiom was of "objective correlates"—Washington Allston's term, popularized by T. S. Eliot—to refer to those literary or artistic devices by which emotion is transmitted without direct connection of object to emotion. The so-called "new" criticism in the early twentieth century was all about moving the art object farther and farther away from any subjective experience, forcing it to stand or fall on the basis of its own intrinsic merits—pure art, as it were. The difficulty with this thoroughly scientific approach is that art and beauty by their very nature are subjective, if for no other reason than their origin is subjective—human beings. The only possible ultimate result was that art and beauty in the twentieth century Western world were more often than not matters of confusing critical or popular fashion and had lost any real meaning. Objectification had produced the perverse effect—by dehumanizing art and beauty it had destroyed the sight of the beholders. No one could tell, and few cared, whether the magic of Mona Lisa's face lay in the perfect triangle or in her smile; or which of the Giverny gardens was real.

NOTE

1. Wallace Stevens, "Sunday Morning," *The Literature of the United States*, ed. Walter Blair (Glenview, Ill.: Scott, Foresman, and Co., 1966), 974.

CHAPTER 26

Behaviorism and the Nature of Human Capacity

> Freedom of choice is not a formal abstract capacity which one either "has" or "has not"; it is, rather, a function of a person's character structure.
>
> Eric Fromm[1]

When behaviorism took over psychology in the early twentieth century, it did so with mind-numbing suddenness. Nothing had ever so quickly and so thoroughly captured the psyche of Western civilization. But this radical new way of nonthinking immediately entered the popular domain for at least three reasons. First, the inventor of behavioristic psychology, Thomas B. Watson, was not only its strongest advocate, he was also a fervent evangelist. He was a popular writer and speaker, always ready to bear testimony, convincing in both style and argument, to his doctrine of sensory adaptation. Second, most psychologists of this time were ready for something other than the traditional mentalistic approach to the subject. They had become rather sated by always grappling with things they could not see, hear, feel, smell, or taste. The most active version of mentalistic psychology, introspection, had become hopelessly bogged down in the question of whether imageless thought were possible. The profession languished. The cost of living increased. Third, behaviorism was eminently practical. One could actually do something with it, and that greatly added to its marketability.

Once more we see the artful dodge of science: Unable to provide an answer, it simply changed the question. Watson took the position that psychologists should forget the mind of the organism and concentrate strictly on its response to stimuli—in a word, behavior. The study must be based on objective observation. In one fell swoop, meaningless speculation gave way to meaningful clinical observation. Furthermore, Watson's science was the perfect combination of the Darwinian legacy of biological continuity and the growing body of contemporary research on animal learning and sense-organ functions. One might say, behaviorism was predictable.

STIMULUS VERSUS THOUGHT

The negation of thought in favor of stimulus–response as the source of human action and behavior had three critical implications. First, mentalistic psychology had been concerned with the nature of consciousness, that is, as a state of mind. Behaviorism contends that there is no such thing as consciousness, existence being merely the continuing musculo-skeletal responsive adaptation, often exploratory, of the organism to changing circumstances. Philosophical behaviorism denied that the term "consciousness" had any referent. Later behaviorists such as B. F. Skinner contended that all mentalistic terms are unscientific and have no place in psychological research. Whether or not the organism actually "experiences" anything is a moot point because behaviorism is interested only in the reaction to, and to which, stimulus. The real significance of the denial of consciousness is not that the human being is rendered just another instinctive animal or even that the individual becomes essentially the result of external forces but that he or she, despite all the emphasis on sensory response, has no sense of time. But timing is all that matters. The concept of timelessness requires an understanding of time. Behaviorism simply does not acknowledge time—except as the interval between stimulus and response (timing). The net effect is that the human being loses any sense of past, present, and future and moves in a kind of sensuous eternal now. Everything is of the moment and for the moment. Satisfaction, which is nothing more than successful adaptation, is a constant lonely struggle, exciting with the slightest victory. Life becomes a mélange of sensations. And nothing lasts, not even the memory.

Second, traditional psychology had been given to the study of feelings, that part of the mind that transcends even the rational. The admission of feelings transcends the rational; it declares emotions (passion) and spirituality (intuition) to be naturally human—probably distinct from other animals. Behaviorism dismisses feelings as nothing more than the nervous reactions of the organism to stimulation. What this means is that there is no such thing as human being—human existence, perhaps, but not being. In the personal context, any sense of self is possible only as a perception of one's own reactions. Loss of feelings means loss of being. As the loss of consciousness removed any sense of time, the loss of feelings removes any sense of dimension—not only the dimensions of the person but also that person's place in the world. Being is always a matter of place. Obviously, that is not a physical place but a mental (perhaps spiritual) place where the mind is able to identify itself by its own breadth, length, height, and depth. All this is denied by behaviorism. According to that doctrine, the human exists only in patterns of behavior, all immediately on the other side of stimulus. Anger, hatred, and fear, like pain and pleasure, are merely physical reactions. There is no such place as state of mind—and no reference points, no context. So it is impossible ever to find oneself. Or to act out of compassion. Or to be in love.

Third, traditional psychology had been built on the assumption that the highest expression of mentality was the intellect, the part of the mind that involves the innate ability to learn; that is, to perceive, understand, reason, and judge. The traditional definition included not only cognition but also intuition and imagination. Because of the peculiar linguistic–grammatical relationship of cognates separated at birth (L. *intellegere*) and reunited in maturity, during the past five hundred years or so there has been less than absolute precision in the distinction between "intellect" (L. *intellectus*) and "intelligence" (L. *intellegentia*). Although today the words are used more or less interchangeably, even in learned discourse, it is safe to say that "intellect" is usually taken to refer to a mental attribute of a person (although Jacques Barzun, using a truly apt metaphor—"house of intellect"[2]—proposes that term also describes the aggregate condition of society). But "intelligence" is used to indicate the quality of the intellect, especially with regard to quickness and accuracy of perception, range of awareness, and depth of reasoning and understanding, as well as the accumulation of knowledge through experience. Intelligence was the manifestation of one's intellect. Although intelligence was considered a single attribute, consistent and complete in each person ("general intelligence" or "g," as it was called), it was subject to various analyses including comparative tests; and it was susceptible to many practical expressions, which ostensibly proved the degree of intelligence.

There was assumed to be a broad range of intelligence, from simple to complex; and there was a vast array of demonstrations of cognitive ability, suitable to a society temperamentally given to the democratic principle of supremacy of the individual and intellectually fascinated by the science and pseudoscience of the times. One's intelligence easily became his or her identity, not because that person or others were able to detect certain abstract features but because of the very personal, practical expression of that intelligence in one's speech, countenance, demeanor, and actions. The concept of "who" has meaning only in terms of both awareness of oneself and the awareness of and by others. Just as a point of reference, in Western literary and theological traditions, it is not uncommon for all living beings, especially spiritual ones, to be called "intelligences."

Behaviorism, ironically, not only refused to accept intelligence as an intellectual force or even as a mental characteristic, it also denied intelligence as sense or sensation. It is a rather curious circumstance that in the vernacular the word "sense" was often used as a synonym for intelligence (as in "common horse sense"); and in the touchy-feely seventies, "sense" virtually replaced "intelligence" (as in this television interview led by a morning show host, "Give us a *sense* of developments in the Middle East"). Even so, for behaviorism, intelligence was simply and only the objective description of the way a human organism dealt with the necessities of living on the planet. When "who" became behavior, personal identity became moot. If identity had any use at all, it was to designate observed habitual response. But loss of identity meant gain in intelligence—for everyone. Once intelligence had been removed from the person to the outside, it was possible to give it the proper scientific treatment. It could be analyzed, categorized, and otherwise manipulated into as many constructs as tendentious research could devise. Aided and abetted by a social conscience, of uncertain origin and a somewhat suspect agenda that eschewed discrimination among people and worshipped at the altar of egalitarianism, and buoyed by popular demand for smartness, intelligence became a bountiful luxury available in scientifically retrofitted fashion for each and every one. The universal grant of intelligence was the ultimate act of patronage by science.

By the mid-twentieth century, the attempt of science to define intelligence had become a farcical, if alliterative, exercise of pedantry, pedagogy, and patronage. In order to make the grand bequest, behaviorism first had to eliminate the old concept of intelligence as a single general attribute (essentially the assumption of both Alfred Binet and Lewis Terman) and create in lieu thereof something called "multiple-intelligences," which were nothing more than convenient categories of ordinary human activities, including grinning and jumping up and down. In 1575, a Spanish physician, Juan Huarte, defined "intelligence" as "the ability to learn, exercise judgment and imagine." In 1775, Samuel Johnson took care to specify that intelligence was "not of the senses, but of the intellect." In 1983, a professor at Harvard University, Howard Gardner, himself a practicing intellectual, set out the criteria not for intelligence but intelligences. According to him, for an intelligence to be verified, it must involve a set of skills in problem solving, entail the potential for finding and creating problems, and have some importance to a cultural setting. Obviously, these are not very precise criteria; there is hedge in every phrase. But evidently, vague premises can produce surprisingly specific conclusions. Accordingly, he identified seven distinct intelligences: linguistic, musical, logical (mathematical), spatial, bodily (kinesthetic), interpersonal, and intrapersonal.[3] He graciously admitted that there might be others; and sure enough, in 1993 he suggested several more.[4] Memory was not one of them. That this condescending jury rigging could be generally accepted as truth and actually incorporated into the educational systems of North America might be just another example of the spell-binding mystery of rationalistic science; perhaps it is an example of group think by an entire civilization already admittedly incapable of thought. (Evidently, as the definition of intelligence expanded, so did the potential for insanity. According to the *Diagnostic and Statistical Manual of Mental Disorders* published by the American Psychiatric Association, the number of possible mental disorders increased from 297 in 1987 to 374 in 1994.) The most rational explanation is that by the end of the twentieth century, unintelligent people (by definition) outnumbered intelligent people (by nature) at least three to one. Nobody could be sure who was who, and most had lost interest in knowing. It was about this time that anything pertaining to the intellect was abandoned completely, and something absurdly tagged "emotional intelligence" was offered as a substitute. At last, it was possible to feel good about being stupid.

CONDITIONING VERSUS CONSCIENCE

There is no doubt that the coup de grâce of behaviorism was the supplanting of the human conscience with conditioned response. From the earliest recorded mental activity of human beings and throughout the development of Western civilization, the idea of conscience was accepted as a constant, if sometimes vexing, force within the human mind. No one, it seems, had the occasion to doubt its presence and for that reason no need to prove its existence. In fact, some of the most enduring Western literature and legend deal with the dilemma of a mortal struggling with conscience almost as if it were another being. Sometimes it was a still small voice in the night; sometimes a desperate shout amid the clamorous streets. The nominal definition of the word, "with-knowledge," suggests an inescapable and constant testing of the person through pitting the expectations of a previously established moral imperative against the present urges of need and ambition. Christianity saw this mental gyroscope not only as a guide but also as a judge, alternately accusing and defending. Pagans searched it for peace of mind. But in either tradition, it was something that could be destroyed—or, more precisely, eradicated—by constant adamant denial and deliberate contrary behavior. That possibility was not lost on behaviorism.

Before Thomas Watson introduced behavioristic psychology to the world, Vladimir M. Bekhteren, a Russian, had developed an approach to "objective psychology" (his term) based on reflexology—that is, the simple "associative" (his term again) reflex action of human beings to various stimuli. His more famous contemporary, Ivan P. Pavlov, after persistent experiments with dogs, metronomes, and powdered meat, established "conditioning" (his term) as not just a matter of association of ideas but a fundamental biological phenomenon. Taken as such, as it was jubilantly by the psychologists of the day, this proud postulation redefined everything about human learning, especially the development of conscience. The very idea of conscience presupposes an understanding above and beyond current conduct. And the very idea of understanding presupposes an active mind with capabilities to absorb, challenge, decide, and accept or reject alternative behaviors.

Conscience is the mind's struggle with the spirit. For centuries it was assumed that this kind of understanding was to some degree innate, always with the capacity for maturation. So understanding was the aim of instruction and guided experience. In every case, such developmental activity arose out of some moral or otherwise values-based context and was conducted with the expressed intent of engendering self-control. Conditioning put an end to all that. Not only was learning redefined as the organism's accumulated patterns of reflex action, otherwise known as "habits," but the conscience was made an entirely obsolete idea because uprightness is determined by the suitability of response and control is never internal. Right was replaced by effectiveness.

Historically and philosophically, conditioning was the final triumph of a relative universe over the moral one—a paradoxical conclusion to the new science. Standards of human behavior dissolved quickly into situational ethics. Practically speaking, conditioning became the means by which people created themselves in their own images, or in the images of others. Here again is the inversion of subject and object. Teaching is based on authority or knowledge greater than that possessed by the learner as subject; conditioning is based on control or information greater than that possessed by the respondent—as object. Both take, or have taken, assumption to judgment. When behaviorism seized upon conditioning as the prototype for all learning, the authority and moral context of teaching were lost. The scientific alternative to teaching was a progressive application of stimuli intended to evoke the desired response. By the mid-twentieth century, the teaching profession itself had generally adopted not only the language but also the techniques of behaviorism. "Positive reinforcement," the simplest form of conditioning, quickly became the buzzword of classroom, pew, and factory floor. The phrase carried that certain je ne sais quoi that seemed to blend scientific authority with sensitive, humanistic concern.

The theory, ubiquitious in application, was that people respond primarily to rewards and recognition and that the way to direct their behavior was to drop bit-sized incentives along a route leading to some desired outcome. The most amazing thing about this scenario, indeed of the whole business of conditioning, is that no one ever thought to question the authority of the conditioners or the prerogatives of the conditioned. But positive reinforcement also had its other side—negative reinforcement—that is, punishment for inappropriate or undesirable behavior. "Reinforcement" really amounted to a euphemism for control through reward and punishment or, depending on the sincerity involved, promise and threat, hope and fear. Throughout the last half of the twentieth century, this was the prevalent philosophy in child-rearing, education, management science, government, and most Western religions. The only question was which side of the force would be applied. Positive reinforcement was a technique that lent itself handily to getting certain people to behave in a certain way at a certain time. The effect was permanent and, ironically enough, it usually required continuing ratcheting-up adaptation of any sustained reinforcement. There was a tendency for the object to become resistant or insensitive to the stimulus and relapse into previous behavior.

No one has ever accused science of lacking ambition. The obvious reasoning was that if external stimuli can change behaviors ("atomistic") why can it not also change behavior ("organismic")—that is, recast the subject (now object) completely and permanently according to the image of what that person could or should be. "Behavior modification," it was called. Innocuous enough as a basic phrase, it sounds almost like one of those intellectual clichés spun out of late night musings when the Johnny Walker wisdom is running high; but the implications were as big as life.

The postulate was that behavior modification, also known as behavior "therapy," could change the whole person or, perhaps more accurately, the persons's characteristic behavior—all according to specifications. In "behavioral shaping" there were two important words, each indicative of the technique and intent of the process. The first term was "demonstration." All specifications for desired behavioral outcomes were written as description of response that could be observed, analyzed, and eventually predicted. Obviously, it had to be that way because behaviorism had forsworn any possibility of mental or emotional reaction.

The second word was "habits"; that is, the accumulation and retention of desired behavior patterns. The issue was never whether the person himself or herself had actually experienced a change of character but whether he or she had acquired enough learned responses to constitute a transformation of characteristic behavior. "True nature," as in what a person really is like, became a matter of habitual response. So the aim of human development was simply the acquisition of a prescribed set of habits—sustained patterns of behavior. Here again, the fix was susceptible to recidivism or, ironically, to other fixes. So, continuous methods of monitoring, such as biofeedback, and instantaneous mechanisms of reward and punishment, such as merits and demerits, were invented, if for no other reason than to reinforce the integrity of science.

A sturdy case had to be made for the credibility of behaviorism, because it quickly ceased to be science and became a program—a program with far more than the objective analysis of individual human behavior on its mind. There were astoundingly seductive social implications in control theory. The ultimate form of conditioning was "brainwashing," so-called, one supposes, because of the patent insistence that humans do not have minds but rather possess brains with relatively complex response capacities. If it were possible to cleanse the brain of the debris of previously learned responses and the residue of conscience, then it would be possible with the application of constructive force eventually to replenish it completely and create another, more desirable reaction. But it was not an easy process.

Typically, brainwashing involved subjecting the individual to intensely stressful conditions, including physical deprivations, isolation, fatigue, and a relentless barrage of taunts and threats with inexplicable intervals of compliments and pleasure. This technique soon became the darling of prisoner-of-war camps, cult cabals, and political campaigns. It made the re-creation of the individual virtual reality. But true to form, the ambition of behaviorism was insatiable. If brainwashing was effective with individuals, why not use it on entire societies? The process was relatively simple, if unexpected. The first requirement for such a massive effort was obviously some form of mass communication, which technology readily supplied. But the second requirement came as something of a surprise, even for those who are guided by the contrariness of the universe.

When the brainwashing technique was applied to society at large, rather than psychological stress, the exact opposite was needed—that is, the creation of euphoria by spinning (even in prospect) a general sense of deserved affluence, of self-importance, of group superiority or righteousness, and by unleashing a loud and steady torrent of reminders about the badness of others and the goodness of us; coupled with an endless variety of distracting entertainments calculated to keep attention away from anything that mattered. By the end of the twentieth century in Western civilization—especially in the North American version—no one could tell the difference between learning and conditioning, between teaching and indoctrination, or between the truth and propaganda. And very few had the conscience to discern the untruth that covered all.

NOTES

1. Eric Fromm, *The Heart of Man: Its Genius for Good and Evil* (New York: Harper and Row, 1964), 131.

2. Jacques Barzun, *The House of Intellect* (New York: Harper and Row, 1959), 57.

3. Howard Gardner, *Frames of Mind: The Theory of Multiple Intelligences* (New York: Basic Books, 1983).

4. Howard Gardner, *Multiple Intelligences* (New York: Basic Books, 1993).

PART V

THE EMERGING ORGANIZATION

CHAPTER 27

The Passing of Old Orders

Things are going to slide in all directions
Won't be nothing
Nothing you can measure anymore
The blizzard of the world
has crossed the threshold
and it has overturned
the order of the soul.
                    Leonard Cohen[1]

As long as the fundamental assertions of Western civilization remained seriously unchallenged as the truth, the corporation-model organization flourished. During this extended heady time, the corporation as both a construct and philosophy of organization gradually came to be the exclusive structure of all social order and therefore to dominate every part of day-to-day life. It was, indeed, the representative institution of the civilization. Average citizens were enslaved to and by that institution. Problems and inadequacies abounded, most of them unsolvable, but almost all were blamed on the person—not the system. Therefore, almost all corrective measures were aimed at fixing people, as in conformity. Even the ubiquitous "continuous improvement" approach, although originating in the mathematical world of operational research, was aimed at increasing the performance of individuals—much in the same way that is had been used to increase the efficiency of machines. Very little effort was directed toward displacing the corporation-model organization itself—

not even in the dysfunctionality of its terminal stage. Finality was unthinkable. It existed in an imperious state of denial.

Ultimately, the real problem—the system—became so obvious that even oblivious rationalization could not deny the inherent flaws in the system itself—flaws that could not be overcome. The problem lay strictly within the assumptions on which the modern corporation-model organization and the antecedent society had been constructed. That foundation, like the assertions, began to crumble with devastating results.

THE END OF RATIONALISM

As empiricism gave way to pragmatism, the philosophy of rationalism, now little more than speculative assertions disguised as science, reached the inevitable point of complete moral and logical relativism. Absolute, objective reality ceased to be plausible as a concept of truth or as a way of life. The very idea of truth became a myth.

THE END OF HUMANISM

The modern version of materialistic humanism reduced the life of human beings to mere material considerations. The original notion of canonizing the best said and done by noble human beings in earnest pursuit of human excellence was replaced by statistical analyses of "quality of life" as judged in quantitative measure; and creativity was replaced by adaptation.

THE END OF DEMOCRACY

The great experiment in democracy proved again at the end to be an ignoble failure. It became painfully obvious that the mass of human beings simply were not capable of governing themselves, collectively or individually. Proof positive was demonstrated in those who were raised up, through dubious political processes, to rule them. Unruly themselves, the rulers personified the irresponsibly selfish nature of human beings when reduced to the lowest common denominator in the name of equality. Stalemate, fragmentation, and confusion were the real rulers of the society.

THE END OF CAPITALISM

The mock capitalism of the modern age inevitably deteriorated into greed, scarcity, and competition—all deemed virtuous by the erstwhile moral centers of society. The church and education not only advocated these pernicious attitudes, they eagerly participated in them. Not surprisingly, the whole culture of Western society was characterized most fully by the same traits.

THE END OF BEHAVIORISM

This insidious philosophy, which dominated the entire twentieth century, reduced human beings to organisms without choice, without power, without hope. Both their innate capacity and sovereign autonomy were all but erased from memory. In fact, memory, as well as all willed action, was denigrated into "habits"—the operative word of contemporary organizational development. Control, always external, resulted only in the perverse effect—the opposite of the announced intent. Conditioned behavior became the sum total of human being.

As dire as the situation had become, as the old orders, the old assertions, inexorably crumbled against vehement protestations and soothing assurances, there was still within human beings the innate genius of creation and the consciousness that they were not made for existing systems, just as those systems were not made for them. Old orders die hard. And so it was with the corporation-model organization and its society. It was unyielding until the end, maintaining its grip on people by dint of either force or inertia and depending for its own survival on the incapacitation of persons trapped within it.

The decline and fall of these once-dominant assertions was nothing short of apocalyptic—each dying alone, unattended by either honor or regret. But in the ruins of the ensuing disequillibrium, human beings were discovering within themselves both the imagination and the will to create new social orders that were neither constructs nor formations: these systems would be human.

NOTES

1. Leonard Cohen, "The Future," *Stranger Music: Selected Poems and Songs* (New York: Vintage Books, 1993), 370.

CHAPTER 28

The Decline of Rationalism

> Someday they will sicken of the touchstones of Freud and Marx, abandon dead-end rationality, give up the futility of dialectics, and open their hearts ... if they have any.
>
> Vrest Orton[1]

The modern corporation-model organization was not only founded on the principles of rationalism, it was the consummate expression of the science. There was not a single aspect of the corporation that did not originate in, or was not defined through, or was not driven by rationalistic principles. But neither rationalism nor the corporation could be sustained in what ultimately proved to be a nonrational world. Unnatural, inhuman artifacts eventually crumble.

At the end of the twentieth century, rationalism struggled mightily against its own obsolescence. Cracks began to appear in the once solid intellectual construct, and new intuitive orders began to emerge. The indicators of rapid and irreversible deterioration were numerous and varied, occurring in every aspect of a once proud and sure civilization: a rash of "waivers" granted by heretofore intractable authorities; downsizing and mergers of corporations; shrinking profits and increased competition: a marked tendency toward laissez-faire economics; incapacitated governments; rampant official corruption; deurbanization; the fascination with chaos; uncontrollable cybersystems; anecdotes as substantial evidence; debt as wealth; and symbols as actual—all these and more became the signs of the times. The demise of this science had been at first imperceptible, ironically because of its own benighting effect on those who otherwise might have seen the truth. Incrementalism was the extent of the popular mentality's grasp of change; and the innate human senses, once acute, had been so dulled that credible perception of new intellective and social realities was all but impossible.

It is incomprehensible that a science founded on the studied observation of nature could have itself overlooked a particularly critical natural phenomenon, that is, the principle of the life cycle. Or perhaps the proponents of rationalism thought it exempt from the very "laws" they touted as the foundation and infrastructure of all rational systems. Whether rationalists knew or would admit it, the whole intellectual construct of rationalism, since it had a beginning, eventually had to come to an end or otherwise create itself anew. Because it had by its own doctrine precluded any other reality, there was no possibility of its originating or willingly giving way to another system—even if one could have been imagined. Diagramatically, the life cycle raises some instructive considerations, as shown in Figure 28.1.

The cause of the decline of any systems is always to be found within the system itself. That is the law of regeneration. And so it was with rationalism. One of its assumptions, as pointed out earlier in this study, was that all artifacts not only could be perfected but also should be. According to the doctrine, this was the rule of progress in every aspect of human life, including civilization itself. And that way of thinking resulted in the extension of systems long past efficacy, to say nothing of relevance. Any change was defined strictly within the context of the system because all discovery and invention occurred within the system and was interpreted or applied by the system. Therefore, real change was resisted.

The system actually never changed. As it turns out, homeostasis is not an option; it occurs only in death. And perfection is simply not possible in an imperfect world inhabited by imperfect beings. Refusing creative self-destruction as the only way to self-preservation, rationalism stubbornly precipitated its own annihilation. Contrary to the soothing doctrine of incrementalism, the end comes suddenly—a virtual crash, unforgiving and irreversible.

That fatal flaw of rationalism lay in the fact that it was, from beginning to end, a contradiction. It manifested this intrinsic characteristic quite dramatically in its terminal stage. There were three kinds of patented duplicity: inversion, diversion, and denial of anything superior to itself. These tactics would become a routine part of every aspect of Western civilization. In science, each was unabashedly demonstrated: rationalism came to depend on illogical faith. It refused the admission of knowledge into its own closed universe, and it became consummately dogmatic. In an earlier discussion, the three phases in the development of rationalism are discussed; observation, application or imitation; and postulation. The last was an open invitation for all kinds of fictive apparitions cloaked under the mantle of science.

Rationalism destroyed its own credibility when science was misapplied to nonscientific subjects. In some cases, the fabrications were elaborate ploys

Figure 28.1

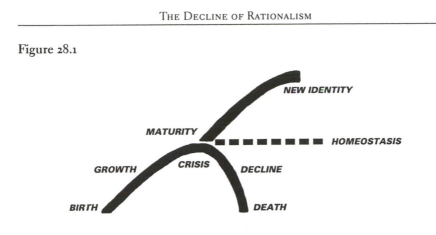

designed to enhance the status, professional and otherwise, of the scientist-pretender, especially in those nondefinable disciplines such as anthropology (the infamous Leakey hoaxes), or psychology (the speculative Dr. Freud and a garrison of clones), or sociology (all the social engineers who convinced politicians that a "great society" could be built). Of course, one would expect that the soft sciences might deal fast and loose with whatever facts they could pan out and that research would consist of questions calculated to produce preconceived answers consistent with the prevailing philosophies.

In the hard sciences, the temptation—as well as the rewards—was often even greater. While a veritable tome of examples could be readily compiled, a front page story in 1996 about the discovery of life on Mars illustrates the many implications of scientific fiction. There were many accounts of this "discovery" in all the media—no doubt reflecting the public-relations efforts of NASA, which was at that very time facing congressional hearings on funding. The account, which reveals as much about the jounalistic tendency to sensationalism as it does about scientific spinning, was in the *San Francisco Chronicle*. The headline blares: "Scientific Evidence of Life on Mars." Orson Wells would have been proud. The immediate impression was that at long last human beings have discovered the opportunity for a close encounter. Little green men and women danced in the fantasy. But the text, presumably based on word from the scientists themselves, held a substantially different story; actually, it was speculation artfully disguised as science. The layers were peeled off slowly:

Space scientists said yesterday that they have discovered the first *compelling* evidence that microscopic life existed on Mars more than 3 billion years ago. . . . The scientists say they have detected what *seem* to be the fossil remains. . . . NASA administration . . . sent an e-mail message to the space agency's Mars experts, declaring: "the evidence is exciting, even compelling, but *not conclusive*. It is a discovery that demands further scientific investigation" [message to Congress].

The story continues, "There is no evidence or suggestion that any higher form of life ever existed on Mars."[2]

While this story was but a single disingenuous hoax foisted on or by the reporters, the Congress, and the public at large, the language itself is indicative of science at the close of the rationalistic age: "seems," "might," "appears," "suggests," "possible." This tentativeness, whether ulterior or desperate, seems rather at odds with the original dedication of modern science to absolute objectivity—not subjectivity—and to irrefutable, not compelling, evidence. Hypothesis is one thing; conclusion quite another. Obviously, this goes considerably beyond the "anthropomorphic subjectivism" about which Clark L. Hull, the co-father of behaviorism, warned early in the twentieth century. But rationalistic human beings seem to have the possible tendency to overestimate their own importance, and that suggests they might underestimate their worth. Or, so it appears.

Regarding the second duplicity, rationalism was predicated on the major premise of the capability of human reason to discover truth through observation and the minor premise of a fixed, rigidly ordered universe—that which was observed. Voilà: The truth lies in "natural laws." Just who (or what) promulgated the laws quickly became an issue of heated and prolonged debate. Nevertheless, Isaac Newton's analogy of the universe as a clock and his three famous laws became the foundation of modern scientific inquiry. The clock imagery gave rise to the happy certainty about the unerring accuracy of prediction, based on the present state of things, and to the unhappy prospect of determinism, based on the future state of things. This cosmic machine operated separate and apart from human beings; it was completely neutral with regard to their well-being and beyond their control. The human being was merely an observer, detachment the only possible stance, and compliance the only course of action. All three of these assertions became well-known towers of rationalistic science. Although never stated as such, it was implicit in all three that the solution to any human problem is always outside the problem.

Newton's famous three laws: inertia, friction, and equal and opposite actions are the basis of modern physics. They were real; it was the truth. And it all could be reduced to mathematical certainty. Then a strange thing happened. At the turn of the twentieth century, observation—so heartily recommended by Bacon and Newton—took on a completely new meaning. A few years earlier, Max Planck followed a clue provided by Clerk Maxwell and concluded that energy is not emitted in a continuous stream but in discontinuous units he referred to as "quanta." The mechanical model was no longer a valid analogy. In 1913, Niels Bohr took the idea to its ultimate conclusion; that is, the entire composition of matter depends on the existence of quanta. The traditional or classical scientific idea of predictability was shattered. But what then was the nature of reality, if indeed there was such? Werner Heisenberg, intrigued and somewhat frustrated by conversations with other scientists, dedicated himself to the quest; and in 1927, he was able to prove mathematically the implausibility of Newton's universe. Because it is impossible to know simultaneously both the position and the velocity of any particle, any causal relationships between and among particles are insufficiently constant to constitute objective reality. The "uncertainty principle" became the basis of a whole new scientific perspective that ultimately suggested that reality was contingent upon the intrusion of human observation. Scientific explanation of the universe shifted from the thing itself—the objectively real— to the human observation of nature—subjective realities.

It was here that science and philosophy met. The romantic poets of the early nineteenth century, for example, believed that human beings "half-create" what they see.

But Heisenberg's famous discovery rekindled another question: that is, was matter made up of "particles" or of "waves." Either theory failed by itself to explain all phenomena. Niels Bohr provided the solution through his principle of "complementarity," which simply suggested that both theories were not only valid but must be taken together. The significance of Bohr's work, along with that of Heisenberg, produced the impetus for an impressive array of expansions, refinements, and new applications over the next fifty years, involving many notable scientists and philosophers, including Albert Einstein. Yet the basic postulates of quantum physics and its ultimate conclusion remained unchanged; that is, there is no absolute reality. Reality lies in the act of observing.

Quantum theory, quite obviously has implications beyond the natural universe. It was there the real trouble began. The third duplicity of rationalistic science forced Western civilization into an historical dilemma of unmeasurable proportions. The premises of all existing rationalized human systems had been thoroughly discredited; and yet those systems, rather than being dismantled, were reinforced, mechanically. As the natural end approached, rationalistic science had proved itself unreasonable; but there was neither the reason nor the will to accept the alternative. Both faith and uncertainty inevitably lead to dogma. Orthodoxy by its very nature provokes resistance. Uncertainty seizes upon any certainty. Although many historians and social critics accurately suggest that during the first half of the twentieth century the quantum philosophy made its way into every discipline of science, as well as sociology and theology, it was not always a welcomed stranger. A stranger, yes. Welcomed, no. Even Einstein was not fully persuaded. Alfred North Whitehead, among others, took note of the intractability of science.

Nothing is more curious than the self-satisfied dogmatism with which mankind at each period of its history cherishes the delusion of the finality of its existent modes of knowledge. . . . At this moment scientists and sceptics are the leading dogmatists. Advance in detail is admitted: fundamental novelty is barred. This dogmatic common sense is the death of philosophic adventure. The Universe is vast.[3]

Having been all but rejected by its own domain of science, quantum theory began to flourish as a popular philosophy, but only after 1986. That is exactly where it had begun—as philosophy. But this time it was translated into the context of human life generally and human organization specifically. Even here it remained outside mainstream thinking. True enough, the new-age secular religionists romanced selected apparent features of the quantum world—namely chaos, complexity, and change—but any implications derived from those intensely vital phenomena were stillborn. Indeed, the various musings about them clearly demonstrated all three. So what if there is order in chaos? So what if there are patterns in complexity? So what if change is the only constant? Nothing in the new science ever approached the seriousness of a tree falling without anyone to hear it, or certainly not that of Schroedinger's cat in the box. There was no meaning because there was no context. And there was no interpretation because there was no meaning.

It is still difficult to imagine a new-age guru, in the early 1990s, explaining to a group of middle managers the creation of a tidal wave by the flutter of a butterfly's wings a thousand miles away. Or perhaps another, in the late 1990s, attempting to convince corporate executives that "visuals" are the "next revolution" in strategic planning. Until then, no one really knew what desperate straits the society was really in.

With all due respect to rationalistic science, that great and earnest inquiry into nature presumed to know the questions that, from a human standpoint, deserved to be answered. Admittedly, most of their actual questions were tendentious, but they were nevertheless serious. So the answers rationalism discovered about nature or created about human beings were defended dogmatically—at least as long as the questioners agreed with them. The questions were invariably about "what" and "how"—never about "why." Analysis of the object and its workings were sufficient knowledge. But the popular version of the "new science," particularily as applied to modern organization, presumed to know answers that did not deserve, much less need, questions. That has to be the final dogma.

The decline of rationalism and its attendant social constructs dramatized at last the need to answer the question, "Why?" Understanding what and how was no longer justification of the perpetuation of any system. That belief actually passed away with the early discoveries of empiricim. But when imitation of natural systems turned to postulating and inventing systems derived strictly from rationalistic thinking, then common sense demanded that they be validated by their benefit to human beings. With regard to human organization, the question became the ultimate question, which very likely had been the original concern. It was, quite simply, Is it possible to create systems that inclusively and completely and permanently serve the universal good of human beings? That is the only reasonable justification for any human organization.

However the question was to be answered, one thing was clear. The future did not lie in the past. Reform was not—nor had it ever been—possible. Neither was improvement. Any attempt to salvage only further wrecked existing systems. Those systems had simply run their course. Nowhere was the collapse more evident than in the major constructs of rationalism, which together had formed the infrastructure of Western civilization: humanistic materialism, democracy, capitalism, and behaviorism were all quickly being absorbed by history. Soon they would be only memories of what they had become: dependency instead of freedom; gratification instead of justice; greed instead of virtue; words instead of action, and, above all, legalism instead of character.

Inexorably, human beings were forced to the unwelcomed and unexpected conclusion that rationalism is unreasonable. Only then could any new concept of organization emerge.

NOTES

1. Vrest Orton, *Vermont Afternoons with Robert Frost* (Rutland, Vt.: Academy Books, 1979), 18.
2. David Perlma, "Scientific Evidence of Life on Mars," *San Francisco Chronicle*, 7 August 1996, p. A1. Emphasis added.
3. Alfred North Whitehead, *Dialogues of Alfred North Whitehead*, ed. Lucien Price (New York: Mentor Books, 1956), 12.

CHAPTER 29

The Decline of
Materialistic Humanism

There are certain sects, which secretly form themselves in the learned world, as well as factions in the political; and though sometimes they come not to an open rupture, they give a different turn to the ways of thinking of those who have taken part on either side. . . . Some exalt our species to the skies, and represent man as a kind of human demigod, who derives his origin from heaven, and retains evident marks of his lineage and descent. Others insist upon the blind sides of human nature, and can discover nothing, except vanity, in which man surpasses the other animals, whom he affects so much to despise.

David Hume[1]

The whole idea behind the modern corporation-model organization was that all human beings, as well as all aspects of human life, are, like the universe they inhabit, strictly materialistic-economic animals, as they were called. And if living excellently were the purpose of life, as the early humanists had argued, then the pursuit of material things was not only natural, it was virtuous. The only problem was that ultimately the obsession with materialism is lethally adverse to life. The corporation-model society produced two extremes, but the same plight. There were those whose lives were consumed by the pursuit of material goods and those whose great material possessions obliterated their persons. There is little wonder that anything so adverse to human being, in the course of time, would be summarily rejected as a way of life. The new prosperity would be defined not as having but as being.

Materialistic Humanism (termed "social humanism" by its proponents) revealed itself early in the twentieth century as the long-sought intersection between, as the phrase implies, the classical idea of humanism and the ancient, though modernized, doctrine of materialism. Although it could be summarized quickly and accurately as anything anti-god, the culminate intellectual disposition had a profound affect on every other aspect of rationalistic science, especially the purpose, psychology, and design of human organization—social, political, and economic. Like all other dualistic and contradictory rationalistic fabrications, it was eminently more materialistic that humanistic, although it claimed equal parts in its heritage. True enough, the philosophy of materialism was not new. In fact, it predates both humanism and rationalism. It could be argued that the early humanists at least courted the idea by their celebration of the enticing beauty and pleasures that lay in the physical world. Yet they were still convinced of a divinely supernatural world and believed that humanity, if it were to achieve its fullness, must partake of the divine nature. The religious themes of Renaissance artistic masterpieces and the unexcelled architecture of cathedrals are eternal testimony to the majestic convergence of the divine and the earthly. That materialism was the progenitor of empirical–rationalistic science, as it was conceptualized in the seventeenth century, however, needs no argument. Even so, its originators were men of religious faith, believing that the physical world was the manifestation of God.

Both humanism and rationalism were motivated by one intense human desire to break out of the stiffling clutches of the tyrannical Church, and to bring the Kingdom of God to the earth and earthy beings. There seems always to be a great gulf between an ecclesiastical order of any kind and the religious faith of individuals. In both cases, materialism had the upper hand, not just because of its longevity and universality but because of its inherent appeal to the baser passions of human beings. It was here and now—not vaguely remote but eternally present. It was easy to understand—not cloaked in mysticism and miracles and dependent on priestly interpretations. Furthermore, it explained and justified natural urges that were condemned by impersonal, nonfeeling icons; and it could easily assuage guilt, that had been heaped upon the conscience of sinners, simply by the abnegation of sin. In its latter stages, it justified sin rather than the sinner. Ironically, those human interpretations were made possible not only because of the Church's own rigid demands and oppressive actions but also because, although waging intellectual and actual war for centuries against materialism, the Church itself had early on become the most materialistic and the most brutal enterprise in the history of civilization—the God of grace and mercy had been given over to cruelty and avarice. The corruption of the Church was a clear indication of the natural power of materialism to co-opt religion long before it quite readily co-opted science. In fact, religion was party to the seduction of science.

There had been traces of materialism in Eastern prehistory, particularly with the mystery religions that divided the universe into the physical and the spiritual—the physical being thoroughly evil. When the idea emerged in the

Western world in the sixth century BC, it was quintessentially simple in its separation of the universe into space and matter. Then, in the fifth century BC, Democritus unbelievably concluded that matter is made up of atoms, of variable shades and sizes. The idea was later denied, of course, by Socrates, Plato, and Aristotle. And when the Church rose to prominence in the first and second centuries, it officially considered anything pertaining to the materialistic philosophy tantamount to heresy: Reality was spiritual—nothing else. In later years, materialistic humanism would play on this rejection by the Church as evidence not only of its antiquity but also of its rightness all along—the truth scorned, as it were: "Democratic secular humanism has been a powerful force in world culture. Its ideals can be traced to the philosophers, scientists, and poets of classical Greece and Rome, to ancient Chinese Confucian society, to the Carvaka movement of India, and to other distinguished intellectual and moral traditions."[2] Only after the authority of the Church was weakened by its own vagaries and the advent of empirical science did materialism resurface as a legitimate, reasonable world view. It soon became the overwhelming force in Western philosophy. Thomas Hobbes even insisted that space was matter (ether). By the end of the eighteenth century, materialism was demonstrably and pervasively the basic assumption of all science; and by the end of the nineteenth century, it had captured the whole mind of Western philosophy. In the United States, it audaciously took the age-old battle into the enemy's camp by infiltrating mainline religion and emerged victorious with the trophy of a completely secular religion. But all its tenets, like the phrase itself, were inherently contradictory; it became a perversion of both religion and reason. Although oversimplified and perhaps not inclusive, Figure 29.1 illustrates the actual lineage of secular humanism.

Although the basic ideas were generally known, if for no other reason than the bitter attacks by traditional fundamental Protestantism, they were not put into a concise formal statement until 1933. Raymond B. Bragg, working with about thirty men from various walks of life, drafted a kind of constitution, titled "Humanistic Manifesto I." That statement would be followed forty years later by "Humanistic Manifesto II"—a postwar elaboration of the original assertions adjusted to the reality of evil in the world but fueled by the free-thinking of the 1960s concerning personal freedom and social justice. This manifesto called for "unified action" to create a "secular society on a planetary scale." And that proclamation, unapppealed and unrescinded, would be followed in 1980 by A Secular Humanist Declaration, which is an elaborate defense of the philosophy cast in the form of an apologia, although drifting from time to time into the shrill cant of eighteenth-century fire-and-brimstone preachers. This declaration introduced the term "democratic secular humanism."

Throughout these successive versions, the one constant from the beginning is contradiction—rife and blatant. This contradiction nevertheless appeals, purportedly, to reason. It was the first example, at least since the Garden of Eden, of linguistic, intellectual contortion—that is, imparting opposite

Figure 29.1

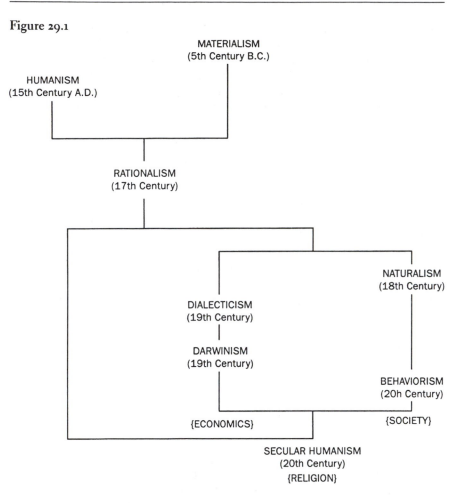

MATERIALISM
(5th Century B.C.)

HUMANISM
(15th Century A.D.)

RATIONALISM
(17th Century)

DIALECTICISM
(19th Century)

NATURALISM
(18th Century)

DARWINISM
(19th Century)

BEHAVIORISM
(20h Century)

{ECONOMICS}

{SOCIETY}

SECULAR HUMANISM
(20th Century)
{RELIGION}

meanings to words—that was used so successfully during the remainder of the century by moral relativists to invert the truth. Satan first appears as an angel of light. "Secular humanism," as it is currently termed, has always had the disconcerting habit of arguing with itself. Searching in vain for some kind of order in a godless world, it scours the philosophical galaxy and collects intellectual debris to fashion its own universe. It is a work in regress. The contradictions within secular humanism are too numerous and too obvious to merit exhaustive analysis, but the following examples demonstrate that the nonfaith, antisystem was more an incoherent attack on reason's child, common sense. It was a strategic assault on religion. Contemporary secular humanists adamantly deny that their philosophy is a religion. The argument is simple, though unconvincing: They ask, rhetorically, how can any human thought or practice that does not accept even the notion of God, the supernatural, or the afterlife be a religion? Yet the "Humanist Manifesto I" describes that philosophy as "religious humanism" and announces itself as a "new religion." Although feigning originality, it can be defined only by that which it opposes.

It presents a remarkable study in contradiction:

Critics often try to classify secular humanism as a religion. Yet secular humanism lacks essential characteristics of a religion, including belief in a deity and an accompanying transcendent order. Secular humanists contend that issues concerning ethics, appropriate social and legal conduct, and the methodologies of science are philosophical and are not part of the domain of religion, which deals with the supernatural, mystical and transcendent.[3]

Today man's larger understanding of the universe, his scientific achievements, and deeper appreciation of brotherhood, have created a situation which requires a new statement of the means and purposes of religion. Such a vital, fearless, and frank religion capable of furnishing adequate social goals and personal satisfactions may appear to many people as a complete break with the past. While this age does owe a vast debt to the traditional religions, it is none the less obvious that any religion that can hope to be a synthesizing and dynamic force for today must be shaped for the needs of this age. To establish such a religion is a major necessity of the present. It is a responsibility which rests upon this generation.[4]

There are many other blatant contradictions in the official statements of the secular humanists. For example: It advocates human "spirituality," but denies the existence of the supernatural.

In the twentieth century scientists, philosophers, and progressive theologians began to organize in an effort to promote the humanist alternative to traditional faith-based world views. These early organizers classified humanism as a nontheistic religion which would fulfill the human need for an ordered ethical/philosophical system to guide one's life, a "spirituality" without the supernatural.[5]

The cultivation of moral devotion and creative imagination is an expression of genuine "spiritual" experience and aspiration.[6]

Even at this late date in human history, certain elementary facts based upon the critical use of scientific reason have to be restated. We find insufficient evidence for belief in the existence of a supernatural; it is either meaningless or irrelevant to the question of survival and fulfillment of the human race. As nontheists, we begin with humans not God, nature not deity. Nature may indeed be broader and deeper than we now know; any new discoveries, however, will but enlarge our knowledge of the natural.[7]

It claims to seek and provide morality, but its definition of moral principles is little more than pragmatic ethics; that is, morality is impossible to know except by its consequences. This conclusion is preferred as an absolute, even though secular humanism adamantly rejects moral absolutes.

We are deeply concerned with the moral education of our children.[8]

We need to extend the uses of scientific method, not renounce them, to fuse reason with compassion in order to build constructive social and moral values.[9]

As secular humanists we believe in the central importance of the value of human happiness here and now. We are opposed to absolutist morality, yet we maintain that objective standards emerge, and ethical values and principles may be discovered, in the course of ethical deliberation.[10]

We affirm that moral values derive their source from human experience.[11]

Thus, secularists deny that morality needs to be deduced from religious belief or that those who do not espouse a religious doctrine are immoral. For secular humanists, ethical conduct is, or should be, judged by critical reason, and their goal is to develop autonomous and responsible individuals, capable of making their own choices in life based upon an understanding of human behavior.[12]

It revels in "free-thinking" and severely castigates all those institutions that would deign to propose truth; yet it rigidly rejects any mention of spiritualism and scorns those who accept it. All other facets of Western civilization presupposed a divine source — even rationalistic science.

The first principle of democratic secular humanism is its commitment to free inquiry. We oppose any tyranny over the mind of man, any efforts by ecclesiastical, political, ideological, or social institutions to shackle free thought.

We recognize the need for intellectual modesty and the willingness to revise beliefs in the light of criticism.[13]

Promises of immortal salvation or fear of eternal damnation are both illusory and harmful. They distract humans from present concerns, from self-actualization, and from rectifying social injustices. Modern science discredits such historic concepts as the "ghost in the machine" and the "separable soul." Rather, science affirms that the human species is an emergence from natural evolutionary forces. As far as we know, the total personality is a function of the biological organism transacting in a social and cultural context. There is no credible evidence that life survives the death of the body. We continue to exist in our progeny and in the way that our lives have influenced others in our culture.[14]

It champions individual and social freedom, and yet it calls for unification of all secular humanists against those who oppose their doctrine.

There are many forms of totalitarianism in the modern world—secular and nonsecular—all of which we vigorously oppose. As democratic secularists, we consistently defend the ideal of freedom, not only freedom of conscience and belief from those ecclesiastical, political, and economic interests that seek to repress them, but genuine political liberty, democratic decision making based upon majority rule, and respect for minority rights and the rule of law.[15]

Indeed, there is a broader task that all those who believe in democratic secular humanist values will recognize, namely, the need to embark upon a long term program of public education and enlightenment concerning the relevance of the secular outlook to the human condition.[16]

In the final analysis, secular humanism was 100 percent rationalistic but completely unreasonable. It is either a fanatical agenda looking for intellectual respectability and historical adjudication or a desperate and naive confusion of fact and fiction. Or, without any fear of contradiction, it could be both.

Secular humanism, therefore, could easily be dismissed as an insignificant aberration. Its dubious origin, its erratic propositions, its material errors and fallacious reasoning, and its illogical conclusions seem the antithesis of the Western philosophical tradition—both religious and secular. Before the end of the twentieth century, this renegade intellection nevertheless had pervaded almost every aspect of Western society, especially where thought is not antecedent to action. If the citizens of the United States in 1933 had been confronted directly with the doctrine of secular humanism, as in some forced imposition of any or all of its tenets upon them, the overwhelming majority would have rejected it out of hand. But there is genius in pure perversity. Secular humanism, as an organized movement, did not overtly challenge the public's belief in the existence of God through advertising campaigns, civil litigation, political clout, or public demonstrations. To the contrary, by design or nature, it surreptitiously infiltrated the heart and soul of Western society—its religion and its philosophy; its churches and its schools—the only places it would be understood and accepted. These were also the only aspects of that society with the potential of shaping all the others, and both proved disappointingly pervious.

There is no need here to recount the long history of the corruption of religion in America—from the incendiary atheistic promulgations by Robert Ingersoll in the nineteenth century to the defense of the theory of evolution by Clarence Darrow in the 1920s to the announcement of the death of God by Harvey Cox in the 1960s, the erosion of theistic religion (to say nothing of traditional Christianity and Judaism) ultimately became a landslide. It would not be appropriate here to argue the merits of this religion or any other, but it is certainly apropos to consider the effect of rationalism on Christianity. As a quick example, at a religious symposium sponsored by Duke University's Divinity School in 1998, seven scholars openly denied essentially all the foundational precepts of the Christian religion. According to them, "Jesus was not born of the Virgin, never walked on water, did not deliver the sermon on the mount, did not claim to be divine, and was not resurrected from the dead."[17] Some said he did not have twelve apostles and never convened a last supper with them. When a member of the audience asked what the Church's purpose was without miracles, one panel member replied, "I'm amazed by the question." Of course he was.

But it was in education that secular humanism realized its greatest triumph. The disciples of this pseudophilosophy have the annoying habit of audaciously dropping names to bolster the respectability of their assertions. For example:

There have been any number of distinguished secularists and humanists who have demonstrated moral principles in their personal lives and works: Protagoras, Lucretius, Epicurus, Spinoza, Hume, Thomas Paine, Diderot, Mark Twain, George Eliot, John Stuart Mill, Ernest Renan, Charles Darwin, Thomas Edison, Clarence Darrow, Robert Ingersoll, Gilbert Murray, Albert Schweitzer, Albert Einstein, Max Born, Margaret Sanger, and Bertrand Russell, among others.[18]

Whether all these could be accurately classified as secular or humanist is indeed doubtful. But there was one signatory to the *Manifesto I* worthy of special note because of his extraordinary influence on "progressive" education—not only in the United States but throughout Western society. John Dewey was a pragmatist, believing in no transcendental or supernatural reality and convinced that rationalistic science was the only "instrument" by which human beings could adjust themselves to their world. Science was the only morality; democratic interpretations of experience the only solution to changing circumstances; and utilitarian work the only righteous vocation. It would be an unfair exaggeration, and far too generous, to suggest that Dewey was responsible for the particularly secular cast of both public and parochial education in the twentieth century; but it is true that the critical features of modern education were amazingly congruent with the principles espoused by secular humanism. And that definition of education was a radical departure from the classical tradition of the West. Both Aristotle and Plato would have insisted that the purpose of education was individual freedom—the exercise of one's full powers. St. Thomas Aquinas would have thought its only purpose was proving the will of God. John Milton would have wordily suggested it was that which equips one "to perform justly, skillfully, and magnanimously all the offices, public and private, of war and peace."[19]

Rationalism assigned to education the role of "rationalizing" human beings, just as it had already "rationalized" production and eventually every other aspect of society. The purpose of rationalized education was to conform human beings to the process, uniformity, and precision of a practical, industrial world and, beyond that, to conform their minds, and consequently their lives, to a secular humanistic order of society, the corporation. By the

end of the twentieth century, it had become abundantly clear that every specific educational initiative undertaken in the name of rationalism had succeeded only in producing the exact opposite of its much-heralded intent.
The most significant study of education ever undertaken concluded in 1983,
"Our Society and its educational institutions seem to have lost sight of the
basic purposes of schooling, and of the high expectations and disciplined effort
needed to attain them."[20] But no one, not even the distinguished Carnegie Commission, took the warning as a serious indictment of what the system had become—an instrument of secular humanism. They urgently proposed that the
solution was to "reform"—not to replace—the existing system. As a result,
the entire reform movement that subsequently swept the nation served only
to reinforce those inbred features that were adverse to the original purpose.

- First, it advocated education as a "social project," rather than the development of
  individual human beings. In fact, in the early 1970s, the U.S. Department of Education developed comprehensive and detailed guidelines and regulations to bring
  about the radical shift from teaching and learning to creating a rationalized social
  order. As far as anyone knows, contrary to all the political rhetoric about the redemption of America's hapless educational system, that was the last official word
  or action from the federal government regarding the purpose of education. The
  result was two losses, both devastating. The first was widespread illiteracy and
  general carelessness with respect to historical and cultural facts, to say nothing,
  paradoxically, of fundamental ignorance of mathematics and the sciences. Newton would have been proud. In fact, at the beginning of the twenty-first century,
  the educational system of the United States was ranked among the lowest in the
  so-called "industrialized nations." At least it satisfied the nation's obsession for
  always being preeminent.

- Second, there came the horrifying development of social divides wider and more
  intense than any since the original colonization of the Americas. In outright contradiction of their own doctrine, politicians parlayed racial, economic, and cultural divisions into political advantage, pitting citizens against citizens in destructive
  social conflict and making a mockery of E pluribus unum. School lunchrooms,
  classrooms, and playgrounds were but the natural microcosm of that severely rup-
  tured society. Clubs turned into gangs, proms into political causes, extracurricular
  activities into a juvenile version of class warfare. The primary concern of schools
  was no longer teaching and learning but the prevention of violence. Schools became citadels of security; classrooms corrals. The noble purpose of creating a
  social order was lost in the desperate attempt to maintain order.

- Third, education boldly proclaimed "critical thinking" as the "highest order" of
  intellectual skills. Virtually every school district in the United States and Canada
  by 1990 recited this mantra in its public mission or "vision" statement and had
  interjected a "program" of critical thinking into its curricula. Dewey had, in fact,
  changed the whole paradigm of Western thought when he suggested that the re-
  vered methodology of science could actually be considered not a means but an
  end. He maintained that since real objective truth could never be known it was
  only through the experimental method that human beings could constantly ad-

just their reality to that which is real. The foregone conclusion: there was no "essential" truth beyond human experience. Truth was at best only verisimilitude. The attractiveness of this idea is obvious: The person is able to control the conclusion simply by controlling the hypotheses and experimentation. In this remarkable reverse twist, the belabored denial of essential truth became itself little more than a preconceived essence. However, critical thinking, if honestly understood, is impossible without judgment; and judgment, even in scientific inquiry, is impossible without some moral basis. "Testing" experience may be empirical, and it may be rational; but it is not the highest order of thinking—for two reason. First, it is purely analytical. Synthesis is impossible simply because nothing has meaning except in the interpretation; situational analysis provides little by way of permanence. Second, it refuses to accept the immeasurable truth that can be discovered in creative thinking—organic, intuitive, imaginative. There is a great paradox here. If critical thinking is a skill, then creative thinking is a power. If critical thinking conforms, then creative thinking frees. If critical thinking is mental, creative thinking is spiritual. If critical thinking results in the confusion of subjective truths, then creative thinking culminates in the harmony found only in objective truth.

The most critical issue facing education at the beginning of the twenty-first century was whether it could and would dedicate itself to discovering the ultimate power of the human mind. That discovery, when made, would prove to be the historical equivalent to the discovery of fire. The only thing that could prevent that discovery was education itself.

• Fourth, it spoke wistfully of morality, but only as derived from human experience. Especially in the 1980s, when the spirit of community was high, public education made a perfunctory nod in that direction. But, again, following the strict guidelines of the Department of Education against cultural or religious bias, U.S. schools adopted not a curriculum that taught specific values but one of "values clarification"—which simply meant exploring some of the ramifications of a "values"-related decision, and understanding the consequences. Officially, there was no right and no wrong, except as defined by beneficial or adverse consequences. When something termed "outcomes-base education" surfaced in the 1980s, a discipline that included a component on values, the strongest opposition came from religious groups who were concerned with the question of whose values would be taught. The results of this farce was not just more moral ambiguity but the loss of the concept altogether from an institution whose only reason for existence is to educate ("to lead out") and which, by law in the United States, must act in loco parentis. In the first instance, it refused to lead anyone anywhere. In the second, it was afraid of the real parents.

If those were the cardinal principles of secular humanism, that emphasis did not diminish the vigor with which several other agendas were pursued—all of which were eagerly welcomed by a vacuous education establishment too bland and too political to have ideas of its own. Anything dubbed "progressive" was immediately embraced as the new gospel. For example, education became the chief proponent and vehicle of egalitarianism. From school uniforms to academic achievement, "equal" came to mean "same." A little book titled *The Rainbow Fish* began showing up in elementary school libraries. Classifying students according to intelligence or ability was deemed too competitive and thoroughly prejudicial; "tracking" was out, "mixed ability grouping" was in. In the mid-1990s, all traditionally respected achievement tests were normed down or eliminated altogether to accommodate the lowest common denominator. All "standards" became minimums for both students and teachers. Educators began to speak with a forked tongue: They praised excellence but refused to let anyone fail; they said they believed that all children could learn—if given enough time and the appropriate conditions—but they provided neither adequate time nor conditions. To raise test scores for their districts, they simply cheated. And fawning state legislatures, in the name of "equalization," made sure the same amount of money was spent on every child—as if that could really produce equal results.

However, if there was an overriding agenda item, it had to have been something referred to as "multiculturalism" or, in its redacted form, "cultural diversity." Secular humanism's most violent political rant was reserved for the condemnation of culture and nationalism in the generic and of Western culture and the United States in particular. Jefferson and other founders of constitutional democracy were firmly convinced that only education could so enlighten citizens that they would be capable of self-rule as a single, unified nation. Patriotism was not a bad word. For generations, immigrants—admittedly, from European countries—were quickly assimilated into the "melting pot" of democracy. But multiculturalsim was the countertrend. Although it mellifluously preached the secular humanistic doctrine of tolerance, respect, and compromise, and even peace on earth and good will, it actually succeeded only in segmenting the nation into consolidated racial, ethnic, and religious groups, with deep-seated enmity toward one another. In the process, the common culture was completely obliterated. In United States schools, American citizens began pledging allegiance to the flags of their "home" countries; and everyone was hyphenated as a mark of his or her true nationality. Citizens became foreigners in their own land. If that were not enough, the education establishment took great delight in dignifying as "cultures" all kinds of morally deviant and socially reprehensible groups and extended to them undue respect along with all the rights and privileges thereunto appertaining.

Here are two final examples: First, education gladly surrendered the concept of authority so roundly denounced by secular humanism, choosing to redefine instruction as "facilitation," and learning as the sharing of ignorance. Second, education somehow came to the conclusion that "self-esteem" was the prerequisite for achievement and acceptable conduct, rather than disciplined achievement and moral uprightness being the prerequisites for self-esteem.

Notably absent from all the groups of secular humanism, and likewise missing from all curricula, were those qualities that ultimately each human being must see reflected in the mirror: virtue, morality, honor, love, purpose, compassion. It is little wonder that, by the year 2000, in some school districts in the United States as many as half the students dropped out before graduation. There was nothing there for them—or about them. That was the legacy of materialism.

NOTES

1. David Hume, "Of the Dignity or Meanness of Human Nature," *The Oxford Book of Essays*, ed. John Gross (Oxford: Oxford University Press, 1991), 81.

2. *A Secular Humanist Declaration*, drafted by Paul Kurtz (Amherst, N.Y.: Prometheus Books, 1980), 7–8.

3. Fritz Stevens, Edward Tabash, Tom Hill, Mary Ellen Sikes, and Tom Flynn, "What Is Secular Humanism?" 30 May 1997. Available at DavidNoelle/admin@secularhumanism.org.

4. "Humanist Manifesto I," *Humanist Manifestos I and II*, ed. Paul Kurtz (Amherst, N.Y.: Prometheus Books, 1973), 8.

5. Stevens et al., "What Is Secular Humanism?"

6. "Humanist Manifesto II," *Humanist Manifestos I and II*, ed. Paul Kurtz (Amherst, N.Y.: Prometheus Books, 1973), 15.

7. Ibid., 16.

8. "The Affirmations of Humanism: A Statement of Principles" (Amherst, N.Y.: Council for Secular Humanism, 1997), brochure.

9. "Humanist Manifesto II," 14.

10. *A Secular Humanist Declaration*, 15.

11. "Humanist Manifesto II," 17.

12. *A Secular Humanist Declaration*, 15.

13. Ibid., 10.

14. "Humanist Manifesto II," 16–17.

15. *A Secular Humanist Declaration*, 13.

16. Ibid., 23.

17. "UM (United Methodists) in Action Briefing," Washington, D.C., Institute on Religion and Democracy, July 1988, 3.

18. *A Secular Humanist Declaration*, 16.

19. John Milton, "On Education," quoted in *The College Survey of English Literature*, ed. Alexander M. Witherspoon (New York: Harcourt, Brace, 1951), 378.

20. *A Nation at Risk: The Imperative for Educational Reform*, A Report to the Nation and the Secretary of Education by the National Commission on Excellence in Education, Chairman David P. Gardner (April 1983), 7.

CHAPTER 30

The Decline of Democracy

From this view of the subject it may be concluded that a pure democracy, by which I mean a society consisting of a small number of citizens, who assemble and administer the government in person, can admit of no cure for the mischiefs of faction. A common passion or interest will, in almost every case, be felt by a majority of the whole; a communication and concert result from the form of government itself; and there is nothing to check the inducements to sacrifice the weaker party or an obnoxious individual. Hence it is that such democracies have even been spectacles of turbulence and contention; have ever been found incompatible with personal security or the rights of property; and have in general been as short in their lives as they have been violent in their deaths.

Publius[1]

Quite frankly, the corporation never knew how to deal with the concept of democracy, so it used any expression of democracy like any other expedient, for its own purpose. The corporation was, in fact, caught in an unreasonable ironic dilemma. On the one hand, the modern corporation could not have come into existence without the conditions implicit within a democratic state, most fundamentally individual freedom. On the other, the very purpose, structure, and disposition of the corporation, a secular version of religious order, could not tolerate the freedom of individuals. It responded by exercising its own freedom even outside the boundaries of its governmental patron even to the point of forswearing any allegiance to that government and putting it at risk; and it cynically held out the false promise of individual participation in its business. Both were perversions of democracy—one on a national scale, the other eminently personal.

Democracy, from the standpoint of the individual, was supposed to be the crowning achievement of rationalism; but it was a pretender to the throne. It held out the promise of liberty, but in order to insure that freedom it had to take away personal freedom. It promised justice, yet was born in defiance of law and ultimately resorted to legalistic injustice to overcome its own moral injustice. It spoke eloquently of equality but saw equality as a mutual privilege among peers, not as a universal right. One would think that the originators of modern democracies, particularly those who drafted the United States Constitution, might have been discerning enough to realize the inconsistencies of their own words and actions; but they were neither political scientists nor philosophers nor moralists. One would also think they had learned the impossibility of a democratic system of government from the disappointing experiments of Solon or the mature yet severely limited democracy of Athens. But they did not. Those dutiful, sincere patriots were concerned only with creating the most practical system of government that could guarantee their life, liberty, and pursuit of happiness. Like all other revolutionaries, they did not escape the constructs of the past. So they began exactly where the Greeks had left off—even to the detail of adopting their basic structural arrangement of government; and they overlaid that with the trappings, along with the pomp and circumstance, of the parliamentary monarchy they had rejected. Also, it is particularly important to remember that the Constitution of the United States was drafted more than a century after the first corporation was established on the North American continent. The pervasive influence of the corporation-model organization was thoroughly impressed in that evolving interpretation of democracy. Predictably, the influence was not reciprocal.

To their eternal credit, the framers realized the risks associated with self-government; and they struggled mightily with various options in order to create conditions and safeguards that would best preserve the original idea. Only in recent times has it become possible to appreciate fully the impossibility of the undertaking. The situation presented a classic dilemma: how to take an essentially antigod construct, with its origin in the pagan world, and reconcile it with the fundamental beliefs that reflected the historical, and their personal, Western belief in a divine creator.

Some of the issues they settled upon became an integral part of the democratic system's basic structure. For example, they chose not to put in place popular democracy, one that was sustained and perpetuated by the direct involvement—specifically, voting—of all citizens. That, they reasoned, would be susceptible to the transient whims of the general population, which is sometimes swayed by emotions. It also would compromise the sovereignty of the several states, which had come together to form a "more perfect union." Rather, they, like Solon, established a "representative" democracy, a republic. Only, in this modern version, the representation was not of numerically constituted groups; it was the representation of citizens of political entities, called states. That was true even before United States' senators were elected popularly rather than by the states, ending an obvious carryover from the British tradition of lords. The wisdom of this course of action—that is, representative democracy—has been hailed, if not always honored in practice, over and over during the past two centuries. On the other hand, the founders' attempts to impose reasonable limits on the actual processes of democracy have not been as enduring; for example, the restriction of enfranchisement to male landowners and merchants (which, by the way, provides an early indication of what "life, liberty, and the pursuit of happiness" came to mean) has long since ended. Issues like this precipitated a continuing legacy of debate and protest, usually settled by constitutional amendment or Supreme Court decision, to say nothing of legislative action. Needless to say, all those questions and their answers, however tentative, were essential not only to the dynamics of self-rule but also as a permanent test of the principles of democracy. Even today, there is passionate debate about exactly what the founding fathers intended, but even more significant, whether it still matters. Democracy was and is an experiment.

The implicit contradiction between divine and human systems resulted in serious tension between ideal assumptions and practical artifacts. For example, the American version of democracy assumed that citizens had both the intellectual capacity to understand the immediate issues and the right to be fully informed. It also assumed, by its very name, that those who were admitted into democracy would participate in all matters—public and private, hostile and peaceful—pertaining to that democracy. It assumed further that those involved in the processes of democracy would be "enlightened," after the intellectual cant of the time; that is, able to reason logically and possessing a historical world view. Above all, it assumed that they would be dedicated to common interest—"general welfare," "common defense," "domestic tranquillity." But the fundamental assumption of this democracy was that its citizens were, or at least aspired to be, virtuous. That assumption acknowledges a moral universe not of human origin: "In God we trust," they said.

Recently, Professor Michael Sandel has argued, and rightly so, that any democratic form of government should be, and in fact is, a "formative" enterprise shaping the character of its citizens simply because self-government is impossible without it.[2] Even the likes of Hamilton and Jefferson, although political opponents on many issues, ultimately were concerned with the effect of public policy and action on the character of society, individuality and collectively. However, in practicality, none of the four assumptions were realized; they were constantly eroded by incessant adversity, ironically because the democratic system itself destroyed the concept of a moral universe, moral uprightness, and responsible individuals and in its place substituted one completely amoral. Rationalism would eventually destroy everything that in a Godly world was true, honorable, good, selfless, and righteous. When democracy, rather than shaping the character of its citizens, was itself formed by the character of its citizens, it ceased to be a reasonable idea of government.

If the form of democracy is the idea, and if its spirit is the ideal, then its soul must be ideology. And therein lies its fatal flaw. Even before constitutional democracy was established in the Americas, ideology had emerged as the vital force in an otherwise hypothetical notion of government: In a word, politics; in two words, political parties; in a ceaseless torrent of words, politicians. Political parties certainly were not new in 1776. They had dominated English rule of law since the Magna Carta, especially in seasons of a weakened monarchy. In the contemporaneous eighteenth century, partisan strife was so pronounced that women joined the fray by wearing "party-patches," cosmetically applied to either side of the face as an indication of their political sentiments, when they attended high-class occasions such as balls and the theater. So, it was not surprising that the founding of the United States was accompanied by intense debate between the Federalists and the Antifederalists. The first was the party of Alexander Hamilton and John Adams; the second, later the Democratic–Republican party, that of Thomas Jefferson. For the next fifty years there occurred a continual realignment and evolution of parties until the fight over slavery, an issue already dividing the nation, forged the two current parties of U.S. politics.

There were two aspects of the always tumultuous and often humorous history of political parties during this time. First, it is noteworthy that the dualistic tendency prevalent in rationalistic science manifested itself in the natural development of a two-party system. There was only one brief period, after 1816, in which the demise of the Federalist party left only one party in action. The only conclusion is that, in a political system of majority rule, division is inevitable. Some political scientists and historians argue that the adversarial dynamic is positive — checks and balances. Yet that friendly assessment is based on the assumption that a single system would lead to tyranny, such as that of present-day China, North Korea, or Cuba, and that a multiparty system, such as those of many European democracies, would deteriorate into chaos.

Second, before 1850, the primary issues of conflict were matters pertaining to the democratic system of government itself. It was as if basic ideas had to be sorted out: nationalism versus states' rights, protective versus revenue tariffs, a national bank versus an independent treasury—then, slavery versus universal freedom. Only after 1932, with the introduction of the New Deal social agenda and the adoption of Keynesian economic doctrine, did the issues of political debate dramatically shift to personal interest—specifically, health and welfare. And only thirty years later did they become rights: civil in the 1960s; social in the 1970s; human in the 1980s; and personal in the 1990s. Government had become a patron saint, not a stern schoolmaster. Political parties had, in fact, changed not only the role of government, but also the definition of democracy. The words themselves became obsolete: government was not government; democracy was certainly not democracy.

If democracy was the amoral equivalent to divine sovereignty, then the corporation was the immoral equivalent of political ideology. It became, in effect, a political party, tolerating democratic principles only as long as they served its interests. In fact, of all organized entities on earth, including the Communist Central Party, corporations opposed democracy most. And that is especially critical, since historically the corporations predate the U.S. Constitution. There was first the inherent conflict between the authoritarianism of the corporation and the individual freedom promised by democracy. Second, the corporation rejected both for itself and as social commitments the four assumptions underlying democracy—especially the common interest. All other interests were subordinated to the creation of stockholder wealth. Taxation was resisted; natural environments destroyed; lives ruined; families broken up; ethics mocked; the national economy weakened and security compromised by traitorous off-shore business activity and foreign entanglements; and the public will and good denied by the blatant undermining of representative governmental process through politics. By 2000, the role of government was dictated by the largest corporate contributors to political campaigns.

Ironically, the closer to its citizens democracy becomes, the more cultural its interpretation. The more cultural the interpretation, the more it departs from the original idea. That principle alone accounts for the wide range of variations in modern Western democracies. For the purposes here, "culture" is defined as the usually accidental (natural) but sometimes deliberate (artifactual) accumulation of myth and legend, wisdom and constructs, experience and conviction that distinguishes a social order. It has already been pointed out that the idea of democracy is culturally based. It is a Western philosophy; and, in practice, both the ancient and modern originators attempted to erect a protective firewall between the actual system of government and the synchronistic cultures; most notably, representation and bureaucratic processes. In the United States, two forces enthralled democracy to culture: The first was the movement from monoculturalism to polyculturalism; the second, as might be expected, was excessive information.

The first was gradual, albeit predictable by even nonscientific observation. It is mildly curious that, although civilization by its very nature is the antithesis of culture, the democracy of the United States was begun with that assumption but ended with a quite different disposition. During the first phase, up until 1918, the national sentiment was anticultural; that is, opposing and willing to destroy other "inferior" cultures in order to perpetuate the dominant value system. There was an overwhelming sense of rightness and righteousness that could not be compromised. From 1918 through the 1970s, the prevalent attitude was one of virtuous noncultural balance; the "melting pot theory" reflected the mood of the times; equality, normalization, uniformity, and equity became the major issues. Beginning in 1980, the attitude shifted to what was termed "multicultural." Even if this idea can be taken as a serious admission that the first two approaches did not work, it is still probably the most destructive of all, simply because, as long as power is defined as material wealth, it will always provoke irreconcilable conflicts among cultures—and within democracy itself. The popular word and tragic warning is "Balkanization." It is a sad reality, perhaps, but true that at the time the European nations—which had intentionally maintained their distinct cultural identities, even to the point of policing their languages—were transcending culture and uniting in a common market, the United States was breaking up into smaller and smaller cultural segments. Confounding yet further the variance of special interests was the insistence, no doubt a holdover from the industrial mentality, that equality (sameness) is compatible with rule by the majority; that is, that there be a single uniform course of action applicable to all groups of citizens. Democracy attempted to make reality out of the real, rather than accepting the real as reality. Having already forsworn the rule of democracy as the agent of character formation, it had neither the legitimacy nor the ability to do so.

The second was cataclysmic. Information technology created a virtual direct democracy. The citizenry could be informed instantaneously and continuously of events, circumstances, issues, and especially the divergent, politically calculated interpretations thereof. Electronically, it was possible not only to govern by immediate popular polling on so-called major issues but also to operate the daily activities of governing simply by reacting to public opinion. In effect, the historical structures that were intended to provide an orderly, deliberate process of reason and debate were no longer necessary—or possible. It was politically unwise to ignore the prevailing winds, the direction and velocity of which were reported by professional opinionologist—pollsters, political analysts, legal experts, news commentators—on a twenty-four-hour basis. Obviously, this inescapable avalanche of information was fraught with many dangers: The information, even in its purest form, did not always constitute real knowledge; polls easily could be rigged with tendentious questions; analysts were swayed by their own political bias; legal experts could fabricate any reality simply by changing the meaning of words (now there were three kinds of definition: real, nominal, and legal); and electronic journalists were by nature instigators of controversy—information often became misinformation, and no one knew the difference. The greatest danger, warned of in earlier decades by a host of critical seers from historians to novelists alike, was not that information control politics but that politics control information. Abraham Lincoln, as it turned out, was only two-thirds correct when he said, "You can fool some of the people all the time and all of the people some of the time. But you can't fool all the people all the time." As any despot knows, the way to control the masses is by controlling information, creating a public truth based on grand lies.

By the end of the twentieth century, these two factors—cultural conflict and information manipulation—had combined to produce inverted chaos, best described 150 years earlier by Matthew Arnold:

> Here we are as on a darkling plain
> Swept with confused alarms of struggle and flight
> where ignorant armies clash by night.[3]

Democracy had become indefensible as a reasonable practicality. By its own attitudes and devices, it had produced at least four intolerable, unjustifiable, and unsolvable predicaments: fragmentation, polarization, separation, and mediocrity. With regard to the first, it was fairly evident early in the 1980s that for any number of reasons—the need for personal identity in increasing globalization, preservation of indigenous language and culture, political prowess—each of the various cultural groups in North America was consolidating rather than assimilating. But the greatest reason was the fear of not being acknowledged in the total composite, that is, of being left out of things of national scope or of not receiving fair treatment. Sensing that politics responds to political pressure, each group in effect became a political action committee, attempting directly to affect, if not effect, the machinations of government. Consensus thus destroyed, agreement—even majority agreement—was frustrated.[4]

At this time, national politicians—although still erroneously defining consensus as rational mutuality—began publicly to speak of "majority consensus." Lost completely was any hope of the common good or, for that matter, of any commonality.

The second was more a matter of the functioning of democracy than of pluralism. Polarity has always been assumed to be a natural condition in any social intercourse—religion, economics, law, politics. In fact, it was thought to be an especially beneficial dialectic because both in processes and substance it would identify and achieve moderation—the much heralded but seldom seen "political center." According to the theory, that would not only please (or displease) both extremes equally, it would actually be the wisest course of action as judged by consequences. So far, so good. However, in a mature democracy, which neither the ancient Greeks nor the founding fathers had foreseen, a strange thing happens. In fact, it is the only sure sign of the maturity of the system. This is the stage at which the polarity is no longer based on issues but on values. The poles destroy the center by sucking everything between into one of the extremes.[5] The result is an open wound that will not heal. Not only is unity destroyed; the nation is permanently divided. That is the inevitable condition of democracy.

Third, political systems eventually separate the government from its citizens; consequently, also citizens from their government. In the United States during the twentieth century, this occurred in two ways. First, the representation of the people—their values, will, and aspirations—through government order was supplanted by the mendacious interjection of special interest cabals—their demands, threats, and litigations—aimed at inciting government disorder. Second, elected officials—politicians first, last, and always—aided and abetted this coup by their lust for power and their greed for perpetual campaign funds, which could handily be converted into personal use. Treason does not always mean selling out to foreign interests.

It is little wonder, then, that in any national election in the United States, barely one-third of eligible voters make the effort. And the rampant ignorance and detachment demonstrated by otherwise responsive citizens would be inexcusable were it not for the fact that, for them, government has become irrelevant.

The fourth predicament was simply this. Originally, democracy was based on the assumption that ordinary citizens could ably participate in the necessary processes of self-government. "Ordinary," however, did not mean "mediocre." However, in the general leveling that takes place in every aspect of democratic life, the natural consequence is the elevation of mediocrity to the ideal. Any pretense of actually leading is immediately exposed as fraud; any idea of excellence is reduced to norms and minimums; examples become warnings; and words are parsed to bestow approval or praise on that which is coarse, mean, and immoral. How is it possible that the United States, the paragon of democracy, lags far behind other industrial nations in almost every significant educational index? And how is it possible that the twentieth century closed with a raging congressional bloodbath over the legal definition of basic morality and honesty—a debate fostered by the conduct of the chief elected government official? The debate personified the culmination of democracy—the dilemma of microrationalistic legalisms versus the innate idea of morality beyond justice and of self-governance outside political ideology. The situation might have been "intellectual chaos" in politics; but the same confused mental condition in a person would have been diagnosed as insanity.

Any system of government ultimately will be judged by the kind of people it brings to power. Mediocrity is not merely a matter of objective comparison; it is a spiritual state of being; and any system of government, whether in its origin or by its intent, that calls forth less than the best of its citizens is no better than a system that accepts the worst.

NOTES

1. *The Federalist or the New Constitution*, papers by Alexander Hamilton, James Madison, and John Jay (Norwalk, Conn.: The Easton Press, 1979), 59.

2. Michael J. Sandel, *Democracy's Discontent: America in Search of a Public Philosophy* (Cambridge, Mass.: Harvard University Press, 1996), 220.

3. Matthew Arnold, "Dover Beach," *The Norton Anthology of English Literature* (New York: W. W. Norton, 1968), 2: 1039.

4. In 1992 and in 1996, the United Sates elected its first president by minority vote. It seems the presidency is not as well connected as a monarchy and therefore not as enduring. One has divine authority; the other only the leverage of a constantly diminishing minority of self-interest seekers.

5. Recent elections in Israel, Poland, and Ireland were won or lost by less than 1 percentage point. And the United States in 1998, both the House and Senate were within 0.02 percentage points of parity.

CHAPTER 31

The Decline of Capitalism

> If you have not acquired more than a bare existence . . . it is because you
> have either not learned the laws that govern the building of wealth, or
> else you do not observe them.
>
> George S. Clason[1]

When capitalism, the raison d'être of the corporation, was at last forced into
the world of ideas, it could not compete. Like all other artifactual systems, it
learned too late that the seeds of its demise were planted at its beginning.
Supply does not elicit demand. But the irresistable demand for economic
systems other than capitalism, even in capitalistic countries, by the 1990s had
reached critical mass. Supply had to follow. It came in the form of a new kind
of human organization.

Capitalism was battle tested, all right, if not battle weary. It had survived
not only attacks from outside forces but also failure from within the system
for over a century; so it was not surprising that it had the undaunted determinism to soldier on as if the war had long since been won. Little by little,
over the years, its line of defense caved.

The decline of capitalism can be best understood in the context of historical economic transitions, especially in the United States.

In the early 1980s, a book called *Megatrends* introduced Americans to something called the "age of information" and generalized the historical transitions in
the economy of America.[2] The fundamental concepts are both accurate and
intriguing; but the most significant issues involved in these transitions are yet
to be fully realized, even by historians, to say nothing of futurists.

The basic approach holds that "ages" or "eras" are characterized in terms of what the majority of the nation's population does to make a living. So, the thesis goes, as late as the mid-nineteenth century, about 70 percent of Americans were involved in agriculture as their primary source of income. The "agricultural" or "agrarian" age historically extends all the way back to precivilization, even to the beginning of the human race. That means, as a conservative estimate, that the "agricultural age" is about 25,000 years old. In 1998, less than 1 percent of Americans made a living farming; and that percentage continues to decline.

The shift from agriculture came with the Industrial Revolution of the nineteenth century. It is not generally noted, but in America the movement into and through the "industrial age" came over a period of at least ninety years—from 1860 to 1950—and occurred in three approximately thirty-year increments. The first was that of private industrialization, characterized by the entrepreneurial industrialists of the middle and late 1800s. The second was that of corporate industrialization, characterized by corporate enterprise, as opposed to purely free enterprise. The third was government industrialization, which manifested itself in the complicated economic interrelationships between the federal government and all corporations. A final surge of government industrialization came in the frantic rush into outer space during the ten years immediately following the Sputnik surprise in 1957.

Not until the late 1970s did the nation realize that yet another economic transition had occurred, taking the government, industry, and everybody else quite by surprise. According to the popular notion of the time as proclaimed in a variety of pop-futuristic publications, the nation, if not the world, had suddenly been thrust into the "age of information." The experts knew that because, by their count, 65 to 70 percent of the population was making a living in so-called "information" (or service) industries.

During all these economic transitions, capitalism as an economic philosophy was being constantly eroded, by government interference, by capitalism's own pathological avarice, by external forces (sometimes even of its own making), and finally by revolutionary shifts not only in the definition of wealth and factors of production but also in the public's attitude toward consumerism.

First, there was the eviscerating effect of governmental regulations. In 1877, the Supreme Court ruled (*Munn v. Illinois*) that states could regulate businesses when "a public interest" was at stake. Although the ruling was later somewhat weakened by other court decisions, the restraining power of government was permanently established. In 1890, Congress, acting on the theory that "perfect" competition was not only possible but desirable, passed the Sherman Antitrust Act to prevent larger companies from conspiring together to drive smaller companies out of the market. A much stronger version—the Clayton Antitrust Act—was enacted in 1914, probably as a reinforcement of the Supreme Court's decision in 1911 to dissolve Standard Oil, not because of its size but because of "unreasonable" restraint of trade. In fact, the legal principle invoked was termed "the rule of reason." Ninety years later, Microsoft and the U.S. Department of Justice were still debating the issue. Somehow government could never understand that the whole idea of competition is to become, in effect, a monopoly.

Second, capitalism, as both an economic system and a way of life, was severely tested by the catastrophic crash of the stock market in 1929. The tragically amazing thing about this disaster is that, even now, no authoritative analyst is able satisfactorily to explain it. Any diagnostic statistics, such as multifactor productivity indices, that might be meaningful were not kept at the time. But popular consensus is simply that the cause was loss of confidence—panic—on the part of investors. No one has suggested the obvious: the system itself was fundamentally flawed, impossible to sustain. Whatever the real causes, recovery was possible only because of the intervention and assistance of government, which by that time was admittedly capitalistic itself, in the form of subsidies for farmers and increased prices for business, augmented by federal funding through government jobs and entitlements and a national policy of consumption. But salvation by the government is not without a price—in this case, high taxes and the National Labor Relations Board, along with insidious government intrusion into every nook and cranny of business. Again, the fundamentals of capitalism suffered a traumatizing double loss of credibility as a self-sustainable economic system. But the values of the industrial age had already been cast in concrete and steel.

The capitalistic system would not flourish again until the war years of the 1940s. Business and government formed their own trust to destroy the competition overseas. So mutually beneficial was this symbiotic relationship that, fearing its permanent domination of society, General Dwight Eisenhower, in the early 1960s, warned the nation against the consequences of a "military-industrial complex." Today, he might well warn of a corporation-government complex.

Except for the space program and the arms race, the coalition cooled during the 1960s; both business and government were distracted with opportunities and problems of their own. Business was too busy frantically trying to capitalize on the postwar boom in every conceivable market to be concerned with the anticapitalistic fever rising on the college campus. Government was too distracted by its fall into the quicksand of Vietnam while it was attempting to build a great society at home to pay much attention to antiestablishment activity.

Their paths would not cross (collide might be a more appropriate word) again until the mid-1970s—when the government's Murphy's-Law distributive economic policies managed to create inflation and stagnation ("stagflation") simultaneously, while at the same time the government was enforcing rigid civil rights laws, environmental policies, and OSHA regulations—all this just at the moment business was struggling with the seismic turbulence, with all its attendant threats and opportunities, that accompanied the emergence of the information–technological age.

The government's complementary policy of "supply-side" economics in the 1980s ushered in a twenty-year period of unparalleled capitalistic frenzy. Scores of new corporations were started each day. Unemployment reached historic lows. Corporate profits exploded; internet stocks created gold-rush fever as ordinary investors became IPO millionaires; the Dow Jones average more than quadrupled; pension funds swelled; and the treasures of private foundations burgeoned to the point of illegality. It was indeed, a new "gilded age." Opulence and greed were social chic. Yet, it was obvious that something was wrong. In the U.S. government, the national debt soared to more than $5 trillion. Deficit spending became the norm; balanced budgets impossible without political finagling (liars figure). The rate of poverty reached an all-time high. The year 1999 saw unprecedented downsizing and job displacement. Suddenly, there was talk of the possibility that economics was a zero-sum game. The corporate world was still reeling from the effects of technology and the fear of Y2K. Entire commercial systems became obsolete overnight—without warning. The traditional corporate infrastructure was destroyed by virtual organization. Global competition forced the savaging of natural resources and the abnegation of nationalistic loyalty. Offshore manufacturing and foreign outsourcing became de rigueur, despite their social consequences. Downsizing, because of competitive pressure on profits, became the primary corporate strategy—a form of self-cannibalism. Mergers and acquisitions disrupted the natural balance of economic dynamics. And material wealth was concentrated more and more in fewer and fewer hands. By 2000, in the United States, 45 percent of the nation's wealth was held by 1 percent of the population. One individual held more wealth than 44 percent of the entire population. In 1999 the total wealth of the four hundred richest individuals in the United States exceeded the GNP of China. Globally, the disproportionality was as dramatic: almost 83 percent of the total world "income" was received by 20 percent of the world's population. In the United States and other industrialized countries, poverty, joblessness, and homelessness led to dependancy on government for economic well-being, resulting in the acceptance of what was termed a "capitalistic-welfare state" a practical compromise between the democratic capitalism of the nineteenth-century United States and the modern democratic socialism of Western countries such as Spain, Portugal, France, and Germany. When all these altruistic governments, in the 1990s, were finally forced to admit their own practical bankruptcy, irony of irony, they had no choice but to turn to capitalists for salvation from economic ruin. That meant that those who controlled the capital would also control the capitol. Nowhere was that more true than in the United States.

The effect of this massive economic disequilibrium on individual human beings was devastating; the term "human resources" took on a bitter meaning as careers, families, personal economic security, lives were sacrificed to the raging bull of Wall Street. Yet during all this time there were five countervailing forces at work that would presently challenge the very concept of capitalism and create a psychological climate that would ultimately nourish a completely new, more human, economic order.

First, there was the collapse of communism in the Soviet Union. For most of the twentieth century, communism—as a socioeconomic system—had been known to the West only as it was portrayed by friends and advocates of capitalism and only as it was demonstrated by Russia. It was posited not only as the opposite of capitalism in economic doctrine but also as the atheistic enemy of all that is morally good. Ultimately, it was decried as the "evil empire." The conflict between good and evil after World War II escalated into the Cold War, waged heatedly on every front. Political investigations at home, cloak-and-dagger intrigue in foreign intelligence, ideological debates, skirmishes within developing countries, competition for outer space, battles over academic superiority, and ultimately, a prolonged nuclear standoff—all these circumstances had the effect of separating the world into two camps: good and evil, democracy and totalitarianism, capitalism and communism.

And then the wall fell; and the West suddenly discovered, much to its delight, that the world's other superpower was a paper bear. But it was a Pyrrhic victory. There was another surprise, one that did not immediately appear but gradually revealed itself during the next decade. Democratic capitalism's military victory precipitated by the enemy's capitulation, its economic victory arising from the other side's centralized supply-and-demand policies that made the state the customer, and its political victory arising simply from the concession of the opponent were all short lived. Some of the liberated states of the Soviet Union, particularly the Baltic States, readily adopted capitalistic and democratic systems. But for the overwhelming majority of the once expansive empire, the situation represented anything but conversion. Rather than the threat of one big war, the world was faced with the actuality of several small, but intense, military conflicts. Rather than the U.S. brand of capitalism—one geared strictly to an industrial mentality and founded on a Protestant work ethic—ostensibly free citizens, still temperamentally attached to the idea of socialism, were all but forced by the need to survive into the "black" market. Politically, any hope of a democratic form of government went up in the smoke of parliament buildings, as the old guard forcefully resisted loss of power, and of gunfire in the streets, as desperate citizens clambered against the bleak prospect of having to rule themselves.

As the Western bloc of nations watched this confusion unfold, exhilaration turned to horror, horror to introspection, and introspection to skepticism—not about the Soviets, but about their own system. Robbed of its foil, capitalism faced the challenge of justifying itself not by what it was not but by what it was. It soon became evident that capitalism was communism's long-lost evil twin—forsworn enemies, yes, but with the same genetic makeup, the same family history, and the same Western culture. Only one had not had the dubious benefit of a full measure of rationalism and Protestantism. They were polar opposites, to be sure, but merely the extremes of a single continuum.

Admission of the revolting fact came slowly, although the evidence was indisputable. Both communism and capitalism were essentially materialistic; both assumed human beings to be economic animals, not spiritual beings. One was atheistic; the other godless. Both were obsessed with scarcity, and each produced it by its own economic system. Both were given to competition—capitalism, with one another; communism, with everyone else. Both were driven to survival; neither understood what it means to thrive as a human society. One distributed the government's collective wealth to its citizens; the other collected its citizens' wealth for distribution to government.

And China was still there—inscrutable, impenetrable, eternal. Ideologically defenseless yet still avaricious, capitalistic countries themselves began partaking of the unclean meat of Eastern communism through "favored nation" importation of cheap goods and unequally yoked business partnerships with the Chinese government, all the while cynically mouthing protests against human rights violations and deceitfully masking corporate profit making as a righteous, if naive, attempt to convert the heathen, ironically, to the bright and shining path.

It was little wonder, then, that in the 1990s the second force gained momentum: It was a rekindled interest in the philosophy of Karl Marx and his colleague Friedrich Engels. Newly published copies of *The Communist Manifesto* and *Das Kapital* began appearing in New York bookstores alongside other similar economic and philosophical works. Marx was first and foremost an economist. Only a relatively small portion of his works deal with social philosophy, yet all his conclusions about the dynamics of economics have direct societal implication. Perhaps that's why they still reverberate. The first thing a modern reader comes to understand is that he was not a totalitarian ogre, like many of his professed disciples such as Lenin. But he was a brilliant thinker who earnestly attempted to understand social change, not in terms of historical personalities or philosophical ideas but as the result of impersonal economic causes. While any effort to summarize his conclusions would fail in the attempt, there are some salient principles that resonate plausibly in the economic theories of today.[3]

- He alleged that, at a certain stage of their development, the material forces of production (that is, technology) would come into contradiction with the existing productive relationships (that is, social institutions). The results: immediately, disequilibrium; and ultimately, revolution. Further, he believed that capitalism itself would become a static institution, eventually blocking the full application of scientific knowledge and technology. The only solution was public ownership of the means of production. Because of the authoritarianism implicit in most Western democratic states, force was the only means of obtaining public ownership.

- He believed that capitalism would eventually destroy itself. In his famous "grave digger" theory, he argued that the more capitalism succeeds, the more it creates a class-conscious proletariat that will eventually unite against big business. As a part of this theory, the "law of the falling profit rate" insures that the dilemma is inescapable. As the capitalist class accumulated more and more capital, that supply of capital would necessarily result in the decline of price (that is, interest) and the return (that is, profit) of capital. In a truly amazing prophetic analysis, he suggested that capitalists would seek to overcome the falling profit rate in two ways: by "rationalizing" industry to make it more efficient (this would eliminate smaller inefficient enterprises) and by investing capital in underdeveloped countries where the cost of production is disproportionately low.

- He also foresaw rather dire circumstances in the wake of capitalism—namely, unemployment, concentration of economic power, and the increasing proletarianization of society.

If all this did not seem exactly new or radical in the Western democracies in the late 1990s, perhaps it was because they recognized it as their own reality. One of Marx's most prophetic observations was made in 1872 before a friendly audience in Amsterdam: "We know that we must take into consideration the institutions, the habits and customs of different regions, and we do not deny that there are countries like America, England . . . where the workers can attain their objectives by peaceful means."[4]

Since that time, unremitting reform in Britain has incrementally moved that nation's social system, if not its economic system, squarely into the camp of socialism. As early as 1884, Sir William Harcourt had lamented in Parliament, "We are all socialists now." In the United States, the drift became a radical shift. In 1932, the United States Socialist party platform contained forty-seven planks. By the end of the century, all but five had been realized through legislation or other government action. Two of those not accomplished dealt with military intervention and sales of munitions; two others with proportional representation and direct election of the president and vice president; the fifth was the abolition of the Supreme Court's power to pass on the constitutionality of legislation by Congress.[5]

The third great force creating a noncapitalistic environment was inverted capitalism. There were three aspects: first, there was the obvious chasm between the original principles of capitalism and the actual application of capitalism as exhibited by the economic systems of the United States. Adam Smith had postulated four conditions or assumptions of capitalism: private ownership of property, free markets, competition, and profit. It could be argued that the four never existed at the same time in any sociopolitical structure, but it is beyond reasonable dispute that, by the end of the twentieth century, none existed in its pure form. Private property rights were compromised by perpetual property and inheritance taxes; all markets—except those on the Internet—were controlled by government; competition was redefined as "survival of the unfit"; and profit was limited by progressive tax rates.

Second, new practical realities began to take shape as the plates of the world's economic surface entered an extended resettlement period. One of the most straightforward analyses of the implications of these upheavals was that of Lester C. Thurow.

He cast this latest period of "punctuated equilibrium"—a term borrowed from biological evolution, describing a time of flux, disequilibrium, and uncertainty—as the collision of five "economic tectonic plates" with each other and with the previous tectonic order: the end of communism; the technological shift to manmade, brain power industries; radically changing democracy worldwide; a global economy; and the vacuum of no dominant economic, political, or military power. The trouble with most brilliant analyses is the conclusion reached. And, here again, there is a distinct possibility that Thurow may be too optimistic:

The danger is not that capitalism will implode as communism did. Without a viable competitor to which people can rush if they are disappointed with how capitalism is treating them, capitalism cannot self-destruct. Pharaonic, Roman, medieval, and mandarin economies also had no competitors and they simply stagnated for centuries before they finally disappeared. Stagnation, not collapse, is the danger.[6]

That assumption seems a bit inconsistent with his own understanding of punctuated equilibrium.

Normally evolution proceeds at a pace so slow that it is not noticeable on a human time scale. The top-of-the-food-chain, survival-of-the-fittest species usually only become more dominant—bigger and stronger. But occasionally something occurs that biologists know as "punctuated equilibrium." The environment suddenly changes and what has been the dominant species rapidly dies out to be replaced by some other species. Evolution takes a quantum leap. Natural selection, which normally works on the margins, suddenly alters the core of the system.[7]

The third challenge was philosophical. This one drew the most blood. Reason gave way to passionate emotional arguments, using facts and facsimiles to adamantly contend foregone conclusions. One of the most startling episodes in the history of philosophical discourse (if it can be called that) involved George Soros, one of the forty wealthiest men in the world, and Robert J. Samuelson, one of America's most astute authors, a mild-mannered but straight-talking, straight-shooting son-of-a-gun. In February 1997, Soros's jeremiad, "The Capitalistic Threat," appeared in the *Atlantic Monthly*. The thesis was simply that "the untrammeled intensification of laissez-faire capitalism and the spread of market values into all areas of life is [sic] endangering our open and democratic system."[8] The term "open society," he said, had specific significance to him since he had lived under both Nazi and communist rule in Hungary. Some salient passages capture the tone, as well as the argument, of the piece. Believing that in their present weakened condition

may be tempted by the power that lies within the ambiguity of language or the remoteness from those they represent to pursue their own agendas—to the point where it becomes impossible to tell the Yahoos from the Houyhnhnms. It is here that authority first gives way to power. Authority demands precise language and accountability; power thrives on the obsfucation of both. Tyranny can be exercised by an individual, a group, or the majority. So no matter whether a consequence of misconception or manipulation, of deception or delusion, the sad net effect is that laws are placed in the hands of outlaws; knaves rule the righteous; and slaves think themselves free.

The second condition is unchallenged assumptions. Assumption is the basis for all forms of governance, political or corporate. Even systems based on scientific rationalism are so conceived and so dedicated. Therefore, it comes as a shock to many, if it comes at all, that democracy is based on assumptions that are unnatural as well as irrational. That apparent paradox is explained by the observation that by the time the proponents of scientific rationalism got around to creating political systems they had gone beyond merely reporting how things work and begun to postulate how they should work. Most people, either impressed by clever scientific language or willing to be fooled, could not or would not discern the difference.

There are five such assumptions within democracy. The first is that all people know what is best for them. Self interest, it is alleged, is either a correlative or a source of this knowledge which, in the ultimate democratic system, is undeniable and unchallengeable. Even the great democrat Tom Jefferson admitted trouble with this assumption. He defined knowledge strictly in terms of the "eternal verities"—the knowledge that frees. In fact, the test separating data and information from knoweldge was freedom toward the exercise of one's full powers. He insisted that the only way genuine knowledge could be assured among the masses was development, through education and other cultural experiences, of an "enlightened" citizenry. He realized that a society's system of education defines its moral character far more than its practice of religion or its establishment of government.

Two hundred years later, however, national leaders in the United States assert that "even the most ignorant people know what is best for them. Jefferson would have found it inconceivable that anyone would use the words "ignorant" and "best" in the same sentence. Indeed, that kind of blighted optimism overlooks one of Jefferson's more cryptic observations to the effect that if you pool ignorance, you get pooled ignorance. Any form of governance must be judged by the kind of people in whom authority is placed. Plato noted, "With a magnificent indifference to the sort of life a man has led before he enters politics, it will promote to honor anyone who calls himself the people's friend."[2] Unfortunately, democracy has always been the form of governance most likely to make rulers of those who are intellectually deficient and morally bereft. For this reason, democracy is also the form of government most likely to self-destruct.

The second assumption is that the majority is always right—not in the moral sense of right makes might but in the rationalistic sense that might makes right. Majority rule is the rule of democracy. That means, obviously, that democratic processes are not intended to make—and cannot make—decisions that benefit the whole group. Furthermore, it is a logical impossibility that all people have equal rights when the majority rules. In the final stages of democracy, even proportional representation—a concept that promised to more accurately reflect the interests and attitudes of the various segments of a society—was abandoned and condemned so as to create "mandates" not upon minorities but upon the majority. From this assumption emerged the philosophy and practice of the two-party system of politics that dominated American and British democracies. The object of each party was the imposition of its will on the other. Democracy was ever the choice of bullies. As long as there are minorities, there can be no true democracy.

The third assumption logically follows; that is, E pluribus unum to the contrary notwithstanding, division is always preferable to unity in governance. Whether the terms are "shadow government," "backbenchers," or "liberals" and "conservatives," the net effect is the same: In every democracy, there is always a significant percentage of the population (up to 49.9%) disenfranchised by the very process they believe to represent their best interest. Democracy is always characterized by winners and losers. The house is always divided, and that is a desirable circumstance in the dualistic universe of rationalism. It, however, is the antithesis of the principle of mutuality uncompromisingly put forth by the Hebraic–Christian tradition. Furthermore, when winning is pursued at all cost, the first thing spent is moral conviction. That is why a democratic system is an easy choice for those who have already made the initial investment.

Thus, the fourth assumption: finality in anything that pertains to governance is both impossible and undesirable: impossible because absolutes do not exist in the pursuit of incrementalized improvement and undesirable because of the eternal prospect of power. In the first instance, democratic solutions ultimately settle nothing but continue to provide even more complicated, unsolvable problems, until the contraption inevitably collapses under the weight of its own ambition. This is why democracy is the choice of pettifoggers. In the second instance, democratic processes are calculated to cause the consolidation of special interest factions and to avoid or negotiate conflicts, not to solve problems between them, in an attempt to create control above the legal machinery of a process that would otherwise be dangerously free. As any psephologist knows, voting does not always mean choice; and choice does not always mean democracy. Voting becomes only a temporary stay against anarchy. For this reason, democracy is the system of choice among fleeing felons and others temperamentally opposed to law.

The fifth assumption of democracy is that authority and responsibility are severable. While democratic systems are eager to advance the authority os-

sive, unjust, predatory, destructive, it violated human dignity and human rights, as well as the natural environment. This new attitude was not the warmed-over pabulum of the 1960s but a mature and reasoned sense of the commonality and common interests of all human beings. It would be that attitude that eventually fostered the revival of the idea of commonwealth—but with an entirely new meaning.

NOTES

1. George Clason, *The Richest Man in Babylon* (New York: Hawthorne Books, 1955), 22.

2. John Naisbitt, *Megatrends* (New York: Warner Books, 1982), 11–38.

3. The most compelling critique of capitalism, and the most respected, is that of Joseph A. Schumpeter (*Capitalism, Socialism, and Democracy*, Harper and Row, 1942). He reasoned, like Marx, that capitalism will eventually self-destruct because of its own success: The falling profit rate would accelerate to intolerably low returns, and competition would exhaust markets. His opinion was that capitalism would be succeeded by centrist socialism. But he also believed that the new order would foster a burgeoning entrepreneurism. Schumpeter acknowledged Marx as a "prophet," but he proved to be a prophet himself. By the year 2000, a new economic philosophy had arisen: "The third way," as it was termed, emerged as a combination of capitalism and socialism—not from theory but from the actual practice of former capitalistic-socialistic nations.

4. William Eberstein, *Today's ISMS* (Englewood Cliffs, N.J.: Prentice Hall, 1961), 10.

5. Harry W. Laidler, ed., *Socialist Planning and a Socialist Agenda* (New York: Falcon Press, 1932), 243–248.

6. Lester Thurow, *The Future Capitalism* (New York: William Murrow, 1996), 325.

7. Ibid., 7.

8. George Soros, "The Capitalistic Threat," *Atlantic Monthly*, February 1997, pp. 47–48.

9. Ibid.

10. Robert J. Samuelson, "Crackpot Prophet," *Newsweek*, March 10, 1997, p. 50.

11. Ibid.

CHAPTER 32

The Decline of Behaviorism

People here used to believe
that drowned souls lived in the seals.
At Spring tides they might change shade.
They loved music and swam in for a singer
who might stand at the end of Summer
in the mouth of a whitewashed turf-shed,
his shoulder to the jamb, his song
a rowboat far out in evening.
When I came here first you were always singing,
a hint of the clip of the pick
in your winnowing climb and attack.
Raise it again, man. We still believe what we hear.

Seamus Heaney[1]

Of all the constructs of rationalism, behaviorism was the most critical to the effective and efficient functioning of the corporation-model organization. It turned the metaphor "vital machine" into a science and took the degradation of human beings even further than the label "servomechanism." Behaviorism became a psychology-inspired management dictum that limited all human action to automatic neuromotor response. Performance was defined and measured by reaction to external stimuli calculated and engineered to produce a predetermined result, and the ability to adapt was the trait prized most highly in human beings.

What was in practice a means to an end within a specific corporate structure became the end in the larger societal philosophy of inevitability. Creativity, energy, and enthusiasm existed only outside the confines of the corporation. Inevitably, nothing so diametrically opposed to the intrinsic nature of human beings could survive the practicality of human experience or the truth within human reason.

At the end of the twentieth century, behaviorism was in critical condition. The philosophy had the residual strength of almost a full century's exercise and the vitality that arises from the domination of mainstream thought, not only in psychology but in all other tangential disciplines, for over fifty years. B. F. Skinner, perhaps its most influential proponent, had argued convincingly that human behavior is strictly the result of external stimuli. Although he recognized that individuals possessed inner or mental states, they were only internalized responses caused by external circumstances. Other behaviorists maintained that such states could not be proved objectively and so were of no practical consequence. But these interfaith squabbles were themselves inconsequential technicalities in an otherwise solid, purely scientific philosophy. Or so it seemed.

But behaviorism was lately delivered two potentially mortal blows. The first, intellectual, came from an unexpected opponent—a linguist, another kind of scientist. In the late 1950s, Noam Chomsky had developed a theory of "transformational grammar": The basic idea, oversimplified perhaps, was that grammar consists of two structures in the individual—surface (that is, the actual sounds and words) and deep (that is, the meaning). The inner meaning is converted to language by an ordered set of rules, inherently perceived by the individual. Chomsky's conclusion was that human beings are born with knowledge of the principles of the structure of language—of all languages. The theory sent shock waves through his own discipline of linguistics, but when he published a review of Skinner's analysis of language, he ignited an explosion that seriously injured all advocates of behaviorism. Chomsky contended that Skinner's terms were in fact either implicitly cognitive or logically indefensible. Behaviorism would never be the same.

The second blow came a few years later from the unlikeliest of sources—technology. As a result of the experiences with computer science and artificial intelligence, there was a general recognition that the "behavior" of computers could be attributed to the internal rules and representations of their programs. Some scientists even observed that in the most sophisticated systems there seemed to be a kind of organic integrity that would reject anything foreign—such as, say, a replacement part. Although some of the more philosophical would convincingly argue, as if that were necessary, that the human brain cannot be compared to a computer—analogous, perhaps—the point had already been made with enough credibility to take the form of a distinct philosophy—functionalism.

But the crisis of behaviorism was not confined to the ethereal realm of the philosophical. It was played out in dramatic fashion on a life-sized stage. There were two prominent attitudes regarding behaviorism—appropriately enough, one explicit, the other implicit. Explicitly, it remained a dominant presence in every institutionalized component of society. That, after all, was the legacy of the century. That presence was especially vivid in business (public and private) and educational systems. Here it still held sway over the lives of those persons involved, whether or not they were conscious of it. For example, in both arenas, one of Skinner's signature techniques, "operant condition-ing," was used overtly and routinely to shape the random activity of both individuals and groups into desired behaviors or to alter undesired behavior by means of punishment and reward. In public schools, that kind of condi-tioning was the modus vivendi between the educational authorities and stu-dents, specifically in matters pertaining to discipline—quite poignantly in something designated "alternative" education.

In business, performance was spurred onward and upward and compli-ance was ensured with instructions and policies reinforced—always positively, of course—by an array of incentives, qualitative and quantitative, and by an equal if not greater number of "disincentives." Termination was the ultimate disincentive. And tons of books, articles, and videos on the amorphous sub-ject of management were filled with the cant phraseology and ideas of behav-iorism. In both business and education, virtually all methodologies and formats for personnel evaluation were based strictly on behavioral criteria—not, ironi-cally, on actual results.

Implicitly, behaviorism was either completely supplanted or completely ignored. It was supplanted by a legion of spiritual and supernatural doctrines; it was ignored by everyday pragmatism. In both cases, things such as mental images, spiritual states, sensations, will, consciousness, and conscience—all those things Skinner had denied—were ordinary realities. The first category was dominated by more-or-less traditional religions, which generally believed that human beings are created in the image of deity, and mysticism, which typically insists that humans are spiritual beings in a physical body yet still somehow an inextricable part of the external and universal *spiritus mundi*. The second category consisted simply of the collective, common experiences of living in a practical world. Ironically, of all the injuries inflicted on behav-iorism in its latter years, this was the most cruel.

Much was made of the new millennium, so much in fact that it was cel-ebrated a year early. But all the hoopla and mayhem were a temporary dis-traction from the real turn of events—and attitudes. Human history cannot be understood in terms of a calendar—all calendars are accidental estimates of when. The most revealing story of human life on this planet is written in epochs—those extended periods of order (and disorder) that have occurred with certain regularity since the beginning of time. Some scholars have sug-gested that in recent history, say, the past six thousand years, the duration of epochal intervals has been four or five hundred years. Because the end of one is the beginning of another, the transition is anything but smooth. It is a collision, usually attended by upheaval, disequillibrium, and considerable chaos and conflict. The rapid deterioration of the older principal constructs of the age—rationalism, secular humanism, democracy, capitalism—was al-

ready evident. The end of behaviorism may be considered the ultimate conclusion of an age that began with the bright elevation of human beings to the
center of the universe, created and creator both, and ended with their being
denigrated as little more than accidental material objects, subject only to
external forces over which they have no control.

The contemporaneous generation of Western Society had seen too much
not to realize that there was something terribly wrong with the existing order
of things. It was the profound and inexplicable contrasts that caused them to
begin rethinking all the assumptions on which their present civilization was
based. For example,

- Citizens of the United States, especially, lived in a time of peace, yet terror stalked
  them—from graphic accounts of ethnic cleansing, holy wars, and rogue nations
  intent on building vast arsenals of destruction to the violence in their own neigh-
  borhood streets.
- They enjoyed unparalleled prosperity, yet every day they confronted the fact and
  the prospect of abject poverty all around them.
- They lived in a time of economic stability, yet turmoil and fantasy ruled the financial markets and threatened their own financial security.
- They were told globalization was the inevitable and happy result for their own
  philosophies and technologies, but everywhere they witnessed the worst racial,
  ethnic, and cultural tensions the globe had ever experienced.
- They rejoiced in the best health and health care and in the longest life spans
  human beings had ever known, and yet they were faced with new, insidious, and
  incurable diseases and uncontrollable pestilence.
- They revelled in personal freedom and yet were little more than slaves of abusive
  economic systems and intrusive government authority.
- They were avowed proponents of truth yet they willingly had been deluded into
  settling for lies on a grand scale.

It gradually became apparent in all this travail that if members of this generation were going to witness the beginning of a new epoch and, indeed,
participate in it, they would begin as had those of all previous cusp generations before them—with bold, diligent, and unprecedented inquiry and with
the understanding that although the questions were ancient the answers could
not be. They would begin also with the confidence that the answers would
actually negate not only the existing systems but also, quite possibly, this time
render moot the questions themselves by arriving at final answers.

Ironically, behaviorism had forced the questions; but the answer lay only
within the human. There were four cardinal questions. First, What is the
nature of the human being? This was fundamental because all the other
questions would be answered accordingly. Whether there was any national or
international consensus was not the issue. Nor was negotiation possible.
Rather, it was a matter of deepest introspection. Each person was forced to
face himself or herself without the distorting lenses of dogma and ideology.

The same question had been posed in many forms historically, with varying answers: a plaything of the gods, an innate godly being, a slave of tyrants and despots, a product of accidental biological and chemical evolution, a dual or triune composite of beings. Surely, the ancient notion of *soma, psyche,* and *pneuma* was appealing to philosophical minds. Fully developed, it encompassed the wholeness of the human nature, as shown in Figure 32.1. Was it possible that an entirely new understanding of humanity might emerge— one that transcended the neat and logical fragmentation of philosophical and scientific analysis with a wisdom born of wholeness?

The second question, following closely, was, What is the nature of human systems? Here also, the age-old question had been resolved in any number of ways, at different times, in different aspects of society, and under different presuppositions. But, throughout the history of Western civilization, the fundamental assumptions remained the same—whether manifest in family, nation, or megacorporation—features such as those that characterize social order (authority and rank order) and those that are the structural basis of artifacts whether intellectual or physical (mathematical and scientific principles) seemed constant, changing only within themselves, despite revolutions. But as those systems failed to satisfy, even in their very purpose, was it possible to discover completely new concepts of order heretofore unimaginable? The greatest danger lay in seeing with old eyes.

The third question was a reprisal of the ponderings of centuries, What is the definition of knowledge? Western civilization itself was the personification of philosophy—"the love of wisdom." But in the course of time, the affection for, and the pursuit of, wisdom was replaced by a fascination with knowledge, even though it was often diluted to information. This occurred for good, logical reasons: Knowledge is debatable; wisdom is not. Knowledge is transient; wisdom is not. Knowledge is commercial; wisdom is not. The sage warnings, "The more we know, the less we understand; and virtue is not the child of knowledge," pithily capture the irony.[2] In the Western world, the epidemic pursuit of knowledge by both religion and science assumed that there was, in fact, in anything around or within the human being, a certainty that one could trust—be it esoteric truth or something as basic as pi. The only discussion was how that knowledge was acquired—whether through reason and revelation or empiricism—and how it was apprehended—whether intuitively, cognitively, or sensuously. However that dispute was settled, the knowledge thus defined became the foundation, walls, and ceiling of all hu-

Figure 32.1

PNEUMA	SPIRIT	SPIRITUAL	INTUITIVE
PSYCHE	SOUL	MENTAL	INTELLECTIVE
SOMA	BODY	PHYSICAL	INSTINCTIVE

man constructs. The unresolved issue is whether knowledge brings people to wisdom (as traditionally supposed) or wisdom brings them to knowledge (as suspected by some). If the answer is the latter, then a new era could emerge — an era in which human beings, rather than being servants of knowledge, become its masters.

The fourth question is so old it is all but forgotten: What is the definition of wealth? This may prove to be the final test of the nature of the human being. Throughout modern history, it has never been the definition of wealth (except in arcane economic terms) that was the issue. That was settled long ago, even before the advent of Western civilization. The only questions were about its possession. Wars were fought over the answers, governments destroyed by them, and the human being's highest aspiration reduced to the service of Mammon. Surely, there was still in the heart, no matter how much the treasure, a deep feeling of unfulfillment. Wordsworth's lines still rang true:

> The world is too much with us; late and soon,
> Getting and spending, we lay waste our powers.[3]

Questions that cannot be resolved are generally the wrong questions, so any answer dissatisfies. It is only natural — or, more accurately, human — that in the epochal cusp, the question was, for the first time, being popularly recast, not in quantitative measures, but in terms of qualitative well-being and the common good.

There is actually a fifth question. It is the only reasonable derivative of the other inquiries — the specific context for the answers. That is, What is the nature of (the) human endeavor? (under consideration). Whether commercial, educational, governmental, religious — all existing organized pursuits will of necessity be reconceptualized, virtually de novo. This will require nothing less than sustained abandonment of the old and creation of the new in every human enterprise.

The very fact that these questions reemerged with passionate urgency after almost a century of being stifled by behaviorism is dramatic testimony not only to the errancy of that adamant philosophy but also to the indominability of the human spirit. That spirit would radically transform every aspect of society and consequently create systems of organizations eminently conducive to the common well-being.

NOTES

1. Seamus Heaney, "The Singer's House," *Opened Ground: Selected Poems, 1966–1996* (New York: Farrar, Stras and Giroux, 1998), 153.

2. John Henry Newman, *Apologia pro Vita Sua* (New York: Macmillan, 1931), 294.

3. William Wordsworth, "The Word Is Too Much with Us, A Sonnet," *The College Survey of English Literature* (New York: Harcourt, Brace, 1951), 724.

CHAPTER 33

Aspects of the New Society

But I reckon I got to light out for the territory ahead of the rest, because
Aunt Sally she's going to adopt me and civilize me, and I can't stand it.
I been there before.

Mark Twain[1]

In the early chapters of this book, it is proposed that the dominant organization system of any civilization is a direct reflection of the aspects of that society, especially its wealth production. Nine other such aspects were charted, each having its own sphere of influence and each constituting a distinctive kind of discipline of thought and behavior: reality, faith, relationship, knowledge, order, system, control, governance, economy, and wealth. Furthermore, there was the implicit assumption that as these features of society undergo change, each in its own way and time, the organization of that society would also change accordingly, in kind and degree.

At the beginning of the twenty-first century, that was precisely what was occurring in Western civilization. It was clearly evident that each aspect of that society had undergone radical transformation, especially in the course of the preceding century. Everything about that society—once so certain of its rightness if not its righteousness—was being challenged by both its own inability to satisfy human demands and emerging views and ways of life far more practical that philosophical.

That is not to say, however, that each of these features was yet fully formed. In fact, all were still being discovered through reflected experience and being realized more by impression than by expression. Although the impressions were made by countless accumulating experiences, there was no historical precedent on which to base any judgment or critique of the emerging forms of society.

There is often a fine line between the actual and the speculative; but one thing was certain: Change itself had changed. The old concepts such as dualism, progress, incrementalism, cause and effect, and complexity slowly receded before juvenatingly different realities. Moreover, the new ways were authenticated by a mature practicality. If these impressions seem more fond wish than actuality, it is for a reason. The corporation-model organization, like its society, had run out of options. The trends suggested here, taken together, represent the only hope of avoiding the calamity of total collapse. It may be said with confidence, however, that future systems of organization will thrive only to the degree that they partake of certain identifiable qualities of society. These are shown schematically in Figure 33.1.

Ideas were much out of fashion. And it was just as well. The old ideas were worn and tattered, yet they doggedly persisted in the habituated thought and activity in all the constructs of the antiquated civilization. They had become an intricate, multifaceted infrastructure. It became easy, even chic in some circles, to accept the "memetic" theory of Richard Dawkins, a preposterous notion that so-called "memes" exist, outside the immediate control of human beings, in a seething ethereal pool of fragments of thought, language, and myth (a kind of collective subconsciousness) that, through involitive recollection, intrusively pervade and shape human consciousness and perpetuate a society's distinctive culture. That was the ultimate form of conditioning.

Figure 33.1

ASPECTS OF SOCIETY	Phase IV
• Reality	Virtual
• Faith	Anthropoistic
• Relationship	Quantum
• Knowledge	Contextual
• Order	Holistic
• System	Organismic
• Control	Generative
• Governance	Consensual
• Economy	Commonweal
• Wealth	Well-being
• Organization	Syntagma

In any form, the old ideas about human being and becoming were tedious, boring, irrelevant.

Of course, many adventurers attempted to break out of the old mold (traditional revolutionaries in the new age); but in a rationalistic age everything else is nonsense. So, even their most radical ideas were conceived in and patterned after the old constructs—all variations on superstition, mysticism, and romanticism. But there was a startling difference this time. Marx had observed, as one of his major premises, that knowledge and technology always outpace societal change. However, in this case—and perhaps this is true of all epochal shifts—change in the societal aspects far outdistanced the atavistic constructs of the society. The very best rationalistic thinking only served to retrofit and reinforce obsolete systems.

But there is wisdom born of travail. The struggle with and against rationalistic order, almost four centuries old, ultimately proved that the world rationalism had created was a fabrication unfit for human habitation. Long before the advent of rationalism, the Greeks had spoken of a wisdom that is discovered not in knowing but in doing, and that may be exactly what happened here, only on a significantly larger scale.

This time a whole generation, perhaps without deliberate conscious intent, slowly realized, for generations to come, an amazing new world—a world not found in their enterprises, or in their economic, social, or political systems, or in cyberspace, but only within themselves. Two new truths soon became evident: The most powerful force on the planet is the human spirit; and human beings, left to their own devices, will always do what they perceive as good. These truths would radically change every aspect of their society—change beyond reformation, beyond transformation. It was an entirely new reality.

REALITY

The concept of reality is a fundamental aspect of any society. It is the foundation of and the context for all definitions, including that of truth. As philosophical as that may sound—and it is indeed the basis of all philosophy—the fact is that some accepted world view is the overarching reference for all human beings, and thus for all human affiliation—what is, and how the what works. Like a map, this construct provides the orientation for thought, establishes the benchmarks and the coordinates of behavior, and identifies the locus of being human. But, also like a map, any reality is an anthropomorphic overlay of supposition, assumption, and wish upon the vast raw material of the universe and therefore is constantly subject to changing perspectives, evidence, and desires. It is the ironic condition of humanity that it must always chart position and course by stars that have burned out.

Philosophers through the ages have all known that reality is a matter of perspective. The sincere among them have sought a single perspective that satisfies all curiosity, that settles everything, although, by now, humanity is the dubious beneficiary of tomes of theoretical cartography. In the final analysis, it all comes down to the perspective of the individual. That perspective is more a matter of person, place, and time than all the philosophy in the world — and more a matter of choice than anyone will admit. The very same evidence can be seen as, and thus become, either true or false; and things may exist only as they are observed. A work of art is great only if it is different each time it is viewed. Probably the most debilitating condition that can be experienced by human beings is the confusion of the "real" with "reality." The greatest illusion has been that the ideal and the real are opposites. The result is hopeless fantasy. That unhappy misapprehension leads to either imbecility or dementia. And the greatest delusion is that the reality is truth or that the truth is real. This is the definition of fanaticism.

While in the general ebb and flow of the happy hysteria of ordinary life, the subject of reality is seldom broached in philosophical terms of debate, it is nevertheless as prevalent an influence in any society as commercial advertising, political platforms, and the reporting of the news. It is always the same question: What is reality? Perhaps even more acute is the perception of reality that people hold with regard to themselves — their own definition of personal realism, of what is "realistic" for them in their world. So, the question of reality can be, and will be, answered at three levels: the philosophical, the practical, and the personal.

Philosophically, one is immediately faced with the eternal debate, waged classically by thinkers such as Aristotle and Plato, over whether reality is that which is immediately observable or that which is ideal. The way that question is answered determines the fine line between the possible and the impossible. Practically, the only answer is what works at the time, and, since that depends upon inconstant human participation, the subject of reality quickly becomes the object of reality. Personally, the inevitable conclusion is that one's notion of reality is the source of all human motivation, since that reality is the basis of both hope and despair.

Lack of a certain reality, or lack of confidence in it, produces the same result as a bad map — people get lost, quickly and irretrievably, whole groups of people. No matter what reality is for individuals, all human societies and their organizations proceed from the general acknowledgment of a common personal reality. Without that, there can be no organization, no affiliation, by any definition.

The emerging concept of reality in Western civilization promises to transcend the old irreconcilable dualistic conflicts. It will render argument and persuasion moot. Philosophically, the great historical, if sophomoric, debate between the real and the ideal will dissolve with the understanding that they are, in fact, the same. Because the only reality is that which one sees, and since what one sees is strictly a matter of choice, individual and collective

ORDER

Order (*logos*) is about place and relations within, between, and among the five components of the universe, namely: time, energy, motion, space, and matter. It also is about the physical, intellectual, and spiritual arrangement that everyone seeks to make to coincide with that universe. It also is about the social, ethical, and moral conduct that human beings, thrust together as they are, come to exact of each other. In every case, order proves what is right; it is the only basis of justification. Wallace Stevens poetically opined that humans have a blessed "rage" for order, even though he himself aggressively challenged traditional concepts of it. Evidently, human beings, being creatures with a low tolerance for ambiguity, place a high premium on both the idea of predictability and the compulsion to have everything in its proper place rule the rationalistic mind. The issue of whether either is possible has never been seriously raised.

The matter is at once simple and complex. Just as the basic question with knowledge is whether it exists a priori, here the question is whether order is actual or perceptual. If actual, it is absolute truth that reveals itself only to those who, through diligent quest, discover it. If perceptual, then it takes on the form of the perceiver. So, the overriding question becomes, rather ironically, is order order? That is, does all order consist of the same qualities? The reductionists of the twentieth century, from Whitehead and Russell on, answered in the affirmative, alleging that all order, physical and nonphysical, was ultimately coherent and unified. However, a century later, there is no agreement as to the correspondence between the physical and the nonphysical, especially in human experience such as consciousness and intuition. The assumption still provokes considerable debate. Theses so intricate they evaporate have multiplied, each a derivative of another; and some more philosophical scientists have given up on the idea altogether, conceding that human beings simply are not equipped to understand gauzy speculations associated with the inquiry, to say nothing of the answers.

Obviously, the answers to the question of order will not come from rationalistic science alone. The problem all along seems to have been the adamant refusal to recognize spheres of order other than the physical and the tendentious superimposition of physical "laws" on every aspect of human experience. True, in the natural world, where the order is more likely to be actual, readily discernible order exists. It can be described in terms mathematical (linear, sequential, sets), logical (cause and effect, cycles), and universal (consistency, uniformity). But to extrapolate all that into other domains is fundamentally unreasonable, if not unscientific.

If there is anything the current scend of mysticism and spirituality has done, it is to provide new vistas for thinking about order. Some scientists are still reeling from the shock of new realities that seem to be characterized by chaos and complexity. Expecting to see familiar patterns and processes, they were themselves shocked into confusion by strange orders almost beyond human comprehension. Here are orders of innumerable possibilities and unimaginable dimensions and definitions. It was the conditioned imposition of the rules of physical order that created the confusion, not any inherent order.

From the exhausting struggle to understand order, at least three new truths have emerged. First, it has become evident that there are, in fact, different spheres of order with correspondingly different kinds of order. Until now, one was sure (physical); the other was being grudgingly admitted (nonphysical). But it now appears conclusive that there is order that is purely and only human. It is an order that potentially redefines those of the physical and nonphysical. And why not? It is in the human that the others meet, and it is the human being who ultimately provides the shapes and forms. Second, perspective does indeed matter. While it may not be the final determinant, even the staunchest rationalist will admit that perception creates a "level of reality." Far beyond that, it is now clear that, at least since the seventeenth century, Western thought has perceived order as seen from the outside—not the inside. Even the hardest empirical analyses are objectifications by the observer. But only when the subject can be seen from within, on its own terms as it were, will the barrier of objective understanding give way to subjective discovery.

So, the third new truth is that order will become, if it is not already, the interplay of energy between the actual and the perceptual. And that means that order will be variably and constantly redefining, reconceptualizing, and re-forming, increasingly so from the natural to the social to the intellectual to the spiritual. Order will cease to be a noun; it will become an active verb, both transitive and intransitive, at once actual and perceptual.

SYSTEMS

Systems are the only refuge against isolation and fragmentation. On the one hand, they not only impart meaning, they are meaning. On the other, they promise both the connectedness and dynamism necessary to life. All other aspects of society, therefore, depend on systems for their definition and vitality. It seems order can exist without systems, even though that order is not discernible; but systems cannot exist without order. Furthermore, all systems are self-defining and self-affirming, even when control is external. Their identity is established by common referents throughout. And all systems are characterized by tensions within themselves and between themselves and their own meaninglessness. Ironically, it is the nature of systems to be at risk. It is the nature of rationalism ultimately to destroy them.

The history of Western civilization represents the most frenetic, and certainly the most extended, attempt by human beings to apprehend, create, and deal with systems. That was, in fact, the obsession of rationalism and why experimentation is its persistent mode.

State-of-the-science reasoning declares that there are two kinds of systems, although it still seeks to find a hypothetical order common to both. Equally convincing is the evidence of a third kind of system, the spiritual. Allegedly, the natural systems—universal and discernible by all persons—contain and constitute truth as it can be known. Artifactual systems are those that do not exist in a state of nature; they range from simple utilitarian tools to complex intellectual constructs and social organization. Typically, they are judged by their effectiveness and efficiency. Supposedly, artifactual systems are justi-fied by natural laws and are viable only to the degree they abide by this omni-present and unyielding order. Since spiritual systems are not reducible to strict empirical terms, laws here are less discernible and, therefore, are ex-pressed in code circularly ranging from superstition to metaphysics to mysti-cism. During the past four hundred years, there has come to be general agreement as to the systems of nature, little with regard to those artifactual, and none about the spiritual.

Beyond the issue of kinds is the still-unsettled question about the nature of systems themselves—or, more accurately, the nature of system itself. Predi-cated on the speculative assumption that all systems are alike in their order and dynamic and are therefore subject to the same kind of analysis, for at least two millennia in Western civilization the debate has been over whether systems are atomistic or organismic—that is, comprising severable parts or essentially one. This is at once a fundamental and profound question be-cause of its obvious implications. If, in fact, all meaning is derived from con-text, then the answers lead to completely divergent worlds. And the answer cannot be both. Since 1908, Western thought has been dominated by the atomistic view, which has stamped every aspect of society and life. The ulti-mate result, at last evident at the end of the twentieth century, was the ironic, compulsive analyzing of systems out of existence, much as reductio ad absurdum logic obliterates reason.

Rationalism was a perverse, Setebos-like god. It not only insisted that all systems exist outside human beings but also required them to submit and adapt to those systems. Imitation was the highest human aspiration. But in the post-rationalistic age it is already clear that the human being is the system and that all things—natural, artifactual, and spiritual—will both give and be given new meaning—meaning conducive to human life and of human potential.

First, as the old quantitative structures of scientific analysis dissipate—struc-tures that themselves proved contradictory and adverse to natural systems—naturally qualitative systems will emerge. These new systems will be based on the simple understanding that the natural world actually conforms to the human being. Whether it was created for humans or humans evolved from it becomes a moot question. The fact is, nature provides everything necessary for human beings to fully realize their humanity. Even Dante in *Paridiso* admonished the people of his time to accept their natural state.

> If men on earth were to pay greater heed
> to the foundation Nature has laid down,
> and build on that, they would build better men.[2]

The order this time will be harmony and congruence, not with natural laws that ultimately become unnatural but with a natural order that serves the human.

Second, rationalistic artifactual systems—physical, intellectual, social—will crumble. Such systems have a terrible legacy of diminishing and impoverishing human beings and of wreaking irreconcilable conflicts among them. The emerging systems, although by definition artifactual, will nevertheless be human systems, transcending artificial designations, that are inherently moral and liberating. This will be the context that at long last makes it possible for good people to realize their full powers.

Third, rationalistic religious systems will be as abandoned as any arid wasteland. Life present or future will not be found there, only the relics and markers of life departed. Life will be discovered in spiritual systems that at once justify the individual and reconcile each to others in mutual service. Anything less has no spiritual traction.

Finally, the ancient debate over the constitution of systems will be resolved in the human being. Distinctions between the whole and the parts become specious and irrelevant. When all things are seen as that which is human, there is an integrity in all systems that is indivisible—beyond analysis and synthesis—but not beyond reason.

CONTROL

During all the long history of Western civilization, there is one aspect of society on which its religion and its science have consistently agreed. Both are, in fact, predicated on and constructed with the assumption that control, whether in the physical universe or human society, is always external to the system itself. The tacit admission is that internal control, especially in all things human, is destructive if not impossible. One is subject to natural law; the other to divine dictate. But the assertion has trapped both in an irony so blatant it is hardly recognized. For example, rationalism insists on personal autonomy yet even contorts language, as well as thinking, so that self-rule (autocracy) becomes the rule of people (democracy). And religion preaches a gospel that promises personal freedom yet binds its converts to doctrine and demands their blind obedience. Both define freedom by laws and rules, the ultimate expression of perverse control, and both reduce the human being or powerlessness and dependency.

The corollary assumption of both science and religion—indeed, the issue within the issue—is that the purpose of control is to restrain and compel human conduct according to some predetermined pattern ostensibly aimed at a predetermined end. But the result is always the same: the incapacitation of the person and society. In an overwhelmingly tragic irony, human beings are rendered totally dependent upon the controlling powers of a society which itself is incapacitated.

There is an incontrovertible principle at risk here. Locus of control is the life-or-death issue for all systems, for this reason: control is capacity. The operative force in control of any kind is power, and the relationship within systems is always reciprocal. That is, the application of power in the form of control is always at least equaled by countervailing power, as in resistance; or exceeded, as in release. If it is true that nothing creative ever happens until energy is pressed into a discipline, then capacity is always a direct result of control within or upon the energy within the system. In a human context, control is not a matter of constraint versus freedom; it is a matter of creativity versus dissipation. To insist on total freedom is to forswear creativity or productivity. Freedom is always a means—never an end. The whole purpose of control in any system is to expand capacity. And increasing capacity is tantamount to increasing performance or, in the case of human beings, increasing possibilities.

When controls are exercised as the discipline required to generate creativity, there is naturally no limit to a system's capacity within its kind. But when so-called control mechanisms restrict or prevent the continuous development of capacity, they cease to be controls and instead become constraints. The release thus engendered is in the form of waste. The forte of rationalism was the application of external control that destroyed human capacity and wasted human potential.

When the locus of control shifts to inside the human being, the whole world will be transformed into a place worthy of the human race. But changing the world means changing the person. Conventional wisdom has it that when society is out of control so is the individual. But the opposite is true. Self-control is the only real control possible in any society. The transformation will be fourfold. First, as autonomy is rediscovered by human beings, both dignity and ambition will be restored to the person and, consequently, also the individuality and individualism necessary for community. Respect for self is a prerequisite to respect for others. Self-interest is the necessary condition of common interest. Second, as independence is redefined in terms of personal capability and responsibility, the age-old conflict between the individual and the group disappears. Each person, no matter the social arrangement, will pursue and achieve his or her own projects, but always in concert with the pursuits of others. Neither the person nor the society will settle at the lowest common denominator; both will pursue the highest. Third, as freedom is recognized as the inherent state of being human, the exercise of the individual's full powers will be possible in the life of every person. And the exercise itself will prove to be the only moral discipline that invariably leads to good. Finally, as creativity is realized to be the greatest gift possessed by all human beings, the creation of the world and everything in it will become not some debatable historical event or process but a continuing work in process in which each person owns his or her own unique, original signature on the continually morphing mosaic. This will be as close to divine as human beings can come on this earth.

GOVERNANCE

If the system is a human community or, in a larger cast, a society, then the discussion of control turns to an examination of governance. Strictly defined, governance is the continuous mediation of interests of parties—person to person, person to group, and group to person. That is, it's always busy in the establishment and enforcement of codes of behavior, and that means that by its very nature governance is a restraint on the various energies and interests within a group. If taken in its fullest implication, as most assuredly the complexity of human life and the possibility of evil demand that it must, governance sooner or later necessarily involves the relation of every individual human action within the broader context of the group.

Essentially, it is a matter of determining the relationship between personal freedom and personal responsibility, between self-interest and the exigencies of community. The broad continuum of options becomes immediately apparent—from absolute license (which some might say is the antithesis of governance) to absolute domination (which some would contend is the perversion of government). But in all instances, the relationship is settled by resolving the issue of authority—who has it and to what degree; and is it over self or over others, for self or for others? It is important to remember that freedom is always the last resort of the oppressed.

The three questions basic to all forms of governance are these: who will govern (all, some, few); by what right (granted, assumed, imposed); and to what end (the good of the governors, the good of the governed, the good of the whole group)? The matrix of possible answers to these questions explains why governance, as perhaps the most serious form of human negotiation, is always such a messy affair and seems to thrive on irresolution, upheaval, and transience.

The experience of Western civilization during the past 2,000 years has done little to settle the issues. About the only thing certain is this: There is no system capable of governing human beings. The most notable attempts, monarchy and democracy, have come to be the defining orders of that society, each alternatively opposing or affirming the other. In fact, it may be said that Western civilization is the history of kings and presidents. Historically, perhaps inherently, it is the condition of both to be at risk. Monarchies are the more steady and enduring; democracies the more volatile and short lived. Both have a marked tendency toward either totalitarianism or anarchy. Democracies can devolve into both simultaneously. Monarchies are taken by force; democracies fall by deceit. Monarchies become so distant from their subjects that the governors cannot see the right thing; democracies, so close that they cannot do the right thing.

Neither has been able to find balance between the individual and society, to prevent one class of people from ruling others, to legislate private (or public) behavior, or to insure personal freedom. Ironically, all four dilemmas belie the only justification for government of any kind—that is, the assumption, or the actuality, that human beings are not capable of governing themselves. Even more ironically, all government efforts to resolve these dilemmas have succeeded only in exacerbating the problems, invariably producing the opposite effect from that intended.

It may soon prove that human beings are far more able than all the systems of governance (or nongovernance) ever devised by their predecessors, who had a rather limited view of both themselves and, especially, others. Therein lies the flaw in all those systems: They were (are) designed to govern others; they neither proposed nor expected that other individuals are capable of governing themselves or that, if they were, the result would be mayhem. Only a new concept of governance, predicated on the assumption of personal autonomy, will finally displace the archaic systems of virtual slavery by recognizing and upholding not only the sovereignty of others but the innate capacity of each individual to govern self. Self-governance is the only governance.

In true autonomy, right and responsibility are synonymous. It is naive to speak in terms of proportion or correlation. They are separated and meted out only in monarchies and democracies. So it is only in individual autonomy that the historical dilemmas are resolved. The interests of the individual and of the society are the same; since each person governs self, no one rules anyone; autonomy is its own discipline; personal freedom becomes not an end but a means of service to common good.

ECONOMY

Economy, reduced to its basic terms, is the philosophy and arrangement by which goods are defined and distributed among individuals and groups within a society. Economics—with all its ruminations of scarcity, utility, transferability, and other technical attributes of material wealth—is the "dismal science" by which the system is adjudicated and sustained. The agent of both economy and economics is governance, which justifies and perpetuates its own existence by the regulation of material wealth.

That is not to say that the other aspects of a society—faith, knowledge, and order—do not have their own specific influence on economy; but it is in governance that all economic issues are supposed to be finally settled, whether consistent with economic principles or not. Ironically, government, by its very nature, is incapable of originating wealth of any kind. But there must be some arbiter of economic matters; and since government is the society's ultimate authority, it is at once benefactor and beneficiary. Government's role is doubly ironic because nothing has ever been settled by governance. That probably explains the universal, abject, running confusion about everything pertaining to economics. If there is any absolute principle, it is this: Government is the only means by which consumption of wealth can exceed production of wealth.

Nevertheless, there are three issues of material wealth with which governance must grapple: Who has a right to what wealth; what is the best use of wealth; and how shall wealth be? As for the first consideration, right to wealth, any and all answers to that question will be based on value systems that define right and wrong—in a word, morality. Wealth can be had only by acquisition, assignment, or gratuity; it is the justification of possession that defines the moral character of governance. It is the attitude toward and disposition of the right to wealth, not the rules of human behavior, that ultimately manifest the morality of governance.

As for best use of material wealth, what at first glance may seem only a values-laden issue (as indeed it is) is also exactly a matter of knowledge— knowing ends and means. Best use is impossible to ascertain without awareness of options toward some accepted purpose. Both presuppose choice. The definition of best use, therefore, is subjective to the degree that choice is present; objective to the degree that options are available. Best is relative always to the knowledge that ascribes it so.

As for the representation of material wealth, both practically and theoretically, there must be common recognition of certification and symbols—that is, coin, currency, or other instruments of reckoning and exchange. The two obvious questions are these: Is the representation fair and accurate, and is the representation a cause or an effect of value? The first question can be settled only in a marketplace devoid of government influence but full of intense bargaining; the second is probably not answerable—at least, not until government begins to act as if the representation of wealth were wealth itself (the ultimate legerdemain). When wealth becomes an illusion, there is no difference between those who have it and those who do not. The effect is always terminal, so understanding the cause is as unsatisfying as other things academic.

More than any other civilization, Western society has been defined by the pursuit of material wealth. It transcends all art, science, philosophy, and religion. Progress is measured by acquisition. All institutions have been founded and dedicated to that one ambition. The characteristic organization of that society, the corporation, exists for no other reason. The modern version of capitalism is generally accepted as the paragon of both fairness and justice, the manifestation of natural law. Yet, after 2,000 years, Western civilization is not able to deal conclusively with three fundamental principles implicit in its own economy. First, inevitably the rich get richer; the poor get poorer. Second, individual production of goods is converted to government revenue and used by officials to buy political advantage. Third, the value of currency and other negotiables is secured strictly by promise and the authority to tax production and consumption.

By the end of the twentieth century, it had become evident that the re-vered system of faux capitalism was neither moral, natural, nor practical be-cause the system would not, could not yield to new orders. Unlikely permutations appeared both as actuality and as idealization. The capitalistic welfare state had emerged early as a reluctant compromise between capital-ism and socialism. By 1994, the so-called "third way" had become the philo-sophical, and to an astonishing degree the popular political, rendition of that oxymoronic hybrid. Finally, in the mid-1990s, intellectualism flirted with pure fantasy in theoretical perambulations about the desirability of a "stakeholder society," an idea advocated most convincingly by Will Hutton. But all these practices and philosophies were doomed to ultimate failure because all were predicated on the same basic error—the definition of wealth in material terms.

WEALTH

The fundamental issues of material wealth are two: its status and the status of people with regard to it. Regarding its status, every society must decide whether wealth for them is going to be absolute and fixed or relative and expansive. If the former, then there usually follows mutual, if not equal, shar-ing of that wealth. If the latter, the creation and growth of wealth, which, if allowed to run its course freely, will result in competition for and inequality in the possession of goods. The only thing that can limit the growth of wealth is the separation of the control of wealth from the creation of it.

But there is an even deeper issue here, and that is the status of people with regard to wealth. It is a matter of independence versus dependence. If, on the one hand, wealth is static, every person in the society is dependent upon the total for an adduced proportional share and upon the goodwill of other citi-zens in sharing. If, on the other hand, wealth is created and limitless, then one is dependent only on his or her ability to produce and control it. The same would be true of groups, communities, or entire societies. Simply stated, if wealth is in fact created, wealth production determines whether people are masters or servants. If it is not, the question itself is impossible.

Western civilization was founded on the dual proposition that wealth is relative and expansive and that it is created and limitless. That explains why the society's dominant organization, the corporation, has been one that pro-duces ever more material wealth with increasingly disproportionate sharing of that wealth. Ironically, those philosophies ultimately destroy any social order simply because the effect of having abundant wealth or no wealth is the same—that is, disregard for the common bonds required to hold a society together.

But the emerging concept of wealth will proceed from that common bond. In the new system, the original meaning of wealth will be reclaimed. And there is much more than word play involved here. Until the sixteenth century, the old English *weal* and the middle English *wealthe* were used interchangeably but with the same meaning: that is, common well-being—especially the general good, the public welfare, the prosperity of a community. Early on, the word *weal* was sometimes used alone in reference to riches and possession, but even in those rare instances it was contrastingly qualified as "worldly weal." But that definition became obsolete during the Middle Ages, at least in mainstream usage. The original meaning of "the general good" was always inferred from the phrase "common weal." It was never defined in narrow economic terms, although the state of the economy certainly would have been implied in community prosperity. When "commonwealth" was adopted as a designation of the whole body of people constituting a state or nation in the sixteenth century, it displaced the older meaning, but not the significance. "Commonwealth" is still used generally to refer to any body of persons united in a common interest.

It is more than prophetic when Peter Drucker, archchampion of the corporation and defender of the institution, suggests that, "the challenge of the new millennium . . . is to maintain the focus on the narrow and specific function that gives [the institutions] the capacity to perform, and yet the willingness and ability to work together and with political authority for the *common good*" (italics added).[3] Almost, but not quite. The critical fact this earnest admonition overlooks is that true commonweal cannot be realized within or among existing organizations. The corporation-model organization by its very construction and philosophy is diametrically opposed to the principles of the common good: abundance for all; optimal individual good; and mutual well-being. But it will be these tenets on which the new wealth will be based and by which it will be defined.

NOTES

1. Mark Twain, *The Adventures of Huckleberry Finn* (New York: Holt, Rhinehart and Winston, 1948), 274.

2. Dante Alighieri, *The Divine Comedy*, Vol. III: *Paradise*, trans. Mark Musa (New York: Penguin Books, 1984), 97.

3. Peter F. Drucker, "The Rise, Fall, and Return of Pluralism," *Wall Street Journal*, 1 June 1999, p. A2.

CHAPTER 34

Words, Meanings, and Systems

The issue . . . is not whether we use our language accurately to describe
the world that is really there but whether we see that the things created
by our language have the impermanence of foam on the face of the
unnameable, the unknowable, the unutterable.

James P. Carse[1]

The typical first response to the idea of an emerging new organization is,
"What will it look like?" Old mindsets are indeed difficult to escape. The fact
is the new organization will not look like anything. It cannot be drawn or
otherwise depicted. It cannot be described in quantitative or geometric terms.
It will not be reducible to scientific analysis or synthesis. It cannot be seen.
The new organization will be simply a matter of dedicated relationships —
among individuals and between the individual and all others.

That human beings always have joined and always will join others in some
kind of affiliation, either to guarantee an enduring common benefit or to
accomplish a project of mutual interest none could do alone, was never the
issue. It is fundamental to their inherent nature. Besides, practical necessity
demands it. So the question about this perpetual human phenomenon is not
why it occurs but how. While there are many interpretations, the question
has never been resolved. In fact, much to our eternal discredit and harm, it
has never been clearly articulated. Even a basic assumption has never been
seriously challenged; that is, there is no difference between those arrangements effected in view of a specific task to be done and those intended to
create a permanent, purportedly beneficial situation. So the organization of

one is the same as that of the other. For over three centuries now, that organization has been some version of the modern corporation. The previous historical analysis of that particular social arrangement makes abundantly clear the need to acknowledge and pursue something beyond, something that would actually serve human beings, as opposed to demanding that they serve it—something intrinsically human. It just may be that the unprecedented circumstances surrounding the present generation constitute an imperative to begin the search.

This discussion must now proceed from very rudimentary inquiries: two about language; two dealing with systems. First, are the terms of reference to be considered metaphors or words with actual meanings in context, and do these words carry the tenor of nouns or verbs? Second, in systems, must the organismic and the atomistic be at odds, and what is the difference, if any, between constructs and formations?

Before discussing the first questions, some acceptable rationale is necessary. It is indeed quite simple: No new system can emerge within the constraints of the existing vocabulary. As Marx insightfully pointed out, technology always advances more rapidly than social institutions. That is to say, the forms of society seriously lag the forms of thought. If language is the expression of thought, then we would expect that a radical change in vocabulary would necessarily precede any radical change in the forms of society. The basic problem with all attempts at reform of social orders is that new ideas are suffocated straightway by old terminology.

The contemporary corporation-model organization has been built into a construct of language that reduces all human beings within it to marginal existence. Until the language is abandoned, any idea of the emergence of new systems is purely academic. Here are some of the archaic terms that must be eliminated:

Accountability	Directives	Paradigm
Activity	Empower	Policies
Administration	Group decision making	Positions
Administrator	Headquarters	Rank
Benchmarks	Human resources	Re-
Best practice	Implementation	Reform
Bottom-up	Job	Reinvent
Bureaucracy	Job accountabilities	Restructure
Central office	Job descriptions	Scenarios
Centralization	Layers	Site-based management
Chain of command	Leadership	Standards
Committee	Level	Standard operating procedure
Consensus	Line and staff	Structure
Continuous improvement	Management	Subordinates
Data-based	Market driven	Superiors
Data-driven	Models	Teaming
Decentralization	(The) organization	Top down
Delegation (of authority)	Organizational chart	Vision

In regard to the first inquiry, a metaphor is "an implied analogy (logic) which imaginatively identifies one object with another and ascribes to the first one or more of the qualities of the second."[2] This is just one indication that people do not always mean what they say, or vice versa. So it seems that a brief etymology of the two operative words in contemporary social order might indeed reveal their true meanings. Both the words "corporation" and "organization" came into the English language from Latin (*corporare* < *corpus* and *organizare* < *organum*). It appears likely that by the time any derivation of *corpus* was absorbed into the Anglo-Saxon language, its metaphorical dimension already had been lost through common usage. That is, there was no longer any sense of comparison by conscious reference to an actual physical body. Although the word remained the same, the meaning had been transferred to the direct context of a social or political group. The original meaning survived only in words such as "corporeal" and "corpse." In fact, when the Apostle Paul, late in the first century wrote his famous extended metaphor on the body of Christ, he was probably using a metaphor his readers understood, in a secular context, only as the real definition.

Early in English history, the word was applied to any group of people who identified with one another as, say, a town—"the corporation of the town of Plymouth" (1439). In fact, it was during the fifteenth century that the English courts established the legal principle of limited liability for corporate ownership. By then, the term was applied to any company of traders who were granted control, essentially a monopoly, of their particular trade in a borough or other place. Usually recognized by a local authority, such as a mayor, these "corporations" existed independently of any particular membership, and all assets belonged to the corporation itself, which was, in fact, a citizen. By the time the word "corporation" reached its modern definition in the seventeenth century, any implicit allusion to its original meaning—therefore, any necessary inferences of comparison—had been all but lost to legal status. It was as if the qualities of a corporation were ascribed to those of a physical body; the metaphor was reversed.

The word "organization" traveled a similar route. Coming into language later, it first referred to the systemic, dynamic orderliness of the human body and therefore, by easy transference, to that of anything analogous to a "body," even when that term was used metaphorically. Sometime, in the late seventeenth or early eighteenth century, it became a substantive term without prepositional reference to any other thing, literal or figurative; the phrases "the organization," "an organization" began to appear. Lacking the legal specificity of its companion word, the term was used generically in reference to any more-or-less permanent affiliation of several people.

Now, the significance of these etymologies is that in either case the original intent was to convey the idea of relationships among individuals engaged in a common enterprise or bound together by common values. In practice, primarily for legal reasons, the corporation became a nonexpiring, impersonal identity, separate and apart from the individuals in it—even indifferent to them. And human relationships would yield to the organization. Yet, the original metaphor still had significance beyond either logic or legality.

The second inquiry deals with the qualities of nouns and verbs. If the previous argument was somewhat academic, then surely this one verges on the esoteric. Nevertheless, practical lessons may be drawn from the lives of words. Stated simply, the question is whether "corporation" and "organization" are nouns or verbs. On the surface, of course, that is a ridiculous idea since both are defined as nouns by all the rules and general use of language. Yet it is true that both these words belong to a certain category of words referred to as "action nouns," many of which are formed by the suffix "-tion"; for example, "proclamation," "consolidation," "dedication." Each word implies action. "Corporation" came directly from the Latin *compora–ae*, which was used by Tertullian and others to describe something that had been embodied. But, "organization" evidently entered the language as a noun, subsequently became a verb in the sixteenth century, and later returned to the vernacular as a noun in the seventeenth century, with the modernized derivative "organize" surviving as the action word.

Still implicit in the noun form is action—not point-in-time (as "incorporation") but continuing action—even a dynamism. So the question is not as much about the technicalities of grammar as what is actually heard—a kind of synesis; that is to say, when the words "corporation" and "organization" are used, does one hear dynamism or stasis, action or thing? When asked, only approximately 10 percent of respondents reply, "I hear a verb." The others evidently think of "corporation" as being completely independent of active participation by individuals, and "organization" as either a generic designation of the same or similar entity or as the artificial structure of the thing. Lately, complaints about "dysfunctional" organization, in either the specific or the generic, have risen to a loud chorus. Typically, the solution adopted is "reorganization," a musical-chair type exercise in which the pieces are shifted around, some dropped, and others added. It is still "dysfunctional"—but in a different way. All the while the real problem was that the "organization" in trouble was not designed and built with movable parts. It screamed stasis, resisted any movement. Position was more important than action. What was lost was simply not purist language, not even meaning, but the very life of both "corporation" and the "organization."

When a popular textbook opens with the question, "What is an organization?" it asks the wrong question.[3] Rather, the inquiry should be, "What is organization?" That would be truer to the original sense of the word and would, of course, radically change the answer.

The third inquiry is about systems, and immediately the proverbial dichotomy and adversity arises: that is, whether systems are organismic or atomistic. This debate and the concept underlying it are among those logical propositions in which the argument for either side proves the other. It is a wonder that the confusion has persisted for so long, when all along the answer was no. Although the arguments were ancient, the mechanization of the industrial age amplified the contention over a question that never should have been asked and, when first posed, should have settled with dispatch. The only logical question provides the answer: is it possible that all systems are both? Here again understanding lies in the words themselves. There are many very fascinating words in English whose full meanings have been lost, but none more interesting than the word "essence." Its fascination is not in its internal mix of assonance and consonance but in its original meaning. The Latin *essentia* simply means "being"; in a metaphysical sense, "absolute being" or "substance." *Esse* means "to be." Modern dictionaries, in an effort to render the meaning by other words, veer off original center in definitions such as "that which makes something what it is." This definition is almost a verbatim quote from Locke's explanation of the "real" definition, as differentiated from the "nominal" definition: His interpretation was, "that which constitutes the being of a thing." And if all that seems just so much pedanticism, the "real" definition arose from its use in chemical distillation processes whereby that which constitutes the nature of the thing was extracted. (That's why perfumes are termed "essences.") And that is the most common use of the word today—something that is critical to or necessary for. But Locke's explanation of the nominal definition honestly and accurately suggests that distillation is not possible in "essence" or "essential."

The fourth inquiry has to do with the nature of human affiliation, whether existing for task or situation or some other reason; and whether the motivation makes any difference in the system that characterizes the association. The discussion is aided by recalling the traditional notion that there are only two kinds of systems in the world (if there be spiritual systems, they are of another world). There are natural systems—that is, those existing in a state of nature—and there are artifactual systems—that is, those made by human beings. In practical terms, that usually translates to formations and constructs, because natural systems tend to be formations and artifactual systems tend to be constructs. Usually, this kind of discussion presents not an analysis but a choice.

It would be perfectly reasonable to assume that the artifactual systems are those designed, engineered, and built to accomplish some specific purpose (physical facilities, such as dwellings and roads and space vehicles) or to establish some permanent situation (political, commercial, and communication arrangements), or to create a reality for the nonce (philosophy, religion, and science).

Conversely, it seems, natural systems are accepted as those manifested in the states and processes of all aspects of the physical universe, from atoms and galaxies to all manner of living things, typically including human beings. It is not so much the actuality of human nature as the perception of it that dictates the composition of human artifacts. But their actual nature cannot be denied. These are fundamental imperatives—not merely physical and emotional attributes. As such, they inform an omnipresent, natural order transcending and often conflicting artifactual systems. Calamities and catastrophes often have a freeing effect because they reacquaint people with their inherent nature.

It also would be reasonable at least to inquire whether either kind of system is more conducive to task or situation. And the reasonable conclusion likely would be that artifactual constructs ensure permanent situations, whereas natural formations more readily accomplish tasks (a recent very practical example of this is the attempt by corporations to overcome the inherent limitations of structure through the formation of project "teams"). This kind of reasoning takes as its predicate the assumption that formation and constructs are complete opposites. The new age apostles at the end of the twentieth century developed their own organum. Typically, the characteristics of each were described as follows:

Formations	Constructs
Self-identifying	Identity prescribed
Self-organizing	Organized by rules
Relationships	Function
Evolving	Static
Holistic	Particalized
Individual fulfillment	Return on investment

However, as valid as these distinctions may be, they omit the two most critical aspects of any system, unless they are implied in the allusions to identity and organizing; that is, control and energy. In natural systems, the locus of control is always within the system; formation is internally driven. The practical result of a human formation is that everyone in it experiences gain or benefit and that all bear mutual responsibility; should any exception occur, the formation breaks up. That is true in regimented military formations, parade or battlefield, just as much as in the formations of birds. It is also true of game formations in sports, where natural conformity to the action results in continuous change of designs and patterns. Consequently, in natural formations, there is no limit to energy—as opposed to constructs, which by design limit even its application. Disciplines in one actually create energy; in the other, they suppress or dissipate it.

So the ultimate question here is whether it is possible to create, distinct from the conflicted atomistic–organismic concepts, a system of organization that is neither—only human. The answer, if not also already obvious, is a resounding affirmation. In fact, the answer provides a new organum of human organization that will indeed serve the best interest of all involved and will consistently and exclusively guarantee their greatest well-being. If the system truly is to be human organization, it will have five critical attributes.

First, the system will share common referents, both qualitative and quantitative, although neither will be limiting. The qualitative are the permanent moral and ethical convictions that continuously pervade every aspect of the system and adjudicate all its actions strictly by the imperative of its best self. The quantitative referents are those present intents and purposes that represent the best knowledge and highest aspirations at the time, within the existing context. But both are seen only as tentative but necessary states in constant emergence.

Second, it will be characterized by immediate awareness. That is, everyone participating in the system will be so thoroughly informed with the common values, so dedicated to the mutual intent, and so eminently conscious of the system as an organic whole that no one action can be imparted any significance except as it relates to all others. Everything occurs synchronistically and in harmony. Mere activity ceases to exist; nothing can be done that does not affect, or is not affected by, all other action. In a very unusual reverse twist of science turned art, current technologies negate the old barriers to communication and dialogue within the system, no matter what its size.

Third, it will perceive action as discovery. Action is not an end; it is a beginning. All action reveals possibilities that were unimaginable before. No amount of scientific research, no theoretical speculation or stipulation, and certainly no application of effort can discover the possibilities that are found in action. All the other versions of knowledge are rationalistic. But discovery is made by intuitively interpreting each action, not in the context of some preconceived end or conclusion, but within the context of all other action. It is practical hermeneutics.

Fourth, the system will immediately translate discovery as freedom; that is, the freedom of the individual both to do and to be. There is no place for authority or rigid constructs of position and rank—no artificially established limits. Personal freedom is the ultimate capacity. Thriving systems depend on each person's exercise of his or her "full powers." That can be done only outside even the current qualitative and quantitative contexts. Otherwise, how can new contexts be realized? And how can life be sustained? It is here, in the immediate interpretation of action and the intuitive grasp of meaning, that the common good and the good of the individual coincide.

Finally, the new system will be characterized by the generation of energy. Unlike the other forms of action in which energy is either transferred or dissipated, here the energy is the force of life itself. Freed from artifactual constraints, there is no limit to the creative power of the human being. And there is no limit to good.

And what shall this thing, this new kind of organization, be called? Seldom is language successfully dictated by decree, so no attempt will be made to prescribe or predict the ultimate designation. Ironically, common sense and original usage are on the side of "corporation" as the most accurate metaphor for even the emerging system of affiliation. "Body" still speaks to all the dimensions of the ideal human affiliation. But, alas, that linguistic spring has been fouled by so many rationalistic impurities over the centuries that it is forever stained by connotation turned denotation. Corrupted by both history and practice, it can never convey the qualities or intent of the new organization.

One must look far and wide for a term that captures at once both the dimensions and the dynamics of the emerging organization. There is a word that comes as close as any other to accomplishing this. Although surprisingly it may sound awkward to English ears, the word *syntagma* presents itself as the best alternative to corporation. The real definition of the modern Greek term is a "military battalion," or a "constitution." In the center of Athens today is Syntagma (Constitution) Square. The English use of the term has historically been restricted to a collection of formal statements or literary works. And that is now considered archaic. But the nominal meaning, as usual, contains the essential meaning, a meaning probably more contemporary than any real definition. It simply means "together order." That is precisely what the new organization will be — the dimensions and the dynamics of acting in one accord toward mutual benefit.

NOTES

1. James Carse, *Breakfast at the Victory: The Mysticism of Ordinary Experience* (San Francisco: Harper Books, 1994), 24.
2. William Flint Thrall, Addison Hubbard, and C. Hugh Holman, A *Handbook to Literature* (New York: Odyssey Press, 1960), 281.
3. Harold F. Gortner, Julianne Mahler, and Jeanne Bell Nicholson, *Organizational Theory: A Public Perspective* (Chicago: Dorsey Press, 1987), 2.

CHAPTER 35

Explorations and Discovery

One step I have advanc'd thee; if thou dost
As this instructs thee, thou dost make thy way
To noble fortunes. Know thou this, that men
Are as the time is. To be tender-mined
Does not become a sword. Thy great employment
Will not bear question. Either say thou'lt do't,
Or thrive by other means.

William Shakespeare[1]

At this point, this discourse turns from the historical and critical analyses to speculative argument setting forth the characteristics of the emerging organization. The discussion is speculative because so far that ideal organization has not yet been fully realized; argument because there is already sufficient credible evidence to make the case without straining the imagination or reason, even though the features of this organization cannot be reduced to factual reporting and empirical analysis. The proposition is quite simple: syntagma, or whatever the emerging system may be called, has four dimensions and two dynamics. The dimensions are common values, mutual purpose, excess capacity, and creative action. The dynamics are commensuration and essentiality. (Just for the sake of completing the design, it has one essence and three parts— "I," "I" and another, "I" and all the others.)

The conclusions and predictions here are based on three premises, any one of which offers compelling testimony to the reality of the emerging organization, namely, the historical account and critical analysis of the corporation-model organization; the epochal shifts in all aspects of Western society; and actual manifestations of the new concept of organization in contemporary enterprises.

Regarding the first, surely to any discerning critic the contradictions, discrepancies, and inadequacies of the corporation-model organization and its society, as described at length in this book, ironically illuminate by void or negation the human dimensions and the organizational dynamics that will replace it. In short, the corporation-model organization demonstrates the necessity of these attributes in human organization most poignantly by their glaring absence. For example, traditional organization highlighted the importance of common values because it had none except those need-values predicated on economic survival or greed. It dramatized the vital need for mutual purpose by pitting corporate goals against personal interests. It proved the imperative of excess capacity by operating, always maximally, at deficit levels in order to enhance the bottom line. It emphasized the critical necessity for creative action by typically sacrificing real action to either processed activity or strict implementation. Furthermore, wide discrepancies existed among authority, accountability, and information, thus identifying the lack of commensuration as the root cause of the dysfunctionality of corporated systems. And the need for essentiality was clearly revealed by the accentuated polarization, isolation, and internal competition within the corporation-model organization.

Second, there is the readily apparent epochal shift in the aspects of society, as suggested earlier. Old orders everywhere in Western civilization are collapsing; and new, radically different orders are emerging. The very first idea postulated and suggested in this book was that human organization, indeed that of society itself, is a direct reflection of the accumulative aspects and particularly the definition of wealth and the system for wealth production. As Western civilization undergoes metamorphosis, its new attributes, of necessity, will be translated into a new form of organization.

Third, perhaps the most immediately recognizable—if not the most compelling—evidence of the emerging organization is to be found in the somewhat divergent, albeit practical, manifestations of the new dimensions and dynamics of existing progressive corporation-model systems. However, even here it is as if these friendly forces are urgently insinuating themselves into the domain of a reluctant and resistant host. Perhaps that is why so far none has been fully realized and why they do not as yet exist anywhere in proportional combinations—that is, as a single organic system capable of serving strictly and only the common good. Nevertheless, the signs are clear indicators of what is to come, once the forces are freed from the corporation-model constraints.

It is much more than a mere curiosity that the six features have appeared in a natural and necessary progression. That also is testimony to the actuality of the tenets in real contexts, as well as to the inherently developmental character of the new organization. The matter of common values was first to surface, and at present this is still the one receiving most attention in both for-profit and nonprofit enterprises. But it is true that, at this early stage, in most instances values are pragmatically defined by management—usually by the chief executive—and didactically imposed by authority in order to improve morale, employee relations, and, of course, productivity. In most cases, they are handed down as company creeds or as codes of ethics. Or an alternative popular option is to rely on external consultants to audit the existing "values" against some universal standardized set of recommended principles relative to attitudes and behavior and then program corrective measures aimed at effecting conformity.

IBM is typical of the first approach. The company's famous principles, in fact, written by the chairman, contain as much business strategy as moral imperative—probably more.

- The marketplace is the driving force behind everything that we do.
- At our core, we are a technology company with an overriding commitment to quality.
- Our primary measures of success are customer satisfaction and shareholder value.
- We operate as an entrepreneurial organization with a minimum of bureaucracy and a never-ending focus on productivity.
- We never lose sight of our strategic vision.
- We think and act with a sense of urgency.
- Outstanding, dedicated people make it all happen, particularly when they work together as a team.
- We are sensitive to the needs of all employees and the communities in which we operate.

As an example of the second, The Lebow Companies tout themselves as the "Global Standard for the Work Environment." Their "Shared Values Process® Operating System" promises a program that "rapidly translates into bottom-line profits and enhances job satisfaction." Purportedly, this is accomplished through "eight basic Shared Values [that] create a quality company." Whether these attempts and values are authentic is beside the point. Their real significance is that they acknowledge the fundamental place of values in any system of human affiliation. It is "cultural anthropology."

As for mutual purpose, there has been, since the beginning of the modern corporation, the nagging realization that human beings are motivated by their own self-interest. The traditional corporation, although choosing to override that interest by defiance or negotiation, nevertheless slowly accepted the advantage of reciprocity. Chris Argyris was the first seriously to deal with the conflict theoretically. He pointed out the inevitable conflict between the goals of the corporation and the interests of individuals. Pensions and profit-sharing schemes were the first attempts to deal with it practically; however, all sharing was still tied to base compensation and limited by a scale of job classification. And that approach was based strictly on the corporate notion that all human beings are economic animals motivated only by financial gain. It was not until the 1980s that Soichiro Honda recognized that, while there may be many more motives for human behavior than mere economic incentives, there must be a congruence between the goals of the corporation and the interests of the individuals that make it up. Only in the last two decades of the twentieth century did a seismic shift toward common benefit occur. Common benefit is the only proof of common purpose. But the tentacles of the traditional organization, not surprisingly, still maintained a tenacious grip on some of the most mature companies. For instance, in 1999, some companies ignited a firestorm of employee hostility by the attempt to institute a "cash-balance" pension program through which older employees would see their retirement benefits reduced by as much as 50 percent. This incendiary backlash dramatically accentuated the critical importance of mutual benefit.

Perhaps the most promising examples, now almost legendary, are the high-tech firms of Silicon Valley that not only abandoned traditional rank-ordered hierarchies but also moved toward equalizing benefits through shared ownership. For example, Cisco Systems grants 90 percent of its stock options each year to regular employees—not management. The philosophy is that everyone in the company is equal and should share benefits, as well as responsibility. Other primarily nonmanufacturing companies followed suit. One of the most publicized moves to employee ownership was that of United Airlines, which turned its employees into stockholders (60% of the company) and instituted personalized benefits packages that favored individual circumstances and preferences.

The most instructive example, however, came from what only in retrospect appears a quite natural source—Native Americans. Although the examples could be multiplied many times over, the advent of casino gambling on reservations dramatically highlighted an alternative communal system of enterprise. One of the most illustrative and successful ventures is that of the Saginaw–Chippewa tribes in central Michigan. Organized in a communal fashion and dedicated to commercial endeavors as well as political, educational, and social necessities, this community thrives on mutual benefit. For instance, each year every member of the tribe receives a proportionate share of the collective revenues. Ironically, that practice, founded on ancient non-European tradition is still closest to the emerging Western organization.

The issue of capacity was a dilemma for the corporation-model organization. In the corporate mentality, it was always capacity versus immediate profits; and there was never any doubt which would win. While even the most traditional organization grudgingly acknowledged the necessity for employee training and the development of "human resources," it was not until the late 1980s that exemplary companies began to invest in people as "sources." Here again, any number of technology enterprises could serve to illustrate the often-startling

returns on the development of individual capacity outside the existing context. After all, that was the so-called "cutting edge" in product development.
Many such companies, Microsoft for example, created universities dedicated
to exploration and discovery.

But many smaller companies in more businesses not in the tide of the
technology revolution also realized the advantage of building capacity by
investing in human beings, Although their attempts were mostly directed toward training for current responsibilities, nevertheless the emphasis these
companies placed on training and education was driving the development of
human capacity. These companies simply had the foresight to see that there
is a direct correlation between human capacity and profitability. Two of the
most notable, because of their innovation and persistence in building capacity, are Interface and Burroughs and Chapin. The first, an international manu-
facturer of specialized wall and floor coverings, ranked in the Fortune 500,
began investing in the development of its employees from its very beginning.
Admittedly, one could argue—since its business strategy is to specialize and
to create trend-setting and market-dominating products—that such a risk was
merely a prerequisite. But it was just as much the result of the development
and design expected to maintain expertise and awareness far beyond today's
requirements; all those involved in sales, manufacturing, and distribution are
expected to participate in a continuing regimen of training and education,
much of which is in conjunction with a local college. It is little wonder that
this company not only is highly profitable and market dominant but also has
been judged as one of the ten best companies in which to work.

The other, Burroughs and Chapin, by any measure has lately become one
of the most exciting enterprises in the world by discovering and inventing
unique new ways to transform a substantial base of nonproductive raw land
into a galaxy of resort, residential, and entertainment properties. Here again
the open secret has been the dedicated creation of individual capacity within
every aspect of the company. For example, each employee is individually
placed on a career track and provided experience and continuous training to
achieve his or her own goals. In fact, one of the company's published objectives is "to provide for our employees opportunities for compensation, benefits and professional growth that exceed those of comparable positions in
markets in which we operate."

These two companies, without fanfare, have established a new postulate
for the emerging organization: capacity always creates capacity.

Of all the features of the emerging organization, creative action is the least
visible at the present time. Control, it seems, is a difficult thing for tradition-
minded managers to relinquish, and the few enlightened systems that have
dared to trust those individuals who are actually doing the jobs of the enterprise are already fabled in corporate lore. Nordstrom's and the early EDS are
proverbial examples. Many regionals, such as Bankers First, are less well known
but equally appreciated for the excellence in customer service that is a direct

result of immediate action by the person doing the job. Much more than the practice of old-line decentralization, the method of these companies is to bestow on everyone the freedom to decide and act independently and to solve problems rather than to report them to a committee. There is no doubt that, going forward, the most successful enterprises will be those that actually provide personal service to clients and customers; service is impossible without immediate and creative action.

The dynamics of the emerging organization are not as readily apparent in the fin de siècle corporation-model organization. They were fundamentally contrary to the framework and activity of that mechanical system. That is not to say, however, that some serious attempts were not made that all but acknowledged the vital necessity for both commensuration and essentiality in any purposeful human affiliation. In fact, it could be argued that commensuration was the whole idea behind Management by Objectives and Self-Control. Originally, it was intended as a rational process by which goals were mutually agreed upon and the individuals involved then freed to pursue those ends without further permission or instruction—certainly without interference. Unfortunately, the rigidity of the corporation-model systems, along with its basic distrust of the competence and motivation of the person, refused to yield its prescriptive surveillance of performance.

So, there are not many examples of relationships that approximate commensuration. It is said, however, that Lee Iacocca, when he was chairman of Chrysler, practiced something very close to commensuration, at least among the executives and managers, by establishing with them specific objectives, agreeing on the prerogative of action and the resources required to achieve them and reviewing and adjusting them periodically. But one of the most brazen attempts was that of the director of Florida Bureau of Exceptional Education, who in 1995 moved to organize to a strategic plan by declaring all jobs vacant and all job descriptions invalid and building an organizational dynamic based on new accountabilities and new relationships through mutual commitments. Unfortunately, the state bureaucracy, sensing something unorthodox was about to happen, quickly crushed the heresy and the heretic. She was fired. But her attempt to evolve life from a primordial morass was not only illustrative of a breakthrough concept of organic organization but offered proof positive of the developmental nature of syntagma: capacity formation is a prerequisite of commensuration.

The dynamic of essentiality was even more foreign to the corporation-model organization, although the much hullabalooed trends such as decentralization, participatory management, teaming, and even cross-functional training seem to indicate an almost instinctive urge to bring some sense of wholeness to an otherwise fragmented, particularized, often hapless organization. Some modern companies, however, actually approached at least the idea of essentiality not as a result of philosophy but as a practical necessity. For example, vertical integration has long since been a popular tactic of manufacturing and agricultural enterprises. And retail chains such as McDonald's, Wal-Mart, and Home Depot, through franchise-type standardization of products, advertising, and culture achieve a systemic unity ironically not found in most localized companies. But all that is only similar to essentiality.

One of the best current examples of real essentiality is Sonat, a natural gas exploration and transmission company. Of course, the very nature of the business is eminently conducive to essentiality, even though the delivery system itself consists of two distinct operations—pipeline and compressor. Because of this company's philosophy, as well as its uncompromising commitment to safety, the system is essentially one in both operations and culture—so much so, in fact, that a recent chief executive officer insisted that the only company priority on any given day was the part of the system that was in trouble. And that's where he would be—not to fix the problem, but to assure those involved that this site was indeed the company. Here again is another remarkable postulate of syntagma: essentiality is as much about feeling as it is about function.

While there are many other examples of each attribute to the new organization, these are sufficient to constitute credible evidence of the gradual emergence of a radical change in the identity, purpose, and methods of human affiliation. From here it is an easy transition, at least intellectually, to the cardinal features of syntagma.

NOTE

1. William Shakespeare, *King Lear*, V, iii: 29–35.

CHAPTER 36

The Dimensions of Syntagma

The power of the whole gathers in all the power lost in fragmentation. . . .
The power of the alternative lies in recognizing that we have more choices
than we once thought. By imagining new possibilities, we can say no to
the suffocating, unacceptable options we confronted in the past.

Marilyn Ferguson[1]

From the evidence presented in Chapter 35, it is well within the bounds of
reason to propose the specific nature of syntagma—a human nature, and to
assert the full implications within each dimensions and dynamic. Of course,
new systems of this magnitude emerge over a long period of time and seldom
appear exactly as foreseen. However, in this case, the metamorphosis of the
corporation-model organization will occur quickly; and the evolving organization will discover possibilities within human affiliation impossible to imagine.

Unfortunately, constructs and formations, like the poor, will remain always. And each may reveal more about human sympathy than about human
understanding. It is impossible to completely shed the past, to be rid of it forever.
Sometimes it rises in stately monuments to nobility and generosity gleaming in
the sun; sometimes it piles up in the shadows as the rusting junk of meanness and
brutality. In either case, the past is no judge of the future and certainly not its
progenitor; the future will judge the past, but only if the future continuously
creates itself. Already it is emerging, not as an extension of or a reaction to history
but as the inevitable and irresistible assertion of human being. If members of
the race can muster all the power of their inherent intelligence and spirit,
then they can create a new kind of system worthy of their humanity.

First are the dimensions. Since any one of these attributes determines the proportion in kind and degree of the others—change one, change all—perfect harmony is not only desirable, it is at last also possible. Obviously, such a system cannot be reduced to a graphic depiction, as in the traditional corporation organizational chart. It is *intra*active, constantly morphing into original patterns somewhat like a continuously turning kaleidoscope. However, with a nod toward visual learning, perhaps a dynamic hologram could be used to suggest its reciprocally proportioning relationships—occurring within time.

COMMON VALUES

The first dimension challenges every authoritarian construct and corporation-model organization at the core. Conventional wisdom has it that enterprises of this type are driven by mission or, as some less objective-minded have suggested, by "vision"; but that is not the case at all. Mission provides at best only direction; the driving force is, always and only, values. That all social affiliations are based on certain intrinsic values or principles could be convincingly argued simply from the evidence of their overt action, even though the values do not constitute a total congruent value system and do not rise to distinction of moral convictions. Admittedly, this is a positivist approach but, nevertheless, valid. Further, it could be successfully proposed that, whether fragmentary or systemic and whether deemed by observers as "positive" or "negative," values are the energizing force of any collective human endeavor; and, therefore, the energy will be either concentrated or dissipated by organization. Complicating the matter further is the difficulty of ascertaining exactly whose values are in play and whether they are formally or informally expressed. In traditional corporations, those issues were settled by management style. It may be that the values of the corporate entity, as manifested in its behavior or pronouncements and in its policies and practice, are not the values of these individuals who make up the corporation. Which is more likely to be perceived by an outside observation? For that matter, which is acknowledged internally? A traveler can surely tell if the courtesy extended at the airline ticket counter is genuine or simply an effort to comply with the instructions in the customer service guide. And the so-called "grapevine" grows the real culture all over the factory floor. Actuality, in these cases, transcends perception; and the effect can range from disillusionment to despair.

The mere mention of values calls forth a wide range of interpretations: practical opinion about how to go about performing a job or task (is quality built in or inspected in?); circumstantially urgent human needs (hunger, homelessness); or deep and abiding convictions (right and wrong) that are matters of conscience, matters of faith. It is true that opinion, great or small, can have the effect of holding people together as a kind of cohort in argumentation or reaching some end, at least until the subject or task changes. Urgent need can be the strongest bond, at least until the need is satisfied, but only values of moral conviction have enduring power and bestow the unique benefit of community. These values, are best described as "beliefs"; and they are the best meaning of belief—moral imperatives that can be proved not in demonstration but only in personification. All people have them, but not all share them. And that makes the difference.

Beliefs are at once simple, complex, and complicated—simple in their fundamental definition, complex in individual understanding, and complicated in collective interpretation. Fundamentally, there is not an unlimited number of subjects that can qualify as truly moral imperatives. It is true that quite often mere perception of natural conditions or of human nature and behavior reaches conclusions that rise to the level of imperative. Furthermore, certain philosophical axioms are often stated as beliefs. But these conclusions, although often verging on the ethical and frequently admired as "principles" (natural or otherwise), are not issues of morality. Nor do abstract associations, usually posed by linking verbs, qualify: "knowledge is power," or, "to err is human; to forgive, divine." All these are assumptions of truth, all right, and, as such, have at least the temporary compulsion of truth. But even so, none qualifies as a moral imperative. The reason is simple: all the foregoing statements are assumptions, and assumptions are susceptible to verification by empirical evidence; in a world ruled by science, they become merely hypotheses. Once proved, or disproved, they cease to be matters of faith and become instead matters of fact. So what at first appeared as a deeply held belief becomes either acceptance of the fact or rejection of the original assumption. Facts may have the force of values if indeed there is passion sufficient to prompt congruent action; but only in this qualifying way can it be said that agreement on facts constitutes a system of values for one or more individuals.

Distorting the definition even more is the contemporary habit of translating both assumptions about universal realities and logical correlatives into something regarded as "principles," typically understood as trustworthy "rules" or established guidelines for human conduct. Although in many cases, a principle is the implication of moral conviction and presupposes a moral absolute, virtually anything pertaining to either necessity or discretion could be so ensconced. From law to codes of conduct, to corporate policies, to simple etiquette and social grace—all these are grist both for and from the mill of principles. If the sophomoric attempt is made to make principles out of what are alleged to be "natural laws," the whole idea is rightly susceptible to being judged empirically, thus destroying any claim to the status of moral imperative. Furthermore, the formulation of any such principle creates an almost humorous paradox because all such principles are necessarily the result of cultural lenses, and all cultures ultimately are based on perceived moral absolutes. What is moral in one culture is abjectly immoral in another, amoral in yet another. Principles are superficial. Genuine moral imperatives are self-verifying; and while they are most certainly tested, they can never be proved by logic, reason, or empirical evidence. No doubt this is why ancient Greek

and Roman philosophers simply recognized the deadly sins and cardinal virtues and spoke of the eternal verities—without explanation, without apology.

All cultures are made of the same stuff. They are but variations upon themes,
all answers to the same universal and eternal questions. These matters of
faith are the context of culture, the consensus of community. And like one
vast, sustained fugue, they resound to the far corners of the earth. There is an
infinite number of variations, not only in the finer points of substantive distinctiveness but also in nuance, as each idea relates to others, and in depth of
passion for truth. But there are surprisingly few questions.

It is not the intent of this study to recommend any of the variations; that
argument would be countered a thousand times over. The purpose here,
rather, is to suggest the few moral categories and then explain how and why
the answers are critical to any human society and to any specific social organization. For that reason, they are phrased as questions. Furthermore, these
categories are not to be considered as a template for developing dogma or
creed but only as inevitable questions that are answered even in denial.

- First is the question of God (gods) and the nature of that ostensibly divine power
  and personality. This issue is germane to all the other questions and answers alike
  and, consequently, the basis for any conception of moral values. No doubt this is
  the reason religion is at the heart of all the world's cultures. Beliefs about this
  question range from fanatic, militaristic assertions to denial of anything divine.

- The second closely related question is whether there is purpose in or to human
  life. The answer either establishes the context for meaning in life or it admits
  noncontextual meaninglessness. Here again the spectrum of belief ranges to extremes—from the view each person is predestined to abject purposelessness.

- Next is the question of sacredness; that is, whether there are the things that are
  inviolable. The answers resolve the issue of human worth and dignity, the
  hallowedness of places, reverence for that which is understood, and respect for
  that which is not.

- The fourth questions deals with the essential nature of the human being. Here the
  expanse of being is decided, and most probably the end of life. Answers range
  from a tripartite being—body, soul, and spirit—to a blob of protoplasm mauled
  about by uncontrollable forces.

- The fifth is about heritage, specifically whether it is worthy of honor. The issue is
  rather simple: Are the successes of any generation to be attributed to generations
  past? The answer is critical to the validation of the present by generations future.
  It is manifested very poignantly in attitudes toward both age and youth and toward
  the significance of history.

- Sixth, there are the external questions about the value of human life. The first
  issue is whether one life is more valuable than another. The second is the what,
  how, and why of its beginning and end. The answer determines the character of
  every aspect of any society and the way in which individuals see and treat one
  another, and themselves.

- Next comes fidelity. The question is whether there are personal commitments or bonds worthy of undeviating loyalty or allegiance. The answer is not as much an adjudication of the object as it is a judge of the subject. As such, it is the basis of all human relationships.
- The eighth question is about individual freedom. The issues are whether freedom is proportional to obligation, whether it is a means or an end, and whether absolute freedom for all individuals is possible. The answers provide the touchstones of all systems of justice.
- The next question deals with integrity, from basic honesty to being true to oneself. Herein are established the standard and measure of trust. There is no honor or dishonor that is not predicated on the answer.
- Finally, there is the question of personal fulfillment; specifically, in what terms shall it be defined—by what one has, or by what one does not have? Either answer yields wisdom, late or soon, about who one is.

There is something in all this that is profoundly significant for both existing corporation-model organizations as well as the newly emerging affiliations. In the first, it is possible, more or less, to feign a sense of community and thus achieve proportional shares of its power and benefit, despite the variety of fully formed value systems present. The secret of community lies in concentricity. Community exists to the degree that the distinct value systems can discover a common center. Obviously, there is a wide range of possibilities, from cults to clubs. Graphically, it might be illustrated as shown in Figure 36.1. Several observations may be drawn from this graphic, all conducive to understanding the nature of community. One quite significant conclusion is that there are no "opposite" values—therefore no need to reconcile opponents. Dualistic analysis would stipulate x and y as conflicting extremes and then attempt to mediate a settlement in which both would be compromised. However, in community, opposition simply does not exist. "Other" is not opposite. A second conclusion is that only a common core of values can transcend differences that would otherwise separate. In this way, the grudging tolerance so often haughtily granted by collectives is set aside by respect within community; and the patronage so characteristic of antisystems, is trumped by mutual honor. A third observation, in a return to the beginning, is that com-

Figure 36.1

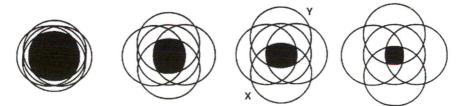

munity entails varying degrees of concentricity, but it is concentric nevertheless. The only requirement is that the center hold. That constant is the only
true consensus. And with that consensus, the community can confront no
problem that cannot be solved by full agreement. Contrary to conventional
understanding and usage, "consensus" is not a rationalized process of decision making in which the majority gets its way and the minorities agree to go
along quietly. The popular term "majority consensus" is an error of either
ignorance or deceit. Nor is it the toilsome settlement at the lowest common
denominator in ridiculous win–win fashion. Consensus, rather, is the exu-
berant moral accord of community; it is the highest common denominator.

Corporation-model organizations can only approximate consensus and
community. But the new system will begin de novo from the center of moral
values. And to that center people of like conviction will be attracted. In existing systems, any common core values, or their facsimiles, are discovered. In
the new system, values atttract their adherents who find one another.

One concluding note: Throughout this discussion of values, reference has
been made to the power and benefit of community. It should now be obvious
that the force of community builds from the concentration of moral imperative. Because there is always a positive correlation between values and well-
being, the benefit of community is nothing less than the general welfare.

MUTUAL PURPOSE

The idea of common welfare provides an easy transition into the discussion of common purpose, a condition that was never possible in previous
systems of human affiliation such as the corporation-model organization, or
even in authoritarian ecclesiastical orders. Common purpose was the bane
of their existence, both as a philosophical ideal and as a practical reality.
From Chris Argyris to Soichiro Honda, the inevitable conflict between the
goals of the corporation and the interests of the individuals in it has been
recognized as a fatal flaw. Even if such organizations had been able to discover a common core of values, there would still remain a thorough and
irreconcilable dichotomy in the economic construct—it's as simple as cross-
purposes. But, the enterprise of the new system will be predicated on common purpose, mutual benefit.

There is an issue that must be addressed early in this discussion; it harks
back to the popular distinction between constructs and formations. The question is simply this: Is it true that a common core of beliefs among human
beings constitutes a formation (that is, culture and community) but that, when
the same community undertakes some enterprise, the necessary systematizing of effort is, in fact, a construct? Given the context of the corporation-
model organization, the answer to both questions is, of course, yes. However,
if removed from that context, the question becomes moot. Outside that context, it is possible to create systems of affiliation in which there is no distinc-

tion between formation and construct; they are, in effect, one and the same. But if that system is ever to be realized, there are two basic tenets that have to be fully appropriated.

First, it is necessary freely to acknowledge that all people are motivated primarily by self-interest as they define it. That is not to say that they are selfish by nature but simply that they have the same instinctive motivation to take care of themselves, beginning with self-preservation. Even the famous entreaty, "Love your neighbor as yourself," necessarily presupposes and implicitly condones the love of self. That, in effect, becomes the standard for all relationships with others. Unfortunately, the concept is seldom understood, and even less frequently practiced; but the secret to common interest lies therein. Common interest actually means that there can be no conflict between one's interest in self and one's interest in others because they are the same.

Second, the common interest is proved only by mutual benefit. Human beings affiliate with others strictly in order to achieve together what no one could accomplish individually, however that end is defined. In the old corporate systems, the stumbling block was equity, in both ownership of and participation in wealth. There were only three possible eventualities: Some would receive more than they invested; some would invest more than they received; and some might break even. But in common interest there is no consideration of equity—or for that matter, equality—because mutuality transcends both. Common interest is never a zero-sum game. If indeed it can be realized, everyone involved in the mutual commitment will experience gain as defined by the common intent. The only reason that is possible is that in common interest, the system itself is not susceptible to the law of diminishing returns. Instead, it results in continuously increasing returns. The corporation thrived only in a world of scarcity, and so worked to produce it. The new system creates its own world of abundance that becomes possible only through the redefining of wealth.

So the question arises as to what the new wealth will be. The "general welfare," as described by the founders of the United Sates, seems hopeful enough, and virtuous, and good; yet it lacks sufficient specificity to be actually achieveable. On one hand, it might be construed as that which does no harm; on the other, and truer to the original intent, it would encompass everything that promotes or brings about the best in and for each person in the affiliation. And while especially the latter is true and highly desirable, there is a specific, knowable, immeasurable wealth.

It is knowledge. For quite some time now, businesses have been much enamored of "intellectual capital," that is, proprietary knowledge with commercial value. Like any other resource or commodity, it is available to others only at a cost. It is a line item on balance sheets; presently it will be capitalized like any other fixed asset. There is no doubt of the financial values thus accrued. W. Edwards Demming spoke of "profound knowledge," but as far as anyone can tell, that meant only the seasoned understanding of the interworkings of a particular enterprise, perhaps even the industry at large. Assuming for the moment that there have been four "ages" identified by systems of material wealth and assuming further that the affiliation of human beings always reflects the primary wealth-producing activity, then knowledge as wealth would not only redefine both the subject and object, it also would require a system that has never existed before. Historically, previous systems are commonly presented as shown in Figure 36.2.

But the new organization will be a radical departure from the previous concepts, moving emphatically from the quantitative to the qualitative, from constructs and formations to the human, from things to persons. Knowledge, as the new wealth, will differ from the resources of past systems in two ways: First, it will not be something to be used up as another resource; it will be created and held as a treasure. Second, it will not be hoarded to produce value by its scarcity and then sold at a profit; rather, it will be returned to the common good, the general welfare, an impetus to real prosperity. The terms of the old organum change radically, as shown in Figure 36.3.

EXCESS CAPACITY

Capacity is the wherewithal of being; it comprises the range and scope of meaning, the breadth and depth of significance. Therefore, it must of necessity always exist in excess. Without it there can be no growth, no development; and so there can be no aspiration but of sustaining the present. There

Figure 36.2

HUMAN SYSTEM	ECONOMIC ERA	PRIMARY RESOURCE	TRANSFORMING AGENT	TIME ORIENTATION
FAMILY STRUCTURE	AGRARIAN	LAND	NATURAL ENERGY	PAST
CORPORATION	INDUSTRIAL	CAPITAL	PROCESSED ENERGY	PRESENT
VIRTUAL NETWORKS	INFORMATION	MIND	COMPUTER	FUTURE

Figure 36.3

SYSTEM	WEALTH	PRIMARY SOURCE	TRANSFORMING AGENCY	TIME ORIENTATION
COMMUNITY	KNOWLEDGE	SELF-INTEREST	COMMON GOOD	BEING

can be wish, perhaps, even hope, but there can be no expectation. There is no real prospect of anything other than that which already is. The human mind is a tremendous power, possibly the most powerful force on earth; its only weakness is that it is self-limiting. That limitation does not occur by some overt act of will that establishes the outer boundaries of its achievement and, thus, its attempts and intentions; nor is it the result of the conscious denial or deliberate rejection of the mind's powers. Rather, limits come from its resistance to fragmentary thoughts; each must be completed immediately within what may often be an arbitrary context. The compulsion is as simple as completing a sentence.

The problem may be this: Once the mind seizes upon an idea—whether trivial or grand, whether in wisdom or in ignorance, whether arising from its own genius or proceeding from conversation with others, often the full construct of the idea is immediately established, in minutely drawn conceptual specifics, even though the actualization of the idea may not occur until after an extended period. If that proclivity were not such an intellectual certainty, it would give credence to Plato's belief that any idea is only a vague representation of the archetypal ideal. Preconception thus takes over, guiding any further thinking or compelling action; it becomes power, overwhelming that of the mind. The idea guards itself, forbidding the intrusion of anything—anything that is other. The thought becomes encased in the idea; the actual becomes slave to the idea. So also does the person who originated it, even to the extreme of doggedly persisting in foolishness—just for the sake of vociferously defending it or otherwise bringing it to fruition, as if, somehow, the idea itself deserved the fullness of life. Even if the idea is ultimately rejected, it does not cease to be; it has merely been supplanted by another, similarly formed through a change of mind. The limitation of anything is always in its prematured completion.

Rationalization destroyed human capacity. No matter its form or its application, the idea of rationalism was supreme; the concept sacred. Science or system, it was the same. Science sought conclusions; human systems were predicated on ends. Yet the only justification for any science is continuous discovery; and the only reason for any human system is the creation of capacity. The corporation could do neither. On one hand, every corporate enterprise, and everything within the enterprise, was based on the achievement of results. For the corporation, the end was profit; in all its busyness, the end was the completion of a task, the achievement of a goal. "Start with the end in mind," became more than axiomatic; it was that mantra of organization.

Everything about any system was engineered to serve the end. The entire system took on the characteristics of its product. Success was measured in terms of the effectiveness and efficiency of activity to that end. Occasionally, the end was temporarily compromised to accommodate the system; but, ultimately, it had to be served. Failure was not an option. But the end was always past tense, preconceived, preconceptualized—always an old idea. The longer it took to achieve it, the older—and the more expensive—the idea became. In most instances, completion and obsolescence occurred simultaneously.

In a rationalized system, the human beings were also means to the end; therefore, just like any other "resource," they were depleted in the process. A typical question posed by a corporate interviewer of applicants was, "What do you have to offer the company?" "Offering" was the fitting jargon of sacrifice. Furthermore, when the corporation-model organization spoke of "capacity," it was always in reference to physical, technological, or financial capability. Of course, it was also much concerned about human capability as measured by qualification, productivity rate, and individual job performance. "Assets" they were called, patronizingly.

But human capacity was of no concern. It could not be, for two reasons. First, capacity—unlike capability—cannot be created en masse, as in training and evaluation, or even by the most sophisticated "human resource development" programs. It is not programmable, not subject to norming. Capacity is individual and personal; therefore, it cannot be conformed to any system. The corporation could not afford fully developed individuals. Second, capacity always exists out of context. And that was anathema to the corporation. Any and all so-called developmental activity on the part of any person of necessity had to be related directly to the job, present or prospective. In fact, all applications for ostensibly developmental experiences required justification by a statement of the expected contribution to their ability to do a job. It was simply a matter of return on investment. Yet all capacity is excess, and thriving systems of any kind are neither efficient nor effective. Human capacity is not created; it is discovered—in, of all places, action.

Capacity development occurs within the action itself, and only within the action. The traditional idea is that capacity is the precursor of action, just as preparation is the prerequisite of work. The problem with such thinking is that preparation is, by its nature and without exception, limiting. Capacity, like work, never exceeds the prescription. When the stored capacity is expended, the action ceases—the battery runs down. Actually, stored capacity—if that were indeed possible—is not really capacity. The moment it is stored, it becomes incapacity. The ultimate purpose of action is not the achievement of a predetermined end but the creation of capacity, of new possibilities unimaginable outside the action. And that is the only purpose of organization.

CREATIVE ACTION

A well-known football coach, who had compiled an enviable record in both collegiate and professional leagues, was asked the secret of his success. His unhesitating response was, "I have always made a distinction between activity and action." The ready inference, of course, is that he was obsessed with winning and therefore concerned only with the effort that would bring about that end. But another answer by another coach—arguably the best basketball coach of the century—may shed more light on the subject. He remarked simply, "I never use the word 'win' with my players; I tell them to do their best." This is a remarkably significant statement, revealing an extraordinary understanding of the nature of human capacity: The best resides only within the individual; and it cannot be known, even by the person, until play begins.

In traditional organization, capability (or ability) is considered to be very much like a storage battery. It is charged by some source (usually external); energy is built up to the maximum; and then, with one turn of a switch, or the shrill of a whistle, it is released in a sustained burst toward the object or objective. Success in any endeavor, it is supposed, is the direct result of intense preparation. As a matter of fact, that is the common definition and the usual practice of "work"—that is, the continuing exertion of effort toward a desired end.

But capacity is not like that. Capacity, rather, as the word itself implies—even in the most practical usage—is about receiving—receiving energy, capability, and insight. Without that quality of being, all work is tedium and will not be done well, if at all, no matter how desired the intended result. The last resort for action is artificial stimulation, internal or external. Capacity is not a matter of motivation, or discipline, or tenacity. It has nothing to do with either commitment, preparation, or the exertion of energy. If, in fact, human affiliation is characterized by a common core of beliefs, and if is committed to the purpose of mutual benefit, and if it realizes the only justification for its existence is the development of capacity in each person, then—and only then—does a great paradox occur: Capacity is found in action—and only in action. That is precisely why, when faced with completely unexpected, extreme circumstances, ordinary people suddenly are capable of extraordinary things—"superhuman" feats, as they are sometimes called. Somewhere in the center of the action they find power within themselves they did not know they had.

The greatest tragedy of the past three centuries is the loss of that power through rationalistic science. Whether by industrialization or information-ization, the human being was critically incapacitated, and so also were human systems. Individuals became dependent on artificial aspiration, systems on artifactual restoration. Again, it is Aristotle who may provide the way. There is much to be learned here regarding the relationship between action and capacity. Writing in practical terms, as opposed to the metaphysical, he distinguishes between three kinds of action—*poiesis*, *theoria*, and *praxis*. And although it may be impossible at this late date to reach complete agreement on the shadings of meaning implied or inferred, there is sufficient core meaning attached to each to be significant today—for both the human being and human societies.

The first term, *poiesis*, was used to describe "artifactual production" as "distinguished both from the sphere of human action and from theoretical philosophizing."[2] More directly to the point, *poiesis* as artifactual production is an activity, guided by *techne* (literally "art"), the product and object that lies beyond the dynamics of the activity itself.[3] In rationalized production, *techne* is scientized, incorrectly, into "technique" or "technology." The art is lost; so is creativity. The person is reduced to mere process activity, as a "vital machine," for example. There is, thus, no implied or necessary connection between the human being and the result of his or her work. One's inherent capacity is limited to doing by the strict requirements of the process. The only concern of this kind of production is with the "performance" of "assigned" "tasks" effectively and efficiently. The person performing in this way does not even have to have an understanding of the why or what of the activity—only the how. Performance is defined not as much by the production of the intended result as it is in accomplishing the process itself. This definition of action is precisely that assumed in all contemporary human systems—especially the modern corporation. Goals and objectives, job descriptions, performance evaluations, standards, best practices, project planning, and all management philosophies such as MBO—particularly TQM—are but the specific or general demonstrations of *poiesis*. In each, human energy is transferred into process activity.

The second kind of action, *theoria*, is most easily understood by contrasting it with *poiesis*. It is not about doing but about knowing. It pursues knowledge for the sake of knowledge, purportedly in search of (the) truth, the "really real." The human faculty involved is not physical or mental capability; it is cognition, reasoned understanding—even intellectual fabrication. The activity becomes a special kind of process, termed "methodology," which must itself be validated and proved relevant. The *techne* of *poiesis* is made into the science of inquiry about things actual or metaphysical, real or supposed. The art of reason and logic is abandoned for an epistemology based on science or an ontology founded in rationalism. In either case, the "knowledge" derived becomes "reality."

The scientific method concludes with "proof," but that which is proved was determined already by the hypothesis; again, the answer is limited by the idea. Anything other is either rejected as invalid (resulting from a flawed methodology) or praised as serendipitous (something completely accidental, but happy, nevertheless). In the practical context of the traditional organization, conclusions take the form of decisions or pronouncements—both a substitute for action, and neither quite activity. In the modern corporation, the whole business of management has been compressed into a single act—"decision making." It is at once both process and result. Management "style" is a description, not of how one goes about getting work done through people, but about how decisions are made within the context of a group. And in education, decision making and problem solving are the twin peaks of "higher-order" thinking, the pinnacle of academic achievement. In administration, especially in government bureaucracies, simply the pronouncement of a conclusion is taken for action. Decision is all the action an institution can stand. Pronouncements as action go all the way to the top of the organizational pyramid. A recent press secretary for the president of the United States cautioned reporters, "You must remember that with him, words are action." In each meticulous process, energy is, at best, appropriated; at worst, dissipated.

The third kind of action, *praxis*, is the only source of human capacity. If the meaning of the word is difficult to comprehend, it is for three reasons. First, the modern translation of this ancient word is usually rendered erroneously as "practice." Sometimes it is translated "deed," "action," or performance. Although these definitions are probably closer to the original concept, they still do not capture the full meaning of the word. Therefore, most scholars do not even attempt to translate *praxis*. It is simply brought into the language in its original form. Second, the concept is admittedly difficult to grasp for persons not accustomed to either complex meanings or creative action. The nominal meaning most likely involves much more than either simple time-present action toward some intent; it is, rather, about the continuously developing reality at the center of the action—time passing. And third, rationalized systems, which exist along a single, narrow band of experience, are interested only in linear, demonstrable cause and effect, both having already been established. So, they reject anything foreign to that reality. And foreign it is.

Since Aristotle's original use, and most especially during the past century, any discussion of *praxis*, and hence any significance, has been relegated to esoteric discourse dealing with philosophy and human sciences—from existentialism (Sartre) to social and economic theory (Marx), from heady discussions of theory and practice to analyses of human communication. It should not be surprising that the more practical inquiries into the nature of communication provide the greatest insights into both individual and group action and go a long way in explaining the dynamics of human organization and, beyond that, the substance of its knowledge—its reality. Reduced to its simplest term, communicative *praxis* is about interpretation. The *techne* of *poiesis* (objective-driven action) becomes, rather, *hermeneutike*—literally, "interpretive art." The art (or science) of hermeneutics, especially as applied to scripture, is particularly exclusive: Nothing outside text is admitted into the text, which is itself its own context. Within that self-context, there is a constant play and interplay of meaning. The words are both means and ends, bearing the message. The interpretation is both objective and subjective, with one simultaneously becoming the other. Understanding and knowledge arise from the continuing dialogues within the text and with the interpreter.

It has already been pointed out that in the first order of action, *poiesis*, action is limited by the object (objective); the artifactual means of production are determined by, and indeed limited to, the end in mind. The objective is the only context. In the second kind of action, *theoria*, the action (conclusion) is likewise limited by the imposition of logical or rational constructs (programs) that anticipate the end result. The process is the only context. There is potentially a similar limiting intrusion in *praxis*. Earlier in this essay, *phronesis* was referred to as a kind of "practical wisdom." That was exactly the meaning Aristotle found in *praxis*—practical wisdom arises from, exists in, the action itself. *Phronesis*, thus, is to *praxis* as *episteme* is to *theoria*. If that action is restricted by preexisting constructs of reality or by the assumption of absolute knowledge, then any emergent wisdom, or knowledge, is rendered inconceivable, if not moot. The consequences are obvious—enervation, stagnation, and incapacitation. Creativity, except as the ingenious, often duplications, rearrangement of old ideas, is impossible. Since stasis cannot occur in living things, the system quickly dies.

It is quite significant that Aristotle used the word *praxis* in reference to a very practical human experience at the time, and for all time—the *polis*: that preeminently ethical social order that provides the context for virtuous living. It was only in the action by and interaction among individuals that the practical wisdom for both the immediate ordering and the continuing creation of the system were realized. The truth was neither absolute nor relative; it was both. Reality was neither objective or subjective; it was both. It is only that kind of action by which any system can hope to continuously create itself. It is the action of constant emergence.

NOTES

1. Marilyn Ferguson, *The Aquarian Conspiracy: Personal and Social Transformation in the 1980s* (Los Angeles: J. P. Tarcher, 1976), 224.

2. Calvin O. Schrag, *Communicative Praxis and the Space of Subjectivity* (Bloomington: Indiana University Press, 1989), 19.

3. Ibid.

CHAPTER 37

The Dynamics of Syntagma

Labour is blossoming or dancing where
The body is not bruised to pleasure soul,
Nor beauty born out of its own despair,
Nor blear-eyed wisdom out of midnight oil.
O chestnut-tree, great-rooted blossomer,
Are you the leaf, the blossom or the bole?
O body swayed to music, O brightening glance,
How can we know the dancer from the dance?
                              William Butler Yeats[1]

If the dimensions of syntagma are not fixed, as indeed is the case, then there of necessity must be some dynamic by which they change both within themselves and in relationship with the others. It is these relationships that, in fact, determine the immediate nature of the holistic organization. "Commensuration" and "essentiality" may seem at first to be rather awkward, even pretentious, terms; however, they are precisely the words to describe the interrelationships of the new organization. This dual dynamic informs and energizes the entire system.

COMMENSURATION

Unfortunately, corporation-model systems violated every principle of commensuration and therefore were doomed to a perpetual struggle of irreconcilable self-contradiction. The contradiction occurred at two spheres within the traditional organization. First, there were contradictions between the fundamental philosophy upon which it purportedly was based and the actual principles by which it attempted to perpetuate itself. For example, and directly to the point, it was genetically authoritarian, yet it ostensibly elicited democratic participation, at least in its latter stages. It expected, or demanded, a community-like loyalty, but demonstrated no regard for community-like values, by artificially fabricating collectives. It demanded obedience but did not feel obligated to justify its own demands. It held rank-order sacred but habitually violated subordinates. It attempted to construct systems yet fostered isolation. Such blatant contradictions are easily attributed to the characteristic cynicism of the corporation mentality. But the contradiction did not end with philosophy or principles.

Second, there was inherent disparity among the matters of management in traditional organization. For example, authority always flowed downward, accountability upward. Middle managers were caught in a crunch that was not only confusing but often debilitating. This kind of disparity accounted for the various so-called "management styles." The styles were either contradictory within themselves or in conflict with the others. In Chapter 12, it is suggested that the five basic assumptions of participatory management, although valid ideas, could not be realized in the confines of traditional organization. More to the point, none could be achieved through the practice of management. The commensuration of syntagma moves those assumptions outside the structures of traditional organization, translates them into imperatives, and allows each its full expression in a view that is both practical and dynamic. These principles, taken together, not only create new natural patterns of organization but also constitute a dramatically new culture. And they themselves are significantly transformed into the organum of a new reality:

1. The person performing any job or task knows more about it than anyone else — even those who performed it yesterday.
2. Everything about a human system is given meaning by the context of mutual purpose.
3. Commitments and expectations, the freedom to act, knowledge, and individual power are proportionate.
4. Decisions and actions are immediately creative.
5. All actions are independent yet in concert.

All organizational issues, past and future, can be resolved only by the adoption of these imperatives. Actually, all are quite basic, but they accomplish at once what traditional organization and management could never do. They give form; they establish expectations; they provide for system emergence. All action is brought into the context of the common values and mutual purpose. And capacity is continuously discovered in action.

One of these new principles speaks directly to the practical realization of commensuration in the emerging organization. The fundamental contradictions in the corporation-model organization made commensuration impossible in the four matters of management and, therefore, in organization itself. Unlike the principles of management, which were, in effect, the process for exercising traditional organization, matters of management were the actual substance of management—the subject and object of action—and the basic ingredients of organization. They were authority, information, accountability, and power. All management considerations involved all matters. The first three were always considered in that order and always proceeded from the "top" of the system downward. But power cannot be placed specifically in the order for two reasons: It was part of all the others; and it was never overtly acknowledged with the others, as though it rose above or fell below rational or deliberate considerations. Yet power was as much a matter of management as the others. Often, especially in incapacitated systems, only power, or force, could ensure that the work of an enterprise was accomplished.

Through commensuration, these systemic contradictions are not simply eliminated, the principles are returned to their natural state and order—probably the pristine form of human organization.

In traditional organization, had the original concept actually been followed, the four matters would not have been separated. But however they were, the first consideration should have been accountability; in a sense, that was precisely the intent of job descriptions. Authority, then, would have been derived, exactly in kind and degree, from accountability—not conversely, as was the practice. Information should have always been available strictly on a need-to-know basis. Most information in the modern corporation is extraneous and confusing; it's not even nice to know. And personal power should have taken the form of leading.

Syntagma, on the other hand, instills commensuration throughout the system by carefully examining and relating all the actions, individual and in concert, of all those who constitute the system. And a completely new kind of human affiliation is the result:

- The old accountability is replaced by the new mutual commitments and expectations; that is, the pledge of each of those within the system both to act on behalf of others and to ensure the success of others. Everyone has a vested interest.

- The old authority is replaced by the new freedom to act; that is, both the prerogative and the wherewithal to do what is necessary at the time to advance the common intent.

- The old information is replaced by the new knowledge; that is, those credible assumptions that merit risking the well-being of the system, even in uncertainty; the ultimate currency is the exchange of security for achievement.

- The old position power is replaced by the new person power; that is, the realization of each individual's greatest gift to others, service of the mutual good.

ESSENTIALITY

Commensuration is critical because it energizes a constant balance between and among the vital actions of the system. Without it, the system would lose control and become an unwieldy monstrosity. It is accurate to say that commensuration is a kind of quantitative regulator, obviously not in a perverse sense but as the discipline of creativity and expanding energy. Essentiality, in contradistinction, is the quality of the system — its life and its motivation. With it, everything about the system is qualitatively the same; without it there is no system — only bits and pieces. It is not easy to understand, but it is easily seen and felt.

It has been noted that there are two generally accepted kinds of systems — natural and artifactual. Further, it was pointed out that historically there has been a great debate, actually a great divide, over the question as to whether the artifactual systems were atomistic or organismic and that the matter in modern Western civilization had been settled early in the twentieth century in favor of the atomistic. That view has served as the metaphor in the construction and operation of the corporation-model organization. The traditional organizational chart depicts it; decentralization effects it; fragmentation and isolation are its results.

During the latter stages of the corporation, some reasonable attempts were made to transform the "construct" into "formation," usually with the announced intent of trying more closely to imitate natural order but always as a clear admission of serious dysfunctionality within the traditional organization. Yet even the "formations" devised as a solution were themselves atomistic in structure and function. In fact, the concept design and language associated with these so-called "natural" systems came most directly from the new-age fascination with the subatomic world.

But there is organization beyond both constructs and formations. It is described, also metaphorically, as "organismic." It is the character of all living natural systems, and it may also characterize artifactual systems; in fact, it makes them essentially human.

Organismic systems do not solve the problems of atomistic systems; they preclude them. "Organismic" simply means that the system is not constructed of components like a machine but is intrinsically one organism like a living body. It is the difference between parts and features. That is not only the concept informing all great art but also the original idea of the corporation (*corpus*).

The modern word "essential" is commonly used in two ways; both are meaningful in organismic systems. First, it indicates absolute necessity; that is, the thing in question is indispensable. And that is true in the new organization: every feature, every aspect, every characteristic is necessary to constitute the whole. That is to say, the concept of holism would be rendered impossible by anything extraneous to the system itself. Essentiality, therefore, may be seen as the other side of holism. In brief, that philosophy holds that there is in living organisms reality other and greater than the sum of its constituent parts. In that sense, essentiality is the bond of the parts. But that is not the whole truth.

There is a second definition, closer to the nominal meaning; and this definition better captures the nature of living things, including the new organization. The word "essential" refers to the essence of the thing itself, its fundamental and thorough nature. The whole is contained in any feature; any feature contains the whole. DNA is an obvious example, but it is difficult to make that analogous to human systems of organization. The concept of essentiality means that there can be no distinction between the organismic and the atomistic, either in the makeup of the human being or in human systems of affiliation. There is a trick of language known as "synecdoche" in which a characteristic part of an object—say, the sails of a ship—stands for the whole thing. But *essentia* means far more than that. A "part" is actually the "whole"; the "whole" is actually any "part." A single individual is the same as the community; and the community is the same as the person. Furthermore, the concept of essentiality means that no "part" is more important than any other; practically speaking, there can be no such thing as ranking the components in order of priority within the system. That is the most nonessential activity perpetrated by the modern corporation—and the most insidious.

Perhaps a more mundane analogy would serve to illustrate the unique qualities of essentiality in organization—say, a jigsaw puzzle, specifically, a 1,000-piece puzzle that actually has 1,007 pieces. This recent perverse trick of extra pieces illustrates the first definition of essentiality: Anything that does not fit is discarded. But more to the point, there are two aspects of the puzzle that are pertinent to organization. The first is the relationship among the pieces. The tenet, succinctly stated, is this: change one, change all—even though the picture, the intent, remains the same. That is, if the shape of only one piece is altered, all relationships are affected, not just those of the contiguous pieces. This concept is shown schematically in Figure 37.1. Obviously, if the image on the piece is changed, the whole picture is different. In artistic composition, this is known as synectics. Figure 37.2 shows the same concept photographically.

Second, there is no rank order among the pieces. In essential systems, there is no such thing as priority. Certainly, the corner pieces of a puzzle may be played first, but that does not mean they are more valuable than the others.

Figure 37.1

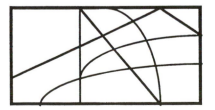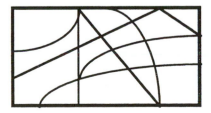

Figure 37.2

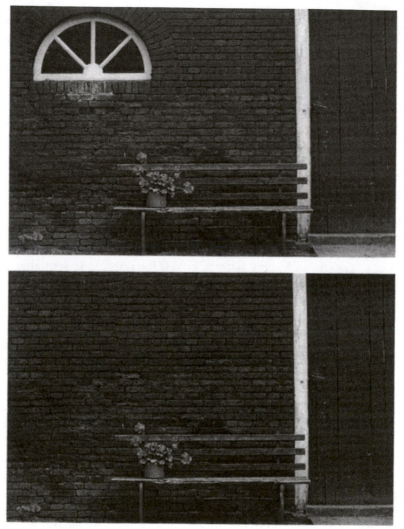

Source: Images®. Copyright 1999 PhotoDisc, Inc.

The timing of action must never be confused with the importance of the action. There is only one instance when relative importance is a consideration; that is, when a piece is broken or missing, and then only because it is critical to the whole.

Of all the features of the emerging organization—common values, mutual purpose, excess capacity, creative action, and commensuration—it is essentiality, with all its implications, that most profoundly separates syntagma from the corporation-model organization. The literal meaning of the word proclaims syntagma's only nature—oneness. Indeed, "together order" is the only concept of human affiliation that holds forth the promise of creating a system that inclusively and completely and continuously serves the universal good of human beings.

NOTE

1. Wiliam Butler Yeats, "Among School Children," *Poetry of the Victorian Period*, 3d ed., ed. Jerome Hamilton Buckley and George Benjamin Woods (Glenview, Ill.: Scott, Foresman, and Co., 1965), 882–883.

Postscript

Looking back on the story this book tells, I realize that it is as much about me as about the emerging organization. Perhaps we are all, indeed, the subjects of this tale. Even so, I still would not shrink from defending my assumptions and assertions about us. My only hope is that, despite its many flaws, this book is seen as an earnest attempt to chronicle the continuing struggle of human beings to deal with contrary things of their own making and to provoke a discovery of that which is essentially human.

No summary will be made here because it would be tedious reiteration. But, taking a cue from the tenets of an earlier Western civilization, these are the assertions of the new organum.

- Human beings are inherently spiritual; they apprehend truth intuitively.
- The common good and the good of the individual are the same.
- Constant emergence is the nature of living systems.
- Human capacity is found only in individual freedom.
- Plenitude arises from shared wealth.

It is impossible to write a conclusion to this story, because the end is in the action of those who believe the story is true. They are the ones who will live happily ever after.

Selected Bibliography

Andrews, Kenneth R. *The Concept of Corporate Strategy*. Homewood, Ill.: Richard Irwin, 1980.

Argyris, Chris. *Integrating the Individual and the Organization*. Somerset, N.J.: Transaction Publishers, 1990.

Argyris, Chris. *Reasoning, Learning, and Action: Individual and Organizational*. San Francisco: Jossey-Bass, 1982.

Aristotle. *The Complete Works of Aristotle*. Ed. Jonathan Barnes. Princeton: Princeton University Press, 1997.

Bean, J. P., and G. D. Kuh. "A Typology of Planning Problems." *Journal of Higher Education* (55/1, 1984): 36–51.

Bennis, Warren. *On Becoming a Leader*. Reading, Mass.: Perseus Books, 1989.

Bennis, Warren. *Why Leaders Can't Lead*. San Francisco: Jossey-Bass, 1990.

Bennis, Warren, and Burt Nanus. *Leaders: Strategies for Taking Charge*. New York: HarperCollins, 1985.

Brandenburger, Adam M., and Barry J. Nalebuff. *Co-opetition*. New York: Doubleday, 1996.

Bridges, William. *Jobshift*. Reading, Mass.: Perseus Books, 1995.

Caldwell, P. "Some Better Ideas from Ford Motors C.E.O." *Planning Review* (September 1984): 8–9.

Carse, James. *Breakfast at the Victory: The Mysticism of Ordinary Experience*. San Francisco: HarperCollins, 1994.

Costa, Arthur L., and Rosemarie M. Liebmann (Editors). *The Process-Centered School: Sustaining a Renaissance Community*. Thousand Oaks, Calif.: Corwin Press, 1997.

Covey, Stephen R. *Principle-Centered Leadership*. New York: Summit Books, 1990.

Cribben, James. *Effective Managerial Leadership*. New York: American Management Association, 1972.

Daly, Herman. *Beyond Growth: The Economics of Sustainable Development*. Boston:
    Beacon Press, 1997.
Darwin, Charles. *The Origin of Species*. Ed. J. W. Burrow. New York: Viking Press, 1977.
Deming, W. Edwards. *Out of the Crisis*. Cambridge: MIT Press, 1986.
Devey, Joseph (Editor). *The Physical and Metaphysical Works of Lord Bacon*. Lon-
    don: George Bell and Sons, 1901.
Donnelly, J. H., J. L. Gibson, and J. M. Ivancevich. *Fundamentals of Management*.
    Plano, Tex.: Business Publications, 1984.
Drucker, Peter F. *Concept of the Corporation*. New York: John Day Company, 1946.
Drucker, Peter F. *The Practice of Management*. New York: Harper and Row, 1954.
Duckworth, A., and R. Kranyik. "What Business Are We In?" *The School Administra-
    tor* (August 1984): 6–8.
Einstein, Albert. *The Meaning of Relativity*. Princeton: Princeton University Press, 1972.
Ellis, Darryl J., and Peter P. Pekar, Jr. *Planning for Nonplanners: Planning Basics for
    Managers*. New York: AMACOM, 1980.
Famularo, Joseph J. *Organization Planning Manual*, rev. ed. New York: AMACOM, 1979.
Fayol, Henri, and Irwin Gray. *General and Industrial Management*. Atlanta: Center
    for Effective Performance, 1987.
Frankl, Viktor. *Man's Search for Meaning*. Boston: Beacon Press, 1992.
Gardner, John W. "Leaders and Followers." *Liberal Education* (March–April 1987): 14.
Gates, Henry Louis. "The End of Loyalty." *The New Yorker* (March 9, 1998): 34.
Geisler, Norman L. *Ethics: Alternatives and Issues*. Grand Rapids, Michigan:
    Zondervan, 1971.
Glavin, G. "The Management of Planning: A Third Dimension of Business Plan-
    ning." *The Business Quarterly* (Autumn 1974): 43–51.
Gortner, Harold F., Julianne Mahler, and Jeanne Bell Nicholson. *Organization
    Theory*. Chicago: Dorsey Press, 1987.
Grossman, Lee. *The Change Agent*. New York: AMACOM, 1974.
Hayman, J. "Relationship of Strategic Planning and Future Methodologies." Paper
    presented at the annual meeting of the American Educational Research Asso-
    ciation, Los Angeles, California (April 1981).
Hegel, George Wilhelm Friedrich. *Hegel's Phenomenology of Spirit*. New York: Ox-
    ford University Press, 1979.
Heider, John. *The Tao of Leadership*. New York: Bantam Books, 1985.
Houston, P. "Involve Your Community in Planning for It." *The School Administrator*
    (August 1984): 11–13.
Humboldt, Wilhelm. *The Sphere and Duties of Government*. Bristol, England:
    Thoemmes Press, 1996.
Kant, Immanuel. *The Critique of Judgment*. New York: The Free Press, 1985.
Kant, Immanuel. *Critique of Pure Reason*. Ed. Norman K. Smith. New York: St.
    Martin's Press, 1990.
Kastens, Merritt L. *Long-Range Planning for Your Business*. New York: AMACOM, 1976.
Kay, Emanuel. *The Crisis in Middle Management*. New York: AMACOM, 1974.
Keech, William R. *Economic Politics: The Costs of Democracy*. New York: Cam-
    bridge University Press, 1995.
Korton, David C. *When Corporations Rule the World*. West Hartford, Conn.:
    Kumarian Press, 1995.
Land, George, and Beth Jarman. *Break-point and Beyond*. New York: HarperBusiness, 1992.

Levi, Margaret. *Consent, Dissent and Patriotism.* New York: Cambridge University Press, 1997.

Lubove, Seth. "Get 'em before They Get You." *Forbes* (July 31, 1995): 8.

More, Thomas. *Utopia.* Ed. George M. Logan and Robert M. Adams. New York: Cambridge University Press, 1989.

Mueller, Ronald E., and David H. Moore. "America's Blind Spot: Industrial Policy." *Challenge* (January–February 1982): 5–13.

Naor, Jacob. "Strategic Planning under Resource Constraints." *Business* (September–October 1981): 15–19.

Naylor, Thomas H. *Strategic Planning Management.* Oxford, Ohio: Planning Executives Institute, 1980.

Neill, S. "Planning for the Future." *Planning for Tomorrow's Schools* (1983): 7–30.

Newton, Isaac. *Mathematical Principles of Natural Philosophy.* London: Dawsons of Pall Mall, 1969.

Ouchi, William G. *Theory Z.* New York: Avon Books, 1981.

Plato. *Complete Works of Plato.* Ed. John M. Cooper and D. S. Hutchinson. Indianapolis: Hackett Publishing, 1997.

Plato. *The Laws.* North Stratford, N.H.: Ayer Company Publishers, 1976.

Reich, Robert. *The Work of Nations.* New York: Random House, 1992.

Rueschemeyer, Dietrich. *Capitalist Development and Democracy.* Chicago: University of Chicago Press, 1993.

Samuelson, Robert J. "Crackpot Prophet." *Newsweek* (March 10, 1997): 50.

Shafritz, Jay M., and J. Steven Ott. *Classics of Organization Theory.* Belmont, Calif.: Wadsworth Publishing, 1996.

Shlain, Leonard. *The Alphabet versus the Goddess.* New York: Penguin Group, 1998.

Siegel, Armand, and Norbert Weiner. *Differential Space, Quantum Systems, and Prediction.* Cambridge: MIT Press, 1966.

Simon, Herbert A. "The Proverbs of Administration." *Public Administration Review* (Winter 1946): 53–67.

Smith, Adam. *An Inquiry into the Nature and Causes of the Wealth of Nations.* Ed. Edwin Cannan. Chicago: University of Chicago Press, 1977.

Smith, Tony. *America's Mission: The United States and the Worldwide Struggle for Democracy in the Twentieth Century.* Princeton: Princeton University Press, 1994.

Soros, George. "The Capitalistic Threat." *Atlantic Monthy* (February 1997): 47–48.

Spencer, Herbert. *Data of Ethics.* Kila, Mont.: Kessinger Publishing, 1998.

Steiner, G. *Strategic Planning.* New York: The Free Press, 1979.

Taylor, Frederick Winslow. *The Principles of Scientific Management.* New York: W. W. Norton, 1989.

Thurow, Lester. *The Future Capitalism.* New York: William Murrow, 1996.

Tichy, Noel M., and Mary Anne DeVanna. *The Transformational Leader.* New York: John Wiley and Sons, 1986.

Tita, M., and R. Allio. "3M's Strategy System—Planning in an Innovative Corporation." *Planning Review* (September 1984): 10–15.

Tocqueville, Alexis de. *Democracy in America.* New York: HarperCollins, 1988.

Urwick, Lyndall. *Golden Book of Management.* North Stratford, N.H.: Ayer Company Publishers, 1979.

Zukav, Gary. *The Dancing Wu Li Masters.* New York: Bantam Books, 1979.

Name Index

Subject Index

ABOUT THE AUTHOR

William J. Cook, Jr., is founder and chief executive officer of The Colonial Cambridge Group, a consulting firm in Montgomery, Alabama, that specializes in strategic planning, design, and organization throughout the public and private sectors. Dr. Cook is the author of several other books and numerous articles, and has had his own daily radio commentary broadcast to more than 70 cities throughout the Southeast.